Dwight D. Eisenhower
An Associated Press Biography

BY RELMAN MORIN
Foreword by retired Col. Jack Jacobs

The Associated Press
200 Liberty Street
New York, NY 10281
www.ap.org

"Dwight D. Eisenhower" Copyright © 1969/2019 – The Associated Press

All rights reserved.

No part of this work may be reproduced, or stored in a retrieval system, or transmitted in any form or by any means, electronic, mechanical, photocopying, recording, or otherwise, without express written permission of the publisher.

All photos from AP Photo Archives – www.apimages.com

ISBN: 978-1-7338462-0-2

Cover Design by Hal Hilliard
Interior design by Kevin Callahan/BNGO Books
Project Oversight: Peter Costanzo
Visit AP Books: www.ap.org/books

Dedicated to the memories of
Relman Morin and Don Whitehead

Contents

Foreword	ix
Introduction	xi
A Gauge of Greatness	1
"I Was Raised to Prize that Code"	6
The Road Opens	18
The Lieutenant's Lady	29
Genesis Of a Leader	37
Fox Conner	41
Preview of Three Battlefields	48
The Tripos Completed	56
The First Star	64
The Reason Why	74
Photo Gallery	*after 85*
"And Over Here"	86
The African Enigma	96
The Glacis of Europe	110
The Fateful Night	123
"A Superb Tactician"	136
Island in the Darkness	149
"Mission Fulfilled"	156
"I Believe Fanatically—"	162
Many Wonderful Hours	173
Human-heartedness	185
Photo Gallery	*after 202*
Hail to the Chief	203
A Cross to Bear	220
"The Cost of One Bomber"	230
Crossroads	244
The Valley of the Shadow	258
Laws and the Man	274

The Bread of Adversity	293
Commander-in-Chief	306
Fulfillment	335
Ike's Enduring Legacy	349
The "Great Deception"	354
Selected References	367
Acknowledgments	370

Foreword

The story of Dwight D. Eisenhower is a uniquely American one.

Raised in rural Kansas, "Little Ike" learned the value of hard work at a young age and gained a sense of determination that would be the driving force behind his eventual rise to Supreme Allied Commander during World War II and then the 34th president of the country he so loved.

His steadfast qualities were a true inspiration to all Americans, but especially those who served in the military during the Second World War and the conflicts that followed in Korea and Vietnam. He provided a legacy that resonates to this day with officers like myself.

As president, Ike was determined to prevent the dogs of war by reaching out to world leaders with thoughtful, pragmatic diplomacy. For this was a man who had seen his share of atrocities and knew all too well the delicate balance required to maintain peace in a fragile, hostile world.

One can't help but wonder how Eisenhower would combat the challenges of modern terrorism, either as a five-star general, president or adviser. Undoubtedly, Presidents Clinton, Bush and Obama would've sought his counsel just as Presidents Kennedy and Johnson did through similar times of crisis.

This was a complex man who could order the D-Day invasion of Normandy; hold the highest office in the nation; champion the Interstate Highway System; become president of New York's Columbia University; and yet play a spirited round of golf with Arnold Palmer and learn to oil paint in his free time.

As someone who's been fortunate to enjoy success after my military career, I am grateful for leaders such as Dwight Eisenhower, who after WWII established a global order that paved the way toward decades of prosperity and freedom for America and our allies.

Because of this, we should all be thankful for his service.

—Retired Col. Jack Jacobs, Medal of Honor Recipient

Introduction

It may be merely wishful thinking, but I cherish the belief that the preparation of this book gave Dwight D. Eisenhower some happy hours in the last years of his life. He was not particularly interested, much less flattered, to learn that it was to be a biography. He never inquired about the title, the organization or emphasis of the material, nor when the book would be published. He granted a series of interviews and answered innumerable questions simply because he was a very generous man.

But my questions in these conversations, and especially about his early life, started him reminiscing and it became obvious that he greatly enjoyed that. His eyes would sparkle and he often laughed heartily as he recalled some distant incident. He described in great detail the riotous reception accorded him and his fellow Plebes on the day they entered West Point. "By golly," he said, laughing and shaking his head, "I thought they were crazy." He rose from his desk and pantomimed an upper classman wearing white gloves and looking for dust in his room. "It was all I could do to keep a straight face," he said. More than once he talked on past the time fixed by his aide, General Schulz, for the interview. When I called attention to the hour, he dismissed it with a gesture and said, "This is an interesting point and I want to finish it first." From his office across the hall, Schulz could hear the laughter. He remarked after one session, "It sounded as though the boss was having a pretty good time this morning."

In one interview, I asked a question that I regretted. It was about how he had trained a horse named Blackie. Obviously, the incident was of no great importance, merely "human interest," and I supposed he would cover it in a few minutes. Instead, he began talking animatedly and went on and on until he had used up almost all the allotted time for that day. When I said I had hoped to cover additional ground that day, he replied, "Well, I'll see you again soon. I guess I got a little wound up about Blackie."

Before the interviews began, I went several times to Abilene to make notes on the Eisenhower family home, the Library and Museum, and to talk with old-timers about Ike as a young man. Over the years, the stories had become encrusted with legend and some myths had found their way into print. I referred to one such story. The General looked up sharply and asked, "Where did you pick that up?" Someone in Abilene told it, I said. He grinned and said, "Well, they tell some pretty tall stories out there and they get better all the time, but the fact is—." Again and again, he de-bunked something I had heard or read about him, minimizing his role in it and downgrading some alleged exploit. But the story about his Homeric fist fight with a boy in Abilene, which is related in Chapter Two, had not been exaggerated. It was then that I discovered his amazing memory. The fight had taken place well over 60 years before but when I mentioned it, he replied instantly, "You mean Merrifield. Well, I don't know just how long the scrap lasted but it seemed like a week."

Through the years, from the North African campaign, through the Presidency and to the time of the interviews, I had seen Eisenhower in many different situations. But I never saw such an expression of warm affection as the one that came into his face when he talked about his parents, about General Conner, and about his friend, "Swede" Hazlett.

For me, the conversations were an inspiration of the highest order. For him, I hope and believe, they were a source of pleasure.

—Relman Morin, AP Special Correspondent

A Gauge of Greatness

In the evening of November 30, 1954, as he closed his desk in the White House, Dwight D. Eisenhower's thoughts turned to an old friend and a happy occasion taking place in London. Winston Churchill was celebrating his 80th birthday. The President always communicated with Churchill on his birthday and his message that day began, "Dear Winston, I know I speak for my fellow countrymen, as I know I do for myself, in sending you warmest congratulations on reaching a landmark in a life that is in itself a series of great landmarks." Now, alone with his memories, Eisenhower pictured Churchill and the glorious days, days of peril and triumph, that they had shared...

The war years had drawn them into a close and unusual partnership, an American commander serving with, but not precisely under, a British Prime Minister. "Churchill is half my boss," Eisenhower would say. (Franklin D. Roosevelt, of course, and the Combined Chiefs of Staff constituted the other "half.") Such an arrangement could not have succeeded so brilliantly but for the fact that "Ike" and "The Prime" very quickly came to like and admire each other. Because of their relationship, the abrasive disputes that plagued the Allied High Command during the First World War simply did not recur during the Second. Eisenhower and the Prime Minister scotched them before they could become venomous.

They met at least twice a week during the period when Eisenhower's headquarters remained in England, lunch on Tuesdays and dinner on Fridays. The dinners were held at Chequers, the Prime Minister's country home. These were working sessions, devoted to planning and strategy. However, with his restless, wide-ranging mind, Churchill often turned the conversation into other channels. He once observed that the ingredients of a good dinner include good conversation, "with me as the chief conversationalist."

And so it happened that at Chequers one night, Churchill and

Eisenhower fell into a discussion of history which turned into a contest. Like two schoolboys, they began vying with each other in pinpointing the details of historic events, dates, cities and terrain features, the protagonists. Churchill, of course, was a professional historian, but Eisenhower was no tyro. For years, he had made a hobby of memorizing dates and as a young officer he often spent his leisure time studying the campaigns of great commanders and the roots of wars. The duelling went on into the early hours of the morning, punctuated with laughter and cheers as one or the other scored a point. A witness reported that Eisenhower won the contest, "hands down." But to accept this as fact would be rouging the cheeks of history; the witness was an American staff officer who idolized his boss.

In spite of their friendship, however, Eisenhower and Churchill occasionally became thoroughly irritated with each other.

Eisenhower incurred Churchill's wrath by sending a communication concerning Berlin directly to Premier Stalin without consulting Washington and London. The question of capturing the city itself set off more sparks. Churchill pleaded with all his strength and eloquence for a headlong sprint across Germany, on a "narrow front," to seize the capital before the Russians could take it. History, perhaps, has vindicated his political intuition. But by the Spring of 1945, Eisenhower considered Berlin a worthless objective from a military standpoint. He insisted that the quickest way to end the war was to encircle the Ruhr, the industrial heart of Germany. With some heat, he reminded Churchill that a Three Power Commission had mapped the Zones of Occupation of Germany in 1944, placing Berlin deep inside the Soviet Zone. "Now look, Mr. Prime Minister," he said, "you were the one who agreed to all these things. I didn't!"

Each was strong-minded. In debating grand strategy, each would cling to his position through hours, and even days, of disagreement. Each had vision and great courage. Churchill looked beyond the war to the political objectives he hoped to achieve when it ended. Eisenhower was fully aware of political motivations, but such matters rested on a higher echelon than his; his main task was to organize and direct a mighty army.

Churchill opposed ANVIL, the project to land troops in Southern France and years after the war ended he still stuck to his opinion that it had been a largely unnecessary operation. In a letter to Eisenhower he wrote that the Supreme Commander had done more for ANVIL than the landings did for him. The potentials of an invasion of Eastern Europe, "the soft under-belly of the Axis," fired Churchill's imagination. Almost up to the 11th hour of the planning for the invasion of Normandy, the Prime Minister remained dubious of the outlook for victory there. Eisenhower forever remembered Churchill's words and he would quote the rolling periods—"My dear General, when I contemplate the beaches choked with the flower of British and American youth, and the tides running red with their blood, I must say I have my doubts." Yet neither man ever shrank from taking the long gamble.

On the morning of June 5, 1944, the gray Channel waters breaking on "Omaha Beach" did indeed run red with the blood of more than 2,000 Americans. Through breathless hours, D-Day appeared to be confirming Churchill's worst fears.

However, even as the battle swung perilously in the balance, Churchill stood in the House of Commons saying calmly, "There is complete confidence in the Supreme Commander, General Eisenhower."

Eisenhower recalled all this at a reception for Churchill given by the Secretary of War and Chiefs of Staff in 1946. "In the course of that association," he said, "there never was a single instance when the full might of the British Empire—and I mean scraping the bottom of the barrel—was not available to an Allied operation once it was agreed on."

The war years were electric years, cruel and dangerous to be sure, but vibrant with a sense of mounting confidence and forward movement toward the great goal. Eisenhower and Churchill shared the toil, the anxieties and disappointments, and at long last, the final triumph. Their friendship was forged in the crucible of the war, a lasting bond between the English aristocrat and the man who came from a poor family in Kansas.

It ended only with Churchill's death. Before then, he and Eisenhower kept in touch with each other in personal correspondence. Churchill's Christmas cards usually were prints of his own paintings, scenes from the French countryside. Eisenhower remembered Churchill's birthday and always received an affectionate reply. When their respective memoirs of the war began coming off the presses, each sent the other a first copy with an inscription. Eisenhower wrote that he approached the work with some misgivings because he believed, "Soldiers only write books to prove that they were right and others were wrong." He also expressed some annoyance because, in his opinion, so many war memoirs emphasized the differences that arose between the British and Americans instead of stressing the largely harmonious relations. Churchill wrote that he still considered ANVIL a mistake, and Eisenhower replied that he still considered it a necessary move. Eisenhower strongly urged Churchill to visit his hometown, Abilene, Kansas, when he came to Fulton, Missouri, to deliver his famous "Iron Curtain" Speech in 1946. Churchill asked Eisenhower for an autographed photograph to be included in his collection of pictures of the principal commanders in the war.

Now, on Churchill's 80th birthday, the great and terrible days were long gone. Nearly a decade had passed. Warm memories remained, however, glowing embers in a flickering fire. Eisenhower sat alone, musing.

A few days later, he set down his thoughts on Churchill in a letter to a friend, Capt. Everett E. Hazlett Jr. They had been friends since their high school days in Abilene. Hazlett, as will be shown, was instrumental in shaping a decision that set the whole course of Eisenhower's life. They corresponded regularly through the war years and after Eisenhower became President. He confided some of his deepest feelings in letters that began, "Dear Swede."

In the letter to Hazlett that he wrote after Churchill's birthday, Eisenhower said, "Winston Churchill comes nearest to fulfilling the requirements of greatness in any individual I have met in my lifetime."

But what is greatness? What are these requirements in the case of a politician and statesman? Eisenhower's letter clearly indicates that he turned over the question in his mind, searching for a gauge.

In working through a problem, Eisenhower instinctively turned away from the abstract and toward the specific. Thus, instead of trying to define the concept of greatness he began thinking of men whom he classified as "great." His letter to Hazlett named Washington, Lincoln and Robert E. Lee as great men. He gave "high rank" to Gen. George C. Marshall, Konrad Adenauer, then Chancellor of Germany, and Henry L. Stimson, one-time Secretary of State and Secretary of War. He said he considered that Senators Arthur Vandenberg, of Michigan, and Walter George, of Georgia, "came close." He later added to his list the name of Air Chief Marshal Sir Charles Portal of Britain.

In these men, as in Churchill, he perceived the same qualities, vision, integrity, understanding, courage, depth of character and the ability to communicate in speech or writing. He set them down in that order. Here was his gauge of greatness.

This narrative of Dwight D. Eisenhower's life will attempt to measure him on his own gauge.

"I Was Raised to Prize that Code"

At the first house on the street, the boy called "whoa" and the horse stopped. He jumped down from the buggy, exploding a puff of yellow dust that curled lazily in the hot Kansas sunshine. The boy was tall for his age, and lanky. He rapped on the back door and when the housewife appeared, he said, "Good morning, Ma'am, you need some vegetables today?" He gestured toward the buggy which was loaded with produce.

Having made a sale, or been turned away, he drove on to the next house and the next, up and down the streets of Abilene.

Most of the housewives were friendly. They called him "Dwight," or said, "What's good today, Ike?"

Some were not. A woman would half-strip an ear of corn, looking for worms, squeeze the tomatoes and pick over the radishes and carrots. Usually, this kind also would complain about the prices, a penny an ear for corn, 5 cents a pound for tomatoes. Then, like as not, she would say she didn't want anything, anyway.

Well, maybe he would make a sale at the next house. The boy hoped so. For this was serious business, and not merely a source of pin money for him. His parents needed his earnings in the summer.

The Eisenhower boys, Dwight and Edgar, grew the vegetables in a garden behind their home. They sold them on the North Side of town. In the classic pattern of American small towns, the railroad split Abilene into a "right" and "wrong" side of the tracks. The North Side was the affluent residential district, the "right" side. The Eisenhowers lived on the South Side.

Edgar fiercely resented the complaints, the dickering, the inferences of inferiority they sometimes encountered. But such treatment left his brother apparently unmoved. The younger boy would stand, poker-faced, detached, seemingly immune to it. (In this, he foreshadowed the man who would occupy the White House 50 years later and remain largely impervious to criticism and derision.) What did irritate him was to have a housewife waste his time. Why did she pick and talk and then not buy anything? He had to get home to other waiting chores. Angry words rose to the tip of his tongue.

But he had learned to keep his temper, which he knew was volcanic, and said nothing. It was not always easy.

Afternoon shadows would be lengthening across the fertile Kansas prairie before he drove over the railroad tracks and came to the white, two-story house on South East Fourth Street where he lived.

The house was comfortable but hardly commodious for a family of eight. An open drawer in the highboy on the second floor sometimes served as a cradle for the newest baby.

Each of the six boys shared a double bed. The room on the second floor that belonged to Dwight and Edgar also contained a chair, a dresser and a marble-top washstand. It was a little cramped for fist fighting, but fights sometimes started there.

Above them, in the attic, the family kept dried fruit. There was a root cellar beneath the house.

A greatly prized piano filled much of the front parlor. A Singer sewing machine, the second model ever made, stood in the parents' bedroom. Ida Elizabeth Eisenhower gave her sons piano lessons, but there was no daughter (much as she and her husband, David, had hoped for one) to whom she could teach sewing.

They kept the large family Bible on a table in the front parlor. On the wall above, they proudly hung David Eisenhower's diploma received from a correspondence school course in steam engineering. The shelves of a bookcase near the front door housed "Silas Marner," "Dick Merriwell," religious tracts, technical pamphlets, and as the years passed, an increasing number of school books. A highly unflattering sketch of "Teacher" came to enliven the last page of one of these books. Today, it is uncertain who drew it, but Dwight is the only one of the six brothers who later took up painting.

The warm aromas of baking bread, Pennsylvania Dutch cooking, and freshly ground coffee came from the kitchen. Every other day, the mother baked nine loaves of bread for her family. They smoked meat, raised poultry and vegetables, and milked their own cow.

They were a self-contained family and certainly a self-reliant one.

In material terms, they could be called "poor." David Eisenhower had failed in business and then taken a job for a very low wage in the Belle Springs Creamery, a few blocks from his home.

His father's failure in business and the consequences of it stamped Dwight D. Eisenhower's thinking throughout his life. In 1953, while touring a drought-ravaged part of Texas, he said, "I know just how these fellows feel. My father was a storekeeper and just such a drought put him under. He gave credit when nobody could pay his bills and then couldn't collect. I know what these people are going through."[1]

But from knowing what it meant to be "poor" he learned something more. When he was a boy, to accept charity, much less to ask for it, was considered shameful. A man, or even a widow with children, would do almost anything to avoid it. In that day, before the concept of state welfare, Americans relied on themselves. Was opportunity more abundant then?

Work was a necessary and natural fact of life for Dwight Eisenhower and all his brothers. When he was 16 and still in high school he worked nights in the creamery and mornings at his chores. The boys wore hand-me-down clothing. When they wanted something better they knew they had to work and earn it. Sometimes, the only money the family had was in an egg dish on the sideboard, the few coins their mother had managed to save.

On a visit to Abilene after World War II, Eisenhower said, "I have found out in later years we were very poor, but the glory of America is that we didn't know it then. All we knew was that our parents could say to us that opportunity was all about us. All we had to do was reach out and take it."

And so, in a larger sense, they were rich. The white frame house radiated warmth and affection. Dwight Eisenhower never heard an angry word pass between his mother and father. The boys loved and respected them. And the parents, returning this affection, instilled in them the beliefs and principles that shaped their lives.

Deepest of these was a religious sense.

. . .

David Eisenhower belonged to a strict religious sect called the River Brethren, a branch of the Mennonites. He met his future bride at a

---

[1] Sherman Adams: "First Hand Report."

school supported by the United Brethren Church. Both held strong religious convictions.

The Eisenhower ancestors came to America from Germany in the 18th Century. Originally, the name was spelled "Eisenhour," which has been translated "iron hewer" or "iron striker." Some philologists take this to mean "armored knight." They settled in Pennsylvania. Thrifty and industrious farmers, they enriched the land and the land made them prosperous. Some made their homes on the Susquehanna River, whence came the name "River Brethren." A colony of River Brethren brought David Eisenhower to Kansas when he was a boy.

Ida Elizabeth Stover's ancestors also came to America in the 18th Century. They settled in Virginia where she was born in 1862.

When she was 20, she entered Lane University, a church-supported school in Kansas. There she met David Eisenhower. They were married Sept. 23, 1885, on his 22nd birthday.

Between 1886 and 1899, seven sons were born to them. The fifth, Paul, died in infancy. Dwight was the third. Early in life, he began to bear a striking resemblance to his mother as she appears in her wedding picture—the same firm, determined chin, the high forehead, the same steady, searching expression in the eyes.

The young couple first lived in Hope, Kansas, where David Eisenhower opened a general store. It failed and they moved to Denison, Texas. He worked on a railroad there. In Denison, Oct. 14, 1890, David Dwight Eisenhower was born.

He never was known as David. His mother decided his first name should be Dwight. It appears that she strongly disliked nicknames and foresaw that he certainly would be called "Dave." As for "Ike," throughout her life she professed to know nothing at all about this nickname. In fact, it attached itself to several of her boys, perhaps most of them. Anyway, when they were in high school Edgar and Dwight both carried it, "Big Ike" and "Little Ike," respectively. Nonetheless, Ida Elizabeth Eisenhower would look puzzled when she heard it, and say, "Ike? Who's Ike?"

Years later, she wrote a letter to Mamie Eisenhower which said, "I am very glad you are having a fine motor trip, but who is this 'Ike' you are travelling with?"

A principal tenet of the River Brethren was to take care of their own. David Eisenhower's family was growing and he needed something better than the railroad job. The Brethren had enlarged the Belle

Springs Creamery, which they owned, and needed an engineer. About 18 months after the birth of Dwight, the family moved to Abilene, Kansas, and David Eisenhower went to work in the creamery.

His salary was $380 a year, according to the vastly informative and entertaining history of Abilene by Henry Jameson.[1]

On this stipend, supplemented later by the earnings of the boys, Ida Elizabeth Eisenhower reared them to manhood.

She was a remarkable woman, all steel beneath a delicate exterior. She looked frail but she cooked, sewed and cleaned from sunup until bedtime. In remaining moments, she read religious tracts.

The boys, of course, were with her more than with their father. In the main, she prepared them for life.

She taught them self-respect and respect for authority. Having had a passion for education herself, she emphasized the importance of schooling, and all her boys were good students. Honest labor, however menial, ennobled the man who engaged in it, she said. When necessary, she did not hesitate to punish the boys. Then she would sit down with the offender and quietly explain where he had disobeyed, why he had to understand discipline, the penalties he would incur in life if he broke the rules. Not least, she spoke to them of love of country. For religious reasons, she abhorred war. Yet, when Dwight announced his intention to become a professional soldier she made no attempt to dissuade him.

Obviously, she could not condone the fistfights that regularly broke out between Dwight and Edgar, but she appears to have looked the other way.

One night a week, the family gathered in the parlor to read the Bible. The boys took turns. Having read a passage, they discussed it, helping each other find meanings that might seem obscure. Before he was 18, Dwight had read the Bible twice, from Genesis through Revelation.

He grew up with faith in the power of prayer.

In 1952, shortly before Eisenhower was to appear before his first press conference as a candidate for the Republican nomination for President, he was in Suite 600 in the Sunflower Hotel in Abilene. Two of his Kansas backers came to the hotel to escort him to the conference. At the door, they were asked to wait. Eisenhower was praying.

---

1 Henry B. Jameson: "Heroes by the Dozen."

A rustle of surprise swept the great audience gathered in Washington for his first Inauguration when he prefaced his speech with a prayer. He had written it himself on the back of an envelope shortly before he was driven to the Capitol to take the oath of office. The President, in turn, was surprised at the widespread comment on what seemed wholly natural to him.

Cabinet meetings opened with a silent prayer. And on more than one occasion, in moments of adversity, he said he felt the need for divine assistance. The instinct for prayer was deeply ingrained.

"Freedom itself means nothing unless there is faith," Eisenhower often said.

. . .

Along with his mother's teachings when he was a boy in Abilene, Dwight Eisenhower also absorbed the standards of conduct of the Old West. Ideally, in that code, a man was honest and above-board. He was physically tough. He was always prepared to defend himself. He met his enemy in a stand-up fight. He was chivalrous toward women. He took a stranger at face value and expected his attitude to be reciprocated.

It was a simple masculine code, born of the dangers and hardships of life on the Great Plains.

Abilene is a town with an impossibly picturesque past. In the beginning, it was authentic Wild West. In appearance, and in terms of the action that swirled through the streets, Abilene was the precursor of all the "Westerns" ever written.

Only a little more than a decade before Eisenhower's birth, cowboys shot it out in front of the Pearl Saloon and Indians lived on the prairie nearby. For this was the frontier and the people were pioneers, the builders and chance-takers.

Any number of men who were only middle-aged when Ike was a boy could have told him about the last Indian fight in 1860. The Indians had trailed a wagon train to a point not far from Abilene. They waited through the night and attacked at dawn in the classic maneuver, circling and shooting. A few broke into the ring of wagons and were clubbed and shot to death. Five other Indian bodies were found outside the ring after the Indians galloped away.

Any number could recall the shootings and knifings, the night a

Texas cattleman lost $30,000 in a poker game at the Bulls Head, and cowpokes dancing in Texas Street with ladies of the evening.

They had a high old time in Abilene before the town sobered up.

It owed its existence to the Chisholm Trail. A year or two after the Civil War ended, the railroads, stretching toward the Pacific Coast, reached that part of Kansas. Almost immediately, some far-sighted Westerners, who were prepared to take the financial risk and face the physical dangers, saw a shining new vista. It might be possible, they thought, to drive thousands of cattle to Abilene and from there ship them by rail to the populous East.

From Texas, across a thousand miles of mesa and uplands, cowboys began coming, driving the Longhorns. Hostile Indians, armed rustlers, drought and storms often menaced them along the Trail.

In Abilene, having drawn their pay, they proceeded to dispose of it on liquor, gambling and women.

"Saloon keepers wore diamonds as big as hickory nuts," Henry Jameson wrote. "All places patronized by Texans had six-shooters handy under bars and counters…The usual first action of the trails-end cowboy was to get a haircut and have his moustache or beard shaped and blacked. Then he visited a clothing store for a new outfit. Emerging with new clothes, the hats and boots embellished with Texas stars, he was ready to go out on the town for fun and frolic. After three months on the trail few blamed him for cutting loose and 'raising hell.'"[1]

Yet, Jameson's history reports, it was perfectly safe to walk the streets of Abilene at night, except for the possibility of being hit accidentally by a stray bullet from a saloon or gambling hall.

No record exists of a woman being sexually assaulted. The cowboys behaved honorably toward the wives and daughters of the town's permanent residents. Hospitality to strangers also was a tenet in the code of the Old West and histories of Abilene report that it was not unusual for a man to stay overnight in a family home, even though the head of the house was absent.

Brothels came soon after the first cowboys arrived. However, contrary to movies and television "Westerns," the bare-shouldered beauties were not permitted in saloons or gambling halls in Abilene.

Gun fights and knifings were common. Records indicate that

---

1 Jameson: op. cit.

between 20 and 25 men were killed in the heyday of the cowboy era, but other killings took place on the trail. Killing a man violated the law, of course, but it appears that the citizens were inclined to regard it as less than a capital offense if it happened in a fair fight.

Not all the cowboys left all their pay in Abilene. Some were well-born young men who rode the Trail in order to earn enough to go to school.

Functioning as "law man" in all the turbulence in Abilene was Wild Bill Hickok, the handsome Marshal with the lightning draw. (Fate never brought him face to face with Billy the Kid, the desperado who may have been equally fast with his gun, and history is the poorer for it.) Another famous "law man," Bat Masterson, is quoted as saying of Wild Bill, "He is not a bad man but he is a bad man to fool with." Hickok, it is said, never killed except in self-defense or in the performance of his duties. However, the bullet that killed him came from behind. He was shot in the head while playing poker in Deadwood, South Dakota. He was holding aces and eights, with a Queen, and this is still known as "the dead man's hand." The story is that Wild Bill's reflexes were so incredibly quick that, even as the bullet pierced his brain, his hands were reaching for both his guns.

Eventually, the citizens of Abilene had enough of the cattle trade, the cowboys, prostitutes and cardsharps. By the time Dwight Eisenhower was born in 1890, the town had become a quiet, respectable community. Handsome homes rose, especially on the North Side, and a number of schools were built. Football and baseball, in a sense, took the place of the shootings and knifings.

But the code of the Chisholm Trail survived long after the cowboys disappeared from Abilene. In 1953, Dwight D. Eisenhower recalled it in a speech. He said:

"It was: meet anyone face to face with whom you disagree. You could not sneak up on him from behind…without suffering the penalty to an enraged citizenry. If you met him face to face and took the same risks as he did, you could get away with almost anything, as long as the bullet was in front.

"I was raised as a boy to prize that code."

He lived for football, baseball and boxing, and his passion for athletics almost cost him his life. It also led to a strange event which seems beyond all explanation.

In a scuffle one day, Dwight lacerated his leg. He paid no attention to the wound until the pain grew sharper and an ugly discoloration began rising in his leg. Blood poisoning. A doctor examined the boy and said it would be necessary to amputate. Otherwise, he warned, Dwight would die. Soon, he went into periods of delirium. Finally, his parents told him the doctor's verdict. Amputation! Never again to run with a football or take his place in the batting order? It was tantamount to a death sentence. And that is precisely what the boy said, "I would rather die."

He turned to Edgar with a fearful request. He begged his brother to stand outside their bedroom and made him swear to block any attempt to operate. Edgar agreed, although in fact he knew that during the day he would be in school, not at home. Perhaps his brother was delirious when he exacted the promise. In the succeeding days, Edgar came to understand that Dwight meant exactly what he said. He would rather die than lose his leg.

The emotions of the mother and father can easily be imagined. However, he convinced them of his determination to fight it out, and pleaded for time. They agreed to wait. Through 10 days, he passed in and out of the attacks of delirium. The poison crept steadily upward. They swabbed the boy's leg and lower abdomen with homely remedies, carbolic acid and alcohol. The acid burned and he screamed. Finally, the awful moment came. "If you postpone it another day," the doctor said, "it will be too late."

Edgar, grim-faced, stationed himself in front of the bedroom door. He had given a promise and he meant to keep it, whatever the consequences.

Throughout the long nightmare of suffering and delirium, the whole family had prayed constantly for Dwight. Now, in this moment of crises, they went down on their knees together. It seemed to be all over, either death or a boy with only one leg.

But somehow, and beyond reason, the poison began to subside a short time later. Little by little, Dwight recovered. Who can say what wrought this miracle? In their prayers now, they gave thanks to the Lord.

The day came when he could walk again. Presently, with his brothers, he was performing his assigned chores.

In winter, they rose before dawn and went into the cold darkness carrying lanterns. They gathered eggs, split kindling, milked the cow, lit the stove. The chores were rotated among them. Then, after a gigantic breakfast that today's dieticians might not approve, they were off to school. Kenneth Davis, who compiled a mountain of details about the Eisenhower family, wrote that on Sunday they came home from Sunday School and did all the cooking and housekeeping while their parents went to Church. They played catch in the kitchen with pie dough.[1]

Dwight lost time in school due to the blood poisoning but he made it up even though, toward the end of his high school days, he worked nights in the Belle Springs Creamery.

He was above average in his grades. He earned the equivalent of "A" in English, history and geometry. In composition, algebra, physical geography and German the grades fell only a little lower. He was no Horace in Latin.[2]

What did the boy's school days foreshadow in terms of the man's two great careers? Very little. Except, perhaps, the power of concentration and the energy to work long hours, physically and mentally. The talent for organization, the ability to absorb a multitude of details and arrange them in his mind in an orderly fashion, the gift of diplomacy in coordinating the often conflicting ideas of strong-minded men—none of this is discernible in an examination of his high school days in Abilene.

. . .

He lived for football and baseball and he might very well have pursued a career in professional sports. He was a natural athlete. Like most high school boys he had no clear view of what he would do, or want to do, in the future. For reasons that Eisenhower never was able to explain exactly, the thought of going to Argentina captured his imagination. Since he knew something about farming, he thought vaguely of trying his hand at ranching in Argentina. The thought of a career in the Army had not occurred to him. His friend, "Swede" Hazlett put that idea in his mind.

Hazlett has left a sketch of Eisenhower when they were schoolmates. "Ike was calm, laconic, sensible, and not the least affected by being the school hero," Hazlett wrote. "There was something fine

---

1   Kenneth S. Davis: "Soldier of Democracy."
2   Ibid

about him that drew me to him—as it is drawing so many today. He had the qualities of leadership combined with the most likeable human traits—candor, honesty, horse sense and a keen sense of humor."

Where a small town has only one high school, everybody idolizes its athletic teams and Dwight was a star athlete at Abilene High. He played right field and was the leading hitter on the baseball team. In football, he played end, and as the West Point days would show, was fast enough for the backfield. He was not heavy but he was physically tough. In blocking and tackling, he hit hard.

He also liked boxing. Before he entered high school, he was known in town as a redoubtable fistfighter.

When he was 13, he had a Homeric battle with a boy from the North Side named Wesley Merrifield. There were North-South overtones to the fight, but it came about largely because some men simply wanted to see a good fight and egged them into it. Merrifield was short and bull-shouldered. Dwight was taller and gangly.

In a ring of men and boys, they squared off and began battering each other. Soon, both were lacerated; bruised and spitting blood. They fought for more than an hour without stopping. ("It seemed more like a week," Dwight D. Eisenhower recalled later.) Neither would give in when the other said, "You had enough now?"

They called it quits only when each was too weary to lift his arms. The fight was adjudged a draw, and a bloody one. Dwight was unable to go to school for two days afterward. History does not say how long it took Merrifield to recover.

Since Abilene High was located on the North Side, the story of the fight no doubt contributed to Dwight's "hero" status when he entered there.

He had little time, and less money, to spend on girls. Now and then he did some visiting and beauing, but no one Abilene beauty seems to have thrown her butterfly net over his attentions and kept it there for long. A story has it that one Abilene father advised his daughter not to "get serious" about Dwight; he thought it unlikely the boy would ever amount to anything in life!

Edgar, having been held back a year by illness, graduated in the same class with Dwight. The customary predictions about the future of each graduate appeared in "Helianthus," the school annual, and they can still be read today in the Eisenhower Museum in Abilene. The editor foresaw Dwight becoming a Professor of History at Yale, and Edgar elected President of the United States. Not such a cloudy crystal ball!

This was in 1909. In that day, college was not the logical next step after high school for every young man. Nonetheless, both Dwight and Edgar wanted a higher education. For financial reasons, it was not possible for them both to start in the fall, so they came to an agreement: One would enter college for a year and the other would find a job and send him money. They flipped a coin. Edgar went to college and Dwight went to work as night foreman in the creamery. He worked an 84-hour week and during that year he sent his brother $200, a small fortune in that day.

Their arrangement, however, was not to continue. Dwight Eisenhower, without realizing it, was approaching the first great turning point in his life.

The Road Opens

On a warm summer night in 1910, "Swede" Hazlett came to the Belle Springs Creamery to pass the time with the night foreman, Dwight Eisenhower. "Swede" often spent an evening there with his friend. They ate ice cream, played penny ante poker, and talked about football and girls, in that order, Hazlett recalled in a sketch of Eisenhower written years later. Sometimes they also cooked a chicken "on a well-scrubbed shovel."

Tonight, "Swede" had something on his mind. A great idea.

The year before, he had received a Congressional appointment to the United States Naval Academy, but failed the entrance examination. Now he had a second appointment and he was taking special studies in preparation for another attempt to enter. His idea: Ike should try to go to the Academy, too.

"Look at it this way, Ike," he said, "here's a chance for an education and you don't have to pay for it." They would have a lot of fun at Annapolis, perhaps even room together. And think of college football! With Ike's proven ability, he would play for Navy, sure as shootin'. It was an altogether attractive prospect. "Why not give it a whirl?" he asked.

What made the suggestion doubly attractive were the words, "an education and you don't have to pay for it." Ike hadn't thought of that.

Now he did start thinking. A year had passed since he finished high school, a year spent working in the creamery. He was sending part of his earnings to Edgar, who was in college. Next year, in their plan, Edgar would work and help finance Ike's first college year. If they continued this alternating pattern, it would be a long time before either finished. "Swede's" suggestion opened a brighter vista. Ike was not particularly interested in becoming a Navy officer (he could scarcely picture life on the sea) but he was vitally concerned with getting a college education.

Soon after this conversation in the creamery, Ike wrote letters to both Kansas Senators, requesting an appointment to either Annapolis or West Point. Next, he sought support in Abilene. Shrewdly, since he knew no politicians, he called on the town's two newspaper editors, Charlie Harger and Joe Howe, in the thought that they would have some influence with the Senators. He also asked a number of businessmen to write letters supporting his request.

Civic pride came into play. Someone pointed out that "Swede" was the first Abilene boy in a dozen years or so to get a Congressional appointment. The last one before him was a boy named Abe Lott. (Lott became a General officer and Eisenhower came to know him in the Army.) The citizens stoutly asserted that Abilene deserved better treatment than that from its representatives in Washington.

Soon, letters recommending one Dwight Eisenhower were in the mail to the Senators. They said he was a good student, industrious, well-behaved (which was stretching a point), a good athlete and a regular churchgoer. They pictured him as a paragon of solid Kansas virtues.

With such backing, favorable replies naturally were expected. The first, when it came, was a disappointment; the Senator had no vacant appointments. For a time, there was silence on the part of the other Senator, Joseph L. Bristow.

Once he started something, Ike could be doggedly persistent. He now followed up his original letter to Bristow with a second one, dated September 3, 1910. Couched in typically forthright language, the letter said:

"Dear Sir: Sometime ago, I wrote you applying for an appointment to West Point or Annapolis. As yet, I have heard nothing definite from you about the matter but I noticed in the daily papers that you would soon give a competitive examination for these appointments.

"Now, if you find it impossible to give me an appointment outright to one of those places, would I have the right to enter this competitive examination?

"Trusting to hear from you at your earliest convenience, I am, respectfully yours, Dwight Eisenhower."[1]

In short, the newspaper report indicated that Bristow, instead of handing out his appointments on a patronage or personal basis, proposed to do it on a basis of may-the-best-man-win.

---

1 This letter, framed, now hangs in the Eisenhower Museum in Abilene.

Ike's follow-up letter brought a response. The Senator wrote that the examination would be given in Topeka in October and Mr. Eisenhower was welcome to compete.

Less than a month to prepare! And Ike was holding a full-time job in the creamery, on duty through the night, from 6 p.m. to 6 a.m.

The odds were stacked against him, but it was like getting into a fight; having started, he would not back away.

He began cramming as hard as he could. No other emergency would ever find him concentrating more intensively, not even those that were to arise in the Second World War when, on short order, he would have to attack a complicated problem and quickly solve it.

"Swede" Hazlett pitched in to help and "Swede" had had some experience, having taken the examinations for Annapolis. He tried to foresee the questions his friend might encounter. He unearthed copies of past examinations and found publications that might be of use in the examinations in Topeka. Time was precious. "Swede" looked for shortcuts. They studied together, in the afternoons from 2 to 5 in the manufacturer's office where "Swede" had a job, and at night in the creamery, in both instances on "company time." They developed a method. First, one would hold a book or examination paper, asking the questions. Then they reversed the process.

All too swiftly the hours passed, the merciless ticking of the clock. September faded and October came.

On the day of the examination, Ike boarded a train for Topeka. He had worked like a Trojan to get ready, driving himself day and night. Now, for what it was worth, he at least could say he had done his best in the time available. In fact, he felt reasonably confident when he entered the office of the Superintendent of Public Instruction in Topeka.

He found himself one of eight candidates.

Four stated a preference for West Point only. The others, playing it safer, said they would take an appointment to either academy. Ike listed himself in the latter group, two chances to one.

The examination proved to be more difficult, in some respects, than he had expected and easier in others. As he rode back to Abilene, he felt certain that he had done reasonably well. But how well had the others done? Ike was never given to underrating his opposition in football, war or politics.

At last, the report came. Dwight Eisenhower, it said, was No. 1

for Annapolis, No. 2 for West Point. He had scored an over-all grade of 87 1/2 out of a possible 100, less than two points below the highest scorer.[1]

Now, assuming he and "Swede" could pass the examinations for entering the Naval Academy, they would be together for the next four years. Whoopee! Annapolis, here we come!

But the dream soon perished. Fate, in the form of Senator Bristow, decreed that Ike would never march under the colors of Annapolis. The boy who had topped Ike in Topeka was unable to accept the appointment to West Point (Eisenhower never knew the reason) and Bristow advised Ike that *he* had the appointment. History often hangs on a thin thread.

Hazlett later wrote:

"This was a cruel blow and Ike didn't like it any better than I did. All his hopes had been aimed at Annapolis and he felt that, through me, he knew a good deal about it. I urged him to write the Senator and tell him that he greatly preferred the Navy, and beg for a reconsideration. He muttered something about 'not looking any gift horse in the mouth,' but he toyed with the idea for some time."

In fact, although neither of them realized it then, Ike already was too old to enter Annapolis.

Academy regulations fixed the age limit at 16 to 20. Ike and his friend interpreted this to mean *through* a man's 20th year. Ike's 20th birthday came on Oct. 14, 1910. On that day, they discovered, he became ineligible for Annapolis.

Hazlett said he suggested that, inasmuch as a birth certificate was not required then, Ike should conveniently lop off a year, "but of course he refused to consider any such stratagem."

So it would be West Point and the Army.

Suppose he had found a way to enter Annapolis? Would there have been an "Admiral Eisenhower"? And would he have sailed the oceans to the Presidency of the United States?

Once the die was cast, Ike turned immediately to the next problem, preparing for the West Point examinations. This hurdle remained and "Swede," as he knew, had stumbled over it. The "cram schools" for the Military Academy were out of the question. Ike couldn't afford to enroll in one.

---

1   Davis: op. cit.

Then he found the alternative. He would reenter Abilene High and try there to shore up his chances.

Overage and oversized, compared with the other students, he sat in the classrooms, boning up on algebra, geometry, history, geography and English. The Academy examinations were to be held in January, two months away. Again, the race against time.

And again, the day came when he boarded a train, this time for St. Louis and Jefferson Barracks. St. Louis all but overwhelmed Ike. It was the biggest city he had ever seen.

He reported in at the Barracks and then went out to see the sights. He took a streetcar to the downtown section of the city. In what he judged to be its center, he disembarked. He walked and walked. To a country boy, the theaters and hotels, the department stores and restaurants, all blazing with lights, were nothing less than dazzling.

Suddenly, he became conscious of time and discovered also that he was lost. Which streetcar takes you back to Jefferson Barracks? He asked a passerby on the street but the man didn't know. Neither did several others. At last, he found someone who could tell him.

It was late when he returned to the Post, much later than he intended.

As he approached the gate, a clammy thought struck Ike. Suppose the Army authorities arrested him, or ruled him out of the examination, or penalized him somehow, for leaving the Post and staying out so late? He knew nothing about regulations or whether they applied to a mere candidate for the Academy.

Anyway, he decided not to take a chance. Instead, he took an even longer gamble. He tiptoed through the darkness, away from the gate, to a point beside the wall. There he waited, listening. A sentry might be on patrol. Hearing no footsteps, Ike jumped, pulled himself to the top of the wall and then slipped into the Barracks.

The next day, still somewhat shaken from the adventure, he took the examination and passed it with grades that put him in about the middle of the group of candidates.

Five months later, in June 1911, Ike stowed a single suitcase aboard a train bound for New York via Kansas City. He said goodbye to his family and friends, goodbye to Abilene.

Once out of the depot, he did not look back. Characteristically, as he always would do, he looked ahead, ahead to the next task, the next problem, the next campaign.

・・・

From the first, Cadet Eisenhower was a popular man in the Class of 1915. He was big and breezy as all outdoors, casual in dress, somewhat irreverent toward regulations, an athlete, a prankster, and altogether a product of the Great Plains and the big sky. "Swede" Hazlett's description of him in high school fitted even more closely in the West Point days—"calm, sensible, laconic."

On June 14, 1911, Eisenhower and the other members of the incoming class disembarked at the railway station below the Academy. It was a blistering summer day. Lugging their suitcases, they began the long climb up to the Plain. Although Eisenhower was physically fit from athletics and manual labor, even he was panting and dripping when they reached the top.

There, waiting to pounce, were the upper classmen. Bedlam exploded, a cross between a riot and the closing moments of Custer's Last Stand. They set upon the Plebes in a manner designed to strike terror in the depths of their souls. "When they got to screaming," Dwight D. Eisenhower recalled, "I thought they were crazy."

The definition of Plebe, of course, is "lowest class." This was drilled into the new arrivals in numerous bizarre ways and they were made to understand that the possibility of them ever blossoming into officers and gentlemen was extremely remote.

For about 48 hours, Eisenhower was as bewildered as the others. Then he analyzed it: an exotic method of testing their mettle and instilling the habit of absolute obedience, the cardinal rule of the Army. Having reached this conclusion, he relaxed. He knew he could take the disciplining, however rough and apparently senseless it might be.

Others could not. A 17-year-old cracked almost immediately and fled the Academy. Eisenhower's first roommate also left after a short time.

But to Eisenhower, West Point presented a golden opportunity to get the education he could not otherwise afford. He determined to survive and grasp that opportunity. Nobody was going to get *his* goat. Nobody ever did.

And so the photographs taken then show a cool cadet. The expression in his eyes is watchful, searching and slightly sardonic.

His registration form, filled out on that first day, shows that he stood 5 feet 11 and weighed 175 pounds.

He wrote that he attended primary school for six years and two months and Abilene High for four years. In his senior year there, his courses included the study of American history, physics, economics, English and civil government. He listed the textbooks used in these courses and named their authors from memory.

Evidently referring to his postgraduate work in Abilene High, he said he had had three months of "special training" for the West Point entrance examinations.

Under "previous occupation," he wrote "refrigeration engineer" and that he had supported himself "partially" for six years and "wholly" for two years.

He was assigned to Room 2644 in the "beast barracks." (Today, a bronze plaque on the wall says, "This room was occupied by President Dwight D. Eisenhower, Class of 1915, during his Fourth Class Year." Fourth Class means the first year in the Academy, not the last.)

On the first Sunday after registration, the Class of 1915 was marched around the granite cliffs overlooking the Hudson River and the grounds around the Academy. In the formation, along with Eisenhower were men destined to become famous soldiers, Omar N. Bradley, Joseph T. McNarney, James A. Van Fleet, Hubert R. Harmon, "The class the stars fell on."

Cadet Eisenhower soon notched a place for himself in the esteem of his classmates and at the same time achieved a certain notoriety in the Academy as a whole. Two upper classmen ordered him to appear in their rooms one night for "special instruction," whatever that might mean. He was to come "dressed in blouse." In his own room he habitually wore a football sweater and lounging clothes.

On the dot of the appointed hour, he rapped on their door. When it opened, jaws dropped. Cadet Eisenhower was only half-clad.

"Where are your pants, Beast?" one of them asked.

"Sir," Eisenhower replied, "the order didn't say anything about trousers. It said to come 'wearing blouse.'"

As the months passed, demerits dotted his record…late to target formation…late to Chapel…brass buttons badly polished…disorderly room on afternoon inspection…other minor infractions.

He seldom managed to keep stony-faced when an upper classman, wearing white gloves, rubbed them over the locker in his room, looking for a speck of dust. Too often, on these occasions, a wide grin would split his face. He recognized the importance of discipline, but he thought this was carrying spit-and-polish too far.

For his frailties, he soon earned a nonscholastic degree, B.A., meaning "busted aristocrat." Frequently, too, he was an A.B., an "area bird."

He played football, of course, but now in the backfield. He was a strong, shifty runner, hard to bring down, a good blocker, and rough on defense. The coaches, watching the Plebe from Kansas, marked him for special attention next year. He also played baseball.

And he developed an avocation, hiking through the woods and hills around West Point, studying the defensive positions of the Revolutionary War. He learned to look at terrain with a soldier's eye.

But for all his outwardly cavalier attitude toward the mores of the Academy, Eisenhower never lost sight of its central purpose, a military education. Without appearing to be "grinding," he studied hard and came through his Plebe year with more than satisfactory grades.

In a class of 212, he stood 10th in English, 30th in Military Engineering, 39th in History, 82nd in Drill Regulations and Service of Security and 112th in Mathematics. Although 43 demerits appeared on his record, he was rated 39th in Conduct. And in the over-all "Order of General Merit," he stood 57th, near the top fourth.

The quality of his competition may be gauged by the fact that the Class of 1915 was to produce two Generals of the Army, two Generals, seven Lieutenant Generals, 24 Major Generals and 24 Brigadier Generals, a total of 111 stars. More than one-third of Eisenhower's classmates later became General officers. To reach the top echelons in such a group took some doing.

On May 31, 1912, the first year ended.

A road had opened and he could look forward confidently to the stretches ahead.

• • •

Fate dealt Eisenhower a cruel blow in his second year at West Point.

As expected, he won his "A" on the Army football team. He played in the backfield. The New York Times predicted he would develop into "one of the best backs in the East."

In a game in which the great Indian athlete, Jim Thorpe, was starring for Carlisle, Eisenhower twisted his knee. It hurt for a few days but, characteristically, he ignored the pain. Soon afterward, he reinjured the knee playing against Tufts College.

Now it became badly swollen. The doctors hospitalized him until the swelling subsided. He still had no idea of the extent of the injury. Nobody warned him against putting too much strain on it.

Had he known, he would not have taken part in a cavalry drill shortly afterward. Or at least, if he had advised the instructor about his weak knee—which he neglected to do—he would have been excused from one part of the drill. In this maneuver, the rider jumped from his horse and hit the ground hard enough to vault clean over to the other side.

Eisenhower jumped. His knee buckled like a jackknife. In the hospital again, the doctors worked for five days before they could straighten his knee. They strapped him up and put him in traction. In all, he lay in the hospital for 30 days.

His athletic career was ended.

With his usual buoyancy, he looked for other outlets to satisfy his love for athletics. He designed the black and gold capes which the cadets put over their uniforms, spelling out "Army," as they sat in the stands. In spite of the obvious danger to his knee, he became a cheerleader. And he helped coach the Plebe football team to a successful season.

Possibly because of his long stay in the hospital, or possibly because of the psychological shock of being forever sidelined from the playing fields, Eisenhower's grades fell off sharply in his second year. In the "Order of General Merit," he stood 81st in a class of 177, barely above average.

They improved again in his last two years. Generally, stood well above average and frequently in the upper third of his class.

He qualified as a sharpshooter with a score of 245, the same as Omar Bradley's. James Van Fleet, who would command the Eighth Army in the Korean War, led the field with 268.

Eisenhower liked to dance and here again, he ran afoul of his superiors "for violation of orders with reference to dancing, after having been admonished for same." He also was a member of "The Misogynists Club," composed of three cadets. All three married within a year after they graduated.

In the manner of most college yearbooks, the 1915 "Howitzer" satirized him as a "Mexican athlete—good at throwing the bull." The written sketch of Eisenhower that accompanies his graduation photographs says, among other raffish assertions:

"He claims to have the best authority for the statement that he is the handsomest man in the Corps and is ready to back up his claim at any time. In common with most fat men…he roars homage at the shrine of Morpheus on every possible occasion."

One of his photographs in the yearbook shows a blocky figure, but not fat, in a wholly unmilitary posture, hands on hips, uniform unpressed, the visor of his cadet's hat pushed belligerently forward.

Whatever Eisenhower may have thought of his own future, the star of the class in his view was the sober Missourian, Omar N. Bradley. He wrote, "If he keeps up the clip he's started, some of us some day will be bragging, 'Sure, General Bradley was a classmate of mine.'"

On June 12, 1915, they graduated. Eisenhower placed 61st in the class of 164 cadets, near the top third. But in Conduct he stood 125th, in the lowest quarter. Many of the demerits on his record came from infractions that he himself reported, under the Honor System. He was anything but a model cadet but he had integrity.

One of his instructors later gave this estimate of him in his West Point years:

"We saw in Eisenhower a not uncommon type, a man who would thoroughly enjoy his Army life, giving both to duty and recreation their fair values (but) we did not see in him a man who would throw himself into his job so completely that nothing else would matter."[1]

In a very few years, as the official record shows, this estimate would be radically revised.

Because of his damaged knee, the question of recommending Eisenhower for a commission hung in doubt when he graduated. Army authorities hesitated to commission any cadet with a physical defect that might cause him to retire early. In that event, the investment of four years' training in the Academy would be lost, and moreover he would be on the pension roll for years to come.

The matter lay in the hands of the medical officers at West Point.

Eisenhower did not attempt to argue about it. He had achieved his objective, a college education, albeit primarily technical. If he was

---

1 Quoted in Kevin McCann: "Man from Abilene."

not to have an Army career, he would have to try something else. A sum of money was due him from a special fund, compulsory savings earmarked to purchase equipment for a newly commissioned officer. He said he would use this money to finance a trip to Argentina and if he liked the country he would stay there.

They offered to recommend him for a commission in the Coast Artillery but he refused it. The prospect of duty at the ocean's edge did not enthrall the man reared on the Great Plains. He wanted Infantry.

The medical officers were sympathetic. At last, although they may have thought they were stretching a point in overlooking his uncertain knee, they told him he would be a Second Lieutenant in the Infantry. However, they attached a stipulation: He must never apply for "mounted service."

It was 1915. Tanks and motorized infantry had not yet come into action in the war in Europe, but the day was not distant when both would replace the cavalry. Ironically, in a few years the United States Army itself would assign Eisenhower to the new "cavalry."

The road lay open before him. It would lead to North Africa and Italy, to Normandy, the Elbe River, and the surrender ceremony in a schoolhouse in Rheims.

The Lieutenant's Lady

The maid in the Doud home was thoroughly vexed that evening when the family returned from a day's fishing. Not that she was unaccustomed to being interrupted in her work by young Army officers telephoning for Miss Mamie. The maid didn't mind two or three calls a day.

But this Lieutenant Eisenhower, well, he was a little too much. The maid said he must have called 15 or 20 times during the day, asking for Miss Mamie. And she had told him the family had gone fishing and then he asked what time they would be back and she said she didn't know exactly. Well, would they be having dinner at home? Yes, she said, she expected them for dinner. And then in a little while he had 'phoned again and asked all the same questions. Oh, he was polite enough, but persistent, mighty persistent. And what with all the running to the telephone all day she hadn't been able to do half the things around the house that needed doing.

And then the telephone again rang and the maid, handing the instrument to Mamie Doud, said, with unvarnished disapproval, "It's him."

Without a dissenting vote, the officers at Fort Sam Houston rated Mamie Geneva Doud among the prettiest and most attractive girls in San Antonio. Considering the well-known standards of beauty in Texas, this was saying a good deal. She was slim and dainty. Her chestnut hair, piled high above an oval face, made her look taller than she was in fact. She had blue eyes, a dazzling complexion and a mischievous smile.

She entertained the officers with grape juice and cookie parties in her home. Sometimes fudge was served. Fudge was one of the two comestibles she knew how to make; the other was mayonnaise. She played the piano by ear and she would gather them into the music room to sing "When You Wore a Tulip" and "Down by the Old Mill Stream."

In effect, you had to stand in line for a date with Miss Doud. But Lieutenant Eisenhower, being new at the Fort, didn't know that.

They met on a Sunday evening in October. As he came out of the bachelor officers' quarters, he heard his name called. Mr. and Mrs. Hunter Harris, with whom he was acquainted, were standing on the front porch of their home along with some friends. "Come and join us, Lieutenant," Mrs. Harris said. "I want you to meet someone."

She introduced him to Mr. and Mrs. John Sheldon Doud and their daughter, Mamie.

Could he stay for dinner? He accepted eagerly. During dinner, he made only a half-hearted effort to keep his eyes off the pretty girl in the white dress. The moment came when the Lieutenant said, with regret, that he must leave to inspect the guard. The term "blitz krieg" was not in common usage in 1915, but Lieutenant Eisenhower obviously had an instinct for the tactics it identified. Turning suddenly to Miss Doud, he said he felt certain that she would find inspecting the guard a most enlightening experience and asked if she would like to come with him. Caught by surprise, Miss Doud heard herself accepting. And off they went.

As they walked around the Post, he learned that she lived in Denver and that her family wintered in San Antonio. She was 18. She had gone to high school in Denver and then "finished" at Miss Walcott's School. Her father owned a Packard twin-six and his Sunday ritual was to take the family on tours of Denver. "We all have to go whether we want to or not," she said with a wry smile.

Winter in San Antonio…a Packard…a "finishing school." It all added up to a background and status quite different from his.

Meanwhile, Miss Doud was observing the Lieutenant. He was tall, trim and good looking. His movements were graceful. She noted his easy, open manner and the expression of fun in his eyes. Altogether, Miss Doud decided that she liked him.

That was Sunday. On Monday, to the great annoyance of the maid, the "blitz" began in earnest. When he finally did speak to Miss Doud that evening, he asked her to a dance. She was engaged. Yes, she was busy tomorrow night, too. Would she go to the Majestic Theater with him on its special night next Saturday? She was engaged. What about the week after that? She said she had dates for the next three special nights at the theater. All right, was she free for the fourth week? Yes, she could accompany him to that one. Fine.

The maid was right. He was, indeed, a most persistent man.

More than a week passed before they saw each other again. Later, she invited him to a cookie and grape juice party. He made it a point to ingratiate himself with her mother and father. They liked the Lieutenant and he liked them.

The Doud family came from Guilford, England, and helped found the town of Guilford, Connecticut, in 1639. John Sheldon Doud was born in Rome, New York. When he was a child, his family moved to Chicago. He attended the University of Chicago and Northwestern University. Then he moved to Boone, Iowa, and joined his father in the meat packing business. He was so successful that he retired at the age of 36. In Boone, he met Elivera Mathilde Carlson and married her. Mamie Geneva was born there, Nov. 14, 1896.

Mrs. Doud's father, Carl Carlson, came to the United States from Dagsos Socken, Sweden, in 1868. For a short time, he lived in Portland, Maine, and there married Marie Anderson. Then they moved to Boone where he farmed and went into the milling business.

The Douds had four daughters, the eldest of whom died. Mamie was the second. Then came Eda Mae and Mable. The younger girls were in San Antonio when Lieutenant Eisenhower first made his appearance.

In the ensuing weeks, it became apparent to the officers at the Fort that 'phoning for a date with Mamie Doud was all but a lost cause. Lieutenant Eisenhower had moved in and taken charge of her social calendar.

On St. Valentine's Day in 1916, only four months after they first met, Mamie accepted an engagement ring from him. It was a full-size copy of his West Point class ring, amethyst set in gold. And then, at high noon of July 1, they were married in the music room of her family home in Denver, at 750 LaFayette Street. The bride wore white lace. The groom was resplendent in his white dress uniform.

He received his promotion to First Lieutenant on his wedding day and his pay now rose to $151.67 a month.

Soon after the ceremony, he took Mamie's sister aside and held a whispered conference with her. He asked her to put Mamie's wedding bouquet in the refrigerator until he could carry out a plan. He then changed his uniform and the family left the house for a wedding celebration. When they returned, he began melting candles and pouring the wax into a large bowl. Then he plunged the bridal bouquet into the molten wax in the thought that, like a bee in amber, it would be preserved for all time. Of course, he succeeded only in french frying the flowers but his bride applauded the knightly gesture.

They had 10 days for the honeymoon. He took Mamie first to El Dorado Spring, Colorado, and then to Abilene to meet his family. Then they returned to Fort Sam Houston to settle into married life.

History does not record whether the Lieutenant carried his bride across the threshold of their first home at the Fort. But Mamie never forgot the shock she felt when she walked into what was to be their bedroom. It was completely empty, four bare walls and an unshaded light bulb hanging from the ceiling. There was a clothes closet but his uniforms completely filled it. Evidently, he had completely overlooked the fact that his bride would need a place to hang her dresses. They began laughing.

Some friends then drove them downtown to a furniture store, and the Lieutenant learned something about Mamie. She was a manager. She carefully picked out the furniture they needed, discussing prices and quality with the clerk, and mentally calculating the total cost of her purchases. Her husband had given her some money from his savings and she also had in her purse some gold coins, gifts for her wedding. When the transaction was closed, she used the gold pieces as well as the greenbacks to pay for the furniture. Thereafter, for the rest of their lives, Mamie was to handle the family finances. Moreover, the day soon came when he gladly turned over to her the matter of shopping for his clothes. On his salary, she had to be a bargain-hunter and it came naturally to her.

Their quarters in the Fort consisted of a parlor, bedroom and bath, all cubicles. It was a far cry from the prosperous home in Denver where she had grown to womanhood. However, Mamie was to discover that it was almost palatial compared with some of the rickety houses on Army posts in which they would live. Before they finally settled down in their own home near Gettysburg, they would move 27 times. "I've kept house in everything but an igloo," Mamie would say.

In the attic of her home in Denver, Mamie found a rug and this covered the floor in their parlor. Her mother gave her four pairs of Brussels lace curtains. Ike hung them. Kitchen equipment included a grill, chafing dish, percolator and toaster. However, Mamie's repertory in the kitchen was severely limited, confined in fact to whipping up fudge and mayonnaise. Not even a doting husband could be expected to live on that, so they took many of their meals in the officers' mess at a maximum cost of $60 a month. When money ran low between paydays, Ike did the cooking at home. He was a good cook.

In the first months of their marriage, he was assigned to night duty with a Military Police patrol. Once a bullet whizzed past him in a dark alley. Whether it was meant for him he did not know. Apart from the occasional danger to him, Mamie was not happy to be left alone every night, but she said nothing to him. One night, the sound of a prowler awakened her. Apparently, he had been trying to remove the screen from the bedroom window. She telephoned some friends who made a search but found nobody. One of Ike's service revolvers was in a chiffonier drawer but Mamie was afraid to touch it. She sat up, wide awake, for the rest of the night.

They entertained as often as their straitened budget would permit. Never mind if their guests stumbled over one another in the sardine-box quarters. Mamie rented a piano for $5 a month and she played while the others danced. She was pretty and vivacious, still in her teens. Her husband's easy charm, which was to be so important in his two careers, already was developing. They soon became popular at the Fort.

This was important to his future. An Army wife, perhaps to an even greater degree than any Organization wife, can either help to advance her husband's career, or she can cripple it. The rules of protocol governing relationships between wives of officers of different rank are tricky and, depending on the particular woman, something to be meticulously obeyed. Mamie soon familiarized herself with these unwritten statutes. She became adept at skating around thin ice on the social pond.

In another way, too, Mamie and marriage influenced Ike for the better. At West Point, largely out of a spirit of independence, he had been a rule-breaker and a cutup. The sketch of him in Howitzer, although written half in fun, indicates that he liked to horse around and was a big talker. It adds that he was always prepared to back up his opinions with his fists.

Had he carried these mannerisms into the regular Army, he would have become known throughout the ranks as a comical cuss but the traits hardly would have commended him to his superiors.

Now, almost imperceptibly, he began to change, to become serious.

He discovered, beneath his wife's gentle and deceptively fragile appearance, a highly determined woman with a mind of her own. Her sole goals in life had become a home and family and he was her sole career. They still enjoyed parties and dancing. But Mamie wanted mainly to build a successful home life, and he settled down to play his part in this.

On their first wedding anniversary, Ike gave her a heart-shaped silver jewel box and she received an English tea service from her grandmother. His parents had set aside for them a "spool bed" of the Victorian Era which his grandfather, the Reverend Jacob Eisenhower, had transported by oxcart from Pennsylvania to Kansas in 1878. That would have to wait until they were given more spacious quarters.

Mamie's father, without saying anything to them, planned another gift. He appeared in San Antonio and began consulting the used car dealers. Eventually, he bought a four-year-old roadster called a Pullman and drove it to the Fort for them. Mamie had never driven an automobile and, for the moment, was not interested in learning. This was to lead her into a hair-raising adventure.

They were happy at the Fort, off to a good start in marriage. It had been a love match and they remained in love.

Only one cloud, a small cloud at the time, darkened Mamie's horizon, the possibility that the United States might be drawn into the war in Europe. In that event, she knew, her husband would pull every string to be sent to France with the troops. Mamie read the newspapers with a pang of anxiety. President Wilson had sent a stiff note of protest to the Kaiser over the sinking of the Lusitania.

However, the election placards of 1916 proclaimed of Wilson, "He kept us out of war."

The slogan emerged from an obliquely chauvinistic speech at the Democratic Convention. A speaker, in Fourth of July cadences, asserted that Wilson had "wrung from the most militant spirit that ever brooded above a battlefield an acknowledgment of American rights and American demands." This was anything but accurate. Nonetheless, the convention exploded into a demonstration that continued for 20 minutes.

Wilson himself disliked the slogan. "I can't keep the country out of war," he growled to Josephus Daniels. "Any little German lieutenant can put us into the war at any time by some calculated outrage." However, it probably was the slogan that reelected Wilson.

In 1917, apparently out of desperation, the Germans adverted to a policy of unrestricted submarine warfare. On March 18, the U-boats sank three American ships. Interventionists, the 1917 counterparts of today's "hawks," cried out louder than ever for war with Germany.

The famous Zimmerman Note provided them with more ammunition. It revealed the Germans' secret effort to induce Mexico to attack the United States, offering as bait the return of former Mexican territory in the Southwest.

Finally, on the evening of April 2, 1917, after months of vacillation and drifting, Wilson rose before Congress to ask for a Declaration of War. "It is a fearful thing to lead this great peaceful people into war," he said, "into the most terrible and disastrous of all wars, civilization itself seeming to be in the balance. But the right is more precious than peace, and we shall fight for the things we have always carried nearest our hearts—for Democracy. The world must be made safe for Democracy."

So, for Mamie Eisenhower, the dreadful moment had come and it now carried a special poignancy. A short time before, her physician had informed her that she could expect a child in September or October. Would her husband be "over there" when her time came?

In fact, almost immediately he had to leave her alone in the Fort. He was ordered to Leon Springs, Texas, for several weeks of target practice. The firing range was about 30 miles from San Antonio. He could not come home on weekends. Mamie was worried and she became desperately lonely for him.

On a Sunday morning, she telephoned Leon Springs and told Ike she intended to come to the camp to spend the day with him. She asked him to meet her at the front gate.

What she did not tell him was that she was going to make the trip in their little roadster—and by herself, although she had never driven an automobile. Her only experience had been in her father's Packard when he allowed her to steer the car.

A sergeant showed her the gears on the roadster and how to engage them. He cranked the motor into life and Mamie set off. Like many a woman before and since, she first ran into the cellar steps, killing the motor. The sergeant, no doubt muttering "woman driver" under his breath, again cranked the car. This time, Mamie managed to reach the street and turned in the direction of Leon Springs. It was a long 30 miles. The Pullman chugged along and at last the gate came in sight. Ike, waiting there, was astounded when he saw Mamie behind the wheel, careening toward the fence. At almost the last minute before she ploughed into it, she cried, "Ike, jump in here. I don't know how to stop it!" He sprinted to the side of the car, reached in and turned the ignition key. They sat in the car looking at each other, both breathless.

They had that Sunday together. It was to be the last for a long time.

On September 20, 1917, he was ordered to Fort Oglethorpe, Georgia. The Army frequently operates with exquisite timing. Four days later, Doud Dwight Eisenhower was born. They called the child "Little Icky."

Meanwhile, across the land, the "citizens army" was taking shape, and it's newly minted officers were described as "90-day wonders." As a professional, Ike had every reason to expect that he would soon be fighting in France.

Genesis Of a Leader

Eisenhower's first command embraced 6,000 men and one tank, a French Renault. With this single vehicle he was expected to train the crews to operate American tanks in France whenever they came off the assembly lines. Somehow, he did. In the process, he exhibited a gift for organization and training and, above all, the qualities of a leader.

The United States of course was ill-prepared to go to war in 1917. In spite of a series of provocations, Woodrow Wilson had long wavered over the question of intervening on the side of the Allies. He had provided no positive leadership for Congress in the matter of preparedness in case the United States might be forced to declare war. Weapons were scarce and six months passed, after the Declaration of War, before the first draftees flooded into hastily built camps to begin their training.

1917.

The paradox of war is that, in spite of its horror, in spite of casualty lists and deprivations, it galvanizes a people, binding them together in a common purpose, and stirs excitement and a macabre gaiety.

And so it was then...soldiers in campaign hats and puttees swaggering the streets...yesterday they were clerks and waiters and farmers, today they are heroes by proxy...War Stamps and Bond Drives... lilting tunes, "The Yanks are coming," "Keep the home fires burning," "Pack up your troubles in your old kit bag," "Oui, oui, Marie, will you do *zis* for me?"...Mary Pickford in a tailored Army uniform selling Liberty Bonds at a street rally...nobody minded meatless, wheatless and sugarless days; nothing was too good for Our Boys...girls swooning over the uniform of the LaFayette Escadrille...in a movie theater, lecherous Germans menace the Gish sisters in "Hearts of the World"...flickering newsreels show gray monsters lumbering through the mud in Flanders, tanks.

In the first months of the war, Eisenhower moved from post to post as an instructor and organizer. He became an instructor in an officers training school at Fort Oglethorpe in the autumn of 1917. The year's end found him at Fort Leavenworth, Kansas, instructing in the Army Service School. From there, he went to Camp Meade, Maryland, where he helped organize the 65th Engineers Battalion. His native talent for organization surfaced, and he rapidly learned how to lead. He acquired the indefinable *look* of a commander, and the air of authority seemed natural to him.

A letter, dated January 1918, and written by a soldier at Fort Leavenworth, says of him, "Our new Captain, Eisenhower by name, is, I believe, one of the most efficient and best Army officers in the country."

On March 23, 1918, Eisenhower reported to Camp Colt, Pennsylvania, under orders to organize and train tank crews with his one tank.

Here was a challenge in a largely unexplored field. For the tank, although men had envisioned it for centuries, was still a relatively new weapon. On Sept. 15, 1916, the Allies struck the German trenches at Thiepval, France, in history's first tank attack. It failed to force a breakthrough. But about a year later, the Canadian commander, Lord Byng of Vimy, hurled a much larger armored attack at enemy positions and it succeeded beyond all expectations. "By 4 p.m., Nov. 20," he wrote, "one of the most astonishing battles in all history had been won."

So here was the weapon of future wars. Eisenhower threw all his volcanic energy into learning about it. He studied the tactics, such as they were, of tank operations in France and obtained all the information he could about the performance of tanks in that area. He drilled his men in armored theory. With the lone Renault, he could not do much about practical maneuvers. However, he succeeded better than he realized. Some years later, he was to receive the Distinguished Service Medal for his work at Camp Colt.

The duty there, however hard, brought one advantage: for the first time since leaving San Antonio, a home life again became possible. Mamie brought "Little Icky," now 6 months old, to Pennsylvania and the family settled into a cottage not far from the camp. This was the first of many moves for Mamie and each brought new problems in homemaking on an officer's pay. She made a dresser for herself out of orange crates covered with a flowered fabric. In her various homes, she became an expert in what the British call "making do."

However rewarding Eisenhower found his professional and domestic life at Camp Colt, it irked him to be there instead of in France, commanding troops. It was all well and good to know that his reputation as an organizer and instructor was growing apace. But combat is the raison d'etre of a professional soldier. No other duty presents the same tests of courage, stamina and judgment, nor offers the equivalent opportunity to exhibit competence under stress. Some of Eisenhower's friends and acquaintances were leading troops in France. He could only stick to the less glamorous duty at home.

Promotions came rapidly, however. At Camp Colt, he became a Major and on his 28th birthday a Lieutenant Colonel.

Not surprisingly the erstwhile rule-breaker at West Point now became a strict disciplinarian. He acted decisively when necessary and he earned the respect of the men at the camps where he was stationed. (A group from Camp Colt were among the first to advance Eisenhower's name for the Presidency almost 10 years before his election in 1952.) He was a stickler for physical fitness. He discovered that many of the men in his commands had never done any manual labor nor participated in athletics. They were soft. He was physically tough and he determined that his men would be tough, too. He never became a spit-and-polish officer. He concerned himself very little about barracks-room neatness, but he did demand discipline, efficiency in the field and physical fitness.

Meanwhile, pulling every possible string, he maneuvered to get duty overseas. One day, to his immense delight, the orders came. Lieutenant Colonel Eisenhower was to prepare to leave for France. The orders read: Embarkation, Fort Dix, New Jersey, Nov. 18, 1918.

One week earlier, on Nov. 11, the Armistice was signed.

Eisenhower would soon see service in France and it would become a link in the chain of circumstances that led him to the peaks of his Army career. But he had missed combat. The "war to end wars" had passed into history and it seemed wholly unlikely to him that he would ever have another opportunity to command troops in battle.

It was some comfort to learn that he might be decorated for his work at Camp Colt. In December 1918, two names were mentioned in correspondence relating to awarding Distinguished Service Medals. It read:

"…Colonel W. H. Clopton Jr., and Lieutenant Colonel D. D. Eisenhower, have rendered especially efficient and satisfactory service under many trying difficulties as camp commanders of the Tank Corps Units."

Eisenhower sent a copy of the correspondence to his father, along with a covering note. "Dear Dad," he wrote, "Just sending you above—as thought you'd be interested. There is no chance of my getting one of the medals—but it shows Colonel Welborn's opinion of me. Devotedly. Son."[1]

Nearly four years later, the Army proved him to be wrong. The citation for the D.S.M. he received said, "While commanding officer of the Tank Training Corps Center, from March 23, 1918, to Nov. 18, 1918, at Camp Colt, Gettysburg, Pennsylvania, he displayed unusual zeal, foresight and administrative ability."

---

1   McCann: op. cit.

Fox Conner

The several turning points in Eisenhower's Army career are clearly apparent. He decides, on "Swede" Hazlett's urging, to try for an appointment to West Point. The medical officers there grant him his commission in spite of his injured knee. At one point, he toys with the thought of leaving the Army. If he had taken different decisions, or if circumstances had been different, would the world ever have heard of Dwight D. Eisenhower, civilian? The strange pattern continues. In later years, he meets and works with certain men who affect his thinking and turn him toward the role he will be playing in the Second World War. Suppose his military assignments had not brought him into their orbit? In one view, these events, even granting that he bent his energies into making the most of them, would be seen as a set of lucky accidents. But the teleologist, who believes that a reason, a final cause, underlies this life, would see the same events as evidence of Destiny.

In any case, luck or fate brought him together with a remarkable man in the autumn of 1919, General Fox Conner. Without Conner's influence, Eisenhower might very well have remained one of thousands of competent but obscure Army officers. Many years later, Eisenhower said that Conner was among the handful of persons who exerted a decisive effect on him and his career.

After the First World War, Eisenhower passed through a period of frustration and indecision. The opportunity to prove himself as a commander in combat had not come to him. In 1920, he reverted to the rank of captain. To be sure, a few months later he was promoted to Major, but even so he calculated that he would not go very far in a shrinking, peacetime Army before he reached the age of retirement. Furthermore, the world had been made "safe for democracy." With the armaments-limiting treaties of the 1920s and the rampant isolationism of the United States, it appeared that a military man was almost as useless as the human appendix. For a time, Eisenhower thought of returning to civilian life where the future might hold more promise.

He entered the Infantry Tank School at Camp Meade in 1919. Two years later, he graduated with an "A" and was given command of the 301st Tank Battalion. The "A" took its place beside the other commendations in his 201 File. The 201 File is the Army's record of an officer's performance from the time he is commissioned, a kind of military Book of Judgment. The entries for Eisenhower's file for that early period indicate that his technical competence already was beginning to be recognized. One says, "Desire detail Major Dwight D. Eisenhower, an exceptionally efficient officer, now on leave, for etc." And another, "Major Eisenhower is preeminently qualified for the detail he seeks. He has force, character and energy as well as knowledge."

Camp Meade was the scene of Eisenhower's first meeting with Fox Conner, a brief encounter, yet something about the General made an impression on him and evidently the feeling was mutual.

These were hard days for Mamie. When her husband first went to Meade, the officers quarters were filled. He found one room in a house in Odenton, Maryland, seven miles from the Camp. It was poorly furnished and without electricity from 6 o'clock in the morning until 6 in the evening, Mamie, as usual, set to work to make it comfortable. Taking "Little Icky" in tow, she went frequently to Baltimore, hunting bargains. She watched the newspapers for announcements of sales and auctions, the homemaker.

Then came the first sadness in their marriage. A few days before Christmas of 1920, the baby began running a fever. The physician who examined him said he thought it was no more than a child's ailment and would soon pass. Instead, the temperature continued rising. They took him to the Post hospital where the doctors diagnosed the illness as scarlet fever. On Jan. 2, "Little Icky" died. He was 3 years and 3 months old. Mamie, grieving, and never fully to recover her earlier lightheartedness, took the body to Denver for burial.

By that time, Fox Conner was commanding the 20th Infantry Brigade at Camp Gaillard in the Panama Canal Zone. He wrote Eisenhower that he would like him to be his senior aide and, if Eisenhower agreed, would put in the formal request. Eisenhower accepted. He and his wife sailed for the Canal Zone on Jan. 7, 1922.

Mamie was stunned when she first saw their quarters there. The house, vacant and gone to seed in the tropical climate, stood on the summit of a steep hill.

A muddy path led up to it and Mamie, skidding and floundering, fell behind her husband. She found herself alone, surrounded by thick tropical undergrowth in which, she was certain, snakes and other loathsome creatures were eyeing her. She called out, "Ike, wait for me. I can't go so fast." Then she struggled up the path to the house. The walls were mouldy. Screens and shutters were rotting. The screen door uttered a raucous screech when Eisenhower opened it and some of the boards in the floor were loose. Mamie said nothing. Her husband looked around and said, with consummate understatement, "Needs a little fixing." He added, "I can do it myself." Mamie later described the house as a "disreputable, double-decked shanty."

At that moment, the screen door squawked again and a sweet-faced woman, slim, with gray hair, entered the room. She introduced herself as Mrs. Fox Conner and said she and the General would like the Eisenhowers to have some iced tea with them. Mamie gratefully accepted. Perhaps life in the Canal Zone, despite the "shanty," would not be too difficult after all.

For months, in his off-duty time, Eisenhower hammered and sawed, patching up the place and Mamie slithered up and down the hill to the PX and the stores, making another home.

The relationship between Fox Conner and Eisenhower soon became one of mentor and protege.

The General, with remarkable prescience, was convinced that a Second World War inevitably must follow the first. The causes, he said, were built into the Treaty of Versailles. A people as dynamic as the Germans would not passively abide by its terms for long…a burden of reparations too heavy to manage…loss of territory in the West and the East and the loss of colonies…the status of a second-class military power. Conner predicted, in 1922, that Germany some day would break out of the straitjacket. When? Within 10 years, he said. Or 15 at the outside.

He urged Eisenhower to prepare himself for high command, to aim for a General's stars. This went beyond Eisenhower's loftiest ambitions but the force of Conner's arguments started him thinking.

Late into the night, they discussed geopolitics. Conner in effect drew a map of the great power units in the world, the United States, Britain, France, Germany and Japan. Russia, still bleeding from the

Revolution, was a question mark, China possessed enormous manpower but China, ruled by feuding warlords, could not be classed as a nation. The first five, and they alone, held the keys to peace or war in the world.

The General went on from this premise to delineate the strategic and commercial spheres of the five nations and where their lines of interest, like huge power cables, intersected. These were the danger points. He spoke of colonies, sea lanes, essential raw materials in time of war. He pointed out that not even the United States was self-sufficient.

Fox Conner was a brilliant, deep-thinking man. The importance of his influence on Eisenhower is beyond estimation.

Their midnight discussions widened Eisenhower's concepts of the interconnections of strategy, politics and trade in the world. They also whetted his appetite to learn more than he had learned at West Point about the sheer mechanics of war.

He outfitted a "workroom" in a screened porch on the second floor of his quarters with a drawing board capable of holding large maps. There, with books and technical manuals beside the maps, he refought old battles and campaigns. He concentrated on those that seemed most instructive, Napoleon's victories at Austerlitz and Marengo, and especially the Emperor's last campaign in Italy. Poring over the Battle of Leuthen, he noted that the precision of the two Prussian columns as they attacked was a key factor in the victory of Frederick the Great. Eisenhower familiarized himself with the details of these engagements so firmly that years later, in retirement, he could still recall them.

When he was not working with the maps, he was rereading Clausewitz's "Vom Krieg," on the philosophy of war and the works of other authorities in this field.

Gone forever was the carefree cadet who had studied only out of necessity.

During this period, Eisenhower's boyhood friend, "Swede" Hazlett appeared in Panama. Hazlett by this time was a submarine commander and his ship put into drydock for repair of a burned-out motor. Of his three weeks at Camp Gaillard, he wrote:

"Ike got me astride a horse again and we rode the bosque trails; and in the evenings—some more poker. This latter was bad news, for Ike and his Army friends set a much higher standard for the five-card game than the Navy. But what interested me most was his work. He was…senior aide (chief-of-staff, in fact) to General Fox Conner and had been largely responsible for drawing up war plans for the defense of the area; he explained them to me with the enthusiasm of a genius."

Eisenhower also showed his "workroom" and Hazlett commented of this new avocation:

"This was particularly unusual at a torrid, isolated post, where most officers spent their off hours trying to keep cool and amused."

When the submarine was operative again, Hazlett took his friend for a dive. He wrote that Eisenhower was so "avid for information" that when the trip ended, "I really believe…he knew almost as much about submarines as I did."

In all, Eisenhower spent three years in the Canal Zone. His principal duty, of course, was to assist General Conner in planning its defenses. He discovered that Conner greatly admired a rapidly rising star in the Army, George Catlett Marshall. Whenever Eisenhower solved a problem, or performed some planning task particularly well, Conner was likely to say, "That's the way George Marshall would have handled it." High praise, indeed!

Another of Conner's habitual remarks was, "Always take your work seriously, never yourself." Except for the word, "always," this had been Eisenhower's philosophy for years. Now he adopted the axiom in toto.

Along with the immense value of Conner's tutelage, another dividend accrued to Eisenhower from his experience in the Canal Zone. Years later, it would help him form a critical judgment. Just as he had soaked up a mass of information about "Swede" Hazlett's submarine, he delved into the mechanics of operating the Panama Canal. And so, during the Suez Crisis of 1956, Eisenhower was *not* one of those who said the technical problems were so great that the Egyptians would be incapable of keeping the Canal functioning without foreign assistance. He knew better.

Most important of all in this period of Eisenhower's development, Fox Conner led him to the next long step, an appointment to the Command and General Staff School. He planted the seeds of this ambition and promised to use all his influence to obtain the appointment for his protege.

Without this, it is wholly improbable that the Colonel of 1941 would have been wearing the three stars of a Lieutenant General in 1942.

...

Throughout the Army, the Command and General Staff School at Fort Leavenworth was known as a backbreaker.

The reason was simple. The order in which an officer graduated could very well determine his future role in the Army. To come out near the top marked him sharply in the eyes of superiors. Therefore, those attending the school competed fiercely. For months, they drove themselves without respite. Some broke down under the nervous strain. Some, it was said, committed suicide.

When he left the Panama Canal Zone, Eisenhower visited briefly with his family in Abilene and returned to Colorado where he went on duty at Fort Logan as a recruiting officer. The work bored him, but the Fort was near Denver, and Mamie, who had given birth to John Sheldon Doud Eisenhower in 1922, was able to see her family often.

General Fox Conner had promised to do what he could to open the doors of the Command School for Eisenhower. However, Eisenhower could not be sure he would receive the appointment.

Nevertheless, he began studying. It was like Abilene, 15 years earlier, when he and "Swede" Hazlett had studied nights in the Belle Springs Creamery to prepare for the competitive examinations for West Point and/or Annapolis. Eisenhower used the same methods now. He managed to come into possession of copies of problems presented at the Command School in other years. He studied solutions.

As in the Canal Zone, he set up a workroom on the top floor of his quarters, equipping it with maps and books. Night and day, he focussed his attention on them.

Months passed without word from Gen. Conner.

With hardly a break in his studies while waiting, Eisenhower rid himself of a potential threat. As part of his duties in Panama, he often mounted a horse and rode long distances through the jungle. During one of these trips, a sharp pain stabbed him in his side and lower abdomen. It passed, but he consulted the Army doctors who diagnosed it as an attack of appendicitis. They said it might never recur, but on the other hand it could strike again at any time. Eisenhower didn't want that to happen if, or when, he entered the Command

School. So in the summer of 1925, he entered a hospital in Denver and had his appendix removed.

He took his books with him and studied while he was recuperating.

Then the electrifying word came—the order to report to Fort Leavenworth in August 1925. With mingled feelings, exuberance and worry, he and Mamie packed again and left for the newest and hardest trial.

Working in the Command School, he passed through the same mental and emotional pattern that he had experienced 10 years before when he studied for the competitive and then the entrance examinations for West Point. Intensive work…a recapitulation of what he had learned…a growing feeling of confidence…then the last big push.

He worked in top gear for 10 months, from August until June of 1926, classes during the day, nights studying in the attic of his quarters.

The term ended. Eisenhower and 274 other officers settled into the final examinations. Then, in hope and fear, some with confidence, many in doubt, they waited.

When the ratings were posted, Maj. Dwight Eisenhower stood No. 1 in the class of 275.

Eighteen years earlier, another officer with whom Eisenhower's destiny would be closely meshed, had accomplished the same feat. He was George Catlett Marshall. In all probability, this was when Eisenhower's name first came to Marshall's attention.

One of the instructors at the Command School was an officer named George S. Patton Jr. He made a remark to Eisenhower the day the rankings were announced.

That night, bursting with jubilance, Eisenhower repeated it to Mamie.

"Here's a big laugh, Mamie," he said. "This fellow George Patton, you know, the instructor, he came up to me and congratulated me and do you know what he said? He said, 'Major, some day I'll be working for you.' How's that for a laugh?"

Preview of Three Battlefields

In the ensuing 10 years, Eisenhower undertook three difficult assignments, each of which in a different way contributed to his education for the role of Supreme Commander. He went to France to study terrain where one day he would be mapping tactics and strategy. He was thrown into the problem of industrial mobilization in the United States, the sinews of the fighting forces. And he served in the Philippine Islands, scene of the first American battlefield in the Second World War.

This work also brought his first meeting with George C. Marshall, who was to turn to Eisenhower when he needed a special man for a special task. It came about in this way—

In the fall of 1926, Eisenhower was at Fort Benning, Georgia, serving as executive officer of the 24th Infantry. The job bored him. He felt let down after the 10 months of preparing himself at top speed for graduation from the Command and General Staff School where he was the star in the class of 275. Always restless, Eisenhower was ripe to move from routine desk work to something interesting.

One day, an inquiry that seemed odd to him came from Washington: Would Maj. Eisenhower care to organize and write a guidebook to the battlefields in Europe where Americans had fought in the First World War?

Why not? At least it would be something new and possibly interesting. A surprise awaited him in Washington.

He reported to the Battle Monuments Commission there, Jan. 15, 1927. The dimensions of his assignment, when he saw them, all but overwhelmed him. This, indeed, looked interesting, a challenge wholly unlike anything he had ever undertaken.

The Commission, almost from the day the war ended, had been collecting maps, photographs, pages and pages of descriptive material, personal reminiscences, information of many types about the scenes where American units had seen action. The problem confronting Eisenhower was to boil down this mountain of material into a manageable guidebook, retaining only the most essential facts, and presenting them in such form as to be crystal clear to tourists with nonmilitary minds.

It staggered him. It would have appalled even a professional writer.

Furthermore, the Commission gave Eisenhower only six months to finish the manuscript, select maps and photographs, and arrange the whole in logical sequence. The guidebook then would be submitted to General of the Army John J. Pershing. At the time, of course, Eisenhower could not foresee that he would be studying battlefields where one day he would be directing battles.

He plunged into the mass of material with his characteristic drive, retaining this, weeding out that, fitting each small tile into the mosaic he envisioned. In spite of the pressure of time (so often in his life he found himself racing the clock!) he came to enjoy the work. The long nights in Panama, when he traced the course of older battles, helped him greatly. A by-product of his work, far more important than he could realize then, was the acquisition of an intimate knowledge of the terrain in France and a thorough grounding in the tactics of the American commanders in the First World War.

He finished the book on schedule. The Encyclopaedia Britannica was to describe it as "an excellent reference work on World War I."

Pershing read it and, noting the systematic pattern that Eisenhower had followed, wrote a glowing letter about the guidebook:

"What he (Eisenhower) has done was accomplished only by the exercise of unusual intelligence and devotion to duty." Another bright bouquet went into Eisenhower's 201 File.

In fact, Pershing's high regard for Eisenhower's ability to write logically evidently reached a point where he asked the Major to read the memoirs *he* was writing and give him an opinion.

Eisenhower did so. Nothing could be more typical of him than his report to Pershing. Another man probably would have said, "It's great, General, just fascinating. Don't change a word."

Instead, Eisenhower said, "Gen. Pershing, everything in that war as far as the Army is concerned, pointed up to the two great battles, Saint-Mihiel and the Argonne. Now, I don't believe you should tell the story in those two chapters in the form of a diary. It takes the reader's attention away from the development of the battles and it just follows your own actions, your own decisions, and your own travels."

Inexorable honesty. Eisenhower always expected truthful answers from his subordinates. When he discovered a half-truth or an outright lie, he promptly fired the man. It did not occur to him to sugarcoat his report to the General of the Army.

Pershing blinked. But all he said was, "Write me something."

Eisenhower returned to his typewriter, still sizzling from the rush job on the guidebook, and rewrote Pershing's two chapters. Pershing liked them. However, he said, "Before I use them, I want to send for Colonel Marshall."

Eisenhower was sitting in an anteroom when an officer with a craggy face, keen, searching eyes, and an air of authority, emerged from Pershing's offices. He was George C. Marshall.

This was their first meeting, and it developed into a minor disagreement. Gracefully, in his soft Virginia accent, Marshall said he liked Eisenhower's writing very much. But he said he had advised Pershing not to use the substitute chapters. "General Pershing likes consistency," he said, "and it would be a very hard thing for him to accept this abrupt change for these two subjects and then go right back into his diary."

"My idea is different," Eisenhower retorted. They eyed each other and a mutual respect was born.

Thus, but for Marshall's advice, two chapters in Pershing's "My Experiences in the World War," published in 1931, would have been the work of a ghost-writer named Dwight D. Eisenhower.

As a direct result of writing the guidebook, Eisenhower was soon to go to France to study the battlefields on the ground. But before this, he pinned two more brilliants to his record.

He entered the Army War College in September 1927, and graduated June 30, 1928—again No. 1 in his class. And he received the Distinguished Service Medal, for which he had been recommended nearly a decade before. His father, remembering the letter that said "There is no chance of my getting one of the medals," must have smiled.

Eisenhower received two offers when he graduated from the War College, to join the General Staff in Washington, or, as a preliminary to revising his guidebook, to go to France. He chose the latter.

A month later, he was tramping the terrain and storing in his memory details of villages, fields, streams, bridges and highway communications where, one day, he would be directing the movements of millions of men.

...

Automatically, as he hiked across France, across the lush fields and through the forests, Major Eisenhower's eyes took in the features of terrain in terms of their suitability for tank operations. Could you use tanks here? They could easily be stopped there.

He had entered a new stage in his training for high command.

Eisenhower came to France in July 1928, to study battlefields preparatory to refurbishing the guidebook he had written for the Battle Monuments Commission. He installed Mamie and little Johnny, now nearing his 6th birthday, in an apartment on the Rue d'Auteuil in Paris. They remained for 14 months.

They were happy months. Eisenhower's work fascinated him. Johnny started school. Mamie enjoyed Paris which, in that period, was like a glorious ripe peach.

From this base, Eisenhower zigzagged across France, almost entirely on foot, studying the sectors of American military operations in the First World War.

Although he had missed combat duty, he knew a good deal about the sites he was now studying...Cantigny...Chateau Thierry...the Vosges...Soissons...Saint Mihiel...the Meuse-Argonne...the heights above Sedan.

He carried separate notebooks for separate types of data. Logistics, for example, the systems of feeding and supplying huge numbers of fighting men. The American Expeditionary Forces had been based, in fact, in the United States during the height of the fighting. Thus, although the logistical problem was not especially relevant to his guidebook, Eisenhower studied it simply out of professional interest. Air power, although by no means appreciated from a strategic point of view in that day, nevertheless might be a factor in the next war, he suspected. So he studied railroad marshalling yards and potentially vulnerable points in the French network of rail and highway communications.

But "tank country" interested him most. This was natural since he had been trained for tanks and had then been an instructor in an armored school. Who could say, in the next war, whether the Infantry would remain "Queen of Battles"?

To a lesser degree, he also learned something of the French Army, noting lines of cleavage he hoped would never develop in the United States Army. French politics; although not yet as Balkan as they would be in the 1930s, left him with a murky, confused impression.

In September 1929, he brought his family back to Washington. They returned to a strange and wonderful land.

The decade was ending, a naive and frivolous decade. A man established some kind of record by dancing the Charleston more than 48 hours without stopping. There were Marathon Dances which went on for days, one partner awake and shuffling, and holding in his or her arms what looked like a sleeping rag doll. In Chicago, Al Capone's "torpedoes" sent St. Valentine's Day greetings to seven of their O'Bannion rivals, lined up in a garage—bullets in the back. Women pawned jewelry and clothing for the price of admission to a booming stock market. You couldn't lose, everybody said. And don't worry about margin, you don't have to put up much cash. Pretty soon, there would be two chickens in every pot and two cars in every garage. It was the Golden Age and not a cloud darkened the skies above the Flapper in her knee-high skirts and the Sheik wearing bell-bottom pants.

If security seemed firmly assured in the domestic affairs of the United States in 1929, the prospect for continued peace seemed equally assured.

In the year Eisenhower returned to Washington, the Senate ratified the Kellogg-Briand Pact which pledged the signatory nations to forever abandon force as an instrument of policy. Naval ratios had been established and as a result, mighty battleships now rocked gently on the ocean floor. Japanese naval officers, watching the sinkings with bleak, expressionless eyes, secretly vowed revenge. Nobody but they knew their thoughts. In Italy, a hyperthyroid type named Mussolini had seized total power and many persons applauded on the ground that Italians needed discipline. The aged Field Marshall Paul von Hindenburg was presiding benignly over a prosperous Germany, and only a handful of plotters and maniacs in Munich had heard the name Adolf Hitler. Civilians held the reins of government in Japan, which had enriched itself greatly during the war as chief purveyor to the Allies. They were conservative men, far more interested in continuing the expansion of trade than in any military adventures. They appeared to have the Japanese militarists firmly under control.

So for a professional soldier, the future looked thin, indeed. Fox Conner's prediction about the inevitability of a Second World War began to seem utterly baseless.

In November, Eisenhower went to the staff of the Assistant Secretary of War. Here began another phase of his education. Part of the work in his office entailed procurement for the Army and its air force. Eisenhower's duties became, essentially, those of a businessman. They threw him into studies of raw materials, labor, costs, management and production. Again, he was called upon to study and absorb masses of detail in a brand new field. The soldier became a business analyst.

During this assignment, he helped establish the Army Industrial College. It dealt with these matters. He attended classes and later lectured in the College.

Meanwhile, he watched economic paralysis grip the nation. In October, a month before he began his new assignment, the stock market crashed in a few cataclysmic days. A chain reaction set in, sweeping across the country, shuttering banks and factories. The mighty generators of economic power stuttered and some went dead.

Soon, long queues of men, shambling and shame-faced, stood in the breadlines. Some sold apples on street corners. A grimly appropriate song became popular, "Brother, Can You Spare a Dime?" A newspaper cartoon showed a squirrel talking to a dissipirited man sitting beneath the tree and asking, "But why didn't you save in the good times?" The man answers, "I did." Savings were swept away or lost in the bank failures.

Now, for Eisenhower, the outlook seemed doubly bleak. The Army, starved for appropriations, was contracting. His prospects for promotion receded instead of coming nearer as time passed. Too many officers senior to him stood ahead. Again, for the second time, he seriously considered leaving the Army. He toyed with the idea of becoming a newspaperman.

However, with unemployment rising rapidly, this was no time to start a civilian career. He remained at his desk in the Assistant Secretary's offices.

At about this time, someone in Washington had a flash of prescience.

The question of possible sources of synthetic rubber was raised. Malaya (which was rapidly overrun by the Japanese in 1942) largely supplied the United States with natural rubber. What would happen if this source should be cut off in wartime?

Eisenhower's superiors sent him into the Southwest to study the possibilities in *guayule*, a desert plant from which the Mexican Indians had been producing a form of rubber for centuries. He kept a diary of the trip—

"Wednesday, April 16. Went to plant and gathered up some loose ends of information...Saw Monterey—Del Monte—artist's colony at Carmel—the Monterey Cypress grove...This section (had one a lot of money) would be ideal for a home. Hope to bring Mamie there sometime.

"April 18. Arrived El Paso after a hot, dirty trip. Cleaned up and went to Juarez for a bottle of beer. Ate dinner there. Most expensive bust I've been on in this trip. Spent over $5. Won't do that again. Went to bed early and read until 2 a.m.

"Saturday, April 19. Went to Post...Fort Bliss...Morale seems to be high—but everyone is terribly anxious about the pay bill. Wish I could be more optimistic about it—but I believe the chances are so slim that it would be only raising a false hope to tell people that 'in Washington it is believed a pay bill will pass soon.' Certainly if we don't get one soon we are going to get only those men in the Army who are sons of wealthy families."[1]

In 1933, Franklin D. Roosevelt came to the Presidency and the "Hundred Days" began, one of the most remarkable periods in American history. Overnight, the economic patterns that had been in existence since the nation was founded were altered beyond recognition. Philosophies and policies changed. The relations between the Federal Government and business, and between the state and the individual, changed.

In the "Hundred Days," 15 messages went to Congress and 15 pieces of major legislation emerged, the Banking Act, the RFC, the Farm Credit Administration, the Railroad Coordination Act, the Tennessee Valley Authority—and more.

"The hazards and responsibilities this combination involved might well have given the most intrepid social explorer some qualms,"

---

1 Quoted in McCann: op. cit.

Raymond Moley, a member of the original "brain trust," observed. "But I was never conscious of a moment's doubt in Roosevelt's mind that he could wisely and safely administer discretionary powers too staggering even to be fully comprehended by the electorate at large."[1]

Dwight Eisenhower, watching this astonishing phenomenon from close range in Washington, must have felt some doubts. His philosophy, based on the teachings of his mother and the self-reliance of men on the Great Plains, was quite different.

In Washington, Eisenhower came in contact frequently with the man who had emerged from the First World War universally recognized as a brilliant soldier, Gen. Douglas MacArthur. Mac-Arthur was serving as Chief of Staff.

The two men were wholly unlike. MacArthur had great style and flair. Eisenhower was simple and down-to-earth. MacArthur was handsome and dressed the part. Eisenhower seldom was conscious of his appearance. MacArthur wrote and spoke in majestic, rolling periods. Eisenhower's speech was laconic, his prose lean and terse.

However, they respected each other as professionals.

In fact, in 1935, MacArthur wrote Eisenhower a glowing letter, commending him for his handling of the many-sided problems that had come across his desk. In that year, MacArthur became Chief Military Adviser to the Government of the Philippines. He asked Eisenhower to accompany him to the Islands as his senior assistant.

The idea did not appeal to Eisenhower. Nor did his wife want to go to the Philippines. He told MacArthur that he would prefer some other duty. Whereupon, MacArthur put the request in the form of an order. Eisenhower swallowed his objections and replied, "Very well, sir."

Those are among the three luckiest words he ever spoke.

---

1 Raymond Moley: "After Seven Years."

The Tripos Completed

Eisenhower's four years in the Philippine Islands were a vital link in the chain of events that carried him to the role of Supreme Commander in the Second World War. They added another dimension to his training to organize and lead a multination force. More immediately, his experience in the work of devising a Defense Plan for the Islands was to be one of the reasons why Gen. Marshall singled him out for a special task one week after the attack on Pearl Harbor.

Before he went to Manila in 1935, Eisenhower had fully demonstrated his competence as an officer. He had graduated No. 1 from both the Command and General Staff School and the Army War College, mastering the complexities of high command, strategy and tactics. He had been decorated for his work in instructing crews in the relatively new science of tank warfare. The citations in his 201 File, even at that point in his career, showed an officer superbly equipped as a military technician.

Next, he had been exposed to the problems of industrial mobilization, procurement, production, "lead time," what is entailed in bringing the weapon from the drawing board or factory to the hand of the fighting man.

Now, in the Philippines, he entered a new world, a politico-military world. His work brought him in contact with the highest echelons of government. He learned something about politicians. He found himself dealing with a proud and sensitive people. Eisenhower was a born diplomat, as World War II would demonstrate, a man well endowed with tact and charm. The Philippines assignment developed these natural qualities.

This, then, was the third leg in the tripos.

He sailed from the United States in September 1935, to take up his post as assistant to MacArthur, the Chief Military Adviser to the Philippines Government. The task was to organize and train the

Filipino Armed Forces and to draw up a blueprint for the defense of the Islands.

The Tydings-McDuffie Act provided that they should become a Commonwealth in 1936, graduating to complete independence 10 years later. MacArthur's name was magic in the Philippines; his father, Gen. Arthur MacArthur, had liberated them in the Spanish-American War. To formulate the National Defense Plan, the President Elect, Manuel Queson, asked for Douglas MacArthur. And he in turn chose Eisenhower to assist him.

MacArthur went to work immediately, before leaving for the Philippines. The Army War College drew up a plan. MacArthur and Eisenhower supervised the formulation of it. Eventually, Mac-Arthur rejected it as too costly. Eisenhower and Maj. James Ord, an instructor in the War College started all over again. MacArthur wanted a plan that could be supported on a budget of Pesos 16 million, or $8 million. Even in the 1930s, this was a pittance. Eisenhower and Ord redrafted the Defense Plan so as to fit into this budget, a professional force of 930 officers and 7,000 enlisted men as the nucleus around which, in theory, 30 Infantry division would be built. They pigeonholed, but only for the time being, they thought, formation of an artillery corps. And they stretched the procurement period from 10 to 20 years. Some disquieting signs had appeared in the skies, but nobody in the Philippines felt any sense of emergency. Curiously enough, it appears that during this period MacArthur did not believe Japan would attack the Islands in case of a Pacific War. He seems to have felt they would seize other objectives first. In any event, on the minuscule budget, nobody could have rushed the Defense Plan.

Mamie did not go with her husband when he sailed for the Islands. She waited until the following year so that Johnny could finish junior high school in Washington.

Nearing the end of the voyage, the ship stopped in Japan. Eisenhower went sightseeing in Yokohama, Tokyo, Kobe and Kyoto. The beauty and splendor of Kyoto, the ancient capital of Japan, dazzled him. And he asked innumerable questions about the country. What he learned indicated that perhaps General Fox Conner's prediction in 1922—"the Second World War is inevitable"—was not so farfetched as it had seemed to be in the era when armaments were being reduced by Treaty.

For by 1935, Japan had changed course to a policy of naked

aggression in China. And in Europe, Hitler and Mussolini were weaving the web that would bring violent death to millions and eventually to themselves.

Before Eisenhower first saw Japan, its conservative, businessman's-type of government had been largely superseded by the militarists. In 1931, they seized Manchuria. Then they set up the puppet state of "Manchuokuo" and began eyeing North China across the Great Wall. Henry L. Stimson, Secretary of State, tried to marshal collective opposition against Japan, but the British, although their investments were vastly greater in China, declined to go along.

By the end of 1932, liberal influence in the Emperor's Court all but vanished, and the ultranationalists, known as the "double patriots," consolidated their hold on the central government. They set Japan on the collision course that would lead to Pearl Harbor.

In China, the Nationalist Government of Chiang Kai-shek had been fighting the War Lords, semi-independent satraps who fielded private armies and controlled vast expanses of territory, then the Chinese Communists. Few persons realized then that the Communists would prove to be a greater threat to peace and stability in China than either the War Lords or Japan.

The first Chinese "Soviet" had been established in Kiangsi, a mountainous province in South China, far from the Nationalist capital in Nanking. The Communists steadily enlarged their hold on that part of China. In four major "extermination campaigns," Chiang attempted to dislodge them. The fifth succeeded. However, the great majority of Communists, fighting men, women and children, broke out of the Nationalist encirclement and started on the famous "Long March," an hegira that covered thousands of miles. They transformed defeat in South China into a brilliant public relations coup.

In October 1935, at just about the time Eisenhower passed through the two Chinese cities, the "Long March" ended in the remote Northwestern province of Shensi. There the Communists dug in again. Meanwhile, all along the fishhook-shaped route they had taken, they made a favorable impression on millions of peasants and probably converted many of them. Communist troops, unlike most Chinese soldiers, treated the peasants well. They neither stole, looted nor raped. Moreover, they executed captured landlords and turned their land over to the hungry farmers. Not that they especially cherished peasants. The Communist policy of calculated kindness grew out of Mao Tse-tung's shrewd observation, "The peasants are the sea and we are the fish who swim in that sea." Thus, the Communists established a solid base of goodwill among millions of politically unsophisticated Chinese a full decade before Mao made his first moves toward the conquest of all China.

In Europe, meanwhile, Hitler became the "Fuehrer" in 1935. He promptly repudiated those clauses in the Treaty of Versailles that prohibited German rearmament and hastened to create a gigantic mechanized army, a new navy and a powerful air force.

In the same year, Mussolini marched against Ethiopia. A half-hearted attempt to invoke sanctions failed to stop him.

The parallel movements, Japan in Asia and the Dictators in Europe, were soon to converge and challenge the world.

This was the setting when Eisenhower stepped off the ship in Manila Bay. It was later than the Democracies realized.

. . .

Manuel Quezon, President of the Philippines, took an immediate liking to Maj. Eisenhower. In no time, Eisenhower became a familiar figure at Malacanan Palace. He saw the President two and three times a week, not always on official business. Bridge, for example. Bridge is a game ideally suited to the military mind, attack, defense, timing, the acceptable loss, the calculated risk. When Quezon discovered that Eisenhower played a shrewd and daring game of bridge, the Major frequently was invited aboard the Presidential yacht, Casiana. He was at once Quezon's favorite partner and favorite opponent.

Further, Quezon's friendliness for Eisenhower came from his discovery that Eisenhower invariably gave him the blunt, unvarnished facts in a situation, however unpalatable. Eisenhower's answers, Quezon said when Eisenhower was receiving a decoration at the end of his tour of duty in the Philippines, were not always those he would have liked to hear. But he could be sure they were open, honest and factual. This was second nature to Eisenhower.

So from the standpoint of his relations with the President, Eisenhower started off well in Manila.

But as he came to grips with the task at hand, setting up a National Defense Plan for the Islands, Eisenhower was appalled at the enormity of it. The immediate objectives as he saw them entailed creating bases, camps, airfields, administrative buildings—all the physical facilities for an army not yet in being. Arms would have to be procured, thousands of officers trained, and administrative machinery built to manage the thousand-and-one details of these operations. The budget, equivalent to a mere $8 million annually, was a straitjacket.

The over-all responsibility for the Plan lay, of course, in the hands of Gen. Douglas MacArthur. His advisers worked out the details.

In addition to these physical problems, imponderables in Washington handicapped the Americans working on the Defense Plan. A kind of apathy about Pacific defenses seemed to overlay the Capital during this period. Congress, for example, refused to appropriate a mere $5 million to fortify Guam. Only some ancient Enfield rifles, 75-millimeter artillery pieces and Lewis and Browning machine guns were made available, and these at higher costs than the Planners had expected to have to pay in the United States.

To be sure, at that time many Americans regarded defense of the Western Pacific as the special responsibility of the Navy and there was no lack of Navy officers to express total confidence that this responsibility would be readily discharged. (One of them, a captain, happily said to this writer in Manila on New Year's Eve of 1941, "If war starts out here, our problem won't be to *whip* the Jap Navy—it'll be to *find* it.")

And finally, MacArthur had enemies in Washington. One of his aides wrote:

"For when he became military adviser to the Philippine government, he found himself facing a movement to supplant him even in this position, on the specious theory that as a retired officer he could not lawfully exercise authority over the active U.S. Army officers assigned to the military advisory group."[1]

In the best of circumstances, the job to be done in the Philippines would have been long and difficult. And they were not the best.

Nevertheless, the work fascinated Eisenhower and he found life pleasant in the Islands. In 1936, Mamie and John arrived from Washington after the boy finished junior high school. Eisenhower took his son on jaunts into the mountains and to an island destined to be immortalized in American history, Corregidor.

In 1918, he had held the temporary rank of lieutenant colonel.

---

1 Major General Courtney Whitney: "MacArthur: His Rendezvous With Destiny."

Now he regained it on a permanent basis. In addition to his regular Army pay, he received from the Philippines government a sum equivalent to about $500 a month.

He wore tropical whites to his office but changed into a Chinese robe with the dragon symbol when he returned to the hotel.

And he took flying lessons from Lts. Bill Lee and Lefty Parker. He was 46 when he qualified for his pilot's license. He logged 350 hours of flying time. He took every opportunity to go aloft, ignoring the dangers of storms that come up suddenly in the tropics. Mamie suffered when she knew he was in the air.

1936—German troops reentered the Rhineland (with far too little strength, as their officers later disclosed) but no reaction came from Britain or France. The Spanish Civil War began, the testing ground for weapons in the next war.

In the House of Commons in London, a lone voice growled, "The Dictators ride to and fro upon tigers which they dare not dismount. And the tigers are getting hungry." Winston Churchill's dire prophecies only bored the Members.

1937—The "Marco Polo Bridge Incident" touched off a new Japanese attack on China. Fighting spread from the North, down to Shanghai, and then into South China almost on the doorstep of Hong Kong, the British Crown Colony.

In Chicago, on the night of Oct. 5, President Roosevelt delivered the "Quarantine Speech." He said:

"War is a contagion, whether it be declared or undeclared. It can engulf states and people remote from the original scene…It seems unfortunately true that the epidemic of world lawlessness is spreading. When an epidemic of physical disease starts to spread, the community approves and joins in a quarantine…Peace-loving nations can and must find a way to make their wills prevail."

But what did this mean? Revising the Neutrality Act? The President refused to specify.

On July 28, 1938, Eisenhower and his family sailed for the United States. The climate in the Philippines and the gruelling work were beginning to tell on him. As in Panama, he lost weight and his temper frayed. Besides, he hoped to find at home some surplus weapons at prices the skimpy budget could afford. He remained until Nov. 5.

In that year, Hitler obtained the Munich Agreement. Again, Churchill rose in the House and he said:

"All is over. Silent, mournful, abandoned, broken, Czechoslovakia recedes into the darkness."

Clearly now, time was running out but the strange paralysis still gripped the Democracies, stultifying action.

More and more, the words of Fox Conner echoed in Eisenhower's memory. Not long after he returned to the Philippines, his conviction grew that Conner had accurately forecast the coming of a Second World War and the United States' involvement in it.

Although the task of setting up the Defense Plan as envisioned for the Philippines now became almost totally hopeless, Eisenhower spent all of 1939 struggling to whip *something* into shape. Very little could be done.

On a warm September night in Manila, Eisenhower was with a friend who owned a shortwave radio. Using the earphones they strained to catch the words of a man speaking on the other side of the world. They heard Neville Chamberlain, Prime Minister of Britain, gravely announce that a state of war now existed between Britain and Nazi Germany.

Early next day, Eisenhower asked MacArthur to release him from his duties in the Philippines. "General," he said, "I want to be home because America is going to have to start getting ready for this war." MacArthur expressed doubt that the United States would be drawn into it immediately. However, he agreed to Eisenhower's request.

Next, Eisenhower went to the Palace to notify Quezon of his decision. The President tried to dissuade him and asked him to come back later. When Eisenhower returned, Quezon pushed a document across the desk. "Colonel," he said, "I want you to read this." Eisenhower recognized it as a form which fixed a kind of living allowance for American officers in the Islands. Then Quezon said, "You fill in any figure you want, any figure you think is reasonable." He added, "As you can see, it's already approved." He literally invited Eisenhower to write his own ticket.

Soberly, Eisenhower thanked him and declined the offer. "It's a matter of personal conviction with me, Mr. President," he said. "I believe we're going to get into this war and I'm going home to try to help do my part in preparing for it."

He left a detailed Defense Plan. It was long and largely technical but it contained a perceptive passage:

"There is one line, and one only, at which the defending forces will enjoy a tremendous advantage over any attack on land. *That line is the beach.* Successful penetration of a defended beach is the most difficult operation in warfare.

"If any attacking force succeeds in lodging itself firmly in a vital sector of the Islands, particularly Luzon, 90 per cent of the prior advantage of the defender will disappear. Behind the protecting lines established by such attacking forces, more and more strength can be brought in, by echelon, until, with superior armaments and with naval and other support, the whole will be strong enough to crush the defending Army...*the Philippine Army must have the numbers to defend all sensitive beaches.*"

Less than five years later, the man who wrote these words, "the most difficult operation in warfare," would himself be directing just such an operation. What he wrote of the Philippines would apply in even greater degree to the beaches of Normandy. The defenders would have the advantage on the beach when the attacking force, in effect, has one foot on land and the other on the landing craft. No doubt he remembered all too well his own summation on the night before D-Day.

On Dec. 12, 1939, Quezon gave a lunch in Malacanan Palace for the Eisenhowers. He made no further attempt to induce them to remain in Manila. The President showed his high regard for Eisenhower in another way. He awarded him the Distinguished Service Star of the Philippines and Mamie proudly pinned it on his tunic. The citation read:

"Through his outstanding achievements in the service of the Philippine Government he has increased the brilliance of his already enviable reputation, and has earned the gratitude and esteem of the Filipino people."

On the following day, the Eisenhowers boarded a ship bound for San Francisco. MacArthur and his wife came to their stateroom to bid them farewell. Three blasts from the ship's whistle echoed across Manila Bay and the liner slowly pulled away from the dock.

It passed a rock called Corregidor. Within two years, American troops would be fighting the brave but hopeless battle to hold that rock.

What would have happened to Dwight D. Eisenhower if he had listened to Quezon and remained in Manila? A casualty on Bataan? A prisoner of war in Japan? His great career, already beginning, might have ended in the Philippines.

The First Star

When Eisenhower returned from the Philippines in 1940, he hoped to attain two objectives, a Colonel's eagles and the command of a tank regiment. In that period, before the Army began expanding, he thought he would be doing well to become a Colonel before retirement.

Characteristically modest, although his official file was studded with commendations, he called himself "small fry" in the Army. The rush of events, and especially his tour of duty in the Philippines, were soon to sweep him to a role beyond his dreams.

His future, as he saw it then, depended greatly on the fate of the Selective Service Act in Congress. If the bill passed, the Army would expand overnight. The professionals, assigned to train and command the new units, would be jumped in grade. Eisenhower himself came home convinced that the United States would be drawn into the war in Europe. However, not many Americans shared his view and even more abhorred the thought of becoming involved. Moreover, 1940 was a Presidential election year and the draft would be politically unpopular. Nobody could foretell whether Congress would enact the Selective Service Act.

Eisenhower first reported to Fort Ord, California, in February. He found that maneuvers involving amphibious operations were to be held on the beaches near Monterey. He had seen operations of this type in the Philippines and being a thorough professional he wanted to learn more. He went to Monterey.

There, for the second time in his life, he met Gen. Marshall, now Chief of Staff. Thirteen years had passed since their first encounter in Washington. On that occasion, they had disagreed about the format for General Pershing's memoirs. Marshall now said, with his slow half smile, "Well, Eisenhower, have you learned to tie your shoes again?" He knew that in the Philippines an officer had a houseboy to perform such chores. "Yes, sir," Eisenhower replied. No further conversation took place between them. Eisenhower moved away to study the landings. The incident shows that Marshall remembered him and that, to some extent, he had been following Eisenhower's career.

From California, Eisenhower went to Fort Lewis, Washington, as executive officer of the 15th Infantry. Another desk job, whereas he wanted to be with troops. He asked for command of a battalion during maneuvers in the summer of 1940 and the request was granted.

After the maneuvers, he wrote a long letter about his experiences in the field to a friend, Colonel L. T. Gerow. The letter glowed with an almost boyish enthusiasm. "We certainly went places and did things," it said. He had frozen at night and gone largely without sleep, but boy!, this was the life.

Meanwhile, the fight in Congress over the Selective Service Act crackled into fury. Eisenhower followed it avidly in the newspapers. Henry L. Stimson, Secretary of State, strongly supported the bill which was sponsored by Representative James W. Wadsworth, a Republican, and Senator Edward Burke, a Democrat. President Roosevelt, however, provided no leadership until Aug. 2 when, at a press conference, he said he favored "a" bill. Not until mid-September did the Act pass. Registration day was fixed for Oct. 16.

Eisenhower launched a quiet campaign to obtain a field command. He wanted tanks. He wrote long letters to friends who might be instrumental in helping him. In one of these, he said, "I know that General Marshall, in person, is not concerned with the assignment of such small fry as myself…"

Nothing happened. However, on March 11, 1941, he achieved the first of his two ambitions, the "chicken wings" of a full Colonel.

Thousands of draftees were pouring into the induction centers. New units were being organized. Now, Eisenhower's hopes soared. He might have a regiment of his own, a tank regiment.

A much bigger boost for his fortune was approaching, the Louisiana Maneuvers.

They were to pit two large and very green armies against each other in a vast operation. Gen. Ben Lear commanded the Second Army, Lt. Gen. Walter Kreuger the Third. Kreuger was putting together his staff. Mark Wayne Clark, later to command the American Fifth Army in the Mediterranean, travelled 60,000 miles that summer, looking over officers potentially capable of serving under Kreuger in the critical test. He knew Eisenhower and his record up to that point.

On June 24, Eisenhower was ordered to report to Third Army headquarters in San Antonio, Texas, for duty with the General Staff. Back to the scene of their courtship and the first months of their marriage went Mamie and her husband. On Aug. 2, Eisenhower was named Chief of Staff to Kreuger.

As has been noted, Eisenhower had proved his technical competence long since. But the size and complexity of the Louisiana Maneuvers gave him by far his greatest opportunity to demonstrate his ability to devise tactics and strategy. He was Chief of Staff in an army of 300,000 men.

Preliminary moves in the maneuvers began in August and the main engagements lasted until late September. The Third Army "won" the initial engagements and by Sept. 25, it was adjudged to have thoroughly "defeated" the "enemy." Among the "enemy" tank commanders was a flamboyant, swashbuckling officer, George S. Patton.

Gen. Marshall watched the maneuvers. No doubt he also saw a syndicated Washington newspaper column which said, "Col. Eisenhower...conceived and directed the strategy that routed the Second Army." Other "war correspondents," who were then as green as most of the soldiers in the two Armies, singled out Eisenhower for special attention and praise. They noted his quick, incisive mind and physical endurance.

However realistic, maneuvers are not war. The imponderables, notably courage and an officer's ability to make a quick accurate decision while shells crash around his command post, do not surface in mock warfare.

Nonetheless, Eisenhower came out of the Louisiana Maneuvers with a brilliant success for his record. He knew he was on his way and he hoped it would lead to the armor.

After the maneuvers, he wrote another long letter to Col. Gerow, listing some of his observations in the performance of officers, troops and equipment. He also found space for a touch of humor about the "simulated" features of the operation:

He said a Corporal marched his detail across a bridge, causing an umpire to yell out, "Hey, don't you see that bridge is destroyed?"

"Of course, I can see it's destroyed," the Corporal yelled back. "Can't you see I'm swimming?"

The dust of the vast maneuvers had hardly settled when Eisenhower received a telegram. It advised him that the President had submitted to the Senate his nomination for the temporary rank of Brigadier General. He had his first star. The telegram was dated Sept. 29, 1941.

On that same day, Joseph C. Grew, American Ambassador to Japan, sent a message to Washington. He strongly urged the President to agree to a proposed meeting with Prince Fumimaro Konoye, Prime Minister of Japan.

The proposal envisioned a meeting between Roosevelt and Konoye in the Pacific, perhaps in Honolulu. It had been presented informally but Japanese authorities advised Grew of a date, Oct. 10-15, that would be acceptable to them and said a ship had been designated to take the Prince and his aides to the conference.

Grew commented in his diary:

"For a Prime Minister of Japan to thus shatter all precedent and tradition in this land of subservience to precedent and tradition, and to wish to come hat in hand, so to speak, to meet the President of the United States on American soil, is a gauge of the determination of the Government to undo the vast harm already accomplished in alienating our powerful and progressively angry country."[1]

Prince Konoye was a moderate. For years he had been fighting a rearguard action to prevent the militarists from acquiring supreme power in Japan.

The suggested date for the meeting passed with no word of reply from Washington. On Oct. 16, Konoye's government fell. To the office of Prime Minister came a man whose name would soon be familiar to every American, Gen. Hideki Tojo.

Six weeks later, on Nov. 29, 1941, a Japanese task force secretly slipped out of its home waters. A flow of dummy radio messages, normal in volume, masked its departure. The dark gray ships steamed on a northeasterly course and disappeared in the fog and lonely wastes of the North Pacific. The commander of the task force sailed under sealed orders. When he read them he learned his mission—Pearl Harbor.

• • •

It was still dark when Capt. Fuchida Mitsue went below decks to dress for his mission.

---
1 Joseph C. Grew: "Ten Years in Japan."

As he walked down the flight deck he knew, although he could not see them, that 26 other warships were on station all around the aircraft carrier. Yet not a sound came down the soft tropical wind and not so much as a pencil of light pierced the darkness. It was 5 a.m.

He bathed his face in cold water and carefully washed his hands. Then he took from his bag a white undergarment, white for death, the traditional funeral dress of his people. He could hardly expect to return from this day's mission.

On deck, he recalled later, "The men were excited but they calmed down when they received the order to attack."

At 6 o'clock, on the dot, Captain Mitsue, commander of the flight groups in the Japanese First Fleet, took off, leading 351 fighters and torpedo-bombers from the decks of six carriers. In the air, they wheeled and turned due south toward the Island of Oahu, 200 miles distant, and the American Naval base at Pearl Harbor.

The date was Dec. 7, 1941.

The date was the apex of a pyramid, a structure composed of tragic and often senseless events in the 1930s and even before. Not all the building blocks were stamped "Made in Japan." In 1925, under pressure from labor unions and political blocs, Congress passed the Exclusion Act. It barred Japanese emigrants from entering the United States while European immigration continued on a quota basis. The senseless action cut a proud people to the quick and was long remembered in Japan. In the same period, a few newspapers trumpeted warnings of the "Yellow Peril," although the *nissei*, American-born Japanese, and their parents set the highest standards of citizenship. They worked hard, payed taxes, kept their children in school, seldom appeared in a police court. They could not understand why they should be the objects of contempt and fear, the "Yellow Peril." In San Francisco for a short time, all Oriental children were segregated in separate schools from the whites.

In the 1930s, Japanese armies moved against China. Sympathy for the Chinese and hostility against the Japanese rose in equal measures in American public opinion. Japanese planes bombed and sank an American gunboat, the Panay, on the Yangtze River in 1937. The property of American missionaries in China was frequently destroyed.

Angry notes began to pass between the two governments. A swift-rushing stream was drawing the two nations, inexorably, toward the brink.

These events and others, moving in swift and contracting spirals, approached the climax in 1940.

When France and Holland collapsed under the devastating German onslaught in May, leaving Britain standing alone, Japanese expansionists turned their eyes toward the French, Dutch and British colonies in Southeast Asia. The region abounds in oil, rubber, valuable minerals and inexhaustible sources of food.

Why not seize them? What was to stop Japan?

Only one fighting force in the world could stop them. The single arm capable of reaching across the Pacific and hitting the Japanese was the United States Fleet, based in Pearl Harbor. The other potential threat to Japan, Russia's Far Eastern Red Army, based in Siberia, was being depleted for use against the Germans.

Thus, it became clear that if the ambitions of the Japanese military were to be realized, the mighty American force in Pearl Harbor must be eliminated.

This fact ultimately led to the attack on Pearl Harbor.

But Japanese military leaders asked themselves whether, in fact, the United States would take military action if they seized the European-held colonies in Southeast Asia. For more than a year, they pondered and probed the question: Will the American people, as apart from their government, fight to protect territory not their own? Will this strange and often inscrutable race enter a major war in defense of an abstract moral principle?

The Japanese didn't know. Neither, for that matter, did Franklin D. Roosevelt.

His biographers have described the President's anxiety over the temper of American public opinion at the time. He seems to have been convinced, before 1941, that the United States must enter the war. And so he authorized some steps…Lend-Lease…convoying in the Atlantic…restrictions on the export of scrap iron, petroleum products, and aviation gasoline to Japan…measures "short of war."

All the evidence indicated that at least half of the American people, and possibly more, opposed involvement in the war. Congress passed the Selective Service Extension Act by only one vote!

The Japanese knew this. And so the possibility of a "deal" suggested itself to them. Why not offer to withdraw from some parts of China? Their armies were bogged down in parts of China anyway. This concession, if such it were, might strengthen the antiwar sentiment in America and bring a partial rapprochement between the two countries.

A special envoy, Saburo Kurusu, joined the Japanese Ambassador, Kichisaburo Nomura, in talks in Washington with President Roosevelt and Cordell Hull, Secretary of State.

An ominous message to the Japanese envoys came from Tokyo. It instructed them to "do your best" to reach an agreement by a specific date, Nov. 29. It said, "Let me write it out for you—Nov. 29th." The next sentence was a fateful sentence, "After that, things are automatically going to happen."[1]

This message was decoded by American cryptographers, who had broken the Japanese code. In all probability, Roosevelt and Hull knew of its existence, if not its full import.

Nov. 29 came and went without bringing an inch of progress to the talks in Washington.

On Dec. 2, Imperial Headquarters in Tokyo came to a decision: "Aggressive action against the United States shall begin on 7 December." This was a decision, but not an order—yet. The Japanese First and Sixth Fleets already were at sea, cruising at a slow 13 knots, some 2,156 miles northwest of Pearl Harbor. The order that unleashed their commanders was not communicated to them until Dec. 5.

The American scene on Sunday, Dec. 7, was serene and homely.

Sunday newspapers, fat as holiday turkeys, reminded people that only 15 shopping days remained until Christmas. Business, beefed up with foreign and domestic war contracts, boomed. People hummed the hit time, "When You Wish Upon a Star." Winston Churchill had just passed his 67th birthday; his cheerful, cherubic countenance had become wholly familiar to Americans in newspaper photographs. President Roosevelt, the papers said, had sent a message directly to Emperor Hirohito. Reassuring? A Sunday commentator thought so. The Japanese, he reported, "having tried threats which did not impress the State Department, are now giving soft answers." An advertisement for a magazine article about the Navy brought cheery news:

"Equipped with amazing new secret, deadly devices that no enemy will ever know about (till it's too late), the biggest, toughest, hardest-hitting, straightest-shooting Navy in the world is primed and ready."

---

1 Quoted in George Morgenstern: "Pearl Harbor."

Inane and sophomoric as this may sound today, it reflects the naive cocksureness of Americans in 1941.

At 7:55 a.m., Hawaiian time, Captain Fuchida Mitsue's plane, followed by 350 others, burst through the rose-colored clouds over the Koolau Mountains. His battle plan, with few revisions, duplicated one drawn by an American officer. On maneuvers about 10 years earlier, Admiral Harry Yarnell "attacked" Pearl Harbor in an almost identical fashion. The Japanese apparently took due note; whether American military men attached the same importance to it is difficult to say.

Both operations, the simulated and the real, succeeded brilliantly from the standpoint of the attackers.

• • •

Brig. Gen. Eisenhower, proudly wearing the single star of his new rank, went to his office as usual on Sunday morning, Dec. 7.

He was busy recapitulating and evaluating the Louisiana Maneuvers which brought him his General's insignia. The Maneuvers had exposed weaknesses at all levels, and of various types, in the newly formed "Citizen's Army." In the two months since the great operation, Eisenhower had been working at top speed examining the findings and suggesting measures to correct them. This Sunday, he thought, would be no different from the preceding weekends, busy.

Another reason impelled him to complete this work as soon as possible. He planned to take two weeks leave around Christmas. He and Mamie prepared to spend it with their son, John, now a Plebe at West Point. The prospects of being able to carry out this plan looked brighter on Dec. 7 than they had a week or two earlier. The news from Washington appeared to be better.

Eisenhower was closely following reports of the talks there between Secretary of State Cordell Hull and the two Japanese envoys. Having spent four years in the Philippines, he felt a special interest in events affecting American affairs in the Far East. No evidence of progress toward composing the differences between the respective positions of the United States and Japan appeared during November. Nevertheless, somehow the impression grew that President Roosevelt and Hull had called a Japanese bluff and that now the crisis was past, if indeed it had ever been present. Eisenhower recalled a newspaper editorial of Dec. 4 which said it was now evident that Japan wanted to avoid war with the United States. Good news came from the Russian Front that day. The Russians had stalled the massive German assault in front of Moscow, Leningrad and Sevastopol. In the Far East, Japan seemed to be making a mysterious move. Japanese troops already were stationed in Indo-China by reason of an agreement with the Vichy government of France. On that weekend, large Japanese troop convoys were sighted sailing southward. Toward Thailand? Singapore? The Dutch East Indies?

That Sunday, Eisenhower stayed at his desk until noon and then went home. He felt very tired. He proposed to take a long nap in the afternoon. "Under no circumstances" was he to be disturbed. He scarcely closed his eyes before the telephone rang and an officer gave him the news of the attack on Pearl Harbor.

He jumped into his uniform and hastened back to his office in Fort Sam Houston, San Antonio, Texas.

Hectic days followed. On the West Coast, something approaching hysteria developed. Civilians heard "enemy bombers" above the clouds, and in at least one instance an officer left newspaper reporters with the impression that such a report was not unfounded. People looked under the bed for spies and saboteurs.

Orders flooded into Fort Sam Houston from Washington. Rush anti-aircraft units to the Coast and the Gulf of Mexico at once. Rush patrols to the Mexican Border. Rush such-and-such units of infantry to potential invasion beaches everywhere. (In fact, the Japanese order of battle did not even include invading Hawaii after the air attack on Pearl Harbor.) The Army sprang into action, which seemed vital at the time.

Five days later, on Friday, Dec. 12, a telephone rang in Eisenhower's office, the direct line connecting the Fort and the War Department.

"Is that you, Ike?" a voice asked.

Eisenhower said it was and asked who was calling him. It was Col. Walter Bedell Smith.

"The Chief says for you to hop a plane and get up here right away," Smith said. "Tell your boss that formal orders will come through later."

"The Chief," of course, was Chief of Staff George Marshall.

Far from being elated by the order to report to Marshall, Eisenhower was disappointed. During World War I, he had been kept at a desk instead of serving with combat troops. Here we go again, he thought. He telephoned Mamie and asked her to pack his bag. Within the hour he was on the way to Washington.

On Dec. 14, one week after Pearl Harbor, Eisenhower found himself making his first critical decision in World War Two, a decision affecting the war as a whole, and critical to his career.

The Reason Why

Out of the thousands of competent officers in the American Army of 1941, Gen. George C. Marshall singled out a newly minted Brigadier General, Dwight D. Eisenhower, to map "our general line of action" in the early stages of the Pacific War. He soon discovered Eisenhower's unusual qualities, his gift for organization and his ability to dismantle a problem and analyze its separate components. Then, in short order, Marshall moved Eisenhower ahead rapidly, paying little attention to seniority among the other officers available.

Eisenhower never learned, specifically, why Marshall did this. The Chief of Staff, a laconic man with the expression of the Sphinx, seldom volunteered more than the necessary information to his subordinates. Nor did he to Eisenhower.

But it seems wholly probable that Eisenhower's experience in the Philippines was the primary reason. When he had time to wonder about it, Eisenhower concluded that some of his contemporaries in the War Department probably reminded Marshall of his four years' service in the Far East. He had helped draft the Defense Plan for the Islands. He had witnessed maneuvers testing the plan to withdraw defensive forces from Luzon to the Bataan Peninsula across from Corregidor, forming a single welded position. He was thoroughly familiar with the potentials, such as they were, of meeting the Japanese offensive.

Since American troops were fighting in the Philippines, and because of the ties with the Filipinos, the Islands were Marshall's most immediate concern in the first weeks after the attack on Pearl Harbor. He needed a technician who could advise him on what could be done in that part of Southeast Asia.

And so he called in Eisenhower, one of the few officers with experience in that part of the world.

Eisenhower stepped off the train bright and early on the morning of Sunday, Dec. 14. Milton Eisenhower, who was living near Washington, met him at the station and drove him directly to the War Department. Dwight, of course, had no inkling of why Marshall had summoned him or how long his duties might keep him in Washington. He was anxious to know and so he immediately reported to Marshall without stopping to drop the one bag he brought from Fort Sam Houston.

Marshall plunged directly into an exposition of the general military and naval situation in the Western Pacific. It was grim.

The Chief of Staff could not say, because the Navy was unable to tell him, when American warships in strength would be capable of undertaking offensive operations west of Hawaii. The Asiatic Fleet had a heavy cruiser in the vicinity of the Philippines and this was the largest of its warships, the Houston. Some submarines were still operable there. Japanese bombers had severely damaged air units in the Islands, hitting bases for 35 bombers, the new "Flying Fortresses," and 220 fighter planes. Ground forces totalled 30,000 men, including the Philippine Scouts, an integral part of the American Army. Included in the total force were three regiments of field artillery, an infantry regiment, two tank battalions and some service troops.

Obviously, these minuscule forces could not "defend all the sensitive beaches," as Eisenhower had written in his final report to Quezon.

As he later wrote, "Gen. Marshall took perhaps 20 minutes to describe all this and then abruptly asked, 'What should be our general line of action?'

"I thought a second and, hoping I was showing a poker face, answered, 'Give me a few hours.'

"'All right,' he said, and I was dismissed."

They gave him a desk in the War Plans Division of the War Department. He spread a map of the Western Pacific before him, measuring distances, possible centers of resistance, potential bases. Could the Netherlands East Indies be held? Once, while he was in Manila, Eisenhower had planned a trip to these Islands. If it had materialized, he could have had a better picture of holding Java or Sumatra, perhaps. Too late now. Anyway, it seemed doubtful. Japanese forces, by agreement with Vichy France, already stood in Indo-China, poised for the attack on Malaya, Singapore and the East Indies.

In logical steps, he came to three basic conclusions. The major base had to be Australia. Secondly, the lifeline to Australia would run through Hawaii, Fiji, New Zealand and New Caledonia. It must be opened and secured at the earliest possible moment. And finally, along with the logistical considerations, Eisenhower saw a psychological factor that might have escaped an officer without his Far Eastern experience—despite the improbability of holding the Philippines, the Filipinos must not be abandoned.

As he worked, a persistent thought nagged at the back of Eisenhower's mind. Marshall had given him an opportunity. He must come up with the right answer. He seldom considered the possibility of failing in anything he undertook, but he sensed that he might be standing at a crossroads in his career now.

He checked his conclusions again, remeasuring the distances between the islands on the route over which men, guns and supplies would be rushed to Australia. Had he missed any factors in the equation? Finding none, he put on his best poker face, swallowed hard, and returned to the office of the Chief of Staff.

First, he tersely sketched his plan to make Australia the main defensive base, with the lifeline running through the South Pacific. Then he came to the morale factor in his thinking.

He said he did not believe the garrison in the Philippines could hold out for long with only "driblet assistance" if the Japanese committed major forces to overrun the Islands. But even so, he continued, everything possible must be done. He told Marshall:

"The people of China, of the Philippines, of the Dutch East Indies will be watching us. They will excuse failure but they will not excuse abandonment. Their trust and friendship are important to us. Our base must be Australia and we must start at once to expand it and to secure our communications to it. In this last we dare not fail. We must take great risks and spend any amount of money required."[1]

"I agree with you," Marshall replied. "Do your best to save them."

And that was all. "Do your best to save them." By what means was left in Eisenhower's hands.

In the language of a game he loved, Eisenhower had hit safely in his first time at bat in the Second World War.

But the fact that Marshall agreed with his conclusions and his estimate of the problem does not entirely explain why Marshall would soon be jumping him over the heads of officers senior to him and of higher rank. Marshall had a second reason for summoning him to Washington.

---

1 Eisenhower: "Crusade in Europe"

Fixing Eisenhower with his stern gray eye, the Chief of Staff said, "Now look, Eisenhower, one reason I've sent for you is that I've heard that you like to make your own decisions."

"Well, I didn't know I was noted for that," Eisenhower replied, "but I guess I do."

"All right," Marshall said, "what I need around here are people who can find commonsense solutions to their own problems and then act, and not bring them to me for solving. I want to see the solutions, not the problems."

Eisenhower went to work. All his past experience, in the Army, in industrial mobilization, in the Philippines now came to his aid. He brought to bear his gift for organization, his tact, and the courage that permitted him to take decisive action, regardless of the risk.

George Marshall had found his man.

• • •

Through the Winter and Spring of 1942, Eisenhower fixed his eyes almost exclusively on the Far East, where Allied outposts and strong points crumbled rapidly under the sledgehammering of the Japanese.

They drove Gen. Joseph Stilwell, "Vinegar Joe," out of Burma and threatened India. Using Indo-China as a springboard, they surged down the Malay Peninsula and, to the surprise and horror of Allied military planners, crossed the causeway leading to Singapore and seized that great British naval base. Hong Kong, dependent on the China mainland, fought heroically and then went under. Wake Island and Guam fell, also after a gritty but hopeless resistance. Japanese troops waded across the golden beaches of Java and Sumatra and crushed the brave Dutch defenders. An announcer on Radio NIROM in Batavia (now Jakarta) broadcast the last tragic words, "Japanese troops are on the outskirts of Batavia. We are closing down now until better times." Now the Japanese stood on the doorstep of Australia. At last, as April ended, the only remaining nodule of resistance lay on Bataan and Corregidor. On May 2, 1942, the Bataan radio went dead, too.

Allied fortunes everywhere in the world plummeted to the depths in this period.

Eisenhower climbed to the top position in the War Plans Division and the Operations Division in those months. He was trying to hold together, in effect with chewing gum and paper clips, the unravelling fabric of resistance in the Far East, and at the same time to build up forces in Australia for the eventual counterstrokes. He was working 18 hours a day.

He kept, not exactly a diary, but a drumfire of sketchy notes that give at least a glimpse of the problems jostling each other across his desk, each demanding priority—

"Australia, New Caledonia shipments leaving Charlestown today. Part leaves West Coast in couple days. Never had much faith in New Caledonia garrison arriving there under current conditions. It goes via X. My own opinion is that the whole works will be so badly needed by ABDA (acronym for American-British-Dutch-Australian joint efforts) we will never get this gang to Caledonia. However, we will see. In the meantime, I am going to start making up another shipment for the Far East. Got Navy and Air Force together on question of getting torpedoes to X for B-26s and making sure crews were trained to use. None of the people I talked to seemed to know anything about the matter; but now everything possible seems done."[1]

His log bristled with exclamation points and underlined words, "bogged down," "get going."

The entries show his increasing concern over the apparent possibility that Generalissimo Chiang Kai-shek's resistance in China might collapse, freeing Japanese armies for use elsewhere.

All this, however frustrating and nerve-fraying, proved valuable experience and training for the future Supreme Commander, a post he never dreamed of holding.

Shipping…logistics…moving men and munitions on the vast checkerboard of the Pacific…trying to coordinate operations of different branches of the armed forces and of different nations…sea lanes…procurement…scrounging…and always the problem of ships, ships, where to find ships?

"What a mess," he told his log. "We are going to regret every damn boat we send to Iceland."

Using submarines, he managed to send some critical items of *materiel* into the Philippines, short fuses for anti-aircraft and artillery, for example. A more exotic scheme—smuggling—was undertaken. He sent officers to Australia carrying large sums of cash to hire smugglers

---

1   Quoted in McCann: op. cit.

for the attempted run into the Philippines. Money was no object. Not many of them slipped through the Japanese blockade.

Ships! German submarines, laying off the eastern and southern coasts of the United States, sank ships until the oil slicks spread for miles. A Japanese submarine, prowling the coast of California, boldly surfaced and lobbed shells into Santa Barbara.

Note in Eisenhower's log—"Events move too fast and keep me too busy to permit writing of notes! Day by day the case looks worse in ABDA."

Another sounded a prophetic note—"We have got to go to Europe and fight—and we have got to quit wasting resources all over the world—and still worse—wasting time. If we are going to keep Russia in, save the Middle East, India and Burma, we have got to begin slugging with air at West Europe; to be followed by land attack as soon as possible."

Mamie arrived in Washington, Feb. 6. Until then, Eisenhower lived in Falls Church, Virginia, with his brother, Milton, and Milton's wife, Helen. Milton Eisenhower had held various offices in the federal government over a period of 16 years. He was in a position to give his brother invaluable advice on how to thread his way through the labyrinth of official Washington. It is bad enough in peacetime; during the war it was almost impenetrable.

It was rare, during this period, for either brother to return to Falls Church before midnight. Eisenhower wrote later that he was unable to recall seeing his brother's home by daylight. Helen Eisenhower had coffee and sandwiches waiting at night. For a moment or two, Eisenhower could lean back and breathe.

Three months after he came to the planning offices in Washington, Eisenhower received a second star, becoming a Major General on March 27, 1942. A log entry shows, however, that he still hoped for a command with troops. A year or so earlier, he looked no further than command of an armored regiment. Now, with two stars, he thought he just might get a division.

His professional relationship with Marshall moved on well-oiled bearings. On a personal basis, the two men grew steadily closer. A goose-pimply incident illustrates—

One morning, Eisenhower learned that the giant British liner, Queen Mary, was in port in New York. Ever on the alert for ships, he asked the British for permission to use her. She could take a full division to Australia. The British agreed and the Queen Mary steamed out to sea with more than 15,000 men jammed together below decks.

Eisenhower was armed with wide authority. He did not advise Marshall of what he had done.

The Queen Mary ran so fast that she could operate without escorts—but she could be intercepted by a submarine laying in ambush along her course. Having commandeered her on such short notice, Eisenhower could feel reasonably certain that no enemy agent knew her course when she pulled away from the dock.

A bad shock awaited him.

The liner reached Rio de Janeiro without incident. She stopped there to refuel. As soon as possible, she resumed the voyage, laying a southward course for Cape Horn.

Not long after this stop, a code clerk handed Eisenhower a copy of a secret message. It had been sent in code, intercepted, and decoded by American cryptographers. When Eisenhower read it, clammy sweat glistened on his high forehead.

An Italian spy in Rio de Janeiro advised his government of the Queen Mary's general course southward, and her final destination, Australia!

Cape Horn was the obvious point for an ambush. If the liner could round the Cape she could lose herself in the vast expanses of the South Pacific. But a submarine wolf pack waiting near the Cape, or even a single U-boat—. Eisenhower thought of 15,000 men and the badly needed liner. He tried to put the whole unimaginable picture out of his thoughts.

He said nothing to Marshall nor anyone else in their offices. All he could do was wait, carrying the burden of anxiety alone. Or so he thought.

The great day, the impossibly joyous day, came bringing news that the Queen Mary had docked safely in Australia. Eisenhower went straight to Marshall.

"General," he said, "I want to tell you something. I sent a division to Australia via the South Atlantic and then we got word that she had been sighted and the Italians knew where she was going. Of course, they passed that on to the Germans."

He had to stop to catch his breath. Then he continued:

"I have lived a long life in these past days until I could tell you. It's all right now. She is there. I didn't want to show you that message until now. There was nothing you could do about it, so I just didn't want to show it to you and let it bother you."

Marshall looked at Eisenhower in silence for a long moment. Then he said, "I saw that telegram. I hoped you didn't. It was enough for one of us to be worried about that darned thing. There you were, trying to keep it from me and I was trying to keep it from you."

Eisenhower, relating the incident years later, said, "I think that was the nicest thing any commander has ever said to me."

In this manner, they worked together. Very soon, the partnership was to prove even more fruitful.

After the fall of Bataan, Eisenhower's attention turned largely to Europe.

He soon concluded that the main weight of America's growing military strength should be thrown against Germany and Italy rather than divided more or less equally between Europe and the Pacific. Among many considerations, two stood out prominently in his thinking: In Europe, the Allies could hit two of their three enemies, Germany and Italy. And in the summer of 1942, apprehension was increasing over the possibility that Russia might be knocked out of the war, or sign a separate peace with the Germans, as she had done in the First World War. To throw huge forces against Japan would not help the Soviet Union; neither Germany nor Italy would deplete their forces in Europe and Africa to help the Japanese in the Pacific. No, the main thrust must be directed first in Europe with large-scale American operations supporting Britain as soon as possible. Britain, obviously would be the major base for them, the "unsinkable aircraft carrier."

Planning began at once in the Operations Division, which Eisenhower headed.

It envisioned, basically, the strategy for invasion which was to take place in fact in 1944—overwhelming air strikes, an enormous concentration of naval firepower battering German fortifications in and near the invasion zone, and then the infantry assault across the beaches.

This general plan by no means sprang into existence, full-blown, like Venus rising from the sea. One school of thought held that it would be sheer insanity to strike across the Channel, crashing head on against the massive concrete-and-steel walls of Fortress Europa. Moreover, concealed and well-protected submarine nests dotted the whole coastline. Expose a tight-packed armada of warships, ammunition ships, tankers carrying gasoline, and troopships to the submarine wolf packs? Madness!

In effect, Eisenhower and those who supported the concept replied, "Where else? Anything less is merely pecking at the outer perimeter of the German defenses."

In part, the plan depended on faith in air power. The old airplane-versus-battleship argument had been largely settled when the Japanese sunk the British capital ships, Repulse and Prince of Wales, off Singapore in the early days of the war. But the role delegated to bombers and fighters in this invasion plan, reducing the heavy fortifications, smashing the submarine pens, and helping to hold back counterattacks as men and supplies flowed ashore—well, it just seemed too much to the doubters. Eisenhower, like George Marshall, would not countenance defeatism in his staff, but he welcomed honest differences of opinion. The opposition party had its say.

Eventually, the completed plan was taken to Marshall, the Chief of Staff. "The burden of proof was on us," Eisenhower wrote, "but the critical point, the whole basis of the whole plan, had to be taken almost on faith."[1] Marshall listened, asked questions, probed for weaknesses, sought out details. After a long presentation, he said, "This is it. I approve."

To speed up the conferences that led up to completing the plan, Eisenhower devised a kind of automated communications system. He had his office "bugged," completely wired for microphones. Theoretically, the "bugs" picked up every word spoken anywhere in the room and captured it on a recording machine. The give-and-take in a conference, often a rapid cross fire of statement and rebuttal, then would be transcribed by his secretary. Eisenhower thought this a "most effective" system.

His secretary, Miss Joan Dunbar, did not. She found it insufficiently sensitive, causing her to spend hours piecing together parts that came through indistinctly to her.

Miss Dunbar, a tall, strikingly handsome girl from Buffalo, New York, kept a diary of these days. Being highly circumspect, she recorded next to nothing about war reports or the work in Eisenhower's office. But she wrote a good deal about her boss—

"There is never anything discourteous, questionable or sloppily

---

1 Eisenhower: op. cit.

said in any of his letters or interoffice memoranda. Everything is suitable and polished. He can draw words out of his mind like MacArthur and his memory is meticulous."

She refers to a paper on Philippine defense that he had dictated to her—

"It was six pages long, detailed, specific and beautifully written—all of it from memory and it was accurate.

"He uses every opportunity and chance and every person who comes along, not to the other's disadvantage, as others do, but justly and equally. His time is planned for and he makes the most of it. To be with such a person continually for 2½ months was wonderful and I hope to profit from it."

She notes that the planning conferences begin every morning at 8 o'clock. Regularly, there is a "blitz," a session that runs without interruption for 12 and even 14 hours. She keeps him supplied with Philip Morris cigarettes and vitamin pills for the "blitzes."

He is always in a rush. In Miss Dunbar's first days as his secretary, he told her to get another General on the telephone. She thought he was waiting when she signalled Eisenhower. Instead, it was Eisenhower who had to wait. When he hung up, he said, "Miss Dunbar, you get the other guy on the 'phone first or I'll wring your neck. I can't lose a second around here." She notes, "His eyes twinkled as he spoke but I got the message."

He returns from a trip and Miss Dunbar writes, "Ike is sick, poor fellow. He's got the sniffles." However—

"This morning I arrived at 8 and went in. All the Generals and one or two Colonels were there talking about what was going to happen. I sat down in their midst. Ike started talking about his trip back from England and how they had played poker with wire and lead."

Originally, Eisenhower tried to organize a bridge game on the return flight but the "fourth," it developed, barely knew a spade from a diamond, so they switched to poker, using bits of metal for chips.

On this trip, taken in mid-May, Eisenhower took a sharp look at the American officers already stationed there. He found them capable and efficient, but he concluded that they should be returned to duty in the United States to familiarize themselves with the rising tempo of preparations, of which they knew little.

When he returned, he advised Marshall, "You ought to organize our forces in Europe as a theater because we are going to have a campaign there some day. It is time to start an organization of good men, giving them all their logistics, tracing plans, communications systems and so on."

"I think you're right," Marshall replied.

"I will write a directive for a future theater commander," Eisenhower said.

On June 8, Eisenhower brought the Chief of Staff the draft of a document, "Directive for the Commanding General, European Theater of Operations." He said he believed Marshall would want to read it in detail "because it may have a very strong influence on the future of the war."

Marshall said, "I certainly do want to read it. You may be the man who executes it. If that's the case, when can you leave?"

Eisenhower was dumbfounded. He had recommended Gen. Joseph McNarney for the post. In this instance, as when he brought Eisenhower to Washington in the first week after Pearl Harbor, the Chief of Staff never explained the reasons behind his choice.

When she heard about this, Miss Dunbar wrote, "…I'll miss Ike. There's something about him that is so fine—he's such a live wire and such fun, to boot." She also wrote, erroneously, "The more I think about it, the more I think Ike knew long ago that he was going to wear 'Pershing's mantle.'"

She described his last day in the office. All the staff had assembled when he arrived. "It was all light banter…some scene from a book or a movie." He shook hands with each of them, said he would miss them, and hoped to see each one in England. Miss Dunbar had "hijacked" a photograph of him and she asked for an autograph. "You bet," he said. "Matter of fact, I'm flattered that you want one. (laugh)."

Eisenhower had been parted from his family many times before. But as he prepared to leave for England, he found the prospect of this separation infinitely more painful. He could not know how long he would be away from them but obviously it would be several years. Moreover, unlike the other occasions, this time he was entering a war zone and bombs were crashing on London.

There was a reunion with John, who came to Washington from West Point. Eisenhower took two days leave and spent them with his family.

Then his plane took off for London where a third star awaited the American Commander in the European Theater of Operations.

Eisenhower had travelled a long way from Abilene along a road studded with "ifs."

If his leg had been amputated when he was a boy…if "Swede" Hazlett had not persuaded him to try for West Point…if the medical officers there had refused, because of his damaged knee, to recommend him for a commission…if Fox Conner had not convinced him of the coming Second World War and urged him to prepare himself for a General's star…if Gen. MacArthur had heeded his objections to the tour of duty in the Philippines…if Mark Clark had recommended someone else to be Chief of Staff of the "Blue Army"…and above all, if Gen. Marshall had not called a relatively obscure Brigadier to Washington and given him a problem to solve…

Each event seems to have led inexorably to the next, as though Eisenhower's career up to this point had followed a predestined pattern. In other circumstances it might easily have been sidetracked.

Yet, running through the apparently fortuitous chain of events is a nexus—hard work. Everything that came to Eisenhower on the long route came from his own efforts, energy, brains and application. He paid his way. He earned it all and there were no silver platters.

Napoleon believed in his star. Winston Churchill, looking back and discerning his good fortune in what appeared to have been a period of extreme bad luck, wrote, "Over me beat the invisible Wings."

Were there "invisible Wings" over Eisenhower? Or can his rise be attributed simply to ability coupled with hard work?

LEFT: U.S. Gen. Dwight D. Eisenhower and Mamie Geneva Doud, 18, pose on a Sunday morning, November 1915. (AP Photo)

BELOW: David Eisenhower, seated left, and wife, Ida Stover Eisenhower, right, pose with their sons at a family reunion in Abilene, KS. Dwight Eisenhower, third from left, was called "Little Ike," 1926. (AP Photo)

Lieut. General Dwight D. Eisenhower, commander of the U.S. Army Forces in the European Theatre, October 29, 1942. (AP Photo)

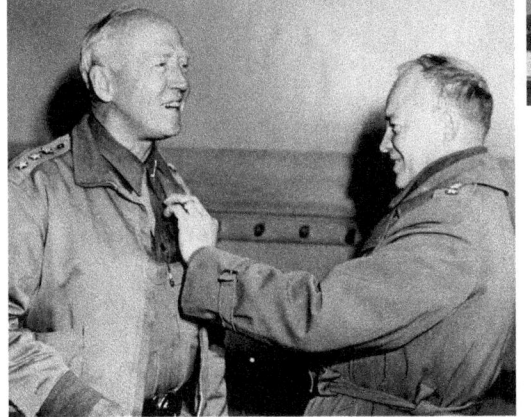

Gen. Eisenhower pins the third star on George S. Patton, making him a Lieutenant General, somewhere in Italy, July 14, 1943. (AP Photo/U.S. Army Signal Corps)

General Eisenhower gives the order of the day, "Full victory—nothing else," to paratroopers somewhere in England, just before boarding their airplanes to invade Europe, June 6, 1944. (AP Photo/U.S. Army Signal Corps Photo)

American soldiers land on the French coast in Normandy during the D-Day invasion, June 6, 1944. (AP Photo)

Gen. Eisenhower talks with Prime Minister Winston Churchill in front of 10 Downing St., London after a luncheon the allied commander attended during a surprise visit, May 16, 1945. (AP Photo)

Cheering crowds greet Gen. Eisenhower as a parade in his honor moves down Grand Avenue in Kansas City, MO, June 21, 1945. (AP Photo)

RIGHT: Gen. Eisenhower stands overlooking Omaha Beach on the Normandy coast in France as he makes an anniversary visit to the scene of the D-Day landing of the Allied troops, June 9, 1951. (AP Photo)

BELOW: President Harry Truman greets General Eisenhower at the White House in Washington, DC, June 1, 1952. (AP Photo/ Charles Gorry)

"And Over Here"

Anthony Eden, the British Foreign Secretary, wrote in his diary for May 31, 1943, "Staff conference at 5 p.m. All went well...I like Eisenhower and Marshall."

The chatty little note is important in that it indicates that Eisenhower was on the way to reaching a first objective, to earn his place with the British. For, along with the tasks of organizing a Theater of War and preparing for an offensive, it was essential that he should win the respect and confidence of America's ally and to create a harmonious relationship between Americans and the British at all levels. This would not happen automatically; it would have to be achieved. After all, in British eyes, who was Lt. Gen. Eisenhower, the American Theater Commander? An unknown quantity as a man and a soldier. Eisenhower was quite aware of this. After the war, he wrote Churchill a letter about the problems of any future Supreme Commander. He said that a man in this position, presiding over the armed forces of a group of nations must first "earn his way" with their heads of state and their commanders. Within a few months after his arrival in England, it appears, he had begun to "earn his way."

It was equally important to him to reduce so far as possible the frictions that inevitably occur when the soldiers of one nation are stationed in the villages and cities of another. British veterans of Dunkerque, looking at the cocky, carefree Americans in their spanking new uniforms, could well ask themselves, "Do they know what it's all about? Can they fight?" In a railway coach in Scotland one day, I overheard two British soldiers talking. "The Yanks are great on production but not much on fighting," said one. His pal replied, laconically, "Blowhards."

The American tendency to exaggerate, bragging about how much bigger and better things are at home, rasped the British. And the

British tendency to understate, and to speak in indirect terms, puzzled and irritated the Americans at first.

The difference in Army pay soon became painfully apparent to the British soldier and a pleasant surprise to the British girl. The American could afford to take a London secretary to the best nightclubs and restaurants and delight her with nylons. He plied her with chocolate bars and tinned food from the PX. The Tommy, who could barely afford to take his girl to the "flicks" once a week, sat alone in the pub with his pint of ale, morosely watching the Americans taking over.

And so, in due course, came the British axiom, "The trouble with the Yanks is that they are overpaid, overfed, oversexed, and over here." It was not always said in a spirit of fun.

Eisenhower's tact and diplomacy, his genius for mediation, were invaluable during this period. It must be remembered that Hitler not only predicted, but counted on, an eventual collapse of the coalition between the United States, Britain and the Soviet Union. He did not believe that people so diverse could long work together. One of Eisenhower's great contributions was to create the climate of partnership that eventually developed in Britain.

With Brendan Bracken, the British Minister of Information, he set about a program of plain public relations.

The GIs received pamphlets which undertook to explain in soldier language some British mannerisms and customs. The tracts mingled meaningful information with some shaky generalizations about the British. But at least it was a beginning.

A drive was organized to collect funds for British war orphans and the American soldier, always a soft touch for children of any nationality, gave lavishly to it.

Bracken encouraged British families to entertain Americans in their homes. At first, the project boomeranged. The people, eager to be hospitable, drew excessively on their rations, and then had to skimp for the rest of the week. (Too late, I discovered that a couple who were little more than acquaintances exhausted their whole week's egg ration to give me an omelet on a Saturday night.) Discovering this, the soldiers began bringing PX food with them on these occasions.

So the bonds were forged. This was Eisenhower's first service in England and the importance cannot be overemphasized.

Inadvertently, he himself made a favorable impression and acquired an influential friend even before he took up his Command.

He came to London in May 1942, to discuss the outlook for an invasion of France. Knowing something of the difficulties and dangers of amphibious operations, he stressed the importance of finding the best-equipped man to lead it. Who should that officer be? Eisenhower replied that he had been told of the exploits of a Lord Louis Mountbatten, adding, "I have heard that Adm. Mountbatten is vigorous, intelligent and courageous...I assume he could do the job."

An odd silence filled the room. Then, Field Marshal Lord Alanbrooke said, "General, possibly you have not met Adm. Mountbatten. This is he, directly across the table from you." Eisenhower reddened with embarrassment and laughter filled the room. As he wrote later, "Almost needless to add...from then on Lord Louis Mountbatten was my warm and firm friend."[1]

Two months after this incident, in July 1942, Eisenhower came to London as American Theater Commander. He jumped off to a good start in the planning sessions with the British Chiefs. They found him modest, tactful, energetic. Rugged honesty shone in his face. His breezy Kansas manner came like a breath of fresh air. He in turn found he could kid them about the English idiom and pronunciation of words. "Some day," he said, "I'll teach you to speak English." His forthrightness touched a chord which sounds in the familiar British expression, "I always prefer to know exactly where I stand." Winston Churchill, in his famous "toil-tears-blood-and-sweat" speech, shrewdly appealed to this national trait and the British response is history. Eisenhower's colleagues also discovered that he was not a man to throw his weight around, a characteristic, incidentally, that would puzzle his admirers and provide ammunition for his detractors when he became President.

Churchill kept himself fully informed about these early planning conferences. His eagle eye took in every detail. He also began forming an estimate of the American Commander and the men closest to him. He later wrote of Eisenhower and Gen. Mark Clark, Eisenhower's deputy:

"I was at this time in very close and agreeable contact with these American officers. From the moment they arrived, I had arranged a weekly luncheon...on Tuesdays. These meetings seemed to be a success. I was nearly always alone with them and we talked all our affairs

---

1 "Crusade in Europe"

over, back and forth, as if we were all of one country. I set great value on these personal contacts. Irish stew turned out to be very popular with my American guests, and especially with Gen. Eisenhower. My wife was nearly always able to get this. I soon began to call him 'Ike.'"[1]

Eisenhower's Boswell during the war was Capt. Harry Butcher. They first met in Washington in 1927 and remained close friends and bridge-playing companions thereafter. Butcher, tall, handsome, urbane, a droll raconteur, went to London as Eisenhower's naval aide. He found this hilarious inasmuch as he knew next to nothing about any ships, let alone warships, and even less about Navy protocol. Fortunately for historians, Butcher kept a diary which later was published under the title, "My Three Years with Eisenhower." It stands as a very useful close-up of Eisenhower at work from 1942 until the German surrender in 1945.

Butcher recorded an incident illustrating Eisenhower's acute sensitivity to actions that would damage the climate of good will he sought to create in Britain—

"One of his men had seen an American officer enter the Mount Royal Hotel dining room for breakfast, juggling two grapefruit. British also patronized the hotel; they scarcely ever saw a grapefruit. He ostentatiously had them cut, pulled a sack of sugar from his pocket, and lavishly spread it over the grapefruit and tablecloth. The CG (Eisenhower) condemned such a display as ungentlemanly and just the kind of thing which will impede progress toward mutual respect. Said if he had been present, he would immediately have ordered the officer sent home by slow boat, preferably without escort."

Similarly, after the costly Allied raid on Dieppe, Butcher wrote in his diary:

"Aug. 20. After Commando raid at Dieppe, Lord Louis full of praise of the conduct of Americans who participated. The CG said he wouldn't bestow medals on Americans until after the Canadians, British and Fighting French had been decorated. He said, 'The tail shouldn't wag the dog.'"

Eisenhower chose to stay out of the limelight as much as possible during this period. He was new to the British, untried as a planner in Europe, and without combat command experience. Had he blossomed into print with photographs and interviews, the impression would

---

[1] Winston Churchill: "The Second World War: The Hinge of Fate."

have arisen that here was just another big-talking, publicity-seeking American. So he hung back.

In this, he differed refreshingly from many an American officer. There was a type who could spot the shoulder patch, "war correspondent," from a mile away and who could not be stopped from explaining who he was at home and what he had done abroad. "Will this write-up get in my hometown paper? I'm, uh, pretty well known and everybody will want to read about me."

Since Eisenhower had come to London with little or no fanfare, British and American newspapermen alike clamored for interviews. Who was this man selected by Gen. Marshall, the Chief of Staff, to command American forces in Europe? They could read his record… Abilene…West Point…highest scorer in the Command and General Staff School…a hotshot in the Louisiana Maneuvers. But they needed to flesh out the bare bones of the record with personality and color.

To one such request, Butcher reported, "As usual, the CG, constitutionally disinclined to personal publicity, put him off." And again, "A color picture is supposed to be on the cover of Colliers. Ike doesn't care when or if they use the picture because he thinks the less he's in the papers the better."

Eisenhower did hold irregular press conferences when he felt both the American and British newspaper readers should know about some developments. But he could be very evasive when questions probed into an area he preferred not to discuss. He gave the impression of having answered—until a correspondent read the answer in his notes.

He also shied away from another sector of the limelight, the social life of London which continued, albeit under the handicaps of the air-raid blackouts and the shortages of ingredients for a good party. Butcher wrote:

"Aug. 10. Social invitations still pouring in. Lady Astor 'phoned Lee a day or two ago to invite Ike down for dinner and an evening. George Bernard Shaw was to be present, who I would like very much to meet. But Ike said, 'To hell with it; I've work to do.'"

After a short time, Eisenhower moved out of his first living quarters in Claridge's Hotel. He found them too luxurious. He and Butcher took a three-room suite, two bedrooms and a bath, in the Dorchester Hotel. He could easily walk to his office at No. 20 Grosvenor Square, which Americans began calling "Eisenhowerplatz." To provide a little respite for his boss, Butcher found a house, Telegraph Cottage, on the outskirts of a village in Surrey. Then Eisenhower found a dog which he named Telek. Now, he said, he had someone to whom he could confide his thoughts and feelings without risking a breach in security.

He wrote regularly to Mamie and John but not at great length. His notes seldom exceeded six to 10 lines. Mamie's letters told him she volunteered for work in the Soldiers, Sailors and Marines Club in Washington. She was waiting table and having some fun in the job. It amused her when, occasionally, a customer brusquely gave his order or said, peremptorily, "and step on it, Sister, I'm in a hurry." If they had known that the American Commander's wife was waiting on them!

Mamie also took up a hobby, interior decorating. She said she liked rose and green as a color combination for a room. A woman friend gave her a gold charm bracelet with seven charms, a shield, helmet, gas mask, American flag, bullet, Sherman tank, and the state of Texas with a dot locating Denison, Ike's birthplace. Later, she added to it a miniature map of Africa, although the operations there had not yet been agreed upon in the planning conferences in London. She wrote that John had built a miniature schooner and given it to her. All was well at home.

. . .

In the winter of 1942, London was cold, damp, foggy, blacked out at night, somewhat hungry, occasionally dangerous, and irrepressibly cheerful. Even gay.

Up to that point, the British had hung on from sheer, iron determination, driven out of France and Norway, mauled in Libya and Egypt, soundly beaten in Crete, Malaya and Singapore. They could only plod through the darkness, unable to see the light that would mark the end of the tunnel. It was all very well for Winston Churchill to assure them that this was their "finest hour," and they tried to believe him. But to the housewife, struggling to stretch her ration coupons from week to week, and to keep a few chunks of coal glowing in the grate, there was nothing fine about it. "Dig for victory," the slogan said, and so she did with her husband, supplementing rations with whatever vegetables they could raise in the backyard. Her husband groped his way through dark streets to catch a commuter train and he knew he would stand up all the way home because so few trains were running now. "Is this trip really necessary?" the railway placard asked. Sometimes he wondered. His son was fighting in the Western Desert and no word had come from him. After an air raid, he and his wife waited anxiously to hear from their daughter, serving in an anti-aircraft battery defending London. "War has become a way of life," a young London secretary said, "I expect we shall always be at war."

Then, in November, the newspapers brought out the biggest type in the fonts to proclaim, "VICTORY!" The Eighth Army had won an electrifying victory in the Western Desert.

In late October, the British opened a pulverizing artillery barrage on the German and Italian positions at El Alamein. Fleets of tanks followed and began punching holes in the enemy lines. On Nov. 2, the great German tactician, Field Marshal Erwin Rommel, sent his wife a message:

"Dearest Lu, Very heavy fighting again, not going well for us. The enemy with his superior strength is slowly levering us out of our position. That will mean the end. You can imagine how I feel. AIR raid after air raid after air raid!"[1]

Two days later, it was all over. Gen. Sir Harold Alexander radioed Churchill, "Ring out the bells!" Churchill, for reasons which will be shown, decided to delay the bells for the time being. But he rose in the House of Commons and said, in vintage Churchill, "This is not the beginning of the end but it may be said to be the end of the beginning." Later, he would write, "It may almost be said, 'Before Alamein we never had a victory. After Alamein we never had a defeat.'"[2]

The London newspapers had shrunk to six and even to four pages. Yet they were bright, alert and miraculously complete. For some days, they devoted almost the entire space to the triumph in the desert. Aerial photographs showed long German convoys streaking westward toward Libya and, unfortunately for Eisenhower, toward Tunisia. As the dimensions of the victory became clear, an infectious nothing-can-stop-us-now spirit began to spread across Britain.

Who cared if a pork sausage contained at least 40 per cent bread crumbs? Americans estimated it was more like 60 per cent. What of it if it had to be plaice and Brussels Sprouts again tonight for dinner?

---

1   "The Rommel Papers"
2   Winston Churchill: op. cit.

Or beans on toast. In the hotels, pantrymen took a sliver of butter and formed it into a curl to make it look as large as a peacetime serving. Nobody grumbled about it now. Victory was in the air. Dig for victory! Setbacks might still lie ahead, almost certainly they did. But somehow, somewhere, in some unimaginably glorious hour, the final victory would come and the guns would fall silent.

Troopships began ploughing across the gray and turbulent Atlantic, long convoys that stretched back as far as 60 miles, bringing more and more Americans. To be sure, they were green troops, untested in battle, and perhaps a little too cocky. But here was the first evidence of America's growing might and the sight of American uniforms increased the lilt in London, the brightening horizon, as they thronged into Audley Street, through St. James Park, across Blackfriars Bridge, into "Eisenhowerplatz." Eisenhower planned to bring two million Americans to Britain. All over the island, the air thundered with the sound of building, warehouses, camps, airfields, repair facilities, the thousand and one installations for housing and training a gigantic new army. A song fitted the new spirit—

"The stars at night—are big and bright."

Clap-clap-clap-clap.

"Deep in the heart of Texas."

In Scotland, British Commandos began training American Rangers in the art of stealth and soundless killing. A full-blooded Indian, Samuel P. Oneskunk, soon surprised his instructors by sneaking up on *them*.

In London, the "Piccadilly Commando" stood in doorways, and the GI, romancing by reflex, was saying, "Now, what's a sweet little thing like you doing here, all by yourself at this time of night?" The soldiers picked up British expressions, which mean something quite different in American, and delighted in using them to describe a good wage or how to be awakened in the morning.

They looked in awe at the ghastly effects of the German "blitz," gaping, empty areas, a house without a wall and the bathtub tilted toward the street, the massive (and somehow, noble) mounds of rubble around St. Paul's Cathedral, the shell of an exquisite little gem of a church near Temple Bar with green weeds already covering its wounds. Scanning the sky, they marvelled at the sight of hundreds of barrage balloons, anchored by cables. And as more American men and equipment poured into Britain, there came, inevitably, the observation, "If they ever cut those cables, this island will sink."

The silvery balloons signified that, although the Battle of Britain had been won in the air, German bombers could still be expected. As dusk fell, heavy blackout curtains closed behind windows. The thinnest pencil of light showing through would bring an air raid warden to the door. He politely suggested that perhaps the curtains could be rearranged to cut off the light, which was perfectly true. Stygian blackness filled the streets so that, in a residential area, the only sure way to walk was to stay close to the curb and kick it with every step or two. Taxis, which were hard to find, moved behind headlight-blinders, thin slits aimed toward the pavement. On a dark or foggy night, London became a sightless world. Americans then discovered the cheery warmth of the pubs and, expensively sometimes, that darts is no child's pastime. Whiskey servings were small, so they took to ordering "doubles" and then "double-doubles." Whiskey, of course, meant Scotch. When it ran out, the pub keeper's ample wife would say, "No more whiskey, Ducks, but I can give you Irish."

On a clear night, especially with a "bomber's moon," the London siren would wail like a soul lost in Hell. People hurried to shelters in buildings or the Underground, the subway.

A story soon circulated about the shelters, to wit: That an air-raid warden entered one and asked, "Are there any pregnant women here?" Out of the dimness, a woman's voice replied, "Give us time. We've only been here 10 minutes." (Curiously enough, The New York Times reported that an identical exchange took place in a group of persons marooned by the great power failure of November, 1965, which blacked out the Northeast. Since The Times acquired a towering reputation for accuracy, long since, it must have been a 23-year-old coincidence.)

During the raids, it was not unusual to go to the roof to watch, although there was some danger of being hit by the falling splinter of an anti-aircraft shell. For the British hung a tremendous curtain of shells and rockets in the path of oncoming German bombers, a "blitz" in reverse. No wonder German pilots sometimes gave up trying to get through, dropped the bomb load on some hapless suburb, and wheeled for home. But many of them bravely came through to their objectives and walls crashed and people lay trapped in the wreckage, dead or dying.

A woman courier enters a small office during a raid and hands a message to an officer. "How is it out there tonight?" he asks. She is pale. She forces a smile. "Noisy, but not too bad," she says. Her voice is thin. "Well, cheerio and good luck." Then out into the thunder again.

Women also manned anti-aircraft batteries. Eisenhower recalled that "…he (Churchill) never ceased to show great concern for my safety, although paying absolutely no attention to his own. His single apparent desire during an air raid was to visit his daughter, Mary, then serving in an anti-aircraft battery protecting London."

In spite of the raids, people crowded into theaters. In hotels and nightclubs, they danced and sang "A Nightingale Sang in Bar-clay Square" and "one, two, three, four, five, six, seven, eight—I got a gal in Kal-amazoo" and an American officer polishing off another double-double, blubbered when the band played "White Christmas."

London in wartime, brave, battered, doughty, cheerful London.

In November, within a few days after the great news from El Alamein, more exciting news came from North Africa. American troops, in numbers for the first time in the war, invaded the French colonies of Morocco and Algeria.

The African Enigma

As early as the summer of 1942, two years before D-Day in Normandy, the American High Command considered the feasibility of a cross-Channel offensive against the Germans in France. Not many American units were yet fully trained and ready for combat. Eisenhower soon discovered the deficiencies of those in England. On the other hand, the German defenses on the Channel coasts were far less formidable than they later became. "We are going to strike," President Roosevelt said, "and strike hard." But where? For the German commanders in France, 1942 was the "year of uncertainty."

They knew that on both sides of the Atlantic the clamor was increasing for a "Second Front" in Europe to siphon off German forces from the gigantic assault on Russia. Stalin had asked for it and suddenly the placards blossomed, "Second Front Now!" The persons who posted them probably were less concerned for the soldiers who would try to establish it than they were for the safety of the Soviet Union.

Admittedly, the situation in Russia was becoming increasingly dangerous. The avalanche of German steel ground ahead implacably, plunging deep into the Soviet heartland, inflicting fearful casualties. Supplies, even food, began running low. On April 21, 1942, the wily dwarf, Joseph Goebbels, German Minister of Propaganda, wrote in his diary:

"We have received a report from a deserter in Leningrad, according to which conditions there must be simply catastrophic...claimed that a great part of the population was now feeding on so-called human flesh jelly made of the flesh of fallen citizens and soldiers."[1]

True or not, such reports accentuated the fear that Russia might be nearing the brink of collapse. The United States and Britain sent tanks, jeeps and trucks and other war materiel via Murmansk at great

---

[1] "The Goebbels Diaries," edited by Louis P. Lochner.

cost in shipping and the lives of sailors. To the seamen, the term, "Murmansk Run," became synonymous with a voyage through the jaws of Hell. But more direct assistance, in the form of a land assault which would force Hitler to pull German divisions out of Russia, was thought to be urgent in that period of the war.

Three possibilities presented themselves: A, send American troops around the Cape of Good Hope to reinforce the British Eighth Army in the Middle East; B, initiate landings in North Africa in Rommel's rear, putting him in a vise; C, strike directly into France, aiming for limited objectives which, hopefully, could be held against counterattacks from enormously superior German forces. For a time, Eisenhower favored the third project. Butcher wrote in his diary on July 8, 1942:

"The British appear to be favoring an attack on North Africa—'to get on Rommel's tail;' in fact, the PM (Churchill) has said that President Roosevelt suggested such an operation before the United States entered the war. Ike, however, feels that if he were ordered to conduct an offensive in 1942, he would prefer to cross the Channel rather than open a new front in North Africa, which he fears would not materially assist the Russians in time to save them."

Gen. Marshall and Adm. Ernest King came to London for conferences on the question of a Second Front. Field Marshal Lord Alanbrooke, Chief of the Imperial General Staff, noted in his diary for July 20:

"After lunch at 3 p.m., we met Marshall and King and had long arguments with them. Found both still hankering for an attack across the Channel this year to take the pressure off the Russians. They failed to realize that such could only lead to the loss of six divisions without achieving any results. The next argument was that we should take advantage of German preoccupation in Russia to establish a bridgehead for operations in 1943. Had to convince them that there was no hope of such a bridgehead surviving the winter. Next discussed alternative operation in North Africa..."[1]

This entry indicates that the wrangling went on for seven hours and the diary says it was "exhausting."

Churchill supported his Chiefs. He messaged the British views to

---

1 Quoted in Arthur Bryant: "The Turn of the Tide."

Roosevelt and on July 24, the decision was taken to invade North and West Africa, French territory.

Conferences on the strategy for TORCH, code name for the projected operation, now filled Eisenhower's days and nights. Should the landings take place as far east as Tunisia? In that event, troop transports and supply ships would have to steam across hundreds of miles of the Mediterranean, vulnerable to attacks by German bombers and submarines. Characteristically, however, Eisenhower for a time considered taking the risk, "putting all our chips" on operations in Tunisia as the quickest way to clamp Rommel in the vise. The gamble, of course, involved his personal fortunes, for if he failed in this first venture as Theater Commander he probably would not have a second opportunity. In the end, for logistical and other reasons, he decided that less distant bridgeheads must first be secured, Casablanca in West Africa, Oran and Algiers in the North. From these bases, he planned to race into Tunisia.

To command the Casablanca operation, Eisenhower asked for an officer already acquiring a reputation for verve and volcanic temper, Gen. George Patton. Patton, he knew, was a bold, follow-up type of commander. In "hot pursuit" of a retreating enemy, Patton literally would race his armor until the tanks ran out of fuel. When Washington agreed to his request, Patton's prophecy of 1925—"Major, some day I'll be working for you" became a reality.

Eisenhower's principal aides in England were Mark Clark, his Deputy, Walter Bedell Smith, Chief of Staff, and the redoubtable Carl Andrew "Toohey" Spaatz, the Air Force Commander.

They drove themselves at a frenzied pace to whip into shape the American forces in England that would be used in TORCH. Eisenhower found serious deficiencies in the training centers. The soldiers by no means met his standards for fitness and discipline. They were poor at the formula for recognizing enemy aircraft, "WEFT," wings, engines, fuselage, tail. "With this outfit," said a disgusted officer, "WEFT means 'wrong every flogging time.'" The GIs were not accurate with either rifles or anti-aircraft weapons. Close air-ground support, so effectively demonstrated by the German Stukas and panzer units, was still sloppy. They wasted rations. These same divisions, it may be said, later became among the finest fighting men in the world.

Eisenhower summoned all his superhuman energies to raise their levels of efficiency. His tours of duty at Camp Colt and other training centers now came to his aid. He knew what he had to do and how to do it. But he lost weight and found difficulty sleeping. He would awaken at 4 or 4:30 in the morning. For the moment, his ability to relax under pressure deserted him.

All too soon, the sands ran low in the hour glass. Churchill, increasingly impatient to see TORCH under way, pressed Eisenhower to give him the date. On Sept. 8, Eisenhower was able to reply, "Nov. 8—60 days from today."

Along with the problems of strategy, logistics, organization and training, Eisenhower also found himself confronted with a complex politico-military situation in French Africa.

The government of Vichy France, headed by the venerable Henri Philippe Benoni Omer Joseph Petain, Marshal of France, had signed a peace with Hitler. Vichy, unoccupied by the Germans, theoretically was now neutral, although one of its highest officers, Pierre Laval, had said publicly, "Je souhaite le victoire Allemand"—"I desire the German victory." And the even more powerful Adm. Jean Darlan, although not pro-Nazi, was bitterly anti-British. Nonetheless, in principle, Vichy was neutral and the French Empire, from Africa to Indo-China, also was neutral.

The British had clashed with Vichy French forces in Dakar, Syria and Oran earlier in the war, leaving, Churchill knew, a residue of hostility. Therefore, to the greatest extent possible, TORCH was to have the facade of an American operation. Churchill even suggested that the British units participating in the landings should wear American uniforms. Eisenhower rejected this.

But even as a primarily American operation, the question remained: Would the French fight, as they had done in Dakar? In the regions of the projected landings were about 125,000 trained men, 200,000 reservists and some warships. This not inconsiderable force could seriously impede, if not entirely stop, TORCH, should it be thrown into action.

Many French commanders had sworn an oath of personal loyalty to Petain. Many others, when the time came, would insist that they could not assist the Allies against the Germans without direct sanction from the Marshal.

Was there any other Frenchman with sufficient prestige to command the loyalty of the civilian administrators and military leaders in North Africa? Could Charles DeGaulle, basing in London as chief of the Fighting French, assume that role? "DeGaulle," a Frenchman there said to me, coldly, "n'est pas legal." In other words, to strike a blow against the Germans the move must be clothed in legality.

Further, DeGaulle's determination to continue fighting the Germans from bases outside France put sincerely patriotic Frenchmen in a painful quandary: If he was the true patriot in the ordeal of France, then they were traitors. And vice versa. Apart from these legal and philosophical niceties, DeGaulle had directed the attack on Dakar in September, 1940, and his countrymen would not soon forgive him for that. No, DeGaulle would not do. Someone else must be found, a man with sufficient authority to order the French military and civilian chiefs in Africa to cooperate with the Allies and to make the order stick.

The more Eisenhower learned, the deeper he wandered in a labyrinth, a maze of factions, rivalries, uncertain loyalties, suspicions and the *mystique* of Petain's towering prestige.

The man entrusted to guide him through the labyrinth was the American diplomat, Robert Murphy, who knew the African problem as well as anyone in the world. After serving in Vichy, Murphy had gone to French Africa as Roosevelt's personal representative in 1940. Of his briefings for Eisenhower, Murphy later wrote, "Perhaps some of the things I said were as incomprehensible as military mappings and logistics would have been to me. The General seemed to sense that this first campaign would present him with problems running the entire geopolitical gamut—as it certainly did. And in those days, Eisenhower, in accordance with military tradition, still preferred to regard himself as a soldier who paid attention to politics only when military operations were affected…Eisenhower listened with a kind of horrified intentness to my description of the possible complications."[1]

There followed one of the great cloak-and-dagger dramas of all time…Murphy finding trustworthy Frenchmen and weaving them into the coming military operations…conspirators coming and going in the night, dodging pro-Vichy police…unresolved questions of leadership…Mark Clark's famous submarine voyage to North Africa and his narrow escape in a police raid…Butcher's diary for Oct. 25 says, "Also asked him (Clark) what motivated the Frenchmen he met: Were they fighting for national liberty, or were they merely schem-

---

1 Murphy: "Diplomat Among Warriors."

ing for personal position? 'Well,' he said, 'until the police came, all I heard was l'honneur, l'honneur, l'honneur.'" Algiers, of course, with its mysterious Arabic backdrop, was the perfect stage for this strange piece of theater.

Next, word reached London that the intelligence networks of both Germany and Japan had informed Vichy that TORCH was in the making. So now, presumably, the French armed forces in Africa had been alerted, if their commanders chose to resist the landings.

This was the reason why Churchill decided not to "ring out the bells" after the British victory at El Alamein. Too many hazards lurked around the landing beaches in Africa.

It was midnight on "The Rock," the night of Nov. 7, 1942. Eisenhower and his staff stood on the headlands of Gibraltar, their headquarters for the past three days, peering into the dark Straits. Below them, ships were passing, steaming eastward toward Algiers and Oran, troopships carrying soldiers, supply ships designed to unload tanks and half-tracks at the water's edge. More ships, coming directly from the United States, were approaching Casablanca. The ponderous, clanking machinery of amphibious invasion was now in motion.

Would the French fight? Would the weather, which had been stormy in the west, whipping up heavy surf, force George Patton to postpone the landings of the "Western Task Force" on the beaches near Casablanca?

Well, they would soon know. In the timetable, the landings at Algiers and Oran were to begin at 1 a.m. and three hours later in West Africa. History was soon to be made, the first American offensive and the first test of Dwight D. Eisenhower as the American Theater Commander. Anxious moments.

H-hour came and passed. As usual in the early stages of such an operation, only shards of information reached Eisenhower on "The Rock."

Gradually, the picture began to take shape…some resistance in all three landing zones…hard fighting near Oran…easier progress near Algiers…a naval battle off Casablanca…communications with Patton so poor that little more was reported from his theater.

In the port of Algiers, French coastal batteries fired point-blank at the British destroyers, Malcolm and Broke. Their mission—to put a unit of Rangers on the mole itself! On the fourth attempt to get through the French fire, the Broke succeeded. The USS Thomas Stone was torpedoed 150 miles from Algiers. The troops aboard, eager beavers, asked to be put in shore in small boats and this was attempted but the seas were too rough. French guns sank two British ships off Oran. However, Gen. Terry de la Mesa Allen and his First Division were ashore. This division, which was to become famous as the "Big Red One," ran into strong resistance as it blasted its way toward the assigned objectives.

Eventually, more details came from Casablanca. Eisenhower's "weather luck" had held. The heavy seas had eased enough to permit landing craft to reach the beaches at Fedala and Port Lyautey. Before that, however, there had been fighting at sea. The Jean Bart, an unfinished battleship, opened fire on the approaching American armada with her 15-inch guns. The USS Massachusetts engaged her, starting fires and then silencing the French ship. Brave but foolhardy action. For the Jean Bart, engines unready, could not move out to sea! Equally brave but pointless, the French cruiser, Primauguet, led a flotilla in an attempt to reach the American troop ships. They ran head on into the warships escorting the convoy. In short order, seven French ships and three submarines were at the bottom of the sea and about 1,000 French sailors were casualties.

Curiously enough, although it had been reported that the Germans and Japanese had alerted Vichy, the landings achieved complete surprise. The convoys had been seen passing through the Straits of Gibraltar but the French had assumed they were steaming for Malta. Apparently only those who had been working clandestinely with Robert Murphy knew they were coming to North Africa. Between Nov. 11-13, more troops landed and seized objectives at Bougie, Bone and Ddijjelli. Resistance all but ended.

Count Galeazzo Ciano, the Italian Foreign Minister, wrote in his diary:

"At 5:30 in the morning, von Ribbentrop (the Nazi Foreign Minister) telephoned to inform me of American landings in Algerian and Moroccan ports. He was very nervous and wanted to know what we intended to do. I must confess that having been caught unawares, I was too sleepy to give a very satisfactory answer…

"During the evening I see General Ame, who brings me up to date. There is still resistance in the cities, but pressure from deGaullists (the General's information was erroneous) and the Americans will soon overcome the small amount of French resistance. Ame believes that within the next week the Allies will have extended their dominion over all the colonies, including Tunisia, and within two weeks they will be able to attack Tunisia from the west. The situation that will result from this is extremely serious. Italy will become the center of attack by the Allies in the offensive against the Axis. Ame says the morale of the Army is sensationally low."[1]

This is an interesting entry. Eisenhower followed this very route, through Tunisia and then into Sicily and into the mainland of Italy. Further, the diary indicates that if the Nazis had in fact alerted Vichy about TORCH they neglected to advise their Italian allies.

Tunisia was one of the objectives uppermost in Eisenhower's thoughts. He was desperately anxious to seize it before the Germans could transform its terrain into a mountainous citadel. He noted, during the early stages of fighting in Algeria and Morocco, "We are slowed up in eastern sector when we should be getting to Bone-Bizerte at once."[2]

Hours of uncertainty. Butcher's diary gives a picture of Eisenhower at this stage:

"Gibralter Nov. 12. Now 7 p.m. 'tunnel time' or 8 Gib. Ike still hard at it, and so are we satellites, but we don't have to make the decisions. He's iron…Despite the pressure on Ike and the irritation caused by the current confusion on political problems, he operates just as coolly as during the planning. But he would be a lot happier if this was simply a military job."

In Washington, meanwhile, Milton Eisenhower had contrived a surprise for Mamie. Through his position in Government, he knew the landings were about to take place but not when the news would be announced. He telephoned Mamie and invited her to dine at his home and spend the evening with his family. She accepted. From time to time, he turned on the radio and finally, at about 8:30 p.m., he left it on. At 9 o'clock an excited announcer interrupted the scheduled program with the news—American troops are landing in North Africa and a communique from Gen. Dwight Eisenhower may be expected shortly.

Mamie and her relatives sat up until the small hours of the next morning, devouring the fragmentary details of the operation her

---

1 "The Ciano Diaries," edited by Hugh Gibson.
2 Eisenhower: "Crusade in Europe."

husband had organized and was directing. Now she could attach an eighth charm, a gold miniature of Africa, to her jingling bracelet.

But costly hours and days were to pass before Africa became "simply a military job" for Eisenhower. First, he would be confronted by the necessity for making a decision in a grave politico-military problem. His decision became known as the "Darlan Deal," and the potentials were so serious that his career might have been chopped off then and there.

Adm. Jean Charles Francois Darlan was a much-hated man. He was the second most powerful figure in the Vichy Government, the Minister of Marine and Vice President of the State Council. This alone would have earned for Darlan the contempt of the Gaullists, other anti-Nazi French groups, and the British. Darlan in turn hated the British, a hatred of 20 years standing, which stemmed from the Washington Naval Treaty. The Treaty consigned to the French Navy a lower ratio of capital ships than it gave to the United States and Britain. He also despised DeGaulle. After the fall of France, Darlan filled the airwaves with invective against everything British or Gaullist and their newspapers responded in kind, picturing him as a political admiral, a contemptible opportunist and a German collaborator. He probably would have been Petain's heir if the Vichy Government had endured.

By the coincidence of his son's illness, Darlan happened to be in Algiers when the landings were about to begin. Here, obviously, was the man who could order the French civilian authorities and military commanders to cooperate with the Allies and not to resist. Robert Murphy who knew Darlan well and knew the extent of his authority, went to see him in the dead of night. He informed the Admiral of the impending invasion and sought his support. At first, Darlan equivocated. Then the Germans, swiftly reacting to the threat developing in Africa, moved into Vichy France, occupying the whole country and ending Petain's regime. With that, Darlan agreed to cooperate with the American and British.

Eisenhower flew to Algiers on Nov. 13. Murphy briefed him on the complex problem and said he would have to make the decision.

Eisenhower was fully aware of the potential consequences to him if he made an agreement placing Darlan at the head of the administrative machinery in North Africa in exchange for his cooperation; Washington and London might reject the "deal." But he was equally aware that if Darlan ordered the French commanders to fight—as Vichy had warned would happen in the event of an attack on a French colony—his carefully planned campaign would, at the least, be seriously delayed and might even collapse before it gained any momentum.

Eisenhower, of course, could have ducked the decision. He could have kicked it back to Washington and let someone else take the responsibility. However, he knew a good deal about wartime Washington and he feared a delay while officials there, not understanding the urgency, discussed the question. There was no time to lose in the race for Tunisia. Moreover, Eisenhower never shrank from accepting responsibility or the possible consequences of a disastrous decision. Time and again he displayed his moral courage.

Without hesitation now, he accepted the "Darlan Deal," set up by Murphy. If the Admiral would order the French civil and military authorities to cooperate with the Allies, he would authorize Darlan to act as a kind of High Commissioner, administering North Africa without interference from them. Darlan agreed.

In "Diplomat Among Warriors," Murphy wrote, "If Eisenhower had not displayed the same aptitude for handling political emergencies as he did for meeting military emergencies, his African campaign might have failed disastrously. In that case, Dwight D. Eisenhower's place in history would be very different, because somebody else would have become Supreme Commander in Europe."

In all probability, too, if Washington and London had rejected the "Darlan Deal," Eisenhower would have been relieved of his command in North Africa.

He stood at a dangerous crossroads.

When the news was announced, a tremendous clamor exploded on both sides of the Atlantic. An arrangement with the arch-Vichyite! A "deal" putting one of the worst of all Anglophobes at the head of French North Africa! What did this portend for postwar France? Were the Allies to deal also with Nazis in Germany and Fascists in Italy? A host of outraged British, Gaullists and Americans protested. The outcry reached such proportions that both Roosevelt and Churchill messaged Eisenhower, asking in effect, "Why Darlan?" He supplied the answer in a long telegram. They did not disturb his arrangement. Roosevelt partially stilled the uproar by saying Darlan was only a "temporary expedient."

It remained for a young man named Bonnier de la Chapelle to close the controversy entirely. On Christmas Eve, he assassinated Darlan.

Eisenhower moved his headquarters to Algiers on Nov. 23. Now he discovered all the shadings of French sentiment to his North African campaign. It ranged from lukewarm welcome to open hostility. Some senior officials hesitated to commit themselves. Junior officers generally were more willing to fight beside the Allies. Among civilians there were those with a why-can't-you-let-us-alone attitude along with those who carried the Cross of Lorraine, DeGaulle's symbol, and abhorred Darlan and Vichy. (With the French, it often seems, matters such as these are seldom simple and uncomplicated.) Resistance ended but as yet no grounds for complacency existed.

By this time, the soldiers were trading tales of their first experiences in combat.

Lt. Jack Sensenny had led his platoon toward a large house, a French officers billet. He fired a few shots through a window. A head appeared and immediately disappeared. Then a bed sheet, in lieu of a white flag, waved from the window. "Those guys had been partying all night," said the Lieutenant. "They'd have surrendered for a glass of ice water."

A GI found romance in his first minutes of war. He jumped into a "wadi," a ditch, taking cover from bursts of fire. Crouching there was a frightened Algerian girl who thereafter became his "steady."

Another soldier fell into step beside a pretty dark-haired girl on the Rue Michelin in Algiers, mistaking a New Yorker for a French mademoiselle. He knew a few words of French, one of which was "coucher." She seemed not to understand. He tried gestures. She started to laugh and said in Vassar American, "I get the idea, Soldier, and the answer is 'No, thanks.' But I'll loan you my French dictionary."

The first contingent of WACS arrived and quickly demonstrated their usefulness in a war zone. Cartoon in Stars & Stripes—A soldier crouching in a foxhole under a storm of shells and bullets says to his buddy, "I'd like to meet the WAC who took over my typing job so that I could get in the fightin'."

Then came the Red Cross, the PX (post exchange), the Commissary, chocolate milk, movies, atabrine tablets to fend off malaria, Coca Cola, Spam, Lister bags, jerry cans and all the other accouterments with which Americans try to make war as comfortable as it ever can be.

Meanwhile, the Germans were winning the race for Tunisia. They rushed in troops, guns and tanks and dug in on such commanding terrain features as Hill 609 and Longstop Hill. The distance from Algiers to Tunis is about the same as from New York to Cleveland. But the roads through the mountains are not superhighways. Trucks and half-tracks broke down. Men and equipment moved at a pace that Eisenhower found agonizingly slow. His "weather luck" now became Rommel's. Heavy storms turned the zone into a sea of mud. Goebbels wrote in his diary on Dec. 12:

"In Tunisia a terrible winter rain has started quite suddenly. This is unpleasant for the enemy but pleasant for us. The more time we gain, the better it is. That enables us to transport a lot of materiel and many troops there and strengthens our position more every day. The American-English airports are completely flooded. They can't start any air operations from there."

Eisenhower established a forward headquarters and went there often, jolting and skidding over ruts, stones and mud. Marshall came to Algiers. Eisenhower, looking pale and peaked, had just returned from the forward area. Marshall told him to take better care of himself, to hire a masseur, to direct the campaign from Algiers. Eisenhower was nettled. He said, "General, I can't run the war the way you would do it. I can't be a General Marshall or a General Pershing. I've just got to run it my way. And of course when I'm not running it well, you've got a lot of people who probably would like my job."

Marshall's slow smile lit up his face. "You're not doing badly so far," he said. And that was the end of any talk of rubdowns or running the war exclusively from a rear area.

On Feb. 15, 1943, Eisenhower received his fourth star.

Not long afterward, on another trip to the front, he stopped to inspect a newly established PX. He was wearing a raincoat. The soldier in charge of the PX did not recognize him until he removed it. His eyes bulged when he saw the four stars. "Holy cats," he said, "it's the Milky Way."

One day when he was touring the Tunisian front, Eisenhower came to an infantry unit which was about to put in an attack. As he walked toward them, he heard the words of a prayer and saw soldiers kneeling on the muddy ground. He stopped to listen and heard the chaplain or an officer (he could not be sure) express a thought that forever remained in his memory "…but we pray for help that none of us may let a comrade down, that each of us may do his duty to himself, his comrades and his country and so be worthy of our American heritage." Eisenhower turned away with tears in his eyes.

Many new place names now entered American military annals as the Battle of Tunisia developed, Gafsa, Sfax, Tebessa, Faid, Sidi-bou-Zid. Two others have been clothed with a special meaning, Kasserine Pass and Hill 609.

In February, Rommel suddenly struck. Faulty intelligence contributed to the confusion in the Allied lines and of course, some American infantry and armored units were still "green." German tanks macerated the American armor in a two-pronged drive on Tebessa and Thala. Had the attack reached its objectives, it could have smashed the Allies' Tunisian front and prolonged the North African campaign indefinitely.

Eisenhower immediately replaced some commanders. (Not long before this, he wrote his friend, Maj. Gen. Gerow, "Don't keep anybody around about whom you say, 'He may get by.' He wont!") Then, when the German drive stalled, on Feb. 23, Eisenhower ordered a series of rapid counterattacks. The Germans fell back in full retreat.

If Eisenhower was displeased with the American performance at Kasserine Pass, he would have been intrigued by what Rommel wrote:

"The American defense had been very skillfully executed. After allowing the attacking column to move peacefully on up the valley, they suddenly poured fire on it from three sides. Buelowius' men had been astounded at the flexibility and accuracy of the American artillery, which put great numbers of our tanks out of action. When they were later forced to withdraw, the American infantry followed up closely and turned the withdrawal into a costly retreat...

"And so ended the Battle of Sbeitla-Kasserine. It had begun with a great victory for the German armor over the 'green' Americans, an advantage which should have been exploited by a deep thrust into enemy territory to collapse the whole of their Tunisian front."[1]

Just as Eisenhower attributed the initial German successes to poor leadership, so Rommel explained the failure of the German drive. Battles often are won by the side that makes the fewest mistakes.

With the capture of Hill 609 and Longstop Hill, key terrain features, the Tunisian campaign neared the end. Both sides fought

---

1 Rommel: op. cit.

grimly to take or hold them. A crack British Guards regiment threw the Germans off Longstop and then lost the hill. "I can't believe it," a British officer said in dismay, "Some 5,000 of the finest fighting men in the world and they couldn't hold…" Next day, the Guards retook Longstop and held it. On Hill 609, the GIs and Germans shot it out, often at point-blank range, and in hand-to-hand fighting. A Midwestern division, the 34th, eventually secured the hill. To Eisenhower, this victory held special importance, for the 34th had been undertrained when this battle began. He called the capture of Hill 609 "final proof that the American ground forces had come fully of age."

By May 10, Butcher was writing in his diary, "Ike is nonchalant. For him this battle was finished some time ago; now his thoughts are on the next job against Hitler—Sicily."

North Africa represents a giant stride for Eisenhower. The events he handled there, military and political, had tested him to the full.

The Glacis of Europe

A rustle of surprise swept the conference room in the Hotel St. George in Algiers when Eisenhower said, "Our next objective is Sicily." He dropped the bomb in a casual, matter-of-fact tone of voice, as though everyone attending his press conference already knew this. The correspondents gasped. So did the Director of Information at AFHQ, Brig. Gen. Robert McClure.

Up to that moment, it was unheard-of for a commander to give more than a hint of his next move except in oblique terms and on a strictly off-the-record basis. Now the boss himself had announced his plans. Clearly, it would be a mighty amphibious operation.

The scene notched itself in memory particularly because of Eisenhower's marble calm. For all the drama in his manner, he might as well have been announcing the arrival of another troup of USO entertainers.

He paused a moment while the words sank in. Then he continued, "We may run into a bloody nose but we think we've got the stuff to do it. You'll be advised when we are going to jump off so that you can make your plans."

Characteristically, Eisenhower said "we." Unlike some Generals he never said, "I am going to jump off," or "*I* am going to take that hill." Further, he took no direct credit for battles won in the North African campaign. He referred to "Ryder's victory" or "Anderson's victory," naming the Generals in the field. He refused to permit correspondents in Algiers to use the dateline, "General Eisenhower's Headquarters." It was AFHQ. He could have disclosed, but did not, an amusing little story about himself: Some of his Army friends congratulated him on the conquest of North Africa and addressed the message to "Ikus Africanus." Eisenhower did not regard himself as a 20th Century Scipio.

Now he added a word to his announcement. "You can't talk about it to anyone," he said, "not even among yourselves. And you can't hint at it in your stories; 'write around it' I think is your expression. Anyone who does will be disaccredited and sent out of this theater."

Nobody could quarrel with that. The censors often seemed overzealous, hinting darkly at something "classified" or "secret." In consequence, the correspondents dreamed up the most highly secret classification of all, "Destroy before reading."

But in this case, Eisenhower shrewdly muzzled them. Reporters covering a Headquarters picked up fragments of information and by piecing them together, could speculate with some accuracy about the next operation in a theater of war. In choosing to announce the news himself, and then warning the correspondents in Algiers to keep it in their musette bags, he choked off such speculation.

Eisenhower had been planning "Husky," code name for the Sicilian invasion, during the winter of 1943 while the outcome of the Tunisian campaign still hung in the balance. He envisioned the biggest amphibious operation in history, an enterprise involving the use of more than 2,000 ships of all types and an intricate coordination of land, sea and air forces on selected beaches. It was a giant jigsaw.

The Casablanca Conference brought Churchill and Roosevelt to Africa in January, 1943. Eisenhower took little part in it, confining himself to one day's explanation of the situation in Tunisia. He had some private talks with both heads of state. In one of these, Roosevelt pressed him for the date when he expected the Germans to be expelled from Tunisia. Eisenhower, somewhat to his own surprise, said, "May 15." He missed by only two days.

At Casablanca, Churchill assured him that the British Chiefs had no intention of scuttling the plan to strike across the English Channel when the Allies' position in the Mediterranean permitted.

He was questioned about the French political situation in North Africa, but otherwise Eisenhower avoided political discussions about DeGaulle (who blossomed into full flower as a politician there, establishing him as the foremost leader of the Free French) and other French officials. Eisenhower found it convenient to go frequently to his forward command post in Tunisia.

Thus, he missed what must have been one of the juiciest scenes in political history, as described by Robert Murphy. He wrote "… Churchill, in a white fury over DeGaulle's stubbornness, shook his finger in the General's face. In his inimitable French, with his dentures clicking, Churchill exclaimed: 'Mon General, il ne faut pas obstacler (sic!) la guerre.' (General, you just cannot place obstacles in the way of winning the war.)[1] DeGaulle, a classicist in his native tongue, must have been more outraged by hearing a noun transformed into a non-existent French verb than by the waggling finger.

Out of the Casablanca Conference, too, came the formula, "Unconditional Surrender." Eisenhower played no part in formulating it, and he did not like it. Obviously, Axis propaganda could use it to steel the men in the armed forces and the civilians in the factories. It could only prolong the fighting. Churchill later attempted to explain it away by saying it did not mean the enslavement of Germany, only that the Nazis had no "right" to any terms.

On June 12, 1943, an interesting sideshow to the war came to North Africa in the form of King George VI of England. He was medium-sized, slim and he had beautifully shaped hands. His features were expressive, alternately thoughtful, inquiring, amused. He flew to the theater to visit armies all the way from Algiers to Tripoli. At dinner that night, he made Eisenhower a member of the Order of the Bath. Capt. Butcher, Eisenhower's faithful chronicler, noted that it did not make him "Sir Dwight."

To the troops, including the Americans and the French, the King's tour was like an accolade, a victory laurel for all of them.

In the Eighth Army he spoke with Englishmen, Scots, Frenchmen, Australians, New Zealanders, South Africans, Indians, Poles and Czechs. The gleaming faces of the black African troops burst into wide smiles when he passed, and they chanted what sounded like "boo-la, boo-la." He saw the stubby, cheerful little Gurkhas armed with *kukri*, a heavy, curved blade. At night, the Gurkhas slipped through enemy lines and, still looking cheerful, took a man's head off with the *kukri*. In spite of the obvious danger of German air attacks, the King then went to Malta on a British cruiser. There, he saw bomb damage even more fearful than in London and found the same indomitable spirit among the people. On his last day, as he prepared to board his airplane, he spoke to Col. John McCormack, conducting officer for the correspondents who covered the King's tour. "I believe this may have done some good," he said. "I certainly hope so." His expression was deeply serious.

---

1 Murphy: op. cit.

Meanwhile, as June melted into July, thousands of men engaged in landing exercises on the flat beaches of Algeria. Ships loaded. Airmen maneuvered. The big show was near.

At 2:45 a.m., July 10, American, British and Canadian troops began hitting the beaches in Sicily, the American Seventh Army and the British Eighth.

The First, Third and 45th Infantry divisions, the Second Armored and 82nd Airborne, and a detachment of Rangers composed the Seventh Army, commanded by Gen. Patton.

Eisenhower, on Malta, waited for the first news. He was worried, as he had been at Casablanca, by reports of unfavorable weather. Winds gauged at 5.6 on the Royal Navy wind scale (maximum, 8) were churning up high waves around Sicily. Luck favored him again. They dropped just before H-Hour. Even so, the waves in the vicinity of Gela and Licata, American objectives, capsized some landing craft.

Italian divisions responsible for holding the beaches quickly crumbled. Two German divisions, and later four, took up the burden of the fighting that ensued. Hitler no longer entertained any illusion about his Italian allies. Gen. Walter Warlimont recorded this exchange in a conference:

"Hitler: Another point—write this down: the ammunition for the anti-aircraft we have down there must be so worked that it can be stopped at any time and that they haven't got too big stocks. Keep them short!

"Warlimont: Yes, the anti-aircraft we've transferred to the Italians.

"Hitler: All the anti-aircraft.

"Rommel: Would it be possible, my Fuehrer, for the Italians to send more troops to Sicily and hold it instead of us?

"Hitler: Anything's possible of course. The question is whether they *want* to defend it. If they really want to defend it then anything could be done. What worries me is not that it *can't* be defended, for with real determination it can be defended, there's no doubt about that…but what worries me is that these people have no will to defend it you can see they've no will. The Duce may have the best of intentions but he will be sabotaged."[1]

In two weeks, Patton raced his tanks and troops across the entire width of Sicily, to Palermo on the north coast and Marsala on the

---

1 General Walter Warlimont: "Inside Hitler's Headquarters."

Western tip. Patton then wheeled eastward where the Germans, on strict orders form Hitler, were fighting desperately from positions around Mt. Aetna. The British Eighth Army captured Pozzallo, Ragusa and Syracuse but then ran into the hard core of German resistance in front of Catania. The American First Division fought off 24 counter-attacks before it could take Tronia. The great and unfortunate First!

Field Marshal Albert Kesselring, "Smiling Albert," fought a masterful battle from the rocky escarpments around Mt. Aetna, giving ground grudgingly. Nevertheless, more towns and cities fell to the Allies, Catania, Taormina, Randazzo. Finally, Messina alone remained as a major objective. The Seventh and Eighth Armies linked up and almost encircled the Germans but Kesselring maneuvered them out of the trap east of Mt. Aetna. Under cover of darkness, he brought the bulk of his forces across the narrow Straits of Messina to the Italian mainland. The United States Third Division entered Messina and the conquest of Sicily was complete. It took longer than Eisenhower had anticipated.

After the North Africa campaign, German records show that Hitler ordered this Headquarters to draw up a general estimate of the situation now confronting him. The report pointed out that Italy and the Italian islands constituted "the glacis of Europe" and must be defended.

By mid-August, 1943, the glacis had been breached and the Allies prepared to set foot in Europe for the first time since 1940.

• • •

At dusk on the evening of Sept. 8, the public address loudspeaker on the troop ship suddenly crackled into life. After a pause, a voice said, "At 6:30 tonight, Gen. Eisenhower announced that Italy has surrendered unconditionally."

For a split second, total silence mantled the ship. Only the swishing sound of the sea boiling up in her wake could be heard. Then the ship exploded into bedlam. Soldiers pummeled and punched each other, cheering, laughing and shouting. "The eyeties have quit"..."It's a dry run"..."We ain't even going to get our feet wet tomorrow" "Hey, Joe, you'll be seeing your relatives sooner'n you thought" "We're just going to walk ashore, nice and quiet. How *about* that? Yippee!"

The troopship had been a Dutch passenger liner. Little Javanese from the Dutch East Indies, wearing brown turbans, served as cabin boys and waiters. They knew no English but they could understand that something fine had happened and they grinned and laughed with the soldiers.

Prior to this announcement, the tension that always grips soldiers about to land on an enemy beach had been building up steadily. The atmosphere was heavy, charged with unspoken thoughts, like the tension in the air before a summer electrical storm. A few men talked, a few played cards. Most remained silent, hiding anxieties. Somehow, they couldn't say to each other, "I'm scared—are you?"

Most of the men on the ship belonged to a green Division, the 36th, composed largely of Texans. They had not experienced combat, much less the ordeal of an amphibious landing, but of course they had heard about both from the other Americans in Oran, where the ship loaded. Religious services held in the ship's main saloon in the afternoon, Protestant, Catholic, Jewish, had been crowded and solemn. But now the Italians had surrendered. There would be no enemy fire from the beaches. A dry run.

At first light, they were to be cruelly disillusioned.

Behind Eisenhower's electrifying announcement lay another cloak-and-dagger chain of events similar to those that preceded the invasion of North Africa. On July 25, Mussolini had been deposed. The King ordered Marshal Pietro Badoglio to form a new government. For a time, both the Allies and the Germans remained in the dark about the situation in Rome. Rommel's diary for July 26 said:

"Situation in Italy still obscure. Nothing is yet known of the circumstances of Mussolini's downfall. Marshal Badoglio has taken office as head of the government on command of the King. In spite of the King's and Badoglio's proclamation we can expect Italy to get out of the war..."[1]

Rommel was right. Soon after the disappearance of Mussolini, Italian emissaries began meeting secretly with Allied officers in Lisbon. Again, there were comings and goings, midnight conferences, persistent uncertainties, an on-again-off-again drama. Badoglio vacillated. Brig. Gen. Maxwell Taylor, later to command the crack 101st Airborne Division, parachuted into Rome while the city still swarmed with Germans. Badoglio could not guarantee to hold the Rome air-

---

1   op. cit.

fields while American paratroops, as planned, were dropping from the skies. On Sept. 8, Eisenhower ran out of patience. He informed Badoglio that he intended to announce, unilaterally, the unconditional surrender of Italy. He advised Badoglio to take the same step. Some of Eisenhower's aides were dismayed. After all, this was largely a political situation and on a very high level, to boot. They thought Eisenhower should first consult the Combined Chiefs of Staff and actually drew up a message to them. When Eisenhower heard of the message, he ordered it cancelled. On his own authority, he made his announcement at 6:30 p.m. It was a bold step.

About an hour later, after the British Broadcasting Corporation had told the world, Badoglio broadcast his surrender.

Thus it was that the men on the Dutch ship, only hours away now from the target beaches south of Salerno, relaxed, congratulating each other on their luck. Off the port bow that night, they saw lurid flashes stabbing into the dark sky. But they interpreted this as a sign that the Italians and Germans were fighting. So much the better for them. (In fact, the explosions came from the first massive demolitions by which the Germans rendered the port of Naples temporarily useless.)

Why Salerno, deep in Southern Italy? The Germans expected Allied landings north of Rome, much further north. Goebbels's diary for Sept. 10 said:

"Naturally we shall not be able to hold Southern Italy. We must withdraw northward beyond Rome. We shall now establish ourselves in the defense line that the Fuehrer always envisaged; namely, the line of the Appenine Mountains. The Fuehrer hopes we can withdraw that far and at that point build up a first line of defense. It would of course be a fine thing if we could remain in Rome. But at Rome our flanks would be too long and too dangerous. We would always be in danger there…"

So in hindsight it appears that the long, grinding, bloody fighting over hundreds of miles of mountains from Salerno through Naples to Rome and beyond, might have been avoided.

But at the time, the region around Salerno seemed to offer the best ground for the operation and the expected quick capture of Naples. Several factors dictated the decision. Fighter cover could be provided; place a pair of dividers on the maps of Allied air bases and the outward arc of their range reached no further than Salerno. Landings north of Rome might bring German paratroops in the Allies' rear. In fact, although it was not known at the time, Hitler had earlier reached the conclusion that "The day of parachute troops is over." Gen. Kurt Student, commander of the German airborne forces, disclosed after the war:

"He (Hitler) only changed his mind after the Allied conquest of Sicily in 1943. Impressed by the way the Allies had used them there, he ordered the expansion of our own airborne forces. But that change of mind came too late—because by then you had command of the air, and airborne troops could not be effectively used in the face of a superior air force."[1]

The Germans swiftly took countermeasures in Italy after Eisenhower's announcement. They disarmed Italian troops there as well as in Southern France and the Balkans. The remaining ships of the Italian Navy, however, sailed to Malta. Sixteen German divisions, seasoned and well-armed, awaited the Allied invasion. Goebbels noted that Hitler felt confident they could "do the job." At the moment they could not be concentrated near any given point on the long Peninsula because Allied command of the seas and air made landings possible at numerous points. The Salerno landings came as no surprise to them. ("We expected you last week," an Italian civilian said later.) But Salerno might be merely a feint. The Germans could not be sure.

On Sept. 3, Gen. Sir Bernard L. Montgomery moved the British Eighth Army across the Straits of Messina to the mainland. They began advancing, virtually unopposed, toward Salerno some 200 miles to the north, and a junction with the American Fifth Army.

Sept. 9, 1942, at first light.

The soldiers climb down the rope webbing hung over the side of the ship and step into a landing craft. When it is loaded, it heads toward the low-lying shore which is barely visible in the morning light. A GI removes his helmet and lights a cigarette. Why not? This is a dry run. The others talk, casually. Suddenly, one of them shouts, "Hey, what in hell's that?" He points to an empty landing craft, damaged and lying "dead" in the water. An instant later, artillery thunders in the distance. A geyser of white water rises in the midst of the boats ahead. An American destroyer cruising off shore returns the fire, guns pointed toward a mountain overlooking the beach. Now the soldiers

---

1   Captain B. H. Liddell Hart: "The German Generals Talk."

begin nervous muttering. An officer says, "Get your helmet on, soldier. It looks as though this isn't going to be any goddamn picnic."

Now you can see the landing area. It resembles the stage in a theater. Hills at both ends like the wings, high purple mountains in the center, forming the backdrop. The mountains, the beaches and the morning sunlight all look very much like Southern California. Supply ships, dozens of ships, are clustered near the shoreline and small boats, like waterbugs, are skittering to and fro among them. The surf, fortunately, is light.

Gun flashes twinkle at numerous points near the top of the "backdrop" and the sharp, cracking sound of German .88s, the all-purpose guns, follow. Evidently, "Jerry" has quite a number of .88s up there, looking down your throat. (Later, it was learned that only two German guns were on the mountain. But they were mobile. After each shot, they moved to a new position. As always, the Germans extracted the maximum effect from the minimum in men and weapons.) Soldiers are sprinting across the beach, staying within strips of white cloth. The strips mark paths that have been swept for mines. A "duck," an amphibious craft, maneuvers clumsily in the surf. Is this the one that carries the radio transmitter that Capt. Jack Le Vien says will transmit the correspondents' stories of the landings?

The landing craft noses into the sand, gently lurching. Out of nowhere, at that instant, two fighter aircraft swoop low over the beach, guns chattering amid the roar of the motors. They are German JU-88s on a strafing run. Soldiers fall. Bullets kick up puffs of sand. In a flash, almost before antiaircraft can be swung toward the planes, they are gone. They will come back, hiding behind the hills where radar can't spot them until the last minute.

More shells hit the beach. Others explode in a fury of white water around the ships off shore. The destroyer's shells passing overhead sound like someone tearing apart a piece of silk. Some soldiers take cover in an empty, partially camouflaged Italian gun pit, with timbered sides, on the edge of the beach. An officer says, "Get out of there, you guys. They say there's a war on."

Back from the beach a peacetime resort restaurant is now a command post. The officers' faces speak volumes: German troops are all over the place and the attack isn't going well.

Nearby there is the shell of a lovely building, Greek, the Temple of Neptune. Crouching in a narrow trench in the foundation stones an Italian woman clutches two terrified children. She looks up with piteous, beseeching eyes. Bodies litter the road to Paestum, a little town up ahead, Germans, Americans and the body of a bald, middle-aged Italian civilian. Already, his face has turned the queer color of death, yellowish-brown, in the hot sun. A packet of letters and a colored postcard of a girl with a red rose in her hair lie beside a dead German. "Better not touch those, Mac. They booby trap everything."

In the afternoon, a sudden burst of fire, mingled with a clanking sound, erupts north of Paestum. German light tanks appear, coming fast. They run into a storm of fire from antitank weapons and bazookas. The soldiers in the 36th Division are learning fast. They turn back the attack; knocking out some of the tanks. They look into one tank. A yellow flame is still guttering inside it. And the body of a crewman who didn't get out, burned to ashes from the waist down.

That night, planes thunder overhead and when they are gone hundreds of flares begin floating downward. Soon the sky is brilliant with white light, an eerie light for the bombers coming in now to hit the ships. Then the bombs and the ack-ack reaching for the planes. A correspondent takes cover in a stone barn. It is crawling with lice but lice are better than bomb fragments. In the darkness someone moves. A GI from Texas. He seems dazed, incoherent. In jerky fragments of speech he says he was in a foxhole when the German tanks attacked and he wanted to raise his head to fire at them but found he was paralyzed with fright. "I'm a coward, a goddam yellow———of a coward," he says. Then he begins to sob.

• • •

That was Thursday, Sept. 9.

During the next three days, two American divisions came ashore with tanks and artillery. The British Tenth Corps, two divisions, fought its way to a toehold north of the Americans. The Germans abandoned the heights overlooking Paestum under heavy artillery fire from the ground and the ships at sea. Yanking the lanyard of his gun, an artilleryman chanted, "This one's for Uncle Ezra"—bang—"This one's for Aunt Cora"—bang—"This one's for Cousin Jim"—bang. He helped silence the German .88s with his relatives.

Around midnight, Sept. 12-13, the Germans counterattacked in strength. They swept over the 36th Division from an unexpected direction and mauled it badly. Had they correctly gauged their own success and kept coming through the darkness, they might have reached the beach and collapsed the American bridgehead. This error canceled out the American error in having been caught by surprise.

Early next morning, as usual, the correspondents crowded into the G-2 (Intelligence) tent to find out what had happened. The Colonel said, "Gentlemen, I can only give you a few minutes today. As you can see, we're being pushed around pretty badly." He pointed toward the map. Circles, arrows and other symbols crayoned on its plastic cover showed the depth of the German penetration. They were on the Sele River, only a mile or two away. No more washing your socks and getting a bath in the Sele for the time being. "Water wings will be issued at noon," said Bill Stoneman of the Chicago Daily News.

Goebbels exulted in his diary for Sept. 13:

"How wrong the Anglo-Americans were about the situation in Italy can be seen from the fact that in New York the telephone books had already been torn and made into confetti to celebrate victory. Now they are sitting before the shreds of their telephone books and the situation in Italy is at present even more favorable for us than it was before the capitulation of the Badoglio gang. For the English and Americans at Salerno are in a bad spot. There is consternation about it in London and Washington...Even that big mug, Knox, had to admit in a press conference that the American troops at Salerno were given a very hot reception and that the battles in North Africa and Sicily could not be compared with those for this bridgehead..."

All too true. For a time it looked to be touch-and-go.

Eisenhower rushed units of the 82nd Airborne Division to shore up the defenses. Brilliant moonlight flooded the jump zone. As the white parachutes spread across the sky, it was like standing on the bottom of a lily pond looking up at the lilies. They were cool troops. One of them hit the ground, laid his head on his pack, and within seconds was snoring peacefully.

Eisenhower came to the fronts on Sept. 16. A garbled message to his headquarters from Gen. Mark Clark, the over-all commander, seemed to indicate that Clark was preparing to evacuate both beachheads. It was erroneously interpreted. As in the Battle of Kasserine Pass, Eisenhower approved the removal of some commanders at Salerno. Meanwhile, he ordered the Air Force to throw everything it had against the German positions. Even B-17S joined the pounding and naval guns added to the tremendous rain of steel and high explosives. Gradually, the Allies regained the initiative.

But Naples with its important port facilities was still nearly 30 miles away and hilly terrain south of the city favored the Germans. There was to be no quick capture of Naples.

After the linkup between the Fifth and Eighth Armies, Montgomery came to the bridgehead for a conference with Clark. Correspondents clustered around the tent. When they emerged, Tex O'Reilly of the New York Herald-Tribune asked, "What's holding us up, General?"

Clark flushed and retorted with some heat, "This is not a press conference. Gen. Montgomery and I are not here to answer questions." But Montgomery, needle-nosed and sharp-eyed, tersely answered, "Mountains and Germans."

And so it was to be throughout the Italian campaign, the slow, slogging push against mountains and Germans.

Some 10 days later, Eisenhower received a message from Churchill:

"I congratulate you on the victorious landing and the deployment northward of our armies. As the Duke of Wellington said of the Battle of Waterloo, 'It was a damned close-run thing,' but your policy has been vindicated."[1]

As the Germans pulled back, their demolition teams destroyed bridges, buildings, anything of possible value to their enemies. They mined roads and fields. They attacked and retreated with equal degrees of skill. In the little town of Scafati, a few miles south of Pompeii, they delayed a column of infantry for two hours with one tank.

Naples did not fall until Oct. 1. They found massive destruction especially in the port areas. Delayed-action mines blew up in the Central Post Office and under the principal boulevards. For a time the city seemed like one great time bomb.

Eisenhower visited it and expressed astonishment over the speed with which the engineers and sea salvage teams were restoring the port facilities. He toured the fighting fronts, making observations from some dangerously forward positions. He has described his amazement when he saw heights taken by American troops who scaled the sheer face of a cliff, using climbing ropes. They captured the German com-

---
1   Butcher: op. cit.

pany commander on the peak and Eisenhower wrote that he said, "You can't be here! It is impossible to come up those rocks."[1]

The Allies, however, held no copyright on the element of surprise. On Dec. 2, in the Adriatic port of Bari, Air Marshal Sir Arthur Coningham held a press conference. He said Allied command of the air had reached such proportions that, "I would regard it as a personal insult if the Luftwaffe should attempt any significant action in this area." The Luftwaffe did so that night. German bombers came over and destroyed 16 ships carrying fuel, ammunition and equipment.

With the capture of Naples and the airfields at Foggia, the Allies had taken their first major objectives in Italy. It now became a secondary theater in the larger planning—which meant across the Channel and into France. Eisenhower toured the fronts for the last time on Christmas Day. He hoped to make Italy a bleeding ulcer for the Germans henceforth, drawing continually on German manpower while he prepared "Overlord," code name for the cross-Channel invasion.

Earlier in December, Roosevelt passed through Tunis on his way back from the Cairo Conference. Eisenhower met him. Almost the first words spoken by the President were:

"Well, Ike, you are going to command Overlord."

He had become the Supreme Commander.

---

1   Eisenhower: op. cit.

The Fateful Night

Dwight D. Eisenhower stretched out in the back of his staff car, closed his eyes, and tried to sleep. He was bone-tired. A feeling of numbness began creeping over him. For many months all his thoughts had been concentrated on this hour, planning and working toward it, and now it was at hand with all the unimaginable consequences for good or evil, for success or the most disastrous military debacle in history. His watch showed 9:10. It was the night of June 5, 1944, the night before D-Day.

The car rolled through the gates of the airfield and started the long journey to his headquarters in Portsmouth, passing through the blacked out towns and villages. His aides in the front seat of the car remained silent. They thought he was sleeping.

Instead of sleep, a montage of memories passed through his mind, pictures new and old. They all pointed toward this hour and came together in it, the apex of a pyramid.

The paratroopers on the airfield he had just left were camouflaging their faces with linseed oil and paint and they had said, "Don't you worry, General. We'll take care of this for you"...men of the 101st Airborne Division...he shook hands and turned away and a tear glistened in his eye...theoretically, to an officer, soldiers are just "bodies"...you don't think of them in terms of Joe Jones or Charlie Smith; you think of casualties in terms of percentages, statistics... some of these men, Eisenhower knew, would be dead very soon and he did not think of them as statistics...he stayed with them until they began boarding the C-47s and gliders and now they were on their way to the drop zones, the Douve and Merderet Rivers and the town of Sainte Mere Eglise.

Would the weather hold?...Eisenhower put his hand in his pocket and fingered three coins, his "lucky" coins American, British, French...he had been forced to postpone the start of the invasion for 24 hours because of near-gale conditions in the Channel...then the meteorologists brought better forecasts, a break in the winds that might last just long enough...not ideal conditions but better than any they could see for the next few days...each day was precious to the Germans, frantically fortifying the invasion coast.

After the meteorologists sketched the weather picture at 4:15 on the morning of June 5, they all sat in silence...the decision lay in his hands and he took a long moment, weighing all the factors while the Generals and Admirals waited, looking at him...finally, he said, "Okay, we'll go."

These words threw the switch that activated the most gigantic engine of war ever assembled...ships carrying more than a quarter million soldiers...planes loaded with 11,912 tons of bombs...carpets of bombs, 800 tons each, for the invasion beaches...8,000 rockets for "Omaha" beach and 5,000 for "Utah"...the guns of six battleships, 21 cruisers, countless destroyers, mine sweepers and other craft... the artificial harbors, "mulberries," first suggested by Mountbatten and the British-invented tanks that could "swim" through the surf, drop their water wings and lumber forward, adding their firepower to the total...grappling hooks with which the Rangers were to scale the heights, barrage balloons for the ships, penicillin, antitank guns, a device that emitted a "croak," like a frog in the swamps along the Merderet, to distinguish friend from foe in the darkness, silk scarves with maps showing German positions...all planned to the last minute detail.

Oh, yes, enormous firepower and all the devices scores of ingenious minds could conceive to help the troops blast out a foothold on the cold Normandy coast...but what effect would it all have on the steel-and-concrete bunkers of the German "Atlantic Wall"?...the soldiers, landing at low tide, would have to cross an open field of fire, 800 yards of it, before they reached the base of the cliffs at "Omaha"... by coming in on the low tide they could avoid the mines and "invasion belts" of underwater obstacles designed to tear out the belly of a landing craft...but 800 yards of flat beach to cross!...G-2 had advised Eisenhower about the bristling guns covering "Omaha"...four batteries of field artillery, eight large bunkers each with one or more .75s, 35 pill boxes, some mounting the deadly .88s, 85 machinegun nests, even some antitank guns...who could live through this?...Eisenhower jingled his lucky coins.

He could hear the voice of Air Chief Marshal Leigh-Mallory solemnly protesting against the "futile sacrifice" of the airborne divisions...the British technical expert estimated casualties would run between 50 and 70 per cent, which meant that the divisions, for all practical purposes, would lose their tactical punch and thus be unable to carry out their missions...yes, if he canceled the air drops, Utah Beach could not be taken...he went over and over the whole, interlocking, step-by-step plan for D-Day...too late now to alter it so radically.

In his mind's eye he saw the key paragraph in the directive to him drawn up by the Combined Chiefs of Staff: "You will enter the continent of Europe and, in conjunction with the other Allied nations, undertake operations aimed at the heart of Germany and the destruction of her armed forces"...easy enough to write.

More than two million men would follow behind the invasion spearheads if all went according to plan tomorrow...of course, in any battle, much less an operation of this magnitude, things seldom went exactly according to plan...there would be three critical stages, getting ashore, digging in for the inevitable counterattacks (Rommel being Rommel, the reaction would strike swiftly), and then break out of the bridgeheads...if these three objectives could be achieved, the intricate schedule for the movements of ships and aircraft to Omaha and Utah and the British beaches, Juno, Sword and Gold, would go into effect, bringing to France overwhelming manpower in successive coordinated waves...Eisenhower had visited virtually every unit in the follow-up force, 26 divisions, 24 airfields, five warships, numerous installations, countless other elements in the complicated machine...it had to work..."We are planning for this to succeed," he had said, blandly...and even Winston Churchill, apprehensive for months, had said during the last full dress review of the D-Day Plan, on May 15, "I am beginning to harden toward this enterprise."

Well, it was under way now...11 p.m...the paratroopers should have been on the ground...when would the first reports come?...Eisenhower could hardly expect to surprise the Germans...for weeks German broadcasts had sounded warnings that the invasion would "come any day now"...Eisenhower would have worried even more had he known that the radio signal, broadcast by the BBC, notifying the French Resistance groups that this was D-Day, had fallen into the hands of the German commanders...it was a couplet by Paul

Verlaine...regularly, the BBC radioed the first half of the couplet but when the *maquis* heard the second half as well they would know that the hour had struck...Overhead, Eisenhower heard the unceasing roar of airplanes swarming across the Channel...but heavy bombing had been going on for weeks, so tonight's raids would not necessarily set in motion the German defensive mechanisms along the coast.

Mounting tension...nothing more he could do now...a while back, in order to break the strain, he had played bridge and badminton and he wrote a letter to an old friend, Charles Case, in Abilene: "Dear Charley, you have a knack for crowding interesting news of Abilene in your letters. I am delighted that you refused to give my letters to the newspapers. Nothing I detest more than to have my private letters made public. Good for you for refusing. This note is going to be a short one, as I am forever on the jump. Kindest regards to you and all the crowd. As ever, Ike"...and there had been a laugh in a planning session...thrice, in answer to Eisenhower's questions about a detail, the answer was that it was "in channels"...He scowled, "Blankety-blank-blank, I'm trying to get *across* a Channel and you guys are keeping everything *in* channels"...and he found another moment of respite when an aide told him a soldier wished to see him..."Says he's from Abilene," the aide said, smiling at the nerve of an ordinary GI coming to see the Supreme Commander. "Says he just wants to chin."..."Probably homesick," Eisenhower said, "send him in."...But the tension returned after each of these moments...now the weight of responsibility on his shoulders seemed all but unbearable.

The minute hand on his watch passed 12 o'clock...D-Day had come.

The Cadillac[1] came to a stop in front of his headquarters in Portsmouth...still no news...he tried again to sleep but there would be no sleep for him that night...he picked up a Western story, the words kept sliding off the page...at last, he strode to his desk, took a pencil and wrote a communique that he would never have to broadcast. It said:

"Our landings in the Cherbourg-Havre area have failed to gain a satisfactory foothold and I have withdrawn the troops. My decision to attack at this time and place was based upon the best information available. The troops, the air and the Navy, did all that bravery

---

1 This staff car is mounted beside Eisenhower's boyhood home in Abilene.

and devotion to duty could do. If any blame or fault attaches to the attempt, it is mine alone."

He put the communique in his wallet. If necessary, he was prepared to issue it. Events would soon tell.

• • •

Low clouds scudded across the sky above the little Norman town of Sainte Mere Eglise on the night of June 5. High grasses in the marshes rimming the Douve River, south of the town, bent double from time to time under gusts of a stiff wind. The cows shivered. A dog, sensing something, began barking and other dogs answered. To the east, the townspeople heard the steady roar of bomber fleets crossing the Channel and the rumbling when sticks of high explosive went off in the distance. Tant mieux! It was not funny, being bombed. The bombs did not distinguish between Germans and Frenchmen but if they hastened the day when the Germans would be forced to leave France—. The townspeople shrugged and said, "Bien, oui." They were a sturdy, laconic, apple-cheeked people. Perhaps the shot of "calva" that a man took, his own apple brandy, accounted for his ruddy complexion. It went well with coffee and a brioche in the early morning. On Sundays, the women dressed entirely in black. Everybody in Sainte Mere Eglise dreamed of the day of liberation and some of the men worked with the *maquis*, the forces of Resistance. They were not at home on the night of June 5.

Elsewhere in France, the Germans detected a higher degree of activity than usual that night. They intercepted *maquis* radio messages in greater volume, unintelligible transmissions probably signifying nothing. More than the customary number of acts of sabotage were reported. Quiet, except for the wind and the thunder of distant bombs, hung over Sainte Mere Eglise.

A German antiaircraft support unit occupied the town. The officers had requisitioned the larger houses, displacing their owners. A few hours later, those who had lost their homes would count themselves among the lucky. German snipers regularly stationed themselves in the upper windows of the church on the square as a precaution against *maquis* night operations. Officers had reconnoitered the marshlands along the Douve River and the thick hedgerows, ideally suited for defense, dotting the countryside. But although a main highway to the port city of Cherbourg passes through Sainte Mere Eglise, the town itself claimed no importance in the German planning for defense of the Cherbourg Peninsula.

Not long after midnight, the pilots and paratroop officers in the leading C-47s peered anxiously downward, trying to catch a glimpse of the ground. They also knew about those swamps and marshes and they knew what it would mean in losses of men and equipment if the paratroops landed in the muck and water. Clouds obscured the view. The pilots knew they were near the drop zone. But how near? Then the clouds parted for an instant and they saw water gleaming below. They mistook it for the Douve. Green lights, signalling "jump," suddenly glowed in the darkened planes. The doors opened and the paratroopers moved toward the open doors and stepped out into the night, 17,000 elite fighting men carrying an average of 70 pounds of equipment.

Now began a nightmare of confusion which could have been the first disaster of D-Day but which the men of the 82nd Airborne were to transform into the first victory, and an important one.

For, instead of coming down near their objectives, the bridges and causeways in the flooded areas around Sainte Mere Eglise and Pont l'Abbe, many landed far away. Units came to earth as much as eight to 20 miles from the drop zones and of course they were not organized units when they freed themselves of the parachute shrouds. They were merely bands of men who found themselves near each other on the ground.

Some landed in the marshes and drowned, borne down by the weight of the equipment they carried. Others, lucky or strong enough to reach dry ground, looked vainly for landmarks and assigned objectives. The great operation involved the 82nd and 101st Airborne Divisions and it had been rehearsed thoroughly in maneuvers. When the moment of actual landings came, however, clouds, darkness, wind and water made hash of the tactical blueprints.

At 1:11 a.m., June 6, the first reports of the landings reached German defense headquarters in the general area. German patrols went out looking for the enemies.

Confused and disorganized, the paratroopers began forming up in the darkness. Presently, they ran into the German patrols and sharp fire fights broke out. The Americans quickly discovered the beauty of the hedgerows for defense and formed behind them into strongpoints.

And by the very fact that they were dispersed over so wide an area, the Germans could not perceive the American objectives. Where were they going? What were they supposed to be attacking? To that degree, the mischance contributed to achieving the main objectives which were, to cut off the Peninsula at the neck, to open paths from Utah Beach, and to secure a line blocking the expected German counterattacks against the beach.

On the 20th anniversary of D-Day, Dwight D. Eisenhower revisited Sainte Mere Eglise. He said to Mme. Simone Reynaud whose husband had been Mayor of the town at that time:

"…So we dropped the paratroopers here in this region, first to capture this town, so they block all the roads that let the Germans through it, and then take care of those openings down there and keep them open for the Fourth Division which came over the beaches. So we landed the 101st here and then just to the west we landed the 82nd Division.

"Now of course they got scattered around and that was quite lucky for us. At the time, we thought it was a disaster but because they were scattered so badly, the Germans didn't know anything we were doing. They were just bewildered and their reaction the next day was very weak…they just thought we were crazy."

Mme. Renaud replied, "They were lost—they were lost. They were terrified. They didn't know what happened, and really, I think it was the first disaster for them to see the airborne troops."[1]

Amid the general chaos, one American unit hit the ground at exactly the right spot.

The townspeople of Sainte Mere Eglise suddenly gaped at the sight of scores of parachutes drifting directly above them. Some landed in the town square itself, others in the big trees surrounding it, still others in the hedgerows nearby. The spire of the church itself presented the weirdest spectacle—four paratroopers, shrouds caught on the steeple, dangling high above the streets. One miraculously lived through it.

Fighting began immediately with the German flak unit. Barns and houses burst into flame. Civilians were killed. The Americans and Germans fought hand-to-hand or shot each other down at point-

---

1 "D-Day Plus 20 Years: Eisenhower Returns to Normandy." Walter Cronkite and the CBS Television Network.

blank range. At length, the German lieutenant commanding the unit withdrew his men. Sainte Mere Eglise became the first French community to be liberated after years of German occupation.

However, the victory meant more than symbolism, more than just a harbinger of the future.

In the morning, German commanders in the vicinity of the invasion coast soon became convinced (unlike the higher German echelons of command in Paris and Germany) that the Allied attack signified more than a mere feint.

They saw the awesome spectacle of the saturation bombings, the carpets of bombs laid in front of the beaches. Clouds of smoke and dust, white, dirty gray, red with flames, rose in the air. Airplanes swooped and zoomed, arcing toward anything that moved on the road. One Allied plane chased a single motorcycle dispatch rider; the pilot could not know that when he killed this courier an important order for a counterattack never reached the commander for whom it was intended, and hours passed before the counterattack began. From the Channel, fire spurted from the gun barrels of the warships and the shells crashed against German blockhouses and screamed through the air toward highways and road junctions leading to the American and British bridgeheads. Sea and air power created an inferno of steel and high explosives in the whole region.

It left no further doubt in the minds of the German commanders standing in and near the fury that the long-expected invasion had begun.

They reacted quickly. Elements of a German parachute regiment, an Air Landing Division and an Infantry Division, moved out toward Utah Beach. Their objective was to seal off the beach and then collapse it before the follow-up waves of American infantry could be landed. One battalion came within four miles which meant, in terms of time, a few more minutes. But near Sainte Mere Eglise the battalion ran into heavy fire from the American 507th Regiment. The Germans could not continue on toward Utah without first eliminating the threat on their left flank; they dared not pass the town. So they attempted to take it. The paratroopers beat off the attacks throughout the day. At nightfall, when the fighting dwindled away, they still held Sainte Mere Eglise.

In his remarkable study of D-Day, the German writer, Paul Carell, noted:

"Only four miles to the coast. All that was needed was for Von der Heydt's Second Battalion to wheel around at Turqueville and to advance over the causeway through the flooded area—and Utah beach, the American beachhead, would be sealed off. Success was so close."[1]

Precious hours gained from the action at Sainte Mere Eglise!

• • •

As darkness came on June 5, the German officers in command of coastal strongpoints in Normandy checked the weather gauges and settled in for what should have been a quiet night. A brisk wind was kicking up the sea, sending relatively high waves hissing across the beaches and gurgling around the rocks. The men in the blockhouses felt they could relax, as did Headquarters in Cherbourg, and the tank crews of the 21st Panzer Division, encamped near Caen, some six miles from the coast. Every day the German commanders checked weather stations asking whether prevailing conditions made an invasion seem probable. They did so on June 5 and as the day wore along the weather looked unusually unpropitious for a seaborne assault. Wind, waves, chances of increasing rain. No cause for worry tonight.

For some time, Field Marshal Erwin Rommel had been attempting to arrange his feverish work on the coastal defenses in order to take a few days leave. He wanted to be with his wife, Lucie-Maria, on her birthday, June 6. And he wanted to see Hitler at Berchtesgaden. Rommel had important questions relating to the defense of Western France to discuss with the Fuehrer. Rommel left on the morning of June 5.

He felt certain the Allies would attempt a large-scale invasion soon. He was surprised that it had not come sooner. Some German commanders had expected it in 1942, "the year of uncertainty." And in March, 1944, Hitler had warned that the blow plight fall at any day. Through the Spring and early Summer, Rommel concentrated all his energies on strengthening coast defenses. He built more Strong points and ordered the reinforcing of those already in existence. He planted millions of mines in the possible landing areas. He was racing against time.

Five months earlier, on Jan. 31, he wrote his son:

---

1   Paul Carell: "Invasion—They're Coming," translated by E. Osers.

"Dear Manfred, there's still an endless amount of work here before I'll be able to say that we're properly prepared for battle. People get lazy and self-satisfied when things are quiet...I feel it essential to prepare for hard times."[1]

And on April 27, to his wife:

"Dearest Lu, it looks as though the British and Americans are going to do us the favor of keeping away for a bit. This will be of immense value for our coastal defenses, for we are growing stronger every day—at least on the ground, though the same is not true for the air."

In his conference with Hitler, Rommel hoped to reopen an unresolved question of defensive tactics when the invasion began. Rommel was the apostle of defense at the water's edge. He preached the efficacy of making the major effort to smash the invasion there. He argued that the enemy would be most vulnerable in the first hour or so, before the assault waves could fully organize and while seasickness beset the men. Moreover, from his experiences in North Africa, Rommel knew that the overwhelming Allied air power could virtually paralyze any movement of men, armor and guns toward the threatened area. "Crush them on the beaches," he urged. In this, his theory paralleled what Eisenhower wrote in his defense plan for the Philippines.

Rommel's chief, Field Marshal Gerd von Rundstedt, disagreed. The Commander-in-Chief West believed in mobile warfare. He envisioned the Allied landings, a penetration inland of some miles, and then swiftly surrounding and destroying the enemy forces. He did not believe that air power could prevent movement into the battle area, isolating it from reinforcements. At his disposal on June 6, 1944, Rundstedt had 51 divisions. A high percentage of them were coast defense units, middle-aged men in their 40s and 50s, and training divisions. Nevertheless, with five Panzer divisions not far from the coast, Rundstedt thought these forces could collapse an invasion force. He clung to the type of mobile warfare which had succeeded so brilliantly in France in 1940.

Hitler, it appears, never resolved the conflicting plans of his two commanders in the West. He seems to have overrated the strength of the "Atlantic Wall," and along with this misconception, he probably

---

1 "The Rommel Papers."

was not receiving from his henchmen all the bad news of the war and thus the picture of it that he saw was out of focus.[1]

His famed intuition (today, the word for it in high government circles is "antennae") did, however, correctly warn him that Normandy would be the invasion zone. German naval officers, thinking of the Allies' need for port facilities and knowing nothing of the artificial "ports," believed they would strike at Le Havre. Army commanders doubted that the invasion force would slam into a position so heavily fortified. They strung 13 infantry divisions along the coast from Le Havre to Belgium, and stationed the Second Panzer Division near the mouth of the Loire. Four other Panzer divisions waited some 50 miles or so from the coast.

Meanwhile, as D-Day approached, the Allies took elaborate measures in England to conceal from the Germans the true assembly areas and the direction from which the attack would come. Huge encampments were built in localities in England that would tend to indicate an assault on the Pas de Calais, some 200 miles east of the actual landing beaches. A nonexistent army presumably was poised in these camps. Radio messages intended for German ears flashed from this "headquarters" to other control centers. The great impersonation did not entirely deceive the Germans. However, their forces in Normandy were much weaker than those further to the east.

D-Day, June 6, 1944.

The first alerts rang shortly after 1 a.m. in the German strongpoints frowning above the invasion beaches. Paratroops! Some time later (records disagree) the German Seventh Army in Normandy sounded the alert. Then the hail of bombs hit the invasion coasts, smashing gun positions, detonating strings of mines, touching off a fury of explosions from blazing ammunition dumps, chewing up telephone communications. In one blockhouse after another, the telephone went dead.

Next came the naval bombardment. In the hours of darkness, a mighty concentration of ships, troopships, supply ships, warships, moved quietly up the Channel and made their rendezvous in the Bay of the Seine. They slipped across completely undetected. German radar stations in the area had been put out of action by earlier bombings. But the weather was the main factor. It had been so bad that German

---
1   Franz von Papen, "Memoirs:" Translated by Brian Connell.

reconnaissance planes stayed on the ground and German outpost ships remained in the harbors. Battleships, cruisers, 122 destroyers, 360 motor torpedo boats and some 6,000 other ships approached unseen.

The same foul weather that worried Eisenhower so deeply, and forced a 24-hour postponement of the attack, now permitted him to achieve a complete strategic surprise. "Weather luck" in reverse!

At 5:30 a.m., a shattering broadside from heavy and light naval guns slammed into the German beach defenses, the hammer blow of a giant. Paul Carell[1] described its accuracy: A field gun from one strongpoint fired at a destroyer. The ship turned broadside and fired back. First shell, long. Second shell, short. Third shell, dead on target, blowing the field gun to bits and killing the crew. Carell pictured the scenes in the blockhouse:

"And then a cry went up: 'The ships!'"

"Jahnke pressed his eye against the scissor telescope. What he saw seemed beyond comprehension. Ships big and small…They were coming by sea in spite of the bad weather. And they were coming at low tide. The 'Czech hedgehogs,' the wired ramming blocks with their mines, the stakes with the primed shells, and all the other cunning underwater obstacles they had built were now standing high and dry.

"'Rommel's blundered!' flashed through Jahnke's head. They were coming at low water."[2] (Rommel had always said the assault landings would be made at high tide.)

The First Infantry Division, the "Big Red," hit the beach at Omaha, followed by the 29th Division. They came under fierce fire and the attack stalled. Pinned down in front of the cliffs, the wounded and dying fell and in those hours the scene fulfilled Churchill's dire foreboding, "the waters running red with their blood."

The planes and warships had done all they could. In the end, it was the raw courage of the soldiers who said, "Come on you guys—I'm sick of this. Let's try it." And in twos and threes they rose and pressed home the attack. Human courage tipped the balance in that perilous hour.

One other circumstance, possibly critical on D-Day, favored the Allies: Hitler was asleep and Col. Gen. Alfred Jodl, at his headquarters, refused to waken him. German commanders in the invasion area

---

1 Paul Carell: op. cit.
2 Carell: op. cit.

telephoned for permission to bring up the First Panzer Corps, which was northwest of Paris. They could not call these units into action without authority from Hitler. Jodl thought the Normandy operation might be a feint. Not until 12 hours later did the First Panzer Corps move toward the scene.

Not long afterward, it became apparent that Eisenhower could forget the communique he had written taking full responsibility for the "defeat" in Normandy. In fact, he already had forgotten it.

"A Superb Tactician"

In a conference with Churchill shortly before D-Day, Eisenhower told the Prime Minister he expected to see Allied troops on the borders of Germany before the winter of 1944. Churchill took this more as an indication of confidence than as a reasoned conviction. It sounded overoptimistic to him. "General," he said, "if by the coming winter you have established yourself with your 36 Allied divisions firmly on the Continent and have the Cherbourg and Brittany Peninsulas in your grasp, I will proclaim this operation to the world as one of the most successful of the war." Then he added, "And if in addition to this you have secured the port of Le Havre and freed beautiful Paris from the enemy, I will assert the victory to be the greatest of modern times."[1]

The United States Seventh Corps took Cherbourg on June 28. French and American troops entered Paris on Aug. 25. And by Sept. 11, Allied forces reached Trier on the German frontier, long before the first chill breath of winter.

Thus, the Battle of France lasted only 80 days, if the liberation of Paris is taken as the event marking the end of it.

But in the 11 weeks after the landings in Normandy, fighting as bitter and costly to both sides as any in history went into military annals. The Germans, outmanned and outgunned, and wholly at the mercy of the Allied air forces, fought heroically to hold on. The steel bars in the door they tried to keep closed were the towns of Caen and St. Lo, through both of which radiated main highways and local roads. Once cut off, Cherbourg could have been left to starve, but the Allies needed its port facilities and so "Lightning Joe" Collins raced up the Peninsula. Gen. Herman B. Ramcke, commander of the fortifications, ordered any man shot, regardless of his rank, who left

---

1 Eisenhower: op. cit.

his position. Along the entire invasion front, through June and into July, the fighting raged, largely a battle of attrition, a meat grinder.

Meanwhile, 19 divisions of the German 15th Army remained idle in the regions of the Pas de Calais. Hitler and some of his commanders still felt that Eisenhower was only feinting in Normandy. As has been noted, Eisenhower did everything he could to prolong this illusion, masquerading a dummy "army" in the southeast of England. When the German divisions did begin moving westward from the Pas de Calais toward Normandy it was too late. By July 2, Eisenhower had nearly a million men in France.

He flew frequently to the battle zones to talk with commanders and soldiers. He also kept in close touch by telephone and radio as the armies swayed back and forth in combat. But fingertip control meant going regularly to Normandy. Besides, he liked to be in the field. More than once, he gambled with his life in these trips.

Once, a sudden storm forced his pilot to land. The only strip of beach available was marked "mined" on the maps. Eisenhower agreed to go in there anyway. Then, in helping the pilot pull the light plane further back from the water's edge, Eisenhower's trick knee, injured 30 years before in a football game, buckled under him. He lay on the sand, writhing in agony. When the pain subsided somewhat, he hobbled to a jeep and made his regular round of visits to command posts.

On another day, the weather over the Channel turned so foul that a huge air attack had to be canceled. Nonetheless, Eisenhower flew to the scene. Gen. Omar Bradley wrote, "'You're going to break your neck running around in a B-25 on a day like this,' I told him. Ike snuffed out his cigarette; a tired smile creased his face. 'That's one of the privileges that goes with my job,' he said. 'No one over here can ground me.'"[1]

Of Eisenhower's close control during the brutal struggles that preceded the Allied breakout, Churchill wrote "…he supervised everything with a vigilant eye, and no one knew better than he how to stand close to a tremendous event without impairing the authority he had delegated to others."[2]

He enjoyed talking with soldiers in the line. He discussed wheat with an erstwhile Kansas farm boy and asked the soldier to hold open

---
1   Bradley: "A Soldier's Story"
2   Churchill: op. cit.

a job for him in the wheat fields, Bradley said. Again, he asked a GI from Kentucky how many experts were in his squad. "Four," the soldier said. "I'm one of them." Eisenhower said it must be a pretty good squad. "Best damn squad in the company, Sir," the boy said. Eisenhower grinned. This was the sort of esprit de corps he would have liked to find in every Army unit, big and small.[1]

On the Fourth of July, Eisenhower returned to the battle zone unannounced. Bradley had ordered every available gun, 1,100 of them, to salute Independence Day at high noon. Artillerymen were ordered to fire "time-on-target," meaning simultaneously. On the stroke of 12 o'clock, 1,100 shells crashed into the German positions within split seconds of each other. Soon afterward, Bradley found Eisenhower had flown over in a fighter piloted by Maj. Gen. Elwood R. "Pete" Quesada, chief of the Ninth Tactical Air Command. Quesada's bosses had forbidden him to fly any longer because of the importance of his work at headquarters. So Eisenhower cautioned Bradley not to let any correspondents know about the flight. "Gen. Marshall would give me hell," he said.

Perhaps. But Marshall's affection for Eisenhower seemed undiminished. John Eisenhower graduated from West Point in June and Marshall, without telling the Supreme Commander, had travel orders cut, sending him to visit his father in England. Father and son went to the front in France. One of the rare disputes that ever rose between them took place there. Lt. Eisenhower asked for a battlefield command. His father reminded him that he had been ordered to Ft. Benning, Georgia, to complete his basic training. The Lieutenant replied, "But, gee, Dad, you've got influence. You know you can keep me right over here."

Eisenhower said, "Look, John, the worst thing I could do for you would be to give you some favor because of my official position. I want you to get ahead on your own."

The Lieutenant went to Georgia. Thus, he did not witness the climactic days in the Battle of the Breakout which soon came.

Eisenhower's tactics misled the Germans into believing that the main attack would be launched from the vicinity of Caen where Montgomery was tieing down five German divisions. Instead, on July 19, the American 29th Division fought its way into Saint Lo in

---

[1] ibid.

bitter, house-to-house, inch-by-inch fighting. But the 29th did not press on with the attack. It withdrew. A ghastly mischance caused the withdrawal. In a carpet bombing, some bombs fell short, killing and wounding Americans. When a second such strike was ordered, the Division pulled back to prevent a recurrence.

As a result, the Germans concluded that Caen, not Saint Lo, still represented the greater threat to their defense lines. On July 24, they moved the Second Panzer Division away from Saint Lo and sent it toward Caen. After a second mighty carpet bombing in and near Saint Lo, the Americans fought their way through the German line, Saint Lo-Periers. The breakout began in earnest.

When Eisenhower entered politics after the war, his detractors attempted with some success to minimize his role as a tactician. Yes, the story went, he was admittedly a good organizer and a good coordinator with a gift for pulling together men of different nationalities who held strong and often conflicting opinions about how to conduct the war. And when Lord Alanbrooke's diaries were published, containing passages critical of Eisenhower, they were cited as evidence to support the fiction. It is significant that the story began circulating only after Eisenhower became the Republican nominee and then President.

No officer worked more closely with Eisenhower than Gen. Bradley and he has written of "…the canard that Eisenhower functioned in Europe primarily as a political commander, unfamiliar with the everyday problems of our tactical war. The inference was grossly unfair, for Eisenhower showed himself to be a superb tactician with a sensitive and intimate feel of the front…Only Montgomery, Devers and I could attest to his rare astuteness in those roles as field commander."[1]

• • •

Not all of Eisenhower's problems during the summer of 1944 concerned the German enemy. Two were created by friends, Gen. George Patton and Prime Minister Churchill.

In his over-all strategy for the invasion of France, Eisenhower had designated Patton to take the Third Army and, once a breakout had been achieved in Normandy, send it racing on a wide sweep toward

---

[1] Bradley: op. cit.

the port cities of Brest and L'Orient. Patton, he knew, was the apostle of speed, bold to the point of recklessness in battle. He was the ideal commander to carry out the demoralizing sweep envisioned by Eisenhower.

Patton was a colorful, volatile officer, emotional, often close to tears and close to anger, personally fearless, known to his men as "Old Blood and Guts." Eisenhower valued him as a commander and therefore generally overlooked his eccentricities. On several occasions, however, Eisenhower reprimanded him severely for his actions, the slapping incident in a hospital, and for his public utterances. Each time, Patton promised to be the soul of prudence thereafter.

Shortly before D-Day, Patton unwittingly burst into the public prints again. He made some informal remarks in London about the desirability of close Anglo-American cooperation to constitute the most powerful voice in the affairs of the postwar world. Patton had been told no newspapermen were present when he was asked to rise and speak. When his words found their way into the newspapers, they caused a stir both in London and Washington. Cablegrams from Washington put the responsibility for handling the case in Eisenhower's hands. The Supreme Commander by this time began feeling serious doubts about Patton's fitness to hold high command.

After examining the question for several days, he came to his decision: Patton would have one more chance.

Summoned to headquarters, Patton appeared immaculately uniformed, as always. His boots gleamed. His highly polished helmet shone like a mirror. He gave Eisenhower an elaborate salute and then stood at ramrod attention.

Eisenhower silently handed him the cables from Washington. A stricken look paralyzed Patton's features. Then he offered to resign to save any further embarrassment for Eisenhower. When the chewing out ended, Eisenhower handed Patton the cable advising Washington that he would be retained as Third Army Commander.

Patton began to weep. He sobbed so hard that his helmet fell to the floor. He picked it up and put it back on his head while the tears continued streaming down his cheeks.

Eisenhower could scarcely smother a grin. "George," he said, "can't you even cry without wearing a helmet?" More seriously, he added, "You owe us some victories; pay off and the world will deem me a wise man."

It was one of the wisest decisions Eisenhower ever made. Patton did "pay off"—and brilliantly.

On July 31, the United States First Army broke through the German defenses at Avranches. This was like shattering a keystone in a dam. Presently the whole line began crumbling. Recognizing the disastrous consequences of Avranches, the Germans counterattacked toward Mortain some days later. They were too late to close the gap.

Patton surged through it at lightning speed. In 72 hours, over a single bridge and road, he moved 100,000 men and some 15,000 tanks and vehicles. Now they went careening into Brittany, as Eisenhower planned.

Patton paid little or no attention to his flanks as the long columns fanned out to the south and west. When some of his division commanders slowed up for fear of flanking attacks, he furiously ordered them to keep going at top speed. Had the German counterattack succeeded, the entire Third Army might have been cut off. Patton refused to worry about that. He was on the high road, fighting the kind of battle he liked best, speed, surprise and demoralization.

Paul Carell, the German writer, quotes Hitler as saying of this astonishing performance:

"Just look at that crazy cowboy general, driving down to the south and into Brittany along a single road and over a single bridge with an entire Army. He doesn't care about the risk, and acts as if he owned the world. It doesn't seem possible."[1]

While Patton's tanks plunged headlong in their wide end run, the roar of the fighting in Normandy rose to a crescendo. In a series of terrible battles, American, British, Canadian and French troops began crowbarring the Germans out of their positions. They took Falaise Aug. 16 and Argentan three days later. They tried to close the noose between the two towns which would have trapped thousands of Germans.

Most of the Germans fought free of the trap. They fought on, bravely and skillfully even though many of their officers now realized total victory in Europe had ceased to be a possibility. Instead, depending on Hitler's caprices, his wild-eyed orders to hold every inch of ground, Germany might be facing total defeat. On July 20, he escaped death in an abortive bomb conspiracy. In light of this

---

1 Carell: op. cit.

incident, and in the face of such heavy odds, correspondents asked a captured officer why he went on fighting. "I am a professional," he said. "I obey orders." Another captured officer smiled urbanely when asked if he thought Germany could still win the war. "I think the side with the least amount of paper work will win," he said. "And we're getting pretty bad in that respect."

While the great conflict raged on in France, Eisenhower and Churchill were locked in a kind of private war of their own.

It pivoted on "Dragoon," the invasion of Southern France to seize the port cities of Marseilles and Toulon. Eisenhower had drawn the blueprints for the operation as an integral part of the over-all invasion strategy. Through these ports, he planned to bring in troops coming from the United States. With a French Army they were then to drive up the Rhone Valley, threatening the Germans from the south.

Eisenhower scheduled the attack for Aug. 15.

In July, Churchill suddenly raised the question of abandoning "Dragoon." He said the troops assigned to it could better be used to hasten the expulsion of the Germans from Italy, and then to press on into the Balkans. The Prime Minister believed firmly in the efficacy of attacking Hitler via "the soft underbelly" of the Axis. Also, he may have been motivated in part by postwar political considerations. Eisenhower insisted on the importance of "Dragoon" from a purely military point of view and refused to cancel it. He said that if political factors were involved in Churchill's desire to move into the Balkans, the Prime Minister should discuss them with Roosevelt. For weeks, during the Battle of the Breakout, they argued the matter. One discussion alone went on for seven hours. Eisenhower refused to budge. He later wrote:

"I felt that in this particular field (strategy) I alone had to be the judge of my own responsibilities and decisions…

"As usual the Prime Minister pursued the argument up to the very moment of execution. As usual, also, the second that he saw he could not get his own way, he threw everything he had into support of the operation…"[1]

It went off as Eisenhower planned. By early September, the armies from Southern France linked up with other Allied forces almost on the doorstep of Germany.

---

1   Eisenhower: op. cit.

This collision between Eisenhower and Churchill, protracted and difficult though it was, merely foreshadowed another and far more important difference of views. This argument involved one of the world's most dangerous friction points today—Berlin. But it would not arise until 1945 when the Allies stood ready to strike the final blow against Hitler.

In Western France, meanwhile, the Allied advance moved ahead far more rapidly than had been anticipated.

By the third week of August, the way to Paris lay open. It was determined that a French division, the Second Armored, should have the honor of entering the city first. This unit, commanded by a general who had taken the *nom de guerre*, Jacques Leclerc, had been fighting for years. It came all the way from Lake Chad in French West Africa, crossed the Sahara, and joined the fighting in North Africa. On Aug. 25, the German commander in Paris formally surrendered to Leclerc at the Gare Montparnasse. Anthony Eden wrote in his diary:

"I congratulated Eisenhower on this happy move to end much argument within the Anglo-French-American triangle…Certainly throughout this business, the Supreme Commander had never failed to practice patient diplomacy."[1] In fact, Bradley chose Leclerc's troops to lead the Allied column into Paris; Eisenhower approved the choice. An American division, the Fourth, entered the city at the same time.

The liberation of Paris, although it had no military significance, touched off a wave of exuberance. It seemed to signal an early end of the war. Optimism spread through the troops and in the Allied governments. "Home-by-Christmas" talk (that unfortunate phrase to be heard again in the Korean War) began to sound.

In statements and a press conference, Eisenhower tried to warn against these high hopes. He quickly pointed out that the Germans could resist powerfully behind the Rhine River, the Siegfried Line, and in the forests and mountains of their homeland.

Would they attempt to do so? German professionals knew the situation was hopeless. Rommel's son quoted his father as saying shortly before his death in the fall of 1944:

"The only purpose of these rumors (about secret new weapons) is to make the ordinary soldier hang on a bit longer. We're finished, and most of the gentlemen above know it perfectly well, even if they won't

---

1 Eden: op. cit.

admit it. Even they aren't so stupid that they can't recognize facts that anybody could work out on the fingers of one hand."[1]

Adolf Hitler was not disposed to recognize the facts.

• • •

Hitler's last cast of the dice took place, as had the first, in the hilly, wooded Ardennes region in France. Before dawn on the morning of December 16, 1944, under cover of fog and heavy clouds, two Panzer armies suddenly struck an American sector. Their intelligence had found the weakest point, a stretch of some 80 miles covered by only four divisions. The armored spearheads quickly overran the Americans there. German infantry divisions followed the tanks; their task would be to hold open the "shoulders" of the gap torn in the American lines. As they rumbled westward, still favored by weather which kept the mighty Allied air forces grounded, they began to wheel to the right, toward the port of Antwerp. So began the Battle of the Bulge, or as the Germans called it, "Operation Watch on the Rhine."

It came as a complete tactical surprise to Eisenhower and the other American commanders. They had taken a calculated risk in the Ardennes in order to beef up the Armies grinding into the German defenses. Eisenhower had been expecting a counter*attack*; he knew the Germans would not remain on the defensive indefinitely.

But as the dimensions of the operations became clearer he saw a counter*offensive* taking shape. Rundstedt was not merely conducting a "spoiling" maneuver, a sortie from behind the Siegfried Line, designed to throw off balance Eisenhower's offensive thrust. It was a major drive.

Eisenhower reacted promptly. He made tactical adjustments south of the ever-widening gap and he placed two American armies under Montgomery north of it. He remained calm, steady, assessing the military threat, dealing with the human as well as technical problems. The British historian, Arthur Bryant, was to write of this dangerous episode:

"Nor in the hour of crisis was the Supreme Commander unwor-

---

1 The Rommel Papers.

thy of the men he led. Calamity acted on Eisenhower like a restorative and brought out all the greatness in his character."[1]

On the day the German offensive opened, Dec. 16, he received his fifth star.

As the battle developed, it tested Eisenhower's qualities of diplomacy to the *nth* degree. Bradley, naturally, disliked relinquishing command of his forces north of the Bulge to Montgomery. However, when he was assured that the shift was temporary, he put aside his feelings. He later wrote, "But Montgomery unfortunately could not resist this chance to tweak our Yankee noses...And while Eisenhower held his tongue only by clenching his teeth, he was to admit several years after the war that had he anticipated the trouble that was to be caused by it, he would never have suggested the change."[2]

Critical reports appeared in some British newspapers, reviving the suggestion that Montgomery should be made Deputy Supreme Commander, directing the Allied ground forces. Bradley said he told Eisenhower that if this step were taken, "you must send me home," that he could not serve under Montgomery, that he would have lost the confidence of his command. For a brief moment, the two men, friends since their West Point days, eyed each other in anger and sorrow.

Eisenhower, of course, firmly rejected the proposal to put Montgomery over the American commanders.

The Bulge also brought him into a collision with DeGaulle. Eisenhower related in his war memoirs that DeGaulle threatened to remove the French army from Eisenhower's command rather than permit the Germans to retake the city of Strasbourg. Eisenhower said he replied tartly to DeGaulle, "I reminded him that the French Army would get no ammunition, food or supplies unless it obeyed my orders."[3]

Anxiety echoed from the home front. The Washington Post demanded "...an authoritative interpretation of what the Rundstedt offensive is all about, how it happened, what its potentialities are. But no authoritative interpretation has been advanced by the War Department. The result has been a babel of voices each with a sov-

---

1 Bryant: op. cit.
2 Bradley: op. cit.
3 Crusade In Europe."

ereign explanation of what is going on and with the end result of increasing confusion."

All the chauvinistic wrangling and rancor, had the Allies but known, was exactly what Hitler hoped to stir up. In fact, he thought it would reach such intensity that the alliance against him would fall apart. In a briefing session five days before the jump-off of the Ardennes offensive, he told his commanders:

"In all history there has never been a coalition composed of such heterogeneous partners with such totally divergent objectives as that of our enemies…If we can deal it a couple of heavy blows, this artificially constructed common front may collapse with a mighty thunderclap at any moment…One day—it can happen any moment—this coalition may dissolve."[1]

Eisenhower, often with the greatest difficulty, kept his temper. He ignored the newspaper clamor respecting greater authority for Montgomery. He mollified DeGaulle by determining that, for both military and psychological reasons, Strasbourg should be defended.

Meanwhile, he took a bold step. The Germans had bypassed a town now immortalized in military history when they found it defended in their original thrust—Bastogne. But as they struggled to maintain the momentum of their drive toward the Meuse River, Bastogne became vital to them. A network of roads runs through the town and they had to have the use of those roads. Movement was difficult enough through the snow and ice on the major arteries, let alone the secondary routes they were using. So the Panzers turned in fury to come back and take Bastogne. Eisenhower put his last remaining reserves, the 101st and 82nd Airborne Divisions, into the town, joining units of the Ninth and 10th Armored Divisions. Eisenhower, Bradley and Maj. Gen. Troy Middleton, commander of the Eighth Corps, had foreseen the necessity of holding Bastogne, but it was the GIs who did it.

Prior to this, however, Hitler thought he had reason for great jubilance. His commanders had been dubious about the feasibility of driving the 125 miles from their jump-off point to Antwerp with the forces available to them. But with the initial successes, it appeared that Hitler might be right after all.

Much depended on the weather. The German commanders

---

1   Warlimont: "Inside Hitler's Headquarters."

counted on a period of wintry fog and clouds to spare them the sledgehammer blows of the Allied air forces. For six days, the weather favored them. Their advance, however, was not as fast as they had hoped it would be.

On Dec. 22, Col. Lowell Weicker, Deputy Director of Intelligence in the United States Strategic Air Force, was studying a map in his headquarters at Marly-le-Roi. A thought struck him. He pointed to Rundstedt's mobile units and said to his boss, Gen. Spaatz, "This may look like a disaster now, but it may give us a great opportunity. Once the weather lets us back in business, we can hit those divisions with everything in the book and knock out more armor here than if they had stayed under cover in Germany." On the same day, Eisenhower voiced the same thought. He issued one of his rare "Orders of the Day" and said, "By rushing out of his fixed defenses the enemy may give us the chance to turn his great gamble into his worst defeat."

On Dec. 23, the weather broke. The sun came out. The soldiers all along the line, and particularly in Bastogne, cheered. They did not have to wait long before they heard the roar of the bombers. On Dec. 26, the Germans reached the point of maximum penetration, about 17 miles from Dinant. The lead division, the Second Panzer, collided head on there with the American Second Armored, commanded by Maj. Gen. Ernest Harmon. For three days, the two tank divisions slugged it out. The Germans advanced no further. A week later, the Allies returned to the offensive and the great threat ended.

Churchill, mindful of the bickering and recriminations between British and Americans during the struggle, rose in the House of Commons on Jan. 18 and said:

"I have seen it suggested that the terrific battle which has been proceeding since Dec. 16 on the American front is an Anglo-American battle. In fact, however, the United States troops have done almost all the fighting and suffered almost all the losses…Care must be taken in telling our proud tale not to claim for the British armies undue share of what is undoubtedly the greatest American battle of the war and will, I believe, be regarded as an ever-famous American victory."[1]

Professional soldiers and amateurs have refought the Battle of the Bulge many times, assessing responsibilities and the critical movements in it. Out of their memoirs, diaries and from conversations

---

1 Churchill: op. cit.

recalled, there is agreement on one point—the performance of the ordinary American soldier, who held the "shoulders" of the bulge, snarled the German communications and eventually threw back the powerful thrust.

Arthur Bryant wrote:

"Yet though the American High Command had been found wanting, the American soldier was not. Wherever he was given the chance he and his junior commanders, many of whom displayed qualities of the highest leadership, proved worthy of the men of Antietam and Gettysburg. At Saint Vith and Butgenbach to the north of the breach and at Bastogne to the south the fighting men of America stood like a rock amid the advancing gray tide."[1]

---

1 Bryant: op. cit.

Island in the Darkness

Long after the war, the mistaken assumption persisted that Eisenhower was responsible for the isolation of Berlin deep inside the Soviet Zone of Occupation in Germany. People frequently asked him, "Why did you let the Russians take Berlin?", during his campaign for the presidency in 1952. It appears that to this day there are some who hold him responsible.

In fact, Eisenhower opposed the Big Three agreement which divided Germany into the Zones and left Berlin in the hands of the Russians. The agreement was concluded on a much higher echelon of authority than his, that is, by Roosevelt, Churchill and Stalin. It was a political decision and, it appears, Churchill later wished to abandon it.

The train of events leading to this dangerous situation began in 1943.

Early in that year, a British committee headed by Clement Attlee, later to become Prime Minister, began studying plans for the occupation of postwar Germany. Eventually, the committee produced a plan very similar to the one actually put into effect after the war ended. This blueprint placed Berlin inside the Soviet Zone but under the joint administration of British, American and Soviet authorities.

In December of 1943, an American Working Security Committee was organized composed of representatives of the Army, Navy and State Department. It was designed to coordinate the planning in Washington on questions in which political and military considerations overlapped.

The European Advisory Council was the next step. It began meeting in 1944 to work out a final agreement on administering Germany after the war. The chiefs of delegation were Ambassador John G. Winant of the United States, Lord Strang of Britain, and F.T. Gusev of the Soviet Union. The Council met in London. With the greatest difficulty, often owing to crossed wires and confusion in Washington, the representatives of the Big Three drew the map of the American, British and Russian Zones of Occupation.

One difficulty, according to the diplomat, Robert Murphy, was President Roosevelt himself. Murphy reported in his book that he went to Washington in September, 1944, and "…to my astonishment, I learned that no American plan was ready yet because President Roosevelt had not made known his own views."[1] The Secretary of State, Cordell Hull, said in his memoirs that Roosevelt told him, "I dislike making detailed plans for a country which we do not occupy."

Meanwhile, the President was deadlocked with Churchill over the projected American and British Zones of Occupation. British forces were advancing into North Germany and the Americans into the Central-South. Therefore, the EAC plan had allocated the Northern Zone to the British and regions south of it to the United States. Roosevelt insisted on reversing the positions. He said the United States would need the great ports of North Germany for embarkation of American troops to the Pacific once the war in Europe came to an end. Churchill would not agree. The impasse between them continued for seven months.

During this period, other designs for postwar Germany came into circulation. One was to dismember the country, splitting it into small states similar to the pattern that had existed before Germany was unified. Another envisioned "pastoralizing" the country, removing all industrial equipment, flooding the Ruhr mines, leaving the Germans wholly dependent on agriculture. In 1944, Henry Morgenthau, Secretary of the Treasury, visited Eisenhower in the field and they discussed the "pastoralizing" plan. Eisenhower, of course, said such matters lay outside his purview as a soldier. However, he added, "You've got to give these people a chance to make a living, or you will have a festering sore forever."

The climate of the times must be remembered. The historians who wrote "The Meaning of Yalta" rightly said, "In each of the countries of the 'strange alliance' relatively few people could think rationally and without emotion about a post-Hitler Germany in the winter of 1944-45."[2] By that time, the dimensions of the Nazi horror were beginning to emerge. As the advancing armies reached the extermination camps,

---

1 Murphy: op. cit.
2 "The Meaning of Yalta": Snell, Pogue, Delzell Lenson.

Eisenhower was revolted by the grisly scenes. So was the ordinary soldier. The postwar dispositions for whatever form they might take seemed of little moment in light of such hideousness.

However, Eisenhower began to feel misgivings about the Zones-of-Occupation plan. He came to Washington in 1944 to advocate a plan of his own. He talked for an hour and a half with Roosevelt, who was in bed suffering from a virus attack. Eisenhower recommended scrapping the EAC blueprint. In its place, he urged that the Big Three administer Germany as a whole. Roosevelt replied, "No, I am committed to that." He added, referring to his dispute with Churchill, "I am going to get the Northwest."

It is interesting to imagine the course of events in Germany if there had been no Zones of Occupation. Berlin then would not have been isolated. No question of the Allies' right of access to the city would have arisen. And how would Stalin have created a Communist East Germany? But it is profitless to speculate; Stalin needed a Soviet Zone for his postwar designs.

On Feb. 4, 1945, Roosevelt, Churchill and Stalin met in the Yalta Conference. There they initialled the EAC plan, partitioning Germany into their respective Zones.

The Conference appeared to set the high-water mark in cooperation between West and East. It looked like a honeymoon. The atmosphere was cordial. The three Chiefs of State each toasted the others for their contributions to the now imminent defeat of Hitler. Who could have foreseen a Berlin Blockade then? Or a Berlin Airlift to circumvent it? Roosevelt obviously expected the Russians, not the Americans and British, to take the city. His chief adviser, Harry Hopkins, reported that "Roosevelt said that during the trip across the ocean, numerous bets had been made as to whether the Americans would get to Manila before the Russians got to Berlin. Stalin laughed and said those who bet on Manila would win."[1]

Yalta came only two months before Roosevelt's death. Churchill and others have written descriptions of the President's physical appearance at the Conference. He looked mortally ill. Murphy, who had seen him shortly before, wrote:

"But Roosevelt was in no condition…to offer balanced judgments upon the great questions of war and peace that had concerned

---
1 Sherwood: "Roosevelt and Hopkins."

him for so long. His conversations illumined for me why the Army during this period was making decisions which the civilian authority for our government normally would have made."[1]

The President's condition may explain a thought he expressed to Eisenhower in their last meeting. He suggested that Eisenhower should send a regiment to Dakar, capital of French West Africa. Why Dakar? The General replied that French West Africa lay far outside his sphere of authority. He could take this action, he said, only on orders from the Combined Chiefs of Staff. Roosevelt said, "I'll take care of that." Eisenhower never heard anything further about the project.

In late March, about six weeks after Yalta, Churchill began to feel concern about Stalin's policy in postwar Europe, about Berlin and about the Allied position in general vis-a-vis the Soviets. He saw, or thought he saw, an opportunity to forestall them by sending British and American forces as far to the east in Germany as they could go before they linked up with the Russian armies.

By that time, German defenses in the west had started crumbling. In the east, they fought furiously to hold every insignificant crossroads against the Russians, as Stalin pointedly called to Churchill's attention. Total collapse now became merely a matter of time. On March 30, Eisenhower issued a proclamation calling on the Germans to surrender. Further bloodshed was senseless.

He poised for the final blow. His plan of battle would first encircle the Ruhr, industrial heart of Germany. Then the armies would advance to the Elbe River, about 60 miles west of Berlin. He intended to halt there to avoid any accidental collisions with the Russians on the ground or in the air. It is not unusual for units of the same army to blunder into fire fights with each other. The potentiality was doubly great with armies speaking different languages. (Later, on the outskirts of Prague, Russian troops opened fire on two American correspondents, Hal Boyle and Ivan Peterman, thinking they were Germans.) A line of demarcation had to be fixed in Germany. Eisenhower chose the river.

Churchill already was thinking beyond purely military objectives and he did not like Eisenhower's plan. He wanted the Americans to cross the Elbe and if possible to enter Berlin before the Russians reached the city. In his memoirs of the Second World War, Churchill

---

1 Murphy: op. cit.

says he had come to regard the Russians as "a mortal danger to the free world," and thus that he considered it vital to establish an Allied "front" as far to the east as possible. On March 31, he wrote Eisenhower, "This has an important political bearing…"

In all wars, military and political objectives become intertwined sooner or later. Berlin, in Churchill's view, had now become important on both counts.

Eisenhower's primary objective, however, was to end the war as soon as possible with the fewest possible casualties. He was not unaware of political considerations but he took the position that political decisions, such as taking Berlin, lay outside his purview. As to Berlin's military value, he messaged Marshall, "May I point out that Berlin is no longer a particularly important objective. Its usefulness has been largely destroyed and even the government is preparing to move to another area."

By contrast, he considered the great complex of industrial cities in the Ruhr the paramount prize. An analogy was used, "When the industrial heart of Germany stops beating, the political heart will die."

Churchill did not agree with Eisenhower's estimate of the importance of Berlin. He messaged, "Further, I do not consider myself that Berlin has lost its military and certainly not its political significance. The fall of Berlin would have a profound psychological effect on German resistance in every part of the Reich."

Eisenhower discussed the question with Omar Bradley who said he estimated it would cost 100,000 American casualties to take Berlin. Bradley says he commented, "a pretty stiff price to pay for a prestige objective, especially since we've got to fall back and let the other fellow take over." The "other fellow," of course, meant the Russians inasmuch as Berlin lay within their Zone under terms of the EAC agreement.

In the exchange of messages about the city, Marshall said, "…I would be loath to hazard American lives for purely political purposes."

Churchill never gave up. On April 1, he messaged Roosevelt, "I therefore consider that from a political standpoint we should march as far east into Germany as possible, and that should Berlin be in our grasp, we should certainly take it. This also seems sound on military grounds." He repeated the thought in another communication to Eisenhower, "We should shake hands with the Russians as far to the east as possible."

Eisenhower advised Marshall, "I am the first to admit that war is waged in pursuance of political aims, and if the Combined Chiefs of Staff should decide that the Allied effort to take Berlin outweighs purely military considerations…I would cheerfully adjust my plans and my thinking so as to carry out such an operation."

On technical grounds, this would be a tall order. Once mighty armies are set in motion in one direction, with the columns of vehicles that support them, it is no simple task to halt them and turn the whole mass off in another direction. However, Eisenhower said he was prepared to do this if the order came from the top.

Churchill, the bulldog, pressed on. He cabled Roosevelt, "If they (the Russians) take Berlin will not their impression that they have been the overwhelming contributor to our common victory…lead them into a mood which will raise grave and formidable difficulties in the future?"

He later commented, "Actually, although I did not realize it, the President's health was now so feeble that it was Gen. Marshall who had to deal with these grave questions."

Bradley was to summarize the situation when he wrote, "As soldiers, we looked naively on this British inclination to complicate the war with political foresight and nonmilitary objectives."[1]

But what about the formula devised by the European Advisory Commission in 1944, which fixed the boundaries of the Zones of Occupation? The Big Three had agreed to this plan. Was Churchill now suggesting that it be discarded, leaving the Americans, British and Russians in possession of the German territory they were occupying when the fighting stopped?

In London, Eisenhower heatedly called this point to Churchill's attention. He said, "Now look, Mr. Prime Minister, you were the one who agreed to all these things. I didn't. I disliked them. Now I make up a plan to defeat the enemy and destroy his forces, and you suddenly come in and bring up Berlin and Prague. I don't know what you are talking about."

Churchill swallowed his feelings and said no more. The Old Warrior still hoped, however, to settle some issues that had arisen since Yalta. When the huge American armies stood on the Elte, well inside the Soviet Zone, the Allies would be in position to negotiate

---

1 Bradley: op. cit.

in a language Stalin understood. Before they pulled back to their assigned Zones, perhaps some solutions could be found.

This was not to be. Roosevelt died and Vice President Truman succeeded him. Five days after the war ended, Churchill messaged the new President, "I am profoundly concerned about the European situation. I learn that half the American Air Force in Europe has already begun to move to the Pacific theater. The newspapers are full of the great movements of the American armies out of Europe…Meanwhile, what is to happen about Russia?…I feel deep anxiety because of their misinterpretation of the Yalta decisions, their attitude toward Poland, their overwhelming influence in the Balkans, excepting Greece, the difficulties they make about Vienna…"

His forebodings were soon to be fulfilled. The Iron Curtain dropped and Berlin was to be a supremely dangerous problem for many years to come.

The American historian, Forrest C. Pogue, places the responsibility on the doorstep of those in Washington at the time. He wrote:

"It is evident that the political leaders in the United States had framed no policy for dealing with an aggressive Soviet Union in Central Europe. It is equally clear that no political directive was ever issued to Gen. Eisenhower by his American supporters or by the Combined Chiefs of Staff…When considered from the purely military viewpoint of the quickest way to end the war in Germany with the fewest numbers of casualties to our troops, leaving the maximum number available for rapid deployment to the Pacific, his decision was certainly the proper one."[1]

During the 1952 presidential campaign, Eisenhower returned to the question. In a speech in Detroit, he said, "Why did I agree to the political decisions of Teheran, Yalta and Potsdam? Well, some of you out there were second lieutenants. Did they ask you? The political leaders and statesmen of our country…did not ask soldiers to participate in political decisions."

So Berlin became an island in the darkness.

---

1 Pogue: "Command Decisions."

"Mission Fulfilled"

On Feb. 1, 1945, Goebbels wrote in the magazine, Das Reich, "The 11th hour seems about to strike." No doubt his purpose was to spur the German armed forces and the weary, bomb-battered people to even greater efforts than they already had made. Yet his statement was more accurate than the Nazi Propaganda Minister realized.

The events of the next few weeks surprised even Eisenhower.

On the afternoon of March 7, a rainy day, the lead elements of the American Ninth Armored Division reached the Rhine near the city of Remagen. To their amazement they found the single-track railway bridge still spanning the river there. It had been damaged by demolitions but it was usable. Within the hour, a dream came true: American troops stood on the east bank of the river.

Eisenhower had expected Hitler to fight with everything he had on this great natural obstacle. When Bradley heard the news, he exulted, "There goes your ball game."

Hitler ordered the execution of the officers who failed to destroy the bridge. He put Field Marshal Albert Kesselring in command of the operations in the West. But it appears that Hitler himself failed to perceive the importance of this first breaching of the Rhine. Kesselring toured all sectors of the front and reported to Hitler in Berlin on March 15. Kesselring said later:

"As I drove back from the Fuehrer's headquarters in the night of 15-16 March, I had the impression that Hitler stubbornly believed we could defeat the Russians in the east, and that what was happening in the west neither surprised him, nor particularly worried him."[1]

More American soldiers soon crossed the Rhine. By March 23, a division of the Third Army went over. Other powerful forces coiled

---

1 Warlimont: op. cit.

to attack across the river. The Ninth Army, after crossing the Rhine, advanced 226 miles in 19 days.

Eisenhower summed up the situation at a press conference in Paris, March 28, in this exchange:

Question—"Do you consider that the main German defense line in the west has now been definitely broken?"

Answer—"I know their main defensive line has been broken but that doesn't mean our troubles are over." (He cited the logistical problems that could arise as the Allied supply lines stretched farther and farther into Germany.)

Meanwhile, quickly exploiting the Rhine crossings, Eisenhower was conducting a great double-envelopment operation around the factory cities of the Ruhr. By April 1, the steel ring closed, trapping 325,000 German soldiers inside.

With these developments coming so swiftly, Eisenhower formally called on the German armed forces to lay down their arms. Their position now was hopeless in the west. No answer came from Hitler. But in spite of his orders, and his threats of reprisals against relatives in Germany, more than a million German soldiers surrendered in the first three weeks of April.

Hundreds of thousands of people, soldiers, civilians, the aged, children, might have been spared if Hitler had capitulated then. It seems clear that by this time he had lost touch with reality. He still thought the V-weapons could turn the tide, along with new jet fighter planes then being developed. On April 15, American troops found a jet factory in a salt mine, 950 feet beneath the earth. They counted the assemblies for 750 fighters. But April 13 was only three weeks away from the total collapse, much too late.

Moreover, the Allies had needlessly given Hitler a powerful propaganda weapon in proclaiming the doctrine of "unconditional surrender." In his book, "Inside Hitler's Headquarters," Gen. Warlimont quotes him as saying:

"It's merely a question who can stand it longer. The one who must hold out the longer is the one who's got everything at stake. We've got everything at stake. If the other side says one day, 'We've had enough of it,' nothing happens to him. If America says, 'We're off. Period. We've got no more men for Europe,' nothing happens. It doesn't change a thing. But if we were to say today, 'We've had enough,' we should cease to exist. Germany would cease to exist."

So he decreed that the hideous Walpurgis night must go on, sacrificing thousands more lives.

American troops reached the Elbe River, the stop line, April 18. They waited there for the meeting with the Russians. Outside Prague also the American Third Army halted, although Czechoslovakian partisans pleaded with Gen. Patton to come in and take the city. The Russian commander, approaching from the east, pointedly reminded Patton that Soviet forces had refrained from taking Wismar in Northeastern Germany at Eisenhower's request. (The latter move was to prevent the Russians from overrunning Denmark.)

Hitler celebrated his 56th birthday on April 20. Champagne was served in his gloomy bunker while Russian shells crashed in the streets outside. His henchmen extended greetings in individual audiences. Then, while there was yet time, some left the bunker and slipped out of Berlin hoping to escape the avenging Furies.

In the battle raging outside the bunker, 6,000 Russian tanks and about 1,000 pieces of heavy artillery ground ahead, pulverizing buildings and houses, many of which had to be taken by assault troops. Against such power, resistance was hopeless. Yet the Germans fought on with fantastic courage and skill.

Eerie scenes were taking place in Hitler's bunker. Twice a day, as though this were years earlier in the war, he received briefings on the course of the battle. He sent radio messages to armies that no longer existed. He married his mistress, Eva Braun, on April 29. Again, the champagne flowed. He then broadcast his "last testament" which said:

"I and my wife have chosen death to escape the shame of overthrow or surrender. It is our wish that our bodies be cremated immediately in the spot where I have carried out the great part of my tasks during these 12 years, which have been devoted to the service of my people."

Hitler poisoned his dog, Blondi. Then, on April 30, probably around 3:30 p.m. he shot himself through the mouth. Eva Braun died by poisoning. The bodies were carried into the garden, drenched with gasoline and set afire.

Goebbels poisoned his six children, his wife and himself. Heinrich Himmler, chief of the SS (Elite Guard) escaped Berlin but was captured, wearing civilian clothes, by the British. He bit down on a cyanide capsule in his teeth and died almost instantly.

That night, Grand Adm. Karl Doenitz received a message at his headquarters at Flensburg, near the Danish border. It came from Martin Bormann, Hitler's deputy, and it informed Doenitz that he was now head of the Reich.

Bormann then disappeared. In the years since, reports frequently circulated that he has been seen alive.

So the Nazi nightmare ended. All that remained was to formalize it with the surrender ceremony at Eisenhower's headquarters in Rheims, France.

Doenitz's deputies, Col. Gen. Gustav Jodl and Adm. Hans Georg von Friedenburg, reached Rheims on Sunday, May 6. They were taken to a room in the red brick building, part of a French technical school, where Eisenhower already was at work on details relating to the redeployment of his forces. He did not see them then. Throughout the years of fighting, when a German commander surrendered, Eisenhower refused to receive him. For him, he said, the war was "far too personal a thing."

It soon appeared to Eisenhower's aides, as they worked out the technical details of the surrender with Jodl and Von Friedenburg, that the Germans were stalling for time. Every passing hour permitted German civilians and soldiers to flee the Russians and pass through the Allied lines. Midnight came and the instruments of surrender remained unsigned. At last, Eisenhower sent out word that unless the signing took place at once he would seal off the fronts.

At 2:30 a.m., May 7, Jodl and Von Friedenburg entered the War Room. A long, L-shaped table stood in the center. Maps and charts showing Allied casualties covered the walls. Auxiliary lamps were turned on, flooding the room with light. Movie cameras whirred. Behind a rope in one corner, 17 Allied correspondents began scribbling. They represented, as a "pool," the hundreds of accredited correspondents.

Except for the sound of the cameras, the room was utterly silent. When the German commanders were seated, Gen. Walter Bedell Smith rose to his feet and handed them the documents of surrender. "There are four copies to be signed," he said. He spoke in a dry, colorless voice.

Jodl and Von Friedenburg signed. Then Smith, Sir Harold Burrough of Britain, Gen. Francois Sevez of France and Gen. Ivan Susloparov of the Soviet Union took the pens and signed. It was 2:41 a.m., British double summer time.

Jodl rose and said, "I want to say a word." He paused and then said, "General, with this signature the German people and the German armed forces are, for better or worse, delivered into the victors' hands…In this hour, I can only express the hope that the victors will treat them with generosity." When he finished speaking, silence again filled the War Room.

Jodl then was conducted to Eisenhower's office. Eisenhower asked, sternly, whether he fully understood the stipulations of the surrender document. Jodl said he did. Eisenhower said he would hold Jodl personally responsible for any violation of its provisions. He concluded, "That is all." Jodl saluted and left. This was the only instance during the war when Eisenhower spoke with a German commander.

Eisenhower's staff, according to Capt. Butcher, immediately began speculating on the language Eisenhower would employ to frame the message to the Combined Chiefs of Staff advising them of the surrender. What grandiloquent adjectives, what majestic, rolling periods, would encase this momentous event in history?

Within a few minutes, Eisenhower sent the message from his office for transmission. It read, "The mission of this Allied force was fulfilled at 0241, local time, May 7, 1945."

The news, however, was to be withheld from the world for the time being. This was an order from the Combined Chiefs of Staff to Eisenhower. The Russians were getting up their own surrender ceremony in Berlin and the two surrenders were to be announced simultaneously. It would have given them a major propaganda coup—if it had worked.

One of the "pool" correspondents who witnessed the ceremony in Rheims was Edward Kennedy, Chief of The Associated Press staff in Europe. Then, at noon on May 7, radio monitors advised him that the Germans themselves were broadcasting the surrender from Flensburg, ordering their submarines, ships at sea and isolated infantry units to surrender to the nearest Allied commanders. Kennedy, on hearing this, felt himself no longer bound to comply with the censor's stop order on the news of the war's end. He advised the censors in Paris that he intended to file his story and did so, using a little-known military telephone line linking Paris and London. A tremendous, and slightly ludicrous, furore followed. In almost a formal "defrocking" rite, the Army disaccredited Kennedy. When it ended, an officer curtly said, "That's all." Kennedy started to leave then, with his waspish sense of humor, he had a second thought. "I almost forgot to return this, too," he said. And he handed the officer his PX card. In the never-ending problem of "managed" news, the Kennedy Case is a landmark. On the one hand, he violated the pledge to abide by censorship which all correspondents signed when they were accredited to the armed forces. But it was wholly wrong, immoral in fact, for Washington and London to withhold news of such transcendent importance—especially for political reasons. It should have been flashed at the moment when the Germans signed, thus notifying millions of anxious families that their loved ones no longer were in danger. Kennedy's moral responsibility transcended the pledge he gave before he went overseas. At the time, very few correspondents agreed. Understandably, they were furious.

When all the facts were known, Eisenhower restored Kennedy's accreditation.

Meanwhile, official or not, the bells were ringing all over the world. Mamie, in Washington, would soon hear her husband's voice on the radio reading his Victory Order of the Day.

At one minute after midnight, May 8-9, the war in Europe ended, the greatest conflict in history.

No other moment would ever mean so much to Eisenhower.

"I Believe Fanatically—"

As early as 1943, long before Eisenhower launched his great military campaigns in Europe, various organizations and individuals in the United States began speaking of him as presidential timber. To such statements he invariably snorted, "Baloney!" When a California newspaperman, Virgil Pinkley, said he should make himself available as a candidate, he replied, "Virgil, you've been standing out in the sun too long." He either laughed at the idea of campaigning for the presidency or turned the idea aside with a derisive remark. He was much too modest to imagine himself in the White House and much too humble to assume that he would have the answers to the domestic and foreign problems of the United States. Apart from that, he knew just enough about politics to recognize that it is a strange world, with its own rules and values, and not for him. A letter from him dated April 7, 1943, tells a friend, "Once this war is won, I hope never again to hear the word 'politics.'" Over and over, in Eisenhower's personal correspondence during the immediate postwar years, this thought reappears.

Nonetheless, and despite his disavowals, politicians of both major parties continued to eye the General with increasing interest. Obviously, he possessed a satchelful of glittering political assets...the genuine war hero, one of the architects of victory in the greatest war ever fought by Americans...a name known in every American home, a face familiar from millions of photographs in newspapers, magazines and newsreels...Franklin Roosevelt's popularity could be invoked on behalf of Eisenhower inasmuch as the President had described him as a "brilliant" soldier...finally, a man who had had dealings with Churchill, Stalin and DeGaulle, had attended the Big Power conferences, and therefore would qualify for the cliche, "soldier-statesman."

When they met him, the politicians immediately felt the force of a million-volt personality. They noted his warm, engaging grin and the air of honesty, his robust humor and instinctive good will.

They found an incisive mind and, when he chose, a blunt, direct manner of speaking. He wore the mantle of authority as though his swaddling clothes had been cut from the same cloth. Thinking of the women's vote, they also noted the electric blue eyes, firm chin and better-than-average looks. To add a bonus, he had a pretty wife. They would make an attractive couple standing on the back platform of a campaign train.

They looked into his background and unearthed a perfect political scenario…the little white house in Abilene was hardly a log cabin but it was a setting with which millions of Americans could identify, especially since it stood in a small town like so many small towns… the barefoot boy who grew and sold vegetables to augment the family income and worked nights in a creamery to help his brother in college…studying nights to prepare himself for the competition that opened the doors of West Point to him…a self-made man in the approved tradition. Here was a Horatio Alger story which could not have been better tailored for a political candidate if his managers had engaged Madison Avenue to write it.

Did he have a political, social or economic philosophy? This was of less moment than the fact that Dwight D. Eisenhower had the winning combination of popularity, personality, looks, an attractive family and an earthy, true-blue American background.

With one exception during his career, Eisenhower had not been closely associated with nonmilitary questions. The exception, of course, was the period in 1930 when he attended the Army Industrial College and studied problems of management, production and costs.

In general terms, however, he had developed a political and social philosophy. A note that he made of a conversation with a Frenchman is illuminating. They talked about France's sudden collapse during the war, the revolving-door governments of the 1930s, disunity and the trend toward Socialism in France. "We defeated ourselves from within," the Frenchman said, "We were working a four-day week as against the Germans' seven-day week." The remark so impressed Eisenhower that he jotted it down and kept it.

In a letter, he recalled Kansas' two senators when he was a boy in Abilene. One, he said, was a "standpatter," and the other a "progressive Republican." His own views coincided with those of the latter.

Another personal letter, written during the war, revealed Eisenhower's beliefs about the relation of the individual American to his country. He emphasized "the obligations as well as privileges of American citizenship"…"the virtues of old-fashioned patriotism"…"the need for a clean, honest approach to problems"…"the necessity for earnest obligation to duty." His simple, homespun philosophy would, indeed, appear to some American circles today to be based on "old-fashioned virtues."

He also wrote a friend in the summer of 1947, "I believe fanatically in the American form of Democracy."

But to the politicians who began beating a path to his door, the important point was that Eisenhower looked like a man who could be elected to the White House, the shiniest of all political prizes. In one way or another, he continued to reply, "Baloney." But the idea soon ceased to be funny or outlandish to him; his correspondence shows that it gradually acquired the proportions of "a problem." People were serious about putting him into the race and he was equally determined to stay out.

An observation attributed to Winston Churchill might have enlightened Eisenhower about all this. The Prime Minister's physician, Lord Moran, quoted him as saying, "In America, when they elect a President, they want more than a skillful politician. They are seeking a personality, something that will make the President a good substitute for a monarch."[1]

Eisenhower was approaching his 55th birthday when the war in Europe ended in May, 1945. He was vigorous and alert. He could and did wear down younger men who trotted after him on inspections in the field. But he was tired.

He looked forward now to peace and quiet after the clatter and stress of the great events with which he had been associated for so long. Nearly four years had passed since that Sunday in 1941, a week after Pearl Harbor, when George Marshall called him to Washington, four years of total concentration on organizing armies, planning their campaigns, and steeling himself to assume full responsibility if they failed. Not only did he need a long rest but he began thinking of retirement. On Nov. 27, 1945, while in the hospital with an attack of bronchitis, he wrote a friend, "For myself, there is nothing I want so much as an opportunity to retire."

He pictured life in a home of his own. No more Army posts or

---

1   Moran: "Churchill."

hotels when the day ended. They would have a house, a place in the country perhaps "miles from a railhead in Texas," or in a small town in the Middle West. Big cities depressed Eisenhower. He once said of New York, "This town scares me." In retirement, he would play with his grandchildren, hunt, fish, ride, play golf. From time to time, he and Mamie would go to Scotland for a holiday in Culzean Castle. In 1945, the National Trust of Scotland gave him a furnished apartment in the Castle which is more than 200 years old and overlooks the Firth of Clyde. Eisenhower's apartment has a drawing room, dining room, study, six bedrooms and four baths. A tourist, passing through the Castle, said she suddenly felt a surge of cold air and saw a ghost. Eisenhower said, "I've been there several times and I never saw the fellow." The Castle might be a good place for him to write. He often thought of trying to write, perhaps for a newspaper syndicate that would be interested in his views on such topics as America's role in the postwar world, isolationism, federal spending, etc. He had definite opinions on these problems. Retirement was a bright dream, but 15 years would elapse before it came true.

First, of course, he intended to carry out his remaining duties in Europe.

He went to London on July 12, 1945, to receive an award and delivered his famous Guildhall Speech (most of which he wrote in bed). In it he said, "Humility must always be the portion of any man who receives acclaim earned in blood of his followers and sacrifices of his friends."

Then he returned to Berlin to assist in organizing the Berlin Council, take the first steps toward rehabilitating Germany, and prepare for the Potsdam Conference.

During the Conference, Eisenhower expressed his view to President Truman on a number of points. He said he considered it would be a mistake for the Western Allies to urge Stalin to enter the war against Japan. (In fact, the secret clauses written into the agreement at Yalta provided for Soviet participation in the Pacific War, along with the cession to Russia of some Japanese territory.) Eisenhower did not then foresee the dangerous developments that would come to be known as the Cold War. But, along with Gen. MacArthur he counseled against giving the Russians a larger voice in the Far East by having the Red Army in the war there.

The news of the first successful test of the atomic bomb came during the Potsdam Conference. Signs of Japan's collapse already were apparent and reports of peace feelers were being heard. The picture was cloudy in that it could not be ascertained whether those Japanese who had made contact with Western intermediaries possessed the authority to speak for the Japanese government. In any event, Eisenhower said he hoped the United States would not use the A-bomb. He was to refer to it later as "this hellish contrivance."

At this time, according to Eisenhower, Truman joined others who were speaking of him as a potential candidate for the presidency. He wrote that he outlined for Truman his general plans for what he would like to do when he came home and quoted Truman as saying, "General, there is nothing you may want that I won't try to help you get. That definitely and specifically includes the Presidency in 1948."[1]

Eisenhower said the statement hit him in the "emotional vitals" but that he passed it off as a joke and assured Truman he would not be his opponent in 1948.

In 1958, Truman denied offering to help Eisenhower win the presidency. The late Edward R. Murrow questioned him about it on a television program and Truman replied:

"No—no. I didn't offer him the presidency. I told him that a great many people who had been in his position had been willing to run for the presidency, but it was my opinion that a man at the top with a military reputation could only have that reputation smeared if he went into politics."

In November, at Truman's request, Eisenhower returned to Washington to succeed Gen. Marshall as Chief of Staff. Mamie provided a bright moment at one of the functions honoring Marshall. A speaker, extolling Marshall for his long service to his country, allowed himself to be carried away by an ardor of eloquence and said, "Now, all the General desires is to return to his land in Virginia with Mrs. Eisenhower." When the laughter subsided, the speaker hastily said, "I apologize to the General." Mamie looked up and said, archly, "Which General?"

Eisenhower had come home during the previous summer to scenes of excitement in New York, Washington and Kansas City that resembled a Roman Emperor's Triumph. Political speculation preceded him. Now that he was in Washington to stay, it redoubled.

---

1 Eisenhower: "Mandate for Change."

Eisenhower thought he could scotch it with a press conference. He told the correspondents, "All I want to be is a citizen of the United States and when the War Department turns me out to pasture that's all I want to be...it's silly to talk about me in politics."

In matters pertaining to politics, Eisenhower was frequently naive. He did not realize that this statement would only add fuel to the fire. The disavowal is one of the hoary traditions of American politics. Hence, Eisenhower's press conference statement merely stirred the customary assertions that he was being "coy." He wrote a friend that this did not distress him, "for the reason that I occupy the enviable position of a man who wants nothing." In another letter, dated March 13, 1946, he wrote, "I cannot conceive of any set of circumstances that would drag out of me permission to consider me for any political post."

The Russians provided part of that "set of circumstances."

When Eisenhower left Europe, the blueprint of Stalin's designs were not wholly apparent. The Russians appeared ready to cooperate with the Allies in the administration of Germany. They had not yet challenged the Allies' right of access to Berlin. Churchill alone among the major statesmen sounded a warning. In March, 1946, he delivered his "Iron Curtain" speech in Fulton, Missouri. Stalin called him a "warmonger" and the speech a "dangerous act." Naked hostility soon developed between Russia and the West.

As Supreme Commander, Eisenhower had been on good personal terms with Stalin and highly placed officers in the Russian Army. He found friendliness and good humor in the individual Russian. While he disliked the Soviet political system, he felt, as did most Westerners then, that the Democracies could live with it in a peaceful world. But then came the enslavement of Eastern Europe and the effort, through local Communist parties or armed guerrillas, to spread Stalin's power over France, Italy and Greece. Eisenhower became alarmed. He wrote his friend, Hazlett, "My deepest concern involves America's situation in the world today."

He served as Chief of Staff from 1945 to February 7, 1948.

These were tedious and often trying years. Eisenhower had hoped that the United States would adopt a system of universal military service after the end of the war in Europe. It was a dangerous world and he felt that America's safety could not be insured by a minuscule Army. Korea was to vindicate his vision. But instead of building a strong peacetime Army, a kind of hysteria for demobilization erupted almost before the ink dried on the documents of the German surrender. Mom wanted her boy home right now and out of uniform at the earliest possible moment. The shrill voices sounded loud and clear in Washington. Congressmen heard them, of course, and took due heed. Pressure blocs formed on behalf of the butcher, the baker, the candlestick maker. Much of this pressure beat against Eisenhower's door. He was disgusted and angry. When an officer congratulated him on the pace of dismantlement, Eisenhower snapped back that he only wished he were out of uniform so that he could "shout from the housetops" against the folly of the headlong process. Churchill came to Washington in March, 1946, and, speaking at the military reception given for him, he quoted a jingle that he said had been written by one of the Duke of Marlborough's veterans—

> "God and the soldier we adore
> "In time of danger, not before.
> "The danger past and all things righted,
> "God is forgotten and the soldier slighted."

He also made his first moves at this time to bring about the unification of the Armed Services. War had become "triphibious," he said, sea and air forces closely supporting the infantryman on land. Salerno and Normandy had been object examples. Apart from these tactical considerations, Eisenhower was well acquainted with the perennial competition between the respective branches for money from Congress. He tried everything in the book to change this. He even advocated a single uniform for all branches, well knowing the pride taken by every soldier, sailor and airman in his own uniform. He wrote in a personal letter, "Each of these men must cease regarding himself as the advocate or special pleader for any particular Service. He must think strictly and solely in terms of the United States."

The experiences in Washington taught him something about the workings of the political mind. Yet he never ceased to be surprised when he found, in his opinion, a politician putting politics ahead of the national interest.

So the controversies swirled around Eisenhower. What had become of that bright dream of the life of a country gentleman in semiretirement?

The honors accorded him in this period no doubt contributed

to his popularity, which seemed to grow rather than to diminish as the war years faded farther into the past. In June, 1947, for example, Princeton University made him an honorary Doctor of Laws and the citation said, "In his postwar missions to other countries, his tact, humor and refreshing frankness left a lasting and happy impression. For his services to his country we owe him a debt never to be forgotten."

His personal correspondence during these years, despite the Pentagon problems and the efforts to strong-arm him into politics, indicate that he was enjoying life to the hilt.

It seems that his friend, "Swede" Hazlett had a daughter, "Buzzie," who, according to her father, had grown up to be a beautiful blonde. Wouldn't it be great if "Buzzie" and John Eisenhower met, fell in love, and were married? It appears that Eisenhower and Hazlett made some tentative maneuvers in this direction. For Eisenhower wrote his friend on Jan. 25, 1946, "I chuckle to myself every time you and I exchange ideas along this line because the spectacle of a couple of old-time Kansas farmer boys timidly sticking their noses into Cupid's business is, after all, a bit on the ludicrous side."

The hopes of the two fathers ended when "Buzzie" fell for an All-America football player at the Naval Academy and married him.

Eisenhower and Hazlett continually needled each other about their respective Academies. Hazlett reported a minor scandal involving a man from Abilene, which came to light in the Navy during the war. In reply, Eisenhower expressed surprise that anything of this nature ever took place in Abilene and he wrote, "It must have been the Navy influence!"

Hazlett read a news story reporting that Eisenhower had been named one of the 10 best-dressed men in the United States. This is not the type of "news" that would catch Eisenhower's eye and he had not seen the story. When Hazlett apprised him of the "new honor" that had come to him, Eisenhower wrote back, "My reaction is that some people must (not?) have a lot to do if they have time to devote themselves to such drivel…One of Mamie's chief causes of complaint is that I will not even buy a pair of socks for myself." He went on to say that "a Jewish friend of mine" had been making his suits, choosing the material and cut, and simply appearing from time to time with a new suit.

Eisenhower's endemic modesty prevented him from realizing the dimensions of his popularity or the fact that he had become a public figure. An editor in a New York publishing house wrote Hazlett suggesting that he and Eisenhower collaborate on a book about their experiences in Abilene as boys and young men. Eisenhower told Hazlett he would not be interested but he would assist his friend in recalling personalities and incidents. (Throughout his life, his memory remained phenomenal.) He said he would do everything he could. Then he added, "I still fail to see, however, how any real amount of interest could be engendered in a study of the commonplace happenings involving a bunch of boys in a small Western town of 45 years ago." Evidently, he could not understand that he had become so prominent.

Hazlett and others regularly informed him of political moves on his behalf in their communities.

For the "Eisenhower-for-President" boom continued to rise like a flash flood in his native Kansas. Few asked whether he was a Republican or Democrat. He might be a Free Silver advocate or a member of the Vegetarian Party. No matter. People just naturally found that they "liked Ike." Some probably found in him a father image. Some felt that, with his military and political experience around the world, he would be the best-equipped man to deal with the Russians. But most simply responded to his charm, the warmth and sincerity, the transparent honesty, the unaffected humbleness.

The clamor worried him. He wrote Milton Eisenhower "...I am getting very close to violating the one underlying principle that I have always believed to be binding on every American. This principle is that every citizen is required to do his duty for the country no matter what it may be. While I am very clear in my own mind that no man since Washington has had any occasion to feel it was his duty to stand for, or to accept, political office, yet the principle remains valid."

By the end of 1947, Communist designs in Europe had become clearer. The Soviet grip tightened on Eastern Europe. Red guerrillas fought on the borders of Greece. Italian and French Communist parties sought greater power in those governments. The Peace Conference in Paris revealed Russian intransigence, an inflexibility which would become boringly familiar in the United Nations and in international efforts to settle disputes. The smell of danger filled the air. Was it Eisenhower's duty to come forward?

"Duty" is the touchstone in Eisenhower's character, a powerfully compelling word in his lexicon. But where did it lie in this instance? Was it the duty of a soldier to make use of his experience in the presidency, assuming he were elected? Or was it the duty of a nonpolitician to steer clear of the almost wholly unfamiliar milieu of politics?

In January, 1948, came the well-remembered exchange of letters with Leonard V. Finder, publisher of the Manchester, New Hampshire, Union-Leader.

Finder advised him that a "genuine grass-roots" movement had started in New Hampshire and that Eisenhower's admirers wanted to enter his name in the state's Presidential Primary election in March. Finder enclosed an editorial in the Union-Leader captioned, "The Best Man," meaning Eisenhower.

Here, the General saw the opportunity to reiterate his position more emphatically than he had yet done. He sat down to frame a reply to Finder and to state his reasons for staying out of politics.

One of his staff assistants, Kevin McCann, says Eisenhower stewed and sweated for nine days composing the letter. When he came in with the final version, Eisenhower said, "It's long and laborious but it's the best I can do. And it's right, too…I'm trying to be honest and realistic about it."[1]

He addressed himself to two questions, a citizen's duty, and whether a soldier should ever occupy the White House.

On the first, the letter said, "…that concept of duty which calls upon every good citizen to place no limitations on his readiness to serve in any designated capacity. (But) unless an individual feels some inner compulsion and special qualifications to enter the political arena—which I do not—a refusal to do so involves no violation of the highest standards of devotion to duty."

As to the second, he wrote, "It is my conviction that the necessary and wise subordination of the military to civil power will be best sustained, and our people will have greater confidence that it is so sustained, when lifelong professional soldiers, in the absence of some obvious and overriding reason, abstain from seeking high political office…" It is interesting to note that Eisenhower first expressed the core of this principle in a Commencement Address he made to the members of the Filipino Reserve Officers Training Corps in Manila,

---

1   McCann: op. cit.

March 24, 1939. He added in his letter to Finder, "Politics is a profession; a serious, complicated and in its true sense, a noble one."

Newspapers throughout the country published the letter beneath blazing headlines, evidence of the interest in Eisenhower's candidacy. Editorials followed. On Jan. 24, the Baltimore Sun said the letter "... withdraws perhaps irrevocably from the political arenas one of the ablest and most popular of the potential Republican nominees. At the same time, it constitutes to American political history a document that should be long remembered."

For the moment the matter was closed. In a letter dated Jan. 30, 1948, Eisenhower told a friend, "You can imagine that I have been experiencing a great sense of relief in the past few days." But this "sense of relief" was to be short-lived. Long before 1952 brought another presidential election, Republicans would be importuning Eisenhower to make himself available.

Evidently, Winston Churchill understood Eisenhower's reluctance completely. His physician, Lord Moran, wrote in his diary on Jan. 8, 1952, "I asked him (Churchill) if he thought Eisenhower would be nominated by the Republicans. His face lit up:

"'Ike has not only to be wooed but raped.'"[1]

However, in 1948, the way lay open temporarily for General Eisenhower to become Citizen Eisenhower in a great University which brought him one of the most rewarding periods of his life.

---

1 Moran: "Churchill."

Many Wonderful Hours

On Sunday afternoon, May 2, 1948, Eisenhower and Mamie entered a large, handsome mansion at 60 Morningside Drive, New York City, the official residence of the president of Columbia University. His new role, he knew, would be a radical change for him after three decades of soldiering. "I know nothing about the workings of a great University," he wrote in a letter to a friend, "and am certainly far from being an educator...The Board of Trustees insists they want an organizer and leader, not a professor." Eisenhower approached every task, even the assault on Normandy with all its hazards, completely confident of succeeding. However, although he had had a vast experience as "an organizer and leader" in the Army, he now imposed on himself a probationary period; if, at the end of one year, he concluded that he was unfit to be president of Columbia, he would resign.

By no definition of the word could Eisenhower be considered an intellectual. In fact, he once said that an intellectual is a person who takes twice as many words as necessary to tell twice as much as he knows. The widely known critic, John Mason Brown, has pointed out that the intellectual usually makes the mistake of "denying intelligence to a person who is not an intellectual." Brown said Eisenhower's associates during and after the war described his intelligence as "fantastically big-sized."[1]

In the academic climate, then, a little-known side of Eisenhower soon began to emerge.

He sent a five-page letter, typewritten, to his friend, "Swede" Hazlett, recounting his conversations at the University with specialists in economics, history, contemporary civilizations, "some branches of natural and physical science," public health and engineering. "You can see that living with a distinguished faculty gives me many won-

---
1 Brown: "Through These Men."

derful hours," he said in another letter reflecting his enjoyment of these discussions.

Eisenhower had formulated a theory about religious faith and man's instinct to be free. He thought they were intertwined, that faith in God is the necessary base for a free nation. As examples, he cited the Early Christians and the Jews. He often mused over the phrase in the Declaration of Independence which says that all men "are endowed by their Creator with certain inalienable rights…" The significant word in it, he said, is "Creator." It signified to him that the American nation was founded on a basis of religious faith. He once said, "A free government without a foundation of deep religious faith makes no sense." He felt that this was one of the great strengths of the Democracies in their conflict with the Communists. At Columbia, he asked faculty specialists to examine his theory.

During this period, too, he displayed an appreciation for writing which seldom if ever appeared in his earlier correspondence. Hazlett sent him a copy of a letter on some current political and economic questions, written by a professional writer. Eisenhower replied in a four-page letter. Much of what he wrote, however, concerned the elegance of the man's writing, not the contents of the letter. He expressed admiration for "nuances" and "shadings of words." He seemed to savor them, like a man rolling a rare wine around on his tongue. And he said in his reply to Hazlett, "Before I go home tonight, I am going to look up the word, 'exegete.'"

Eisenhower often expressed himself poorly, with fuzzy ambiguities when he spoke off-the-cuff. He could not or would not be bothered with grammar and syntax. He was interested in the idea, not the manner of expressing it. (It is difficult to resist the suspicion that he may have done this deliberately at times, in order to fog over the answer to a question he would have preferred not to have been asked.)

But the written word is something else to him. In writing, no amount of revising, rewriting, polishing is too much for Eisenhower; he persists until he has the passage exactly as he wants it. He begins by dictating, often pacing the floor as he talks. When the typewritten copy of this draft is returned he sits down to edit it. He may change a word two or three times, trying different synonyms. On the margins of the typescript, substituted sentences curl around all four corners of a page, sometimes intersecting other changes. Champollion himself would have had difficulty deciphering the maze of hen tracks.

Somehow, Eisenhower's secretaries unravel it. The edited version then is retyped and the process is continued until Eisenhower is satisfied that he is on target. He has been known to redo an entire chapter in his books 20 times.

John Gunther reported that Eisenhower frequently consults Fowler's "Modern English Usage" and a book captioned "Technical English."[1]

However, Eisenhower has never flattered himself about his prose. He once said, "I am unquestionably a hack and I know this. I don't try to reach for style. I have long since thrown away all the purple adjectives I ever knew. I am concerned with logic and accuracy."

His books, he said, "are really reports on matters that came to my personal attention and seemed interesting."

In 1948, he brought out his memoirs of the war, "Crusade in Europe." The title may very well have originated in a private letter written in 1943 in which he said, "I do have the feeling of a crusader in this war." He used the word several times in statements to soldiers when they were about to go into action. The book, 200,000 words in length, became a great success. It brought Eisenhower about a half-million dollars after taxes. Some months earlier, he had purchased an automobile. He paid for it in full by check and then, calculating what remained in his bank account, he pointed to the car and said to Mamie, "Darling, that's the entire result of 37 years' work since I caught the train out of Abilene."[2]

One of the many myths about Eisenhower was that he refused to read a document that ran longer than a page and one-half. It is true that he insisted on having reports and planning documents boiled down to the essentials. But the files of his personal correspondence bulge with letters, written and received, that run to eight and nine pages of single-spaced typescript. His annotations appear on the margins of many letters, terse comments, sometimes a question. Obviously he had read and thought about the letters.

Another myth was that he was a kind of Babbitt who read nothing but Western stories and seed catalogs, confined his interests to bridge, golf and self-made millionaires and lacked all appreciation for culture. In that connection, a number of episodes are illuminating.

---
1   Gunther: "Eisenhower, the Man and the Symbol."
2   McCann: op. cit.

After the Cairo Conference, Gen. Marshall told Eisenhower he looked worn down, which he was, and told him to take several days' rest. Marshall put it in the form of an order. Instead of hastening to the nearest golf course or bridge table, Eisenhower made the long trip from Cairo to Luxor and Karnak, sites of a glorious era in the life of ancient Egypt. Scrambling in and out of the deep-cut tombs and climbing the slope to Queen Hatshepsut's temple palace is mentally and emotionally rewarding, but it can hardly be called a rest. Eisenhower spent the rest of his leave in the Holy Land, sightseeing in Jerusalem and Bethlehem. While he was in Tunisia, he made a special point to visit the ruins of Carthage.

On another occasion, shortly after the war ended, Eisenhower completed some work in Moscow. A free afternoon lay ahead. The Russians asked him how he would like to fill it, and he replied, "I would like to see the Kremlin Museum." With his son, he spent the entire afternoon in the museum. "Magnificent," he said when he left it.

Like Winston Churchill, Eisenhower taught himself to paint. He had no illusions about his ability. One of his first efforts was a portrait of Mamie. Once, when she was asked about it, she rolled her eyes, suppressed a grin, and said, "It's a lulu." Eisenhower often painted late at night, between 11 o'clock and 12:30. In a letter, he said of his hobby, "It gives me an excuse to be absolutely alone and interferes not at all with what I am pleased to call my contemplative powers."

In 1949, when he was barely under way with his work at Columbia, Eisenhower was summoned to Washington by President Truman and James Forrestal, the first Secretary of Defense, to serve informally as chairman of the Joint Chiefs of Staff. Shuttling between New York and Washington, he attended conferences on national security and furthered the projects he had initiated at the University. A friend warned him that not even his exuberant vitality could sustain such a pace indefinitely. He said he was only trying to do his duty. In March, 1949, he broke down, physically exhausted. He entered the Naval Hospital in Key West, Florida. Not until May was he able to resume his work fully in New York and Washington.

Meanwhile, the efforts continued to persuade him to make himself available as a presidential candidate. They came from both major parties. Eisenhower felt it necessary to issue a public statement through the University's information office. He said his position remained as he had stated it in the letter to Finder, and that he would not identify himself with any political party. The statement closed with the sentence, "This implies no intention of maintaining silence on any issue of importance to the country on which I may feel myself qualified to express an opinion."

Accordingly, in letters and speeches he began delineating the rudiments of his political and economic philosophy. A personal letter concerning some domestic problems says, "While there may be little I can do about such matters, I do have the feeling that whatever I try to do is on a national, and not on any partisan, basis."

A recurrent theme appeared in his statements, total opposition to "paternalism" in government and to "collectivism." One passage is typical, "…we combat remorselessly all those paternalistic and collectivistic ideas which, if adopted, will accomplish the gradual lessening of our individual rights and opportunities and finally the collapse of self-government."

On the relationship of labor and management, Eisenhower said, "…intelligent management certainly recognizes the need for maximum income to workers, consistent with reasonable return on investment. With equal clarity, labor cannot fail to recognize the need for increasing amounts of risk capital to provide jobs for our constantly growing population. And—make no mistake about it—no group in our country is more firmly dedicated to the retention and development of private competitive enterprise than is American labor."

Numerous offers of lucrative positions in business and industry came to him. One of his letters reflects a feeling of ironic amusement when he thought of the former "barefoot boy from Dickinson County casually turning down" posts that carried salaries of $75,000 and more.

His years at Columbia were among the happiest of his life. The degree of his success at the University depends on the observer you may question. Opinions vary widely. Eisenhower however took satisfaction in some of the ideas he advanced there, "a study of the Conservation of Human Resources," creation of a Nutrition Center, the establishment of a Chair for Peace. Of this project, he said in a speech, "For me, there is something almost shocking in the realization that, though many millions have been voluntarily donated for research in cancer of the individual body, nothing similar has been done with respect to the most malignant cancer of the world body—war."

A noted American historian, Dr. Edward Meade Earle, was lecturing at All Souls College, Oxford, at the time. Eisenhower wrote Churchill on May 1, 1950, requesting him to meet with Dr. Earle to get the old statesman's thoughts on the Chair for Peace.

As Eisenhower worked toward this objective, war returned to the world. On June 25, 1950, six highly trained and well-armed divisions from Communist North Korea swept across the 38th Parallel into South Korea and President Truman promptly ordered American forces, based in Japan, to meet the threat. The outlook for at least an uneasy peace between West and East had been shattered by the guerrilla attacks on Greece and then by the Soviet blockade of Berlin in 1948. Truman sent Gen. James A. Van Fleet to counter the Communist moves in Greece. And if his advisers had agreed, he would have ordered an armed American convoy to shoot its way into Berlin. The astounding Berlin Airlift eventually forced Stalin to raise the blockade. Greece and Berlin stand as the earliest of a succession of Communist setbacks. Now, in the Far East, they launched another adventure. Nobody but Stalin himself could say if or when they would attack Western Europe. These events soon made themselves felt at 60 Morningside Drive.

Eisenhower and his wife were in a Pullman car in Ohio, waiting to be taken to Heidelberg College on the evening of Dec. 18, 1950. A trainman notified him that President Truman was trying to reach him by telephone. Eisenhower left the car, plodded through deep snow to the freight office, and there talked with Truman. The President asked him to return to Europe as Supreme Commander of the North Atlantic Treaty Organization. The member nations were unanimous, he said. He followed it up with a note on Dec. 19 which said, "The North Atlantic Treaty nations have agreed on the defense organization for Europe and at their request I have designated you as Supreme Commander Europe."

Eisenhower's first reaction was disappointment. He liked his life and work at Columbia.

But he himself had discussed NATO in a letter to a friend about a month earlier. Eisenhower wrote, "I rather look upon this effort as the last remaining chance for survival of Western civilization." As always, he felt the sense of duty and responsibility, and he went on to say in the letter, "Any one of us—no matter what his situation, his position, or what personal sacrifices might be involved—must be ready to do his best."

So his answer to Truman was a foregone conclusion.

In three weeks, he traveled across Western Europe examining the many facets of NATO. The problems were numerous and complicated. How much, in terms of men, arms and money, could each member nation contribute? How soon? How could these forces be integrated into a whole that would constitute the shield to bear the initial Russian thrust if it came?

He rapidly came to some conclusions and a long-range view. "I insist that Europe must, as a whole, provide in the long run for its own defense," he said. "The United States can move in and, by its psychological, intellectual and material leadership, help to produce arms, units and the confidence that will allow Europe to solve its problems. In the long run, it is not possible—and most certainly not desirable—that Europe should be an occupied territory defended by legions brought in from abroad…" Such a situation, he said, would recreate the era when Caesar's legions garrisoned lands far from Rome.

Roy Roberts wrote him a letter about the danger of "complacency" in the United States and Eisenhower replied, "Personally, I agree most emphatically with the last sentence of your note. We must be realistic and tough with ourselves." (His underlining)

On Jan. 27, he returned to Washington and reported to the President. Three days later, he addressed a group of senators and representatives in the Library of Congress. Eisenhower spoke extemporaneously, outlining the problem and his general thoughts on it. He was, as usual, optimistic, confident the job could be done. He said American troops would be required in the task. Here, for the first time, Eisenhower came into opposition with Robert A. Taft, the great Republican senator from Ohio. Taft was to become Eisenhower's political enemy, critic, mentor and finally a friend.

Strange as it may seem today, Taft and other conservatives had challenged Truman's Constitutional right to deploy American troops overseas in peacetime without the consent of Congress. The question of whether the United States should take the lead in building the backbone of NATO also was under debate. Eisenhower, in supporting the NATO concept, inferentially supported the President's position.

A collateral development came from his appearance before the senators and congressmen. He gave a dazzling performance.

He spoke for 90 minutes, clearly and with precision. He knew his subject thoroughly. It embraced much more than the purely military aspects of his task in Europe. He outlined the political, economic and financial factors in the various NATO countries. Then he answered questions from the floor, handling himself equally well. He made a deep impression on his audience, and those who had urged his candidacy, purely on the basis of his popularity, now found additional reason for supporting it. Here was a broad-gauged man, not merely a personable soldier.

A senator whom Eisenhower never named afterward came to his office in the Pentagon for a secret meeting. Eisenhower hoped to enlist his support for NATO. He failed. He found, or thought he found, a mere political gambit aimed at Truman in this and other such conferences. "My disappointment was acute," he wrote later. "I was resentful toward those who seemed to me to be playing politics in matters I thought vital to America and the Free World."[1]

His personal correspondence shows that by this time he had come to see the Cold War as "part and parcel of the struggle between free and slave societies going on for some 3,000 years," only now, he wrote, it had become "polarized" between Washington and Moscow.

He then returned to France to set up SHAPE and to organize a bigger and certainly more complex coalition than the one he led during the war.

His official residence was the Villa St. Pierre, a pleasant, white-trimmed house with fountains in front, near Marnes-la-Coquette. Mamie now had an "igloo" with a French accent. Indian corn is unknown on French menus and almost unknown in French cuisine. Since her husband enjoyed it, Mamie raised corn in her garden.

From this base, Eisenhower tore into his organizational tasks, lavishing physical and mental energy on them. He travelled continually, reviewing new divisions, studying defense plans, talking with heads of state and their aides. He was like a whirling dervish, both in action and in zeal for selling the concept of a united Europe.

Thus, at a dinner in Paris one night, his temper slipped its leash when a prominent Frenchwoman expressed doubt that the French could ever be put in harness with the Germans. Eisenhower blew up. He called this attitude "defeatist" and bluntly said that if everyone

---

1   Eisenhower: "Mandate for Change."

entertained such opinions, the future could hold nothing for Europe but the prospect of more wars. He began talking about the power of faith.

He was still boiling when dinner ended and the ladies temporarily withdrew. He turned suddenly to Col. Jock Lawrence, an aide, and asked, "Have you ever been in the Catacombs?" Lawrence said he had. Eisenhower went into a further dissertation on faith. "What are the Catacombs?" he said. "Nothing but holes in the ground? No, sir. They represent the faith of the Christians during the Roman persecutions." From there he turned to the persecution of the Jews in various parts of Europe, climaxed by the Nazi holocaust. "But through all of this, over many centuries," he said, "they held tight to their faith, and that is the only thing that made it possible for them to survive these ordeals." He paused a moment and continued more quietly, "That is what France needs. They need people with faith in France, not with fear of France."

But with all these matters on his mind, Eisenhower retained an abiding interest in his hometown and state. A disastrous flood swept over Kansas in the summer of 1951. Eisenhower wrote a friend that he had been reading about it in the newspapers. He recalled a similar flood in 1903 after which he and his brothers worked for days shoveling mud from their home and mopping up sludge and water. He said in his letter, "That early experience gives me a real basis of understanding for the thousands of people who have been compelled this year to undergo the terrors and dangers of a major Kansas flood. I trust that things are rapidly returning to normal and I pray that the loss of life and damage incurred were not so great as at first feared." He wrote feelingly about flood control.

Meanwhile, pressures mounted for him to declare himself before the 1952 presidential year dawned. Hordes of visitors came to Marnes-la-Coquette either to wrench from him a statement that he would be available for the Republican nomination, or to divine his intentions. (This writer was one of them.) Talking with him was like trying to fathom the riddle of the Sphinx. However, Norman Chandler, publisher of The Los Angeles Times, emerged from a visit with the strong impression that Eisenhower would run. Numerous letters from Washington told him it was his duty to do so. Roy Roberts, publisher of The Kansas City Star, wrote that Eisenhower told him he was "a good Kansas Republican." At home, other Republicans were actively working for him. Herbert Brownell, one of the shrewdest political brains in the United States, went swinging around the country, sniffing the winds. Everywhere, he found people saying, "I like Ike." In October, Thomas E. Dewey, former governor of New York, asserted that Eisenhower could be nominated and elected. Scores of other prominent voices joined the chorus.

Bob Taft's captains marshaled their forces in what was to be Taft's last attempt to win the nomination and then follow his father's footsteps in the White House. All the elements of an epic political drama were taking shape.

On New Year's Eve, 1951-52, Eisenhower and Mamie invited some friends to dinner at the villa. Among them were Jock Lawrence and his wife, Mary. After the midnight toasts, the conversation turned, as it often did then, to politics. Mamie said, "I think that if Ike should become President it would kill him." Mary Peace Lawrence, the daughter of a professional soldier, quickly replied, "But West Point trains them for the possibility of being killed in line of duty, doesn't it?" Eisenhower glanced at her and murmured, "in line of duty."

He had previously written a friend and cited the axiom that "the voice of the people is the voice of God." But, he added, he was not sure what it was saying with relation to his future.

A political phenomenon in New York early in February, 1952, brought the voice and its message to him more clearly. It jolted him.

Some of his supporters, amateurs in politics, organized an "Ike Rally" in Madison Square Garden. It could not begin until the night's boxing program ended, 10:30 p.m. Because of the hour, and fearing the effects of a poor turnout, other Eisenhower backers urged the sponsors of the rally to cancel it. They went ahead anyway. More than 15,000 people, who had been gathering outside, surged into the Garden when the boxing ended. Cameras recorded the rally. Jacqueline Cochrane, the aviatrix, flew to France the next day carrying the film. She went without sleep for 30 hours. At Marnes-la-Coquette she asked Eisenhower and Mamie to look at the pictures. They did. Eisenhower described its impact in a personal letter, dated Feb. 11. He wrote, "In any event, the film brought home to me for the first time something of the depth of the longing in America today for a change...I can't tell you what an emotional upset it is for one to realize that he himself may become the symbol of that longing and hope."

In March, Senator Henry Cabot Lodge entered Eisenhower's name in the New Hampshire presidential primary. Inasmuch as this election is the first to be held in a presidential year, it carries a psychological impact out of all proportion to the number of votes cast.

Eisenhower remained in Europe, taking no direct part in the campaign. Taft ploughed tirelessly through the snows, hunting votes in every city, village and mountain crossroads. He was an impressive candidate, obviously a giant brain, obviously as well equipped to be President, through a lifetime of exposure to politics and government, as any man ever can be. After a speech, he would stand in the doorway, shaking hands, beaming through his gold-rimmed spectacles, a warm and friendly man not the rasping critic of Democratic Administrations. Time and again, men in the receiving line told him, "I voted for your father, Senator." About a week before the primary a New Hampshire state official said, "They like Taft in these parts, but they like Ike better." And so it was. When the votes were counted, Eisenhower's count stood at 46,661 to Taft's 35,838. The "voice" had spoken.

A week later, on March 18, it spoke again in even more unmistakable terms. In Minnesota, Eisenhower's name did not appear on the ballot for that primary. Thus, the citizen who wished to vote for him had to write his name in on the ballot. Politicians generally are reluctant to try to organize a significant write-in vote, on the theory that not enough voters feel strongly enough about a candidate to take that much trouble. In Minnesota more than 100,000 persons felt strongly about Eisenhower. Many made hash of his name as they wrote it on the ballots, but they knew they wanted him.

The results of the two elections impelled Roy Roberts to write in The Kansas City Star that, in his opinion, Eisenhower would respond to the movement at home only out of a sense of duty and that a genuine draft now appeared in the making. He sent Eisenhower a copy of his article with a covering letter in which he said, "I have felt all along that you would never even look at the presidency for yourself but only out of a sense of duty." Eisenhower replied, on March 28, "I cannot tell you how grateful I am for your letter. It means all the more to me because of its insistence upon a factor that all too many people seem to be able to brush off or explain away, just simple self-respect and personal honor."

When Spring came, Eisenhower felt that his work in organizing the European Defense Community would be finished by June 1. He was now convinced that he should come home and campaign actively for the Republican nomination. He asked to be relieved of his duties as of that date. On April 11, the White House announced approval of his request.

He now prepared to enter the uncharted jungle of domestic politics although he had said he hoped never to hear the word "politics" again.

The dramatic May morning when the Germans surrendered, nearly seven years earlier, had secured Eisenhower's place in history. If he had been concerned solely with this, with his prestige and popularity, he would have retired then instead of exposing himself to the lacerating realities of politics. He was not, and never could be, a politician. But he had been around Washington enough over the years to realize the wisdom of Harry Truman's remark, "If you can't stand the heat, stay out of the kitchen." Further, Eisenhower had predicted (how accurately, as it turned out!) that as a middle-of-the-roader he would be attacked by extremists on both sides. Out of a sense of duty, he put aside his own desires and inclinations and prepared to face up to "the heat."

Human-heartedness

A hush fell in the bull-chested Convention Hall in Chicago. Pulses quickened. All the grotesque antics and the tribal rites of a national nominating convention were finished. The lung-power marathon of nominating speeches and the blast of loudspeakers polling state delegations echoed no longer. The time-worn maneuvers of Taft's men to seat contested delegates had boomeranged, and Eisenhower's captains, Brownell, Dewey and Lodge, had turned it to his advantage. Senator Dirksen's bitter personal attack on Dewey would not soon be forgotten, but the jejune speeches faded into oblivion even as they were being delivered. All this, at long last, had come to an end.

Now the moment was at hand to call the roll, the actual voting, beginning with Alabama and ending with the Virgin Islands. In this uniquely American method, a great political party commits itself to one man, who then carries with him the dreams, ambitions, the power lust of countless men and women in his party. It is always an electric moment, even when the result of the balloting is a foregone conclusion.

On that hot July day in 1952, the conclusion was anything but cut and dried. Everyone present knew the race between Eisenhower and Taft would be close on the first ballot. After that, who could say what might happen? The air quivered with suspense.

It would make a dramatic vignette for history to picture Eisenhower and Mamie, sitting close to the television screen in their hotel, chewing fingernails as his vote raced neck and neck with Taft's toward the winning total, 605. But Eisenhower never was a fingernail chewer in critical moments. In this one, according to his own version, he merely felt numb and tired. Moreover, he was worried about Mamie who was in bed suffering from an infected tooth. As the balloting rolled on, Eisenhower continually left the living room of his suite to ask her how she felt. When he returned, he chatted with his brothers and some friends, paying only cursory attention to the proceedings in the convention hall.

At last the roll call ended. Most of the spectators had kept scorecards and were virtually certain that neither Eisenhower nor Taft had won. Neither had received 605 votes. Nevertheless, silence again settled over the thousands present as they waited to hear the official tabulation.

Finally it was announced—Eisenhower, 595; Taft 500; Governor Earl Warren of California, 81; Harold Stassen, 19; Gen. MacArthur 10.

What now? Another roll call immediately? Or a recess to permit some quick bargaining and horse trading?

Suddenly, Senator Edward Thye, head of the Minnesota delegation, was on his feet, frantically waving the Minnesota placard and shouting, "Mr. Chairman! Mr. Chairman!"

At that instant, Victor Johnston, a seasoned professional aide to Taft, came drifting down the aisle, eyes riveted on Thye and the Minnesota delegates. They had given their votes to Stassen as a "favorite son" in the balloting. Were they going to break away now? Johnston's face was a picture of puzzlement and dismay.

They were. The convention chairman, Representative Joseph W. Martin Jr. of Massachusetts, recognized Thye and ignored other would-be kingmakers who were bellowing for his attention. Thye yelled, "Mr. Chairman, Minnesota wishes to change its vote to Gen. Dwight D. Eisenhower." The Minnesota votes gave Eisenhower more than the necessary 605 and made him the Republican nominee for President.

The great hall exploded. Other delegations boarded the bandwagon as fast as Martin recognized them. Finally, Senator John Bricker of Ohio offered the motion to make it unanimous. And so the long, painful fight with Taft ended for Eisenhower.

Eisenhower brought the news to Mamie's bedroom. Neither he nor his wife, he said later, entertained any doubt that he would go on to win in November. And this was characteristic of him. Once in a struggle, he always expected to succeed, even in the trackless wastes of politics with outriding Democrats waiting to ambush him.

Then he telephoned Taft and asked permission to visit him in his hotel across the street. There, he found the now-meaningless debris of the campaign, Taft buttons, placards, ribbons. Faces mirroring dismay and disappointment, and the sight of people weeping, made a deep impression on Eisenhower. He knew they had worked hard for Taft and he understood their disappointment. What he could not realize then was that Taft epitomized for these people the true political faith, conservatism, a form of isolationism, the necessity for eternal struggle for party control against "Eastern money" and Republican liberals. The cleavage would long remain and even widen. In 1964, a man standing in front of a campaign headquarters in Eugene, Oregon, gritted, "Eastern money cheated us out of our man in 1952, but they're not going to do it again this time, not against Barry Goldwater."

In Taft's suite, Eisenhower said simply, "This is no time for conversation on matters of any substance; you're tired and so am I. I just want to say that I want to be your friend and hope you will be mine. I hope we can work together."

They shook hands and posed for photographs together. But Taft maintained unspoken reservations. Would Eisenhower be the type of Republican President who would work for conservative principles?

In the following September, Eisenhower and Taft held their well-publicized breakfast to talk policy. Taft came out with a statement he had written. When their meeting was over, Taft read the statement to an army of waiting reporters. The whole affair was widely labeled as "the great surrender of Morningside Heights," Eisenhower's capitulation to the conservative doctrines of Taft.

Adlai Stevenson, the Democratic candidate for President, quickly began telling his audiences, "Now we have the spectacle of a candidate who won the nomination seeking out his defeated rival and begging for a kind word. It looks as if Taft lost the nomination but won the nominee." Happily plucking this string in his political harp, Stevenson went on campaigning through the Southwest, delighting the Democrats with a bon mot: "It looks as if the Republicans now have a six-star General."

Sherman Adams, who was to be one of Eisenhower's right bowers in the White House later, conceded that he and other of the General's supporters felt that Stevenson had scored "an embarrassing touche." However, Adams wrote:

"Actually, when you look back again on Taft's statement…there seems to be small ground for the charge of surrender or compromise on Eisenhower's part." Adams pointed out that their views coincided on the intention to reduce government spending, to oppose the trend toward centralized government, to fight "creeping socialism." Their disagreements came in the sphere of foreign policy. Taft tried to minimize these by saying, "I think it is fair to say that the differences are differences of degree." Adams wrote that Taft supported an "isolationist defense concept, a line of thinking that burned Eisenhower up. He could not understand the line of reasoning of people who clung to the outdated notion that the United States could go it alone in world affairs."[1]

Eisenhower began campaigning in earnest after Labor Day. He used airplanes, motorcades and trains. He travelled nearly 21,000 miles by rail alone.

To reporters, this is by far the most rewarding and informative method of campaigning. As the train slows to a stop, it is possible to make a quick estimate of the crowds awaiting the candidate. Then, while he is speaking from the back platform, the correspondents can stand *in* the crowd, seeing the candidate as his audience sees him, and sensing the impact, or lack of it, that he makes by the degree of attention and the whispered remarks. Unhappily, railroad whistle-stopping is becoming steadily more infrequent. The tendency for the candidate is to swish into a city by air, drive through crowded streets to a hotel or auditorium, hold a press conference, deliver a set speech which may not fit his natural phraseology at all, and swish out again. Sometimes, the whole appearance takes place at the airport where he landed. How did he go over? It is often difficult to estimate with any degree of accuracy and there is seldom time to follow up, sampling reactions. After a hit-and-run appearance of this kind, the differences of opinion among reporters, particularly those with pronounced political leanings, is often so great it is difficult to believe they saw the same event.

On Eisenhower's train a car was fitted up as a workroom for the reporters by removing the seats and lining both sides with shelves. When he made a back platform talk, copies of the stenographic transcript quickly were delivered to the car. In the beginning, these extemporaneous talks drove the reporters to despair. They were disjointed, rambling, largely oblivious to the rules of syntax, a tangle of phraseology and backfield-in-motion sentences. It was difficult to determine exactly what the candidate said, much less what he intended to say.

These remarks, of course, contrasted sharply with the precision

---

1   Adams: op. cit.

and elegance of Adlai Stevenson's language. Nor did Eisenhower attempt to tell jokes or invent quips in the Stevenson style. Stevenson once satirized Nixon, Knowland and Taft with a parody of the nursery rhyme, "Winken, Blinken and Nod." And the Democratic candidate could always delight audiences when he said, "If you want to live like a Republican, vote like a Democrat." Eisenhower sometimes essayed a mild irony. Ahead of a meeting in North Dakota, he read a newspaper report which stated that Truman "heavily bombarded" him. Eisenhower turned to an aide and said, "I think I'll say I've been under bombardments before and it doesn't bother me to be shot at with blanks." It drew a mild ripple of laughter when he delivered it in the speech.

He occasionally visited the press car and chatted about the campaign. For the most part, he was genial and accommodating. Once, however, his famous temper flared. A reporter asked if he intended to make a public disclosure of his financial status, adding that the press secretary, James C. Hagerty, had intimated this. The veins in Eisenhower's temples swelled and his face flushed. He rose abruptly from his chair and wheeled through the door with the parting shot, "I can't help what Hagerty told you." Through his two administrations he would take the position that some matters are private and not the business of any reporter.

The photographers on the train painted a sign—"Rewohnesie Club"—and nailed it to the door of the compartment where they kept their equipment and other necessities of travel. Eisenhower burst out laughing when he saw it and said, "By golly, I want Mamie to see this." He walked almost the whole length of the train, brought her back, and introduced her to the photographers, naming each of them.

But he made no special effort to butter up newspaper men. Unlike his predecessors and those who followed him in the White House, he appeared to have no favorites. He remained friendly but slightly aloof. If elected, he would not be one to play poker with the White House correspondents nor to find other means of obtaining a "friendly press."

On the other hand, he could be refreshingly candid in a press conference. He did not pretend to have all the answers to all the questions of 1952. It was rare and very pleasant to talk with a candidate who occasionally said, "I don't know," instead of equivocating.

As the campaign progressed, it became apparent that the throngs who crowded into auditoriums or lined the railway tracks near his train were at least as interested, and possibly more so, in seeing the man than in listening to him. From the first, he captivated the citizens with his incandescent smile, his air of boundless goodwill, his humility. He seemed to communicate, without words, the message that he was interested in the people and their problems.

The cheering began as soon as he appeared on the rear-car platform. He responded with a gesture, stretching his long arms above his head to form a V-sign. It seemed to embrace the audience. At that, the applause would swell sometimes to frenzy. When it began to die down, he stopped smiling and began to speak. A deep wrinkle usually notched itself between his eyes. He looked supremely serious. He seldom said anything that stirred wild applause in these informal appearances. It became evident, as you stood among the crowds, that people had come out to see a famous general and war hero. They liked what they saw. If they came mainly out of curiosity, the majority left under the spell of a warm personality. The Chinese long ago coined one of the most accurate of all terms to describe this type of magnetism. They call it "human-heartedness." And this is what the people saw in Eisenhower.

Having finished a brief talk, Eisenhower would begin to smile again as though a happy thought had occurred to him. Gesturing for quiet, he would say, "And now I want you to meet my Mamie." With that Mamie would appear, pretty, dainty, smiling, supremely feminine. She completed the picture—an honest, sincere man with a happy family life.

Stevenson, of course, had no such political asset to help him.

Eisenhower naturally enjoyed the adulation that welled up around him wherever he went. But he wanted to be something more than merely a popular figure. Sherman Adams relates that in August, before the campaigning truly began, Eisenhower attended a strategy session in Denver. The tone of the meeting annoyed him. When Adams asked him why, Eisenhower replied, "All they talked about was my popularity. Nobody said I had a brain in my head."

And so he tried to develop issues and explain his philosophy. In Abilene, when he started his campaign, he spoke out against centralization in government and against dishonesty and corruption at all its levels. He said he saw in excessive taxation the danger of destroying initiative and he noted "the unreasonable antagonisms among different economic groups" of Americans. He called for more intelligent cooperation between capital, management and labor. In foreign affairs, he criticized the secret clauses in the Yalta agreement, deplored the loss of China and said a policy of isolation was "futile." In sum, he said, "Today, America must be spiritually, economically and militarily strong. She must guard her solvency as she does her physical frontiers. This means the elimination of waste, luxury, and every needless expenditure from the national budget."

As the campaign developed, he emerged more and more as a middle-of-the-roader. He said the Tennessee Valley Authority had done a good job but that he himself was neither a public nor a private-power man.

At about this time, Eisenhower wrote his friend, Capt. Hazlett, a letter that ripples with amusement over the conflicting things being said about him. He was a Fascist warmonger and at the same time a secret friend of Joseph Stalin, a New Dealer and a reactionary, a timid man afraid to win the presidency and a Machiavelli scheming to get the job. The letter does not mention another segment of the whispering campaign. On the day after he won the nomination in Chicago, a man of markedly liberal philosophy said to me, "I'm told he doesn't do his homework." I asked the source of this. He shrugged, "Nobody in particular. It's just what they say." The they-sayers were to be very active regarding Eisenhower for the next eight years. He closed the letter to Hazlett with the sentence, "Anyone who chooses the middle-of-the-road is going constantly to be subject to attack from both extremes." Prophetic words in his case!

In Detroit on Oct. 24, Eisenhower struck a rich vein of political gold. He had previously stressed the necessity for finding means to end the fighting in Korea. In Detroit he said, "That job requires a personal trip to Korea. I shall make that trip. I shall go to Korea."

In a presidential campaign it seldom is possible to pinpoint the issue or the exact statement that tips the balance toward the eventual victor. But the pledge on Korea slammed into the consciousness of the nation with tremendous impact. When I saw it in a copy of the speech, about an hour before Eisenhower delivered it, I did not wait to write the customary resume; I jumped for a telephone and began dictating as rapidly as possible. When I finished, the desk editor asked, "Do you think it's all that important?" "I think it probably has elected Ike," I said. "We'll know more when we see the editorial reaction tomorrow." Editorials left no doubt about the importance of the statement on Korea.

For the nation was deeply divided about the war there. On the Washington level, Harry Truman was under fire for having sent American forces to war without prior authority from Congress. On the street level, Americans asked each other exactly what their boys were fighting for. To contain Communism. Okay, they were all for that, but what difference did it make if we contained it in Korea? The war was wholly alien to American experience. And as the casualties mounted in number so did the general disenchantment with the United Nations.

The high emotionalism shot up to a higher plateau when, in April, 1951, Truman summarily fired MacArthur, stripping him of all his commands in Korea and Japan. MacArthur had his enemies in Washington but he was immensely popular with millions of Americans. In his penetrating study of the Senate, William S. White wrote of the MacArthur case "...there suddenly opened perhaps the gravest and most emotional constitutional crisis that the United States had known since the Great Depression." After MacArthur made his historic, old-soldiers-never-die speech before a joint session of Congress, White quoted a senator as saying, "This is new to my experience; I have never feared more for the institutions of the country. I honestly felt back there that if the General's speech had gone on much longer there might have been a march on the White House."[1]

(What was Eisenhower's reaction? There is only the photograph of the expression on his face when he heard the news. It can be said, however, that had he been confronted with the problem, he would have arranged matters so as to permit MacArthur to resign quietly. This, of course, would not have dramatized the principle of the supremacy of civil authority over the military—in which Eisenhower devoutly believes—so vividly as Truman's action. But that principle is deeply embedded in American thinking. It is an article of faith and MacArthur's many admirers never conceded that he challenged it by his actions in Korea. They therefore questioned whether the principle needed to be dramatized anew, especially at the cost of creating more divisiveness in America at a critical time, and humiliating a

---

1   White: "Citadel: The Story of the U.S. Senate."

soldier who served his country so long and so brilliantly. In any case, Eisenhower would have sought the quiet solution. That was his way.)

. . .

Of all the fascinating episodes in Eisenhower's first campaign, three are notable for the light they cast on him—his insistence on seeking votes in the South, his refusal to panic under terrific pressure over the news of the "Nixon Fund" and his much-misrepresented confrontation with Joseph McCarthy in Wisconsin which is related here in the words of eyewitnesses.

Eisenhower came into the fray fully aware that he knew next to nothing about political campaigning. He listened to the professionals in his entourage, just as, during the war, he had listened to staff officers who were experts in technical fields. But he made the big decisions himself.

During the planning of his itinerary, he raised the question of campaigning in the South. His managers told him it would be an utter waste of time. They doubted that he could jar loose more than a handful of votes there, much less carry any state. He obstinately refused to abandon the idea that he should make some forays into Dixie. They cited the statistics on past voting patterns in the South and reminded him that it had been years since a presidential candidate of either major party had campaigned there. Eisenhower replied (a) that in his perhaps naive view the President was the Chief Executive of all Americans and not of those alone in the states that voted for him, and (b) that, if he were elected, he should have familiarized himself with the problems and currents of opinion in the South. Besides, he had a personal reason, unrelated to the campaign; he liked most Southerners. Finally after tedious hours of argument, Eisenhower slammed the door on the argument. He said he would go South if he had to go alone. He was never more bullheaded.

And so, in early September, he flew to Atlanta, Jacksonville, Miami, Tampa, Birmingham and Little Rock. Later, he made other tours below the Mason-Dixon Line. The response was fantastic. Tremendous crowds greeted him and roared with what certainly appeared to be hearty approval of his speeches. Who could say what it portended? His managers remained dubious. On Election Night, the returns showed Eisenhower carrying Texas, Virginia, Tennessee,

Florida and Oklahoma. To him, this was the sweetest cherry on the cake.

The disclosure of the "Nixon Fund" came as a shattering blow. At first blush, it appeared to be an unmitigated disaster. Eisenhower had been hammering away relentlessly, with documentation, on the issue of corruption in government. Now it appeared that he had a screeching political scandal involving his own running mate, Richard M. Nixon. A blizzard of telegrams and letters engulfed Eisenhower's headquarters and he was subjected to a drumfire of long-distance telephone calls. These messages ran about three-to-one in urging him to drop Nixon from the ticket. The Democrats were delighted and many of Eisenhower's supporters thought this might cost him the election. It was an authentic crisis.

Eisenhower stood firmly against the clamor to rid himself of Nixon, the sooner the better. He said he would wait for the facts. Lawyers and accountants soon brought them to view. Over a period of two years, 76 persons in Nixon's home state, California, had contributed $18,235. Nixon had no access to the money himself; disbursements were made by a Pasadena lawyer, Dana Smith. None of the contributions had resulted in obtaining political favors from Nixon. Nixon then quickly issued a statement about the fund, one section of which said, "It enabled me to keep my speaking and mailing schedule without recourse to padding my federal office payroll, free government transportation, misuse of the senatorial franking privileges, or any subterfuge."

This was all very well. But again, political reality raised its scaly head. Denials seldom fully overtake the original accusation. Despite the accountants' report, suspicion remained. The clamor for Nixon's head increased rather than subsided. He had been a controversial figure long before this. Was he now a political albatross around Eisenhower's neck? Nixon later wrote:

"I could see his (Eisenhower's) dilemma. He had been a winner all his life and his task as a candidate was to win again in a new arena where, as inexperienced as he was, he had to judge the voters' mood to decide whether or not I should be asked to stay on the ticket or resign. He had to win the election before he could lead the country. And his friends and associates, whom he trusts, were telling him that he might lose unless he got rid of me."[1]

Eisenhower's innate "human-heartedness" came into play. He said later, "Quite apart from the fate of the ticket and the reaction to my conduct was the consideration that a young man's personal reputation and future were at stake."[2]

So after the accountants' report, he telephoned Nixon. Nixon offered to leave the ticket but Eisenhower emphatically said "No" to that. They agreed that Nixon should take his case to the people via television and await the public's reaction before coming to any decision. Win, lose or draw in November, Eisenhower determined to give Nixon his day in court.

Countless Americans saw Nixon's televised performance. Many ridiculed it as a juicy bouillabaisse of corn, ham, soap opera and bathos. A great many more, however, saw a man courageously fighting an unjust accusation. It convinced Eisenhower and the flood of approving messages that followed vindicated his judgment. In the end, the whole cacophonous incident probably contributed to Eisenhower's victory.

But as a controversial figure, Nixon was weak wine compared with a burly, black-haired, blue-jowled senator from Wisconsin, Joseph R. McCarthy.

Since February, 1950, McCarthy had been riding a political scooter—Communists-in-Government—for all it was worth, gaining power and publicity which were more important to him than the blood in his arteries. He frightened many Americans, infuriated many, and, be it said, won the enthusiastic applause of many.

Eisenhower also was attacking the Democrats on the issue of unreliable persons in government. But he detested McCarthy's methods and, in a sense, clashed with the senator before they ever met. On Feb. 14, 1951, McCarthy made a vicious attack on Gen. Marshall, whom Eisenhower revered and to whom he owed so much. His speech, some 60,000 words in length, later was issued as a book entitled, "America's Retreat from Victory: The Story of George Catlett Marshall."

At a press conference in Denver, without naming McCarthy, Eisenhower tore into the attacks on Marshall. Part of his long state-

---
1 Nixon: "Six Crises."
2 Eisenhower: op. cit.

ment said "...if he was not a perfect example of patriotism and a loyal servant of the United States, I never saw one. If I could say more, I would say it, but I have no patience with anyone who can find in his record of service to this country anything to criticize." Three times, while he was on this subject, reporters interrupted him with questions about other matters. And three times, Eisenhower brushed the questions aside and went on talking about Marshall's great services to the United States. He did not permit the press conference to move on to other topics until he had dealt thoroughly with idiotic charges against Marshall.

Rivers of words are spoken and written in a presidential campaign and some of them, however important, do not receive the attention they deserve. It appears that Eisenhower's Denver statement was one of these. For, years afterward, the impression remained in the minds of many Americans that Eisenhower had let McCarthy's charges go unchallenged.

Because of his dislike for McCarthy, Eisenhower had not planned to campaign in Wisconsin. When he found that his staff had committed him to appearances there, he blew up so violently that he might have had a stroke or heart attack then. However, there were political realities to consider. (Eisenhower was never to really understand them, much less to reconcile himself to them.) In the early days of the campaign, before Eisenhower's vast popularity became wholly manifest, nobody could say what would happen in November. The high priests of public opinion polls, who had been burned so badly in 1948, were playing more cautiously now.

Walter J. Kohler, a man of high integrity and political acumen, was then governor of Wisconsin. In an analysis for Eisenhower's staff, Kohler reminded them that the state is political quick silver. It has been called "the graveyard of candidates." Because of these unpredictable voters, Kohler said Eisenhower must come into the state; the Republicans should take no unnecessary risks. As for McCarthy's attacks on Marshall, the governor counseled Eisenhower to stand on his Denver remarks, and to avoid providing McCarthy with a new headline every day by giving the reporters a new statement of defense of Marshall. "I think he has said as much as needs to be said on this question..." Kohler wrote.

So, against his better judgment, Eisenhower consented to go into Wisconsin. On that leg of his itinerary, there came the widely bruited report that, at McCarthy's insistence, Eisenhower deleted from one of his speeches a paragraph again praising Marshall's patriotism. It proved erroneous, but it hurt him badly at the time, sickening some of his warmest friends.

He met McCarthy in the Pere Marquette Hotel in Peoria, Illinois, the night before he entered Wisconsin. What followed has been related by Kevin McCann, who was present. McCann wrote:

"Immediately when they were seated, McCarthy began in a high-pitched voice a recital of his position that infiltration by Communists within the government was the critical issue of the campaign and an immediate peril to the security of the republic.

"Hardly had he gotten into his statement when Dwight Eisenhower abruptly broke in that he had come, not to hear a lecture, but to make his own position crystal clear. Then, coldly, savagely, he stripped from the senator all his pretensions of dedication to American security; of incomparable knowledge about the conduct of government; of accurate and massive and unique knowledge about a Communist conspiracy; of any sincerity of purpose or of effectiveness in performance."

When Eisenhower finished, McCann said, he snapped a curt "good night" and left the room. McCann related the episode in a review of a book about Eisenhower's years as President.

On the following day, McCarthy's expression was black and scowling when he appeared with Eisenhower on the rear car of the train. Kohler noted that "…McCarthy kept shaking his head in disagreement and disapproval while the General was talking." Eisenhower appeared to be ignoring him at each whistlestop.

In a confidential letter, Kohler himself took responsibility for the actions that led up to deletion of the paragraph about Marshall in the speech Eisenhower was to deliver in Milwaukee that night. He wrote:

"In the text there was one paragraph which made direct reference to McCarthy's attack on Gen. Marshall and it was that paragraph I believed would cause unnecessary and perhaps very serious problems…a paragraph which would gratuitously alienate many ardent McCarthy supporters could well lose the state…"

To Sherman Adams, Kohler expressed the opinion that the reference to Marshall was extraneous and should come out. Adams agreed. They went together to speak with Eisenhower about it. Kohler's letter said:

"What happened then was remarkable. Adams had barely begun in broad general terms to outline the political background in Wisconsin when the General quickly interrupted and said, 'Are you suggesting that the reference to George Marshall be dropped from the speech tonight?'

"Sherman answered 'Yes' and the General promptly replied, 'Well, drop it. I handled that subject pretty thoroughly in Denver two weeks ago and there's no real reason to repeat it tonight.'

"That's all that was said…There was no lengthy discussion, no argument, no wavering, no pressure. Nor was there any abandonment of either friends or principle…the General went to the heart of the question and quickly for his own reason made his own decision."

At the huge rally in Milwaukee that night, McCarthy's expression was even stormier than it had been through the day. When he rose to speak, he shot a sneering glance at Eisenhower and said he didn't give a tinker's dam about criticism of his methods, adding, with another snarling look at Eisenhower, "I'm going to go on calling 'em as I see 'em." Wild cheering rose from the crowd, showing the correctness of Kohler's estimate.

Next day, front pages blazoned the report that McCarthy had bludgeoned Eisenhower into propping the paragraph about Marshall. McCarthy himself denied it. But, as has been said, denials seldom fully squelch the original accusation, especially in a presidential campaign where events swiftly crowd in on each other. The story remained a seven-days' sensation. It filled liberal-minded persons, regardless of party, with despair and disgust. The Democrats, of course, expressed pious horror. Not only had Eisenhower tacitly endorsed McCarthy, they said, but he shrank from defending Marshall. The incident splotched an ugly smear on the knight's shining armor. "No man," said Thomas Jefferson, "will ever bring out of the presidency the reputation which carries him into it."

The campaign ended in Boston.

Henry Griffin, an Associated Press photographer, had a bright idea for dramatizing the finale. He asked Eisenhower to pose for a picture, sitting beneath a clock with the hands marking one minute to midnight. Eisenhower agreed. Griffin found a heavy clock and mounted it, with masking tape, to a coatrack, Eisenhower, Nixon and their wives took places beneath it. Before Griffin could snap his camera, the clock fell bop! on Eisenhower's bald head. Blood flowed from the lacerated scalp.

Griffin was so embarrassed and upset that tears came to his eyes. As aides rushed around looking for medication and bandages, Eisenhower put his arm around the photographer and said, "Pull yourself together, Hank. It's a good idea for a picture. Set it up again and we'll do it." And he did.

This, although Eisenhower could not know it then, brought him the first of many presidential headaches.

• • •

He stood, unsmiling, amid the din, the moiling crowd, the uproar and excitement in the ballroom of the Commodore Hotel in New York. Klieg lights focused on him, forming a hot bright circle. People climbed on chairs and tables, cheering. Eisenhower raised his arms in the V-sign and the cheering became a tornado of sound. Photographers' flashbulbs flared in his eyes. The pictures would show his swiftly changing moods, one brief smile, the frown above the bridge of his nose, a man already feeling the enormity of the years ahead. But mostly they would mirror his modesty and humbleness, humbleness when he read Adlai Stevenson's telegram conceding the election and his own reply, humbleness when he thanked all those who had worked to achieve this moment. They were going wild with elation. But the expressions flitting across his face were sober and thoughtful. Then they changed again and he looked like a little boy. There was a victory cake waiting upstairs in the hotel, he said, and he grinned when he added, "I've never cut a presidential cake before." He waved goodnight. It was 1:45 in the morning of Nov. 5, 1952.

Before the election returns were complete, they showed a landslide. Eisenhower had won 55 per cent of the popular vote and 442 of the 531 electoral votes.

Among the masses of telegrams and messages that came to him next day he found one especially meaningful. It said, "I send you my sincere and heartfelt congratulations, I look forward to a renewal of our comradeship and of our work together for the same causes of peace and freedom as in the past. Winston." Eisenhower's answering message was signed "Ike." And so it would be between them so long as Churchill lived, through the strains on Anglo-American relations that lay ahead.

There was no real pause for Eisenhower after Nov. 4.

He went to Augusta, Georgia, to rest and play golf. But within a day or two, at Truman's suggestion, Eisenhower addressed himself to the question of "the orderly transition of government." He named his representatives and held long conferences with them as they prepared to go to Washington. He carried on heavy correspondence. He occupied a little white cottage on the edge of the golf course and sometimes it seemed possible to hear the dynamo running inside it.

Two weeks later, Eisenhower went to the White House to hear briefings from members of Truman's Cabinet and to tie up the last threads of the "orderly transition." The meeting was cool, because of the bitterness of the election campaigns, and businesslike. The two men were alone together for about 20 minutes, after which they joined the Cabinet members and Eisenhower's liaison men, Senator Lodge and Joseph M. Dodge, who was to be Director of the Budget.

Long before, Eisenhower's associates had noted that in a discussion of any subject, unless he possessed a good deal of first-hand knowledge of it, or held strong opinions on alternatives, he remained silent, listening. He might ask a question or two, but he was not one to think out loud. He was a listener. Thus, when Dean Acheson, then Secretary of State, reviewed American problems around the world, Eisenhower listened intently but said very little. In his immensely informative book about Eisenhower's first administration, Robert Donovan reported that, during Acheson's review, Eisenhower jotted on a slip of paper, "Call Eden tonight."[1]

After the White House conference, Eisenhower returned to New York to begin forming his Cabinet, discuss legislative policy and, prepare the Inaugural Address.

He was an early riser. An aide, arriving at his desk shortly after 9 one morning was told, "You'd better call the Boss right away. He's been asking for you for 20 minutes."

Adjoining Eisenhower's office were a living room and dining room. Beside his desk stood a small period table, holding a stack of papers and his briefcase.

He ordered his assistants to boil all reports to the barest essen-

---

1   Donovan: "Eisenhower: The Inside Story."

tials. One day a 34-page report on a political situation in the Far West was laid before him. Eisenhower growled, "The whole plan for the Normandy invasion was written in eight pages."

He laid down another rule: In making recommendations for filling offices in his administration, friendship for him, however close, was not to be considered a qualification. What he wanted in a prospective appointee, he said, was ability and character.

There was confusion occasionally during these days and from time to time Eisenhower's temper got away from him.

However, his press secretary, James Hagerty, Said, "But still, when he comes back down from the ceiling, he'll listen if you still think you are right."

Eisenhower kept on his desk a toy which came to be known as "the Eisenpopper." Pushed down, a suction cup held the figure for about five minutes. Then as the suction weakened, it suddenly popped into the air. One of Eisenhower's startled victims of this prank was his wartime deputy, Air Chief Marshal Tedder.

He also had some fun when, through a clerical error, he and Mamie received a formal invitation to his Inauguration. "What should I do with this?" she asked. "Decline it," Eisenhower said, poker-faced. "Say we've got another engagement."

When he left the hotel at night, he invariably paused at doorways as he came down the corridor. He would put his head inside an office and chat for a few minutes with a staff man or a lone secretary. He also attended the equivalent of an office party on Christmas Eve. There, he relaxed completely. He made a point of going to speak with a woman secretary who was standing shyly in a corner. Then he sat down, surrounded by the staff, some of whom sat on the floor, and reminisced about his boyhood in Abilene and about the war. This between bites of the wedge of apple pie that he usually ordered for lunch but had temporarily foregone that day. On another occasion, having no luncheon appointment, he asked a group of second and third-echelon assistants to join him. A starry-eyed secretary said afterward, "I think if he ordered me to jump out the window, I'd jump."

On Nov. 29, in keeping with his campaign promise, Eisenhower secretly flew to Korea. But his purpose went beyond the campaign promise and embraced more than a mere inspection of the troops. He proposed to fit the findings into an over-all strategic concept for the United States. The weather was freezing. Eisenhower happily bundled into his old battle jacket. He flew and motored around the lines, visiting units, listening to briefings by their commanders, peering through binoculars at the Chinese and North Korean lines from forward positions. He learned volumes and the trip led up to his thinly veiled threat, communicated later to the Communists, to use atomic weapons if necessary. This brought them to the conference table.

He also was able to spend some time with his son who was in the lines in Korea. What would happen if the son of the President-elect of the United States were to be captured in battle? They had discussed this during the election campaign. John Eisenhower had said, quietly, "I'll never let myself be captured."

Finally, Eisenhower sought out the 15th Infantry in which he had served as a lieutenant colonel at Fort Lewis years before. He stood in the chow line with the GIs and then sat on an ammunition box with them and ate pork chops and sauerkraut, a far cry from the K and C-rations of the Second World War.

His last action was to go before more than 100 war correspondents in a press conference. "We have no trick ways of settling any problems, no panaceas," he said. "We came over to learn. Much can be done, in my opinion, to improve our position. Much will be done." The cease-fire and Panmunjom would not be long in coming.

Truman called the Korean trip a piece of demagoguery.

Back in New York, after more military conferences in Hawaii, he polished his Inauguration speech, decreed Homburgs instead of the traditional high silk hats in the official "uniform" and sought means to keep the postinaugural parade as short as possible. He had had a surfeit of parades, the salutes of marching men, the cheers of the crowds, a surfeit of glory. But what Eisenhower said was that he himself had marched in these parades and knew what it meant to the men to wait for hours in the winter cold until they were ordered to march.

A day or two before his Inauguration, the brakes failed on a passenger train coming into Pennsylvania Station in Washington. The locomotive broke through the barriers at the end of the track, ploughed across the platform and into the waiting room. Which prompted the comedian, Red Skelton, to observe, "The Republicans were in such a rush to get back after 20 years that they couldn't stop."

The Republicans, yes. But Eisenhower entered the White House in no spirit of exultation. In fact, he secretly told himself that he would serve for only one term and then retire.

An enthusiastic crowd greets Gen. Eisenhower during the first stop of his one-day tour across Iowa, Sept. 18, 1952. (AP Photo/Bill Allen)

President Dwight D. Eisenhower delivers his inaugural address after he was sworn in as the country's 34th president in Washington, DC, January 20, 1953. (AP Photo/WF)

President Eisenhower and first lady, Mamie, wave to spectators from an open car as they leave the Capitol at the start of the inauguration parade, January 20, 1953. (AP Photo)

Left to right: Russian Premier Nikolai Bulganin; U. S. President Eisenhower; French Premier Edgar Faure and British Prime Minister Sir Anthony Eden during the Big Four Conference at the Palace of Nations in Geneva, Switzerland, July 19, 1955. (AP Photo)

Escorted by troops of the 101st Airborne Division, nine African-American students enter Central High School, Little Rock, AR, September 25, 1957. (AP Photo)

President Eisenhower poses with civil rights leaders. (L to R): Lester B. Granger; Dr. Martin Luther King, Jr.; E. Frederic Morrow, White House administrative officer; A. Philip Randolph; Attorney General William Rogers; and Roy Wilkins, June 23, 1958. (AP Photo)

RIGHT: President Eisenhower delivers his State of the Union speech before a joint session of Congress in Washington, DC, January 7, 1960. (AP Photo)

BELOW: President John F. Kennedy and former President Eisenhower at Camp David where the two met to discuss the Cuban situation, April 22, 1961. (AP Photo)

Former President Eisenhower sets the ball on the first tee to start a golf exhibition for the benefit of the Heart Association of Southeastern Pennsylvania in Philadelphia. The foresome who teed off in the match from left, Jack Nicklaus; Arnold Palmer; Ray Bolger and Andy Williams, May 26, 1965. (AP Photo/Warren M. Winterbottom)

President Lyndon B. Johnson chats with former President Eisenhower at Walter Reed Army Hospital in Washington, DC, where Ike was recuperating from a heart attack, June 11, 1968. (AP Photo)

Hail to the Chief

At the close of his first day in the White House, Eisenhower wrote himself a note, "…today just seems like a continuation of all I've been doing since July, '41—even before that."

He knew something of the size and complexity of the presidency and it was not in his nature to be overconfident. However, for more than a decide he had been organizing vast and complex operations, directing their movements, carrying heavy responsibilities. His decisions as Supreme Commander and then as chief of NATO affected the fate of millions of soldiers and civilians and the immediate future of great states. Thus, the possession and uses of great power were not new to him. He had grown accustomed to it long since. Several Presidents have written about the enormous power of the office. "There are men, and not a few," said Martin Van Buren, "who derive so much pleasure from the mere possession of such great power that any degree of dissatisfaction caused by its exercise is not too dear a price…" Eisenhower was not one of these. He would never revel in the knowledge that when he pressed a button, a man on the other side of the world would spring into immediate action. A sense of duty, not the expectation of such rewards had impelled him to run for the presidency and he would have subscribed fully to Woodrow Wilson's observation that "…a man who seeks the presidency of the United States for anything that it will bring to him is an audacious fool." Eisenhower's rewards, if any, would be derived in the changes he hoped to accomplish.

Six months later, he said in a letter to a friend, "So all I am trying to say is that the change is gradual. It is not so rapid as to be completely satisfying even to a person who, I think, is as patient as I am; certainly, I try to be patient."

The "change" he envisioned was broad-gauged, so ambitious that sectors of it would never be achieved. In the world, he sought to create a more favorable climate for disarmament and an assured peace. He bent himself to the task of ending the Korean War. He worked for more freedom of trade between nations, including some Communist countries. In July, 1953, he threw the Communists off-balance by offering East Germany $15 million of food to meet a shortage that had developed there. The offer, of course, was angrily rejected. The President sent the food to West Germany where, since the Berlin Wall had not yet been raised, East Germans came across and bought it. More than once, in his peace-making efforts, he would seize the initiative from the Communists.

At home, he hoped to effect what he would later describe as "dynamic conservatism," based on private enterprise, personal incentive, with fewer government controls (but not to the extent of complete laisser faire), balanced budgets, and rejection of the theory of some economists that "a little inflation" is good for the nation's economic health.

He also hoped to recast the Republican Party, to strengthen it by shaping it in such a way as to attract independent voters and those who could not subscribe to the philosophies of the ultraconservative Old Guard.

All this in four years. Then, he thought, he could retire after one term to a quiet life on his Gettysburg farm, fulfilling the now somewhat dog-eared dream of 1945. He soon began thinking about the men who might be qualified to succeed him and his mind ranged over a number whom he watched and tried to push into prominence. After his heart attack in 1955, he felt that the matter had reached a stage of paramount importance. He wrote a friend that the question, "still unresolved, swirls daily around my mind and keeps me awake at night."

He subscribed to Lincoln's definition of the function of government—"The legitimate object of government is to do for a community of people whatever they need to have done, but cannot do at all, or cannot so well do for themselves—in their separate and individual capacities. In all that people individually can do for themselves, government ought not to interfere."

Eisenhower did not reverse the New Deal policies of his predecessors, but he tried to combat the welfare-state psychology. His thinking appears in a message he sent to Capitol Hill with a vetoed bill. He wrote, "This kind of legislation—this expectation of something-for-nothing—weakens our national fabric and with each occurrence leaves it more seriously impaired. The spread of this expectation and its reflection in an increase of such legislation are profoundly disturbing for the future of America."

As he worked toward the desired change, an image of the President began to take shape. Viewed from without, he sometimes seemed indecisive, hesitant, detached, content to reign rather than rule. At other times, however, he proved to be courageous, unyielding to public or Congressional pressures, steely on issues involving his convictions. When he could not persuade, he used the veto, "Although constrained to disapprove the bill, I urge the Congress, etc…" And the time would come when he would go over Congress' head, taking his case to the people or sending hundreds of letters to influential Americans to enlist their support for his programs.

Unlike other Presidents, Eisenhower was loath to handle patronage matters himself. Patronage is an instrument of enormous usefulness to a President. By dispensing thousands of juicy federal jobs, he can lubricate the legislative machinery for his programs and strengthen his own position at all levels in his party. Instead of keeping this power in his hands, Eisenhower turned it over to others, notably his "Chief of Staff," Sherman Adams. In some instances, the appointments were made without consulting senators and congressmen in the regions concerned. Which, of course, did not tend to make them strong supporters of Eisenhower and Adams. Even Time Magazine, which had supported Eisenhower during the campaign, observed, "Ike seems to find something distasteful in precinct-level party politics. On the one hand, he has bestowed few favors on Eisenhower loyalists, and has avoided giving them active leadership in the Congressional fight against the Old Guard. On the other, he has refused even to show presidential displeasure with those who make political gains by attacking his (programs)…"

And so critics and political opponents began calling him "another Buchanan." In the strong-President, weak-President theorem, a "strong" President is one who dominates Congress and the legislative process, whereas the "weak" President believes he should merely propose and let Congress dispose. "The President is at liberty, both in law and conscience, to be as big a man as he can," said Andrew Jackson. "His capacity will set the limit." And James A. Garfield wrote, "It better be known at the outset whether the President is the head of the government or the registering clerk of the Senate." Eisenhower at first refrained from using strong-arm tactics to impose his will on Congress. By the classic yardstick, then, he was a "weak" President during his first administration. He tried persuasion, not bull-dozing. Yet, his record glitters with achievements, the St. Lawrence Seaway, the first Civil Rights Bill since Reconstruction days, notable changes in the labor laws, the defeat of the Bricker Amendment, creation of the Department of Health, Education and Welfare, the huge highway building program, etc. By that yardstick, he could be placed with the "strong" Presidents. His methods differed from theirs, but much less so in his second administration. In any case, it is the scoreboard of achievement that counts.

His concept of leadership, he said again and again, meant quiet reasoning with men who opposed him on an issue, the effort to persuade. Leadership to him did not mean pounding the table, knocking heads together, conducting a "Pride's Purge," threatening, or putting an opponent in a position from which he could not retreat without loss of face. Eisenhower's gifted speech writer, Emmet J. Hughes, quoted him as saying of his troubles with the Republican Old Guard, "So I'll listen. And I'll answer. And I'll try to get them to understand, to *give*. I'll try to get them to give not everything but—a little here, a little there. And I'll hope something I say *does* get through—and stays with them. I don't know any other way to lead."[1]

The approach was not always successful, but there is no means of casting up a balance sheet of pluses and minuses for Eisenhower's efforts. The noisy failures became known; the quiet compromises did not, except to those in a position to observe them in the making. Relatively speaking, what becomes public knowledge of actions in the inner chambers of Government is only the tip of the iceberg. Only the outsider, unhampered by knowledge of all the facts, can indulge in the luxury of criticism. In any event, to try to persuade was Eisenhower's way.

It worked notably in the case of Taft. On April 30, he attended a Cabinet conference on budget estimates and spending. When he heard the figures, Taft exploded, pounding the table in a scene rarely enacted before a President. He said the figures constituted a repudiation of GOP campaign pledges and, unkindest cut of all, that

---

1   Hughes: "Ordeal of Power"

they meant Eisenhower was walking in Truman's footsteps. When he finished, silence filled the room. Eisenhower, with the help of some deliberate small talk among others present, kept his temper. Then, patiently and quietly, he reviewed for Taft the danger points in the world, the intricacies of building an adequate defense system and defense spending, the care with which the budget had been prepared. Taft remained unconvinced, but at least he was mollified to the extent that he did not throw his great power into an open attack on the budget. More than that, although Eisenhower and Taft could not see eye-to-eye on all policy, they became warm friends. Shortly before his death, the senator told Eisenhower, "I have just one ambition—to come back and help you make this administration completely successful." The extent of Eisenhower's admiration for Taft was reflected in a remark he made later to Roy Roberts. He said he felt that Taft had become less isolationist and had changed his views on foreign policy. He summed up by saying, "If I had known Bob Taft as I do now, I doubt that I would have run for the presidency."

In filling the posts in his Cabinet, Eisenhower said he made his selections on the basis of "experience, ability, character, and standing in their own communities." Martin Durkin, who served briefly as Secretary of Labor, said the Cabinet was composed of "eight millionaires and a plumber." But in a personal letter, Eisenhower wrote that he considered the team he had organized was the "ablest" of any he could remember in all his years around Washington.

The President told the Cabinet he wanted businesslike methods in government. This coincided wholly with the idea of his Secretary of the Treasury, George Humphrey, a charming and strong-minded man. Whether the financial problems of the federal government can be administered in the same way as the financial problems of a great corporation is open to debate. Humphrey was to be criticized as being too concerned with inflation and too concerned with achieving a balanced budget regardless of the condition of the economy as a whole.

But while he wanted businesslike methods, Eisenhower also said he wanted to show the nation that his administration was concerned for the interests of "the little guy." Before he could even get started, there came the distortion, perhaps wilfully, of Charles E. Wilson's testimony when he appeared before a Senate committee prior to his confirmation as Secretary of Defense. He testified that he held $2.5 million dollars in General Motors stock and he was not anxious to sell it to comply with the conflict-of-interest statutes. There was this exchange:

Senator Hendrickson: "...I am interested to know whether, if a situation did arise where you had to make a decision which was extremely adverse to the interests of your stock and General Motors Corporation, or any of these other companies, or extremely adverse to the company, in the interests of the United States Government, could you make that decision?"

Wilson—"Yes, sir, I could. I cannot conceive of one because for years I thought what was good for our country was good for General Motors, and vice versa..."

This was twisted to have Wilson saying, "What's good for General Motors is good for the country." The erroneous impression may persist to this day. At the time, it embarrassed the administration.

Eisenhower consulted extensively, perhaps more than any other President, with his Cabinet, the National Security Council and legislative leaders. As has been said, he was a good listener and a fast learner. When the discussion touched on topics with which he was familiar, NATO, defense, Churchill, DeGaulle, he would speak up. But when it came to the Taft-Hartley Act, the intricacies of the budgets or pork-barrel legislation, he listened.

Some years after he left office, Richard M. Nixon contributed a lengthy oral statement to Princeton University's "John Foster Dulles Oral History Project." The interview has never been published. In it, Nixon drew a picture of Eisenhower's methods of operating in meetings of the Cabinet and National Security Council. Nixon said:

"Eisenhower in conferences followed the usual military habit of going around the table and getting the views of everybody. But when you come right down to the decision-making process, the man in the Oval Room has to make the decision. Eisenhower not only made it—he wasn't just the Chairman of the Board, presiding—but he contributed to it.

"...but Eisenhower's thinking would be stimulated by what the rest of us would say and what Dulles would say. Eisenhower is quite creative in a conference. He feels very free, particularly when it's off the record, very free to throw up almost outlandish ideas just to see what will happen. Jerry Persons used to say he would hit those fungoes[1] out there just to see what would happen.

"Eisenhower would often throw up ideas like that, not with the idea that it was final, but just to see what the reaction would be. And if I had made a diary, which I didn't, there are any number of instances, both on domestic and foreign problems, where Eisenhower originally had the idea; and then there are many, many more instances where he threw out ideas which were rejected. And it didn't bother him.

"I don't go along with the impression that has been created that Eisenhower was weak and didn't really contribute constructively himself to these great decisions. He had such a wide background militarily, and he knew so much about the leaders of the world, personally, and their reactions, that his contribution was invaluable."

Having been long accustomed to holding positions of great authority himself, Eisenhower was not afraid to delegate authority. He often said, "Centralization is the refuge of fear." He recalled George C. Marshall's words, "I want to see the solutions, not the problems."

Naturally, then, Eisenhower brought the Chief of Staff system to the White House. The man who held the post was Sherman Adams, the lean, laconic, hard-bitten former governor of New Hampshire. Adams was a buffer, a watchdog, and a filter for the President. Papers, problems and callers might or might not come to Eisenhower, depending on Adams' judgment. He was efficient, a prodigious worker, quick to get to the core of a situation. He was not popular with the ultraconservative Republicans, particularly those in whose states he dispensed patronage without consulting them. Eisenhower said of him, "The one person who really knows what I am trying to do is Sherman Adams." Correspondents questioned Eisenhower about the extent of Adams' powers and the President replied, "No subordinate of mine, including Adams, can possibly make a decision without getting my general approval or a decision which is inconsonant with the general policies laid down by me."

In his day, James K. Polk could say, "I prefer to supervise the whole operations of the government myself rather than entrust the public business to subordinates, and this makes my duties very great." But even in the 1920s, when the federal government was small compared with its elephantine dimensions today, Calvin Coolidge said

---

[1] A baseball term, meaning high fly balls during fielding practice.

of the President, "In the discharge of the duties of his office there is one rule of action more important than all others: It consists in never doing anything that someone else can do for you."

Eisenhower said he enjoyed the presidential press conference, but he did not always handle himself well in fielding the questions. His press secretary, James C. Hagerty, brought to that office a wealth of experience, having served Governor Thomas E. Dewey of New York in that capacity for many years. Hagerty was tough-minded, deceptively relaxed, humorous, overburdened but always accessible in his office. His task was to release information about Eisenhower and, in the process, to make the President appear in the most favorable light. On occasion, that meant disagreeing with Eisenhower and standing up for what he believed. Hagerty had no hesitation in doing so. Sometimes this angered the President but he admired Hagerty nonetheless.

Before a press conference, Hagerty and other members of the White House staff met to anticipate the questions that might come up and to recommend the answers Eisenhower might return. But all the planning and preparation often went agley for a simple reason—Eisenhower's candor. Instead of saying "No comment" or "That matter is under study and I am not able to discuss it now," he was prone to say, frankly, that the matter had not come to his attention, that he was not fully in command of the details and would look them up, or that he had not seen such-and-such development in the newspapers. Transcripts of the press conference furnish some examples:

On the question of talks about a possible blockade of Red China—"They are under consideration, *I suppose*, in several departments." (Surely, a President would *know* about everything in connection with so grave an action.)

On McCarthy—"I don't know exactly what he is aiming to do but I will say this: It is a question that I will not answer without a bit more preparation...because I haven't thought about his particular function, what he can do and what would happen if he didn't do it."

On discussions concerning the projected St. Lawrence Seaway—"I must admit you caught me to this one extent—I have forgotten whether we agreed to keep these confidential until we can examine them a little bit more among ourselves."

On the actions of his aides—"In a job such as this, all of you realize there has to be a terrific amount of decentralization, and any man worthy to be a chief of a great organizational body must do two or three things: One, pick the people he trusts; two, delegate authority and responsibility to them; three, back them up and particularly take responsibility for any failure or any blunder that occurs. Now some of these people can be doing things which I know they wouldn't bother me with."

Multiplied, such answers could easily give the impression that Eisenhower did not know what was going on in his administration. Fortunately for him, many of his press conference statements were sharp, detailed and to the point. Adams wrote that Eisenhower was aware of the criticisms but that he brushed them off on the grounds that the persons who made them did not understand the meaning of delegating authority and he felt his system was getting results.

Obviously, in a machine so monstrously big as the federal government, no President can know what is being done at all times and in all its parts. A Washington truism holds that it takes a new official six months "just to find the government." But the President can always use methods to conceal the fact that he is not wholly on top of everything, big or small. Calvin Coolidge, for example, required reporters to submit their questions in writing. He then answered only those he chose to answer. On one occasion, he tore up the entire stack of question cards and said, "No press conference today, Gentlemen."

As for snafus, a monumental case developed in Truman's administration. In 1946, James Byrnes, Secretary of State, and Senator Arthur Vandenberg were in Paris, pressing Truman's foreign policy line in conference with the Russians, British and French. Out of the blue, Henry Wallace, Secretary of Commerce, delivered a speech that ran directly counter to that line. Byrnes and Vandenberg were dumbfounded and the Russians found some comfort in Wallace's speech. In the ensuing furore, Truman felt compelled to fire Wallace, and did so. Merriman Smith wrote, "The President during these days of extreme crisis looked worried and hacked. His press conference faux pas seemed to increase and weigh heavily. His manner of speech seemed to tighten."[1]

The correspondents sometimes posed questions to Eisenhower which hardly seemed designed to elicit important and legitimate information for their readers. Two examples:

Q. "Mr. President, I understood you to refer to Governor

---

1 Smith: "The President Is Many Men."

Thornton of Colorado as 'Senator' Thornton. Does that suggest he will run next year against Senator Johnson?"

A. "I think your question merely illustrates the speed with which anyone is ready to pick up a slip. If I did that, I am sorry. I meant 'Governor' and nothing further."

Q. (referring to austerity in government) "For instance, would you be willing to do without that pair of helicopters that have been proposed for getting you out to the golf course a little faster than you can make it by car?"

A. "Well, I don't think much of that question because no helicopters have been procured for me to go to a golf course."

Sometimes, his face would flush and the effort to rein in his bucking-bronco temper would be plainly visible. However he said, "I don't try to play poker with this crowd. I try to tell you exactly what I am thinking when the question is posed." But there were many light moments, too, one of which produced the rare spectacle of a President of the United States blushing. The conference happened to be held on his 43rd wedding anniversary. The first question to him that day was to state his formula for a successful marriage. Eisenhower blushed and said he knew no formula. "I can just say it has been a very happy experience," he said. "A successful marriage, I think, gets happier as the years go by." He looked like a bashful schoolboy.

On the whole, the press conferences were immensely useful to Eisenhower and to the reporters. When he left the White House, they parted as friends, for the most part. He did take a dislike to a particular columnist. In his correspondence, Eisenhower referred to him as a "spherical s.o.b.," meaning that, viewed from any angle, he always looked like one. Eisenhower simply stopped reading some writers. In general, he tended to ignore criticism in the press.

After a press conference or a meeting in which something irritated him, Eisenhower might vent his feelings in no uncertain terms to members of his staff. He put them on notice that there would be such occasions. "You people have got to be my safety valve," he said. Once, he found it necessary to dress down Sherman Adams in private for what he considered an indiscretion and Adams wrote, "He had the most delightfully painless way of taking a person to task I have ever seen. Without saying much, he could make you feel just terrible."[1]

---

1 Adams: op. cit.

But when something went wrong and angered Eisenhower, he, in effect, looked at himself in a mirror to see if he had contributed to it, impersonally examining the causes. He wrote of one such instance:

"After a bit of cool reflection I realized that the cause of the difficulty lay more in my own failure to make myself clear than in the failure of others to understand me. After all, here were some of the most capable men I knew in their field, and apparently all had failed to comprehend the idea I had in mind. It was now up to me to make the best I could of the situation."[1]

Misadventures and crossed wires often moved Eisenhower to ask, humorously, thoughtfully, or in acid irritation, "When does anyone get any time to *think* around here?" Almost every President has felt this about his high office. "I'll be damned if I'm not getting tired of this," said William Howard Taft. "It seems to be the profession of a President simply to hear other people talk." And even the long-suffering Woodrow Wilson once said, "One of the difficulties of the office seldom appreciated, I dare say, is that it is very difficult to think while so many people are talking in a way that obscures counsel and is entirely off the point."

After he had been in the White House about a month, a reporter asked him how he liked his job. The best the President could say was, well, it had its compensations. However, the day was to come, and it may be a gauge of his growth in the office, when he would call it "a wonderful experience."

He learned, as did other Presidents, that the man in the White House is the loneliest man in the world. "To be President of the United States," said Harry Truman, "is to be lonely, very lonely at the times of great decisions." Eisenhower expressed the identical thought when he said, "…one man must conscientiously, deliberately, prayerfully scrutinize every argument, every proposal, every prediction, every alternative, every probable outcome of his action and then—all alone—make his decision."

Further, the mystique that breathes in the chambers of the White House, along with the mantle of great authority, stands between the President and his closest friends. So long as he remains in office, and even after he has left it, his relationship with them cannot be quite the same as it was before his election. Small incidents brought home

---

1 Eisenhower: "Waging Peace"

this fact to Eisenhower in the first few weeks of his presidency. For 40 years, since their cadet days and through their collaboration during the war, he and Omar Bradley had been "Ike" and "Brad" to each other. One day, with a shock, Eisenhower heard Bradley address him as "Mr. President" in a telephone conversation. Few persons could use his nickname any longer. On another occasion, his grandson, David, ran into his office and called out, "Hi, Ike." The President's face lit up with pleasure and he swept the boy into his arms. He continued to sign "Ike" on his letters to Hazlett. But once, in a fit of absentmindedness, he simply initialled a letter, "D.D.E.," as he did with official papers. Hazlett, half-humorously, pointed it out to him. Almost by return mail, Eisenhower apologized and said that if this should happen again, "you send it back to me without reading it and I will get back on the rails."

Early in the term, he began giving stag dinners at the White House. The language of the invitation was vintage Eisenhower. "I wonder if it would be convenient for you to come to an informal stag dinner," it began. If not, he would understand. The President said he would wear a dinner jacket but his guests, if they chose, should wear business suits. He organized these dinners to obtain information and hear the opinions of his guests on a wide spectrum of domestic and foreign questions. He invited, he said, representatives of "government, business, publishing, the professions, agriculture, the arts, labor and education."

When he was not busy at night with formal or informal dinners, he played bridge and read himself to sleep with Western stories. In his office, Robert Donovan reported, Eisenhower kept a Bible and volumes of Lincoln and Jefferson which he regularly read. From reading the works of the historian, Bruce Catton, he became almost a Civil War "buff."

Crude and cruel jokes were invented to create the impression that he spent more time playing golf than working at his desk. He practiced swinging his clubs in his office and putted on a green installed for him on the south lawn of the White House. From time to time he invited influential senators and congressmen to play golf with him. During the time when, in effect, he was wooing Taft he asked the senator several times to be his partner. All these outings were useful to Eisenhower. Theoretically, shoptalk was prohibited but in fact he brought up anything that came into his mind during the play, and that usually was the business of government.

Even in the White House, Mamie found an outlet for her homemaking instincts. She became interested in the collection of chinaware, amassed by earlier Presidents and she made an interesting discovery. Five had purchased no china at all, Andrew Johnson, William Howard Taft, Warren G. Harding, Calvin Coolidge and Herbert Hoover. (Republican thrift?) Through correspondence with their descendants, Mamie set about to try to fill the gaps. For State Dinners she chose a Castleton service with a gold medallion pattern around the rims.

Mamie also conducted an unusual tour of the White House. Her guests were the sons and daughters of former Presidents, some of whom, of course, had lived there. Her husband left his office to join them. He led them to portraits of their parents and, as an amateur painter, discussed techniques used by the artists.

On Feb. 1, Eisenhower joined the National Presbyterian Church in Washington in private rites. He attended regularly. His pew, Number 41, was near the one Benjamin Harrison had occupied. Still another held special meaning for the President; a plaque on the back said, "Ulysses Simpson Grant, General of the United States Army, 1868."

In the raffish tradition of partisan politics, even this act of joining a church, along with the prayer he read at the Inauguration and the silent prayer that opened a Cabinet meeting, was seized upon for ridicule. Critics called it a public relations gimmick to enhance his public image. So early did the campaign begin to twist and distort the true picture of Eisenhower and make him appear less than he was.

For reasons of economy, Eisenhower laid up the presidential yacht, Williamsburg, and he did not use the Presidential quarters at Key West, Florida, to massage the egos of the influential. He wrote Hazlett on July 23, 1953, that he was committed to a policy "approaching austerity." He kept the camp in the Catoctin Mountains of Maryland but renamed it, "Camp David," in honor of his father. He told Hazlett "'Shangri-la' was just a little too fancy for a Kansas farm boy."

Among the few articles Eisenhower kept on his desk were colored photographs of Mamie and his mother and an ebony panel bearing an inscription in Latin, "Suaviter in modo, fortiter in re." It can be translated, "Gentle in manner, strong in deed." Gabriel Hauge, administrative assistant for economic affairs, gave him the inscription, saying it accurately described the Eisenhower manner in the presidency. Eisenhower laughingly said of it, "That shows I'm an egghead."

At about the time he was telling Hazlett about his efforts toward austerity in government, Hazlett wrote him a letter using the red-ink half of the typewriter ribbon. He said the black-ink half had frayed from long use. Eisenhower answered that he disliked red ink in *any* form and advised his friend that he was sending him a new black ribbon. He did so—spooled inside a new portable typewriter.

His devotion to Hazlett was such that, thereafter, whenever Hazlett wrote a longhand letter, the President would inquire anxiously whether the new typewriter was not working properly. If so, he said, another machine would be sent.

Instinctively, he performed these small acts of kindness. They came from the deepest wellsprings of his nature.

One summer, he went to the graduation ceremonies at West Point, and there he learned that an aged general, Chauncey Fenton, was desperately ill in the hospital. General Fenton had been president of the Academy's alumni association. He had undergone surgery, the first of two operations. However, the physicians at West Point had advised the noted surgeon, Dr. Robert H. L. Elliott, that Fenton had not rallied from the first operation, largely because his morale was so low. "He's sunk," they told Elliott. "He doesn't seem to care whether he lives." They advised against the second operation until the general's spirits improved. When Eisenhower heard this, he went to Fenton's room in the hospital. For about 45 minutes, the President sat beside Fenton, reminiscing about the Academy and the war. Army shoptalk, telling him anecdotes about the presidency.

Two days later, the medical officers at West Point telephoned Dr. Elliott. "You can close up General Fenton now," they said. "He's on top of the world." After the operation, with tears streaming down his cheeks the aged officer told Elliott about Eisenhower's visit and what it meant to him.

These were some of the sunny moments for Eisenhower. Many more were somber.

Eisenhower had inherited a painful responsibility, the plea for presidential clemency in the case of Julius and Ethel Rosenberg. They had been convicted of conspiring to deliver to Soviet agents sketches of secret experiments conducted in the Atomic Energy Commission laboratory at Los Alamos, New Mexico. While Truman was still President, they had appealed for presidential clemency but it was not until February, 1953, that the appeal reached the White House. Eisenhower carefully examined the evidence against the Rosenbergs and on Feb. 11 issued a public statement announcing he concluded there was no basis for granting presidential clemency. It said in part:

"The nature of the crime for which they have been found guilty and sentenced far exceeds that of the taking of the life of another citizen; it involves the deliberate betrayal of the entire nation and could very well result in the death of many, many thousands of innocent citizens..."

On June 15, the Supreme Court denied a plea to stay the execution. Thereupon, the President issued a second statement, one paragraph of which said:

"When democracy's enemies have been judged guilty of a crime as horrible as that of which the Rosenbergs were convicted; when the legal processes of democracy have been marshaled to their maximum strength to protect the lives of convicted spies; when in their most solemn judgment the tribunals of the United States have judged them guilty and the sentence just, I will not intervene."

A tremendous outcry rose in the wake of the statement. From around the world came pleas for Eisenhower to reverse himself and the decision of the courts. They came from non-Communist as well as Communist organizations and from persons in all walks of life both in the United States and abroad. I stopped a taxicab on a street corner in Queens, Long Island, one afternoon to listen to a speaker addressing a crowd over a public-address system. First, he cited some details of the physical evidence against the Rosenbergs and found them frail; next, he asked why they should be given the death sentence while Klaus Fuchs, another convicted spy, not only had not been executed but had not even been sentenced to life imprisonment; thus, he could only conclude that the extreme penalty had been imposed because they were Jewish; finally, he reminded his audience that they were the parents of two small children. He closed by exhorting those listening to go to Washington to demonstrate in front of the White House, or if unable to do this, to write and wire the President protesting the sentence.

Evidently, many of them did. The White House mail about the case reached record size. And on the evening of June 19, as the hour of execution drew near, demonstrators knelt in front of the White House, praying and weeping. Others jeered them, shouting obscene and macabre slogans. I was one of three newspapermen who witnessed the executions.

Julius Rosenberg entered the chamber through a door behind and to the left of the electric chair. He peered around the room through his rimless glasses. His movements seemed uncertain, as though he might be under sedation. An odd smile played around the corners of his mouth. He walked quietly to the electric chair. Guards placed a hood over his head and attached the electrodes. When the switch was thrown, in an anteroom, his body strained momentarily against the straps. They creaked. Then he slumped. Two physicians pronounced him dead.

A matron in a white uniform came through the door with Ethel Rosenberg. They embraced and the door closed behind her. She walked with a firm, quick step toward the chair. She looked at the guards, the physicians and the three newspapermen with unwavering eyes. Then, unassisted, she seated herself in the chair. The switch was thrown and the usual sound, like metal objects running down a corrugated washboard, rattled in the anteroom. But when the physician placed a stethoscope against her chest, he stepped back and shook his head. The metallic rattling sounded again. The second charge ended her life.

During the very hours of this grim tableau, disaster threatened Eisenhower's efforts to bring peace on the other side of the world. Syngman Rhee, the doughty old President of South Korea, suddenly released thousands of North Korean prisoners of war. Negotiations for a truce had been going on for several weeks. For a time, it appeared Rhee's action would completely sabotage them, but this was averted.

Robert Donovan wrote that, after the silent prayer with which Cabinet meetings opened, Eisenhower said that he never remembered a time in his life when he felt more in need of help from someone much more powerful than he.[1]

On Aug. 4, the first session of the 83rd Congress ended. Republicans had controlled both houses, but by slim majorities. In the Senate, the lineup was 48 Republicans, 47 Democrats and one independent. In the House, the Republicans held 221 seats, the

---

1 Donovan: op. cit.

Democrats 211 with one independent. The Old Guard held much of the Republican power in Congress and they tended to be followers of Taft, not Eisenhower.

Totting up the work of the session, Eisenhower considered that in 83 test votes on "Eisenhower issues," 74 had been victories for him. But the nonpartisan Congressional Quarterly noted that, on 58 occasions, "Democrats saved the President…their votes providing the margin of victory when Republican defectors or absences imperiled the 'happy glow.'" The Quarterly estimated that Eisenhower obtained 72.7 per cent of his legislative program, a very high figure.

The "happy glow" extended to another sector of the President's work, and one which deeply concerned him, the nation's economic health. On Aug. 27, T. Coleman Andrews, United States Commissioner of Internal Revenue, reported that the government collected $69,687,000,000 in taxes—a record for a fiscal year.

It was a prosperous year. And although there were disgruntled Republican activists who wanted the President to swiftly undo the works of Franklin Roosevelt and Harry Truman, while others of both parties called for bold new adventures in foreign policy, Eisenhower's approach to the problems at home and abroad coincided more closely with the mood of the nation. Americans were still feeling the effects of the strictures and alarms of the Second World War and the Korean War. They wanted peace and prosperity and this, above all, was what Eisenhower was striving to achieve for them.

At times, he seemed hesitant and unsure of himself. But at the end of his first year in office, on Dec. 7, 1953, James Reston wrote in The New York Times. "The wait-and-see phase of his presidency is now coming to an end for a variety of reasons…"

A Cross to Bear

The era of Joseph R. McCarthy reveals more about America than it does about Eisenhower. McCarthy attracted wide support and wider attention during the years when he was blasting lives and ruining reputations under the guise of hunting Communists. Eisenhower displayed his utter contempt for him when they first met in Peoria during the 1952 campaign. Yet, as President, he refused to speak out publicly against McCarthy. His official silence through these eerie and painful years dismayed his friends and gave his critics the opportunity to picture him as detached, indifferent, reigning but not ruling.

The junior senator from Wisconsin, a burly, black-haired man with drooping jowls, was an obscure figure, virtually unknown as a legislator until Feb. 9, 1950. On that day, he stood on a public platform in Wheeling, West Virginia, holding an envelope. He glowered at the paper with an expression of cold anger (which was pure histrionics) and said, "I have here in my hand a list—."

He said it contained the names of 57 persons who were either card-carrying Communists or Communist sympathizers but who "nevertheless are helping shape our foreign policy."

In subsequent speeches, this figure expanded to 81, then to more than 200, and then back to smaller figures as McCarthy talked about the "immense conspiracy" he claimed to have uncovered in Washington. The list was highly elastic but this seemed not to disturb the growing army of his fervent supporters.

The newspapers could not ignore the Wheeling speech and neither could McCarthy's fellow senators, especially after he repeated his charges on the Senate floor. On Feb. 21, a Special Foreign Relations Subcommittee was appointed to investigate his claims. All this made headlines. McCarthy burgeoned into national prominence, a hero to many Americans, an ogre to many others. Still others were sincerely disturbed over the possibility that McCarthy might be right. The late Elmer Davis, while scathingly critical of McCarthy, nevertheless wrote, "But undoubtedly the Communists did some damage; if they were not top-level men they were often industrious assistants to top-level men in the executive departments and on Congressional committees."[1]

In any case, the Wheeling speech ushered in the grotesque McCarthy Era. It lasted about four years. In those years, reputations were lacerated and careers destroyed. Employers' black lists came into existence. A strange and ugly image of America spread around the world.

McCarthy's office became the receptacle for mindless fears, unfounded suspicions, naked prejudice. Sneaks and informers sent him tons of gossip and rumor about their neighbors; in his heyday, the boxes of letters piled so high that they cramped the working space for his staff. To his admirers, for a man merely to be summoned before the Senate investigating subcommittee which he headed, and questioned about past associations or a book written long before, became proof positive of disloyalty or worse. The premise of innocent until proved guilty was reversed. "Guilt by association" was enough. Americans who were outraged by McCarthy's extralegal tactics called him another Hitler or a latter-day Torquemada.

McCarthy laughed at the idea that he tapped telephones. However, a government official who became one of his targets told me an odd story: He said he had received a "scrambled" telephone call from New York, a conversation that would have been unintelligible to anyone listening without the electronic "scrambler." He shrugged and said, "Somehow, McCarthy knew what was said." Of course, someone might have overheard at least one *end* of the conversation, he said. However, he continued, a woman in Washington telephoned him one night. "Two hours later," he said, "one of McCarthy's snoopers was in her apartment building, asking the neighbors if they had ever seen me in her apartment, if I had ever been there late at night and so on." Then his face lit up for an instant. "The lady is 80 years old," he said, "which considerably surprised McCarthy's agent."

McCarthy claimed to have paid agents abroad, watching American Foreign Service officers. Once he tossed a document across his desk to me. It was written in Chinese. He winked and said, "From my

---

1 Davis: "But We Were Born Free."

guy in Shanghai." I pointed out that there was no American embassy nor consulates in Red China. "That's right," he said, "but there are Commies there and Commies here. Get it?" Naturally, I asked what the document contained. McCarthy grinned broadly. (He was an engaging, even a charming, man in private.) "I don't know yet," he said. "I have to get it translated." Sometime later, I again asked about the Chinese papers. "Nothing," he said. "Just trash." Pointing to the boxes of letters, he said, "A lot of that's trash but some of it may come in handy sometime."

Perhaps it did. When a prominent man attacked McCarthy publicly, the senator instantly produced a yellowed newspaper clipping, 19 years old, purporting to show that his critic had had Russian connections.

His following continued to swell until, it was reported, public-opinion polls showed that half the nation either supported him or held a "favorable opinion" of him. He was credited, if that is the right word, with engineering the defeats of four senators who incurred his wrath. He was greatly feared not only in the Senate but apparently in the White House. Richard Rovere reported that when he tried to talk about McCarthy with an Eisenhower assistant, the man said, "For God's sake, please don't ask me to discuss this...Don't even ask me why I don't want to talk about it." Rovere wrote, "The mere mention of the senator from Wisconsin...had reduced this sturdy man to jelly."[1]

A statement that many Americans took as a credo to answer McCarthy came from the illustrious jurist, Judge Learned Hand, on May 18, 1951. He did not refer to McCarthy by name but at a dinner of the American Law Institute in Washington, the wise old man said he thought the nation was "perhaps in greater peril" than it had been in 1941, when war came to the United States. And he said:

"I will not say of my brother that he may be a traitor. Produce what you have. I will judge it fairly...but I will not take it on rumor. I will not take it on hearsay. I will remember that what has brought us up from savagery is a loyalty to truth, and truth cannot emerge unless it is subjected to the closest scrutiny."[2]

Eisenhower's landslide in 1952 swung control of both houses

---

1 Rovere: "Senator Joe McCarthy."
2 "The Spirit of Liberty," collected by Irving Dilliard.

of Congress to the Republicans. (McCarthy ran far behind him in Wisconsin.) Thus, McCarthy became chairman of the Permanent Subcommittee on Investigations. Now he could search his files for targets, issue subpoenas, and watch the victims squirm. He often went back a long way.

During the Depression days of the early 1930s, some Americans joined Communist groups for various reasons. Some were idealists, some found it fashionable. Others thought the great economic disaster represented the final breakdown of the capitalist system. There were those who soon became disillusioned with Communism and abandoned the movement. Many did after Stalin confounded them by concluding the Treaty of Nonaggression with Hitler on Aug. 23, 1939. Such persons looked juicy to McCarthy, especially if they were prominent and their appearance before him would bring headlines.

James Wechsler, editor of The New York Post, was a case in point. Wechsler made no secret of the fact that he had joined the Young Communist League in 1934. He left it in 1937, one of the disillusioned. Long afterward, as editor of The Post, Wechsler found himself confronting McCarthy in a hearing of the investigative committee.

McCarthy said the hearing would be about books Wechsler had written, books which were in United States Information Service Libraries abroad. Wechsler wrote that McCarthy said to him:

"You see, your books, some of them, were paid for by taxpayers' money. They are being used, allegedly, to fight Communism. Your record, as far as I can see it, has not been to fight Communism. You have fought every man who has ever tried to fight Communism, as far as I know."

Wechsler had with him a document he thought proved exactly the contrary. It was a statement of the National Committee of the Communist Party attacking him, and blaming him among others for the poor showing of Leftist parties in the 1948 elections. Offering the document as an exhibit, Wechsler said, "I am rather fond of this tribute, and it may perhaps have some bearing on your comment that I have not been active in fighting Communism."

Quick as a whiplash, McCarthy said, "Did you have anything to do with the passage of that resolution? Did you take any part in promoting the passage of that resolution?"

Wechsler was dumbfounded. He wrote, "Here indeed was a daring new concept in which the existence of evidence of innocence becomes the damning proof of guilt…What a man had said or done could no longer be accepted as bearing the slightest relationship to what he was or what he believed."[1]

McCarthy was a lawyer but he did not permit the rules of evidence to hamper him in these weird hearings.

Nor did he unearth any Communists of any importance in government. I once suggested to him that he might compile a box score, how many cases investigated, how many persons called into the hearings, the results of the questioning, etc. "Hey, you've got something there," he said, with spurious enthusiasm. "I'll get the staff on it right away." Of course, he never did. I doubt that he cared a whit about Communists in government. What he did care about was the power and publicity generated by his witch-hunts, seeing his name in headlines and his face on television, knowing that he was feared.

As he thrashed around, playing cat-and-mouse with lives and reputations, outraged Americans and frightened Europeans (who feared another Hitler in the making) began asking, "Why doesn't Ike do something about McCarthy? Surely, a decent guy like Ike can't sit back and let this go on." One man wrote a letter urging the President to "fire" McCarthy. Some members of the White House staff pleaded with Eisenhower to hurl a thunderbolt at McCarthy in public. Others counseled against this; Eisenhower was having enough trouble with the ultraconservatives in his party, they argued. And the 1954 Congressional elections were approaching. In that connection, I asked Maxwell M. Rabb, Secretary to the Cabinet, whether McCarthy's wide following, and therefore the political implications for the Republicans in the elections, was the reason for the President's silence. Max snorted, "You mean, if people have to choose between Eisenhower and McCarthy in a popularity contest? Pick up the pieces!" Meanwhile, Eisenhower's refusal to speak out gave his critics further material with which to picture him as flabby and indecisive. A newspaper cartoon showed him confronting McCarthy. McCarthy has a meat-ax in his hand and the frightened-looking President is holding a quill pen and is saying, "Have a care, Sir. Have a care."

Eisenhower's intimates knew his feelings. He loathed McCarthy. But he was quoted as saying, "I will not get in the gutter with that guy." Nor would he elevate McCarthy to his level by publicly denounc-

---

[1] Wechsler: "The Age of Suspicion."

ing him. In his concept, the best course was to strike at McCarthy by inference.

Thus, during the 1952 campaign, and with McCarthy sitting nearby on the platform, Eisenhower warned against "violent vigilantism." More pointedly he said, "To defend freedom is first of all to respect freedom...That respect demands another, quite simple kind of respect for the integrity of fellow citizens to enjoy their right to disagree with us. The right to challenge a man's judgment carries with it no automatic right to question his honor."

The thrust could hardly have been lost on McCarthy, and his dark, frosty expression indicated that it had not been. He sat like a graven image during the applause that interrupted Eisenhower. For when it suited McCarthy's purposes, an error of judgment at some point in a man's past did put his honor and loyalty in question.

After the election, while McCarthy was attacking the U.S.I.A. libraries around the world, and the antic cavortings of his two aides, Roy Cohn and G. David Schine, were astounding Europeans, Eisenhower delivered the "book burning" speech at Dartmouth College. He said:

"Don't join the book burners. Don't think you are going to conceal faults by concealing evidence that they ever existed. Don't be afraid to go to your library and read every book, as long as that document does not offend our own ideas of decency...How will we defeat Communism unless we know what it is?"

He used a press conference for another such indirect swipe at the senator. He said, "The administration will continue to hunt for any (subversives) that are present and, of course, any subversives located by a Congressional committee will be removed just as promptly as any others. In all that we do to combat subversion, it is imperative that we protect the basic rights of loyal American citizens."

In a sense, too, Eisenhower rebuffed McCarthy in refusing to withdraw the nomination of Charles E. Bohlen, as ambassador to Moscow. "Chip" Bohlen is a seasoned and brilliant Foreign Service officer, a long-time specialist on the Soviet Union, and he speaks Russian. But—horrors of horrors!—he had served as Roosevelt's interpreter at the Yalta Conference. The Republicans were laboring assiduously to make Yalta a dirty word and in McCarthy's book Yalta was a component of "a conspiracy so immense and an infamy so black as to dwarf any previous such venture in the history of man." Ergo, merely for having been at Yalta, putting Russian into English for Roosevelt, Bohlen was leprous.

McCarthy stepped into the forefront of the fight to block Bohlen's appointment. "We find," McCarthy said in the debate in the Senate, "that his entire history is one of complete, wholehearted, 100 per cent cooperation with the Acheson-Hiss-Truman regime." It was asserted that the FBI files on Bohlen contained damning information. Against the advice of Attorney General Brownell, Eisenhower ruled that Taft and Senator John Sparkman of Alabama could examine the dossier. They did, found nothing of course, and so advised the Senate. Nonetheless, the fight raged on. Eisenhower came under pressure to withdraw Bohlen's nomination, thus appeasing McCarthy and the other senators of his ilk who were fighting the appointment. Eisenhower refused. He had obtained Taft's promise to lead the fight for the approval of Bohlen, and Taft, with his enormous power in the Senate, steamrollered it through. The vote was 74 to 13. But of the 13 who voted "nay," 11 were members of Eisenhower's own party. Hardly a favorable augur for the President's legislative program unless he could continue to draw more support from the Democrats than the Republicans.

But this setback and Eisenhower's inferential condemnations of McCarthy's tactics did not deter the senator. Eisenhower continued to avoid a head-on collision with him.

The core of his reasoning was this: He took the position that "McCarthyism" predated McCarthy and that the senator was merely its rallying point. (Obviously, it has survived McCarthy.) He said, time and again, he would not "deal in personalities." Nor would he enlarge McCarthy's notoriety by dignifying him with a presidential rebuke. He was trying in every way he knew to win support from the Old Guard for his programs, and although the possibility of this seemed slight, he would not foreclose it for the less-important satisfaction of denouncing a demagogue. Finally, as he invariably did, Eisenhower maintained a strict hands-off posture with respect to what he considered the exclusive purview of Congress. If McCarthy was to be censured, he felt, that was the Senate's business, not his, primarily.

Years afterward, Eisenhower remained convinced that he had handled the problem of McCarthy in the most effective manner, to ignore him, and let the Senate or the people of Wisconsin deal with him.

Regarding his view that McCarthy was the Senate's primary responsibility, it must be said that Eisenhower had a good point. While McCarthy struck terror in the hearts of many Senators, a few were too powerful for even he and his snoopers to injure. One such was Robert A. Taft. Jack Bell, an admirer of Taft, nevertheless wrote in his illuminating, tightly reasoned study of the presidency:

"The truth of the matter was that Taft could have stepped on McCarthy at almost any point and squashed him... There would have been no need for presidential action if Taft had moved in to pinch off McCarthy's activities."

Then why didn't Taft "move in"? Bell continues:

"That Taft would not employ the means at his command to gag McCarthy when the latter's anger was turned upon the Eisenhower Republicans was one of those things Taft never satisfactorily explained beyond the obvious fact that he was inclined to regard the party's liberals—but not the President—as enemies akin to the left-wing Democrats. If they hurt a little along with the Democrats, that was all right with the Ohioan."[1]

Taft had gone to his grave by the time the Senate at long last discovered McCarthy's "unbecoming" conduct and plucked up the courage to censure him.

Three events in 1954 brought McCarthy to his Waterloo.

One was the ridiculous Army-McCarthy Senate hearings. McCarthy, having "investigated" virtually every other sector of American society, now toned toward the Army and charged that it was "coddling" Communists. "Tommyrot," snorted Charles Wilson. And Robert T. Stevens, Secretary of the Army, angrily asserted he would not countenance having Army officers "abused and brow-beaten." Earlier, Roy Cohn's henchman, David Schine, had been drafted. Then came an Army report, prepared at the suggestion of Sherman Adams, accusing McCarthy and Cohn of trying, through threats, to obtain a commission for Schine and to shield him with preferential treatment from the rigors of soldiering. The report alleged, among other things, that McCarthy asked Stevens to send Schine to West Point to study the "pro-Communist leanings" in the Academy's textbooks. McCarthy, as always, quickly moved to the offensive. He said the report was "blackmail," designed to stop his investigations of the Army.

---

1 J. Lowell Bell: "The Splendid Misery."

Instead of going to the Senate Armed Services Committee, where it properly belonged, the dispute came before McCarthy's own subcommittee where he could do pretty much as he pleased. (He stepped down temporarily as its chairman.) The hearings were televised and they lasted five weeks. They must have drawn a host of viewers away from the daily fare of soap operas, farces and courtroom dramas, for they served up ingredients of all these in real life. Joseph N. Welch, an impeccably dressed Boston lawyer with elegant manners, represented the Army. He brought some semblance of legality into the shenanigans. Welch, like many another trial lawyer, was something of an actor. (He later played the role of a judge in a motion picture.) But he probably was not acting when tears came into his eyes and he said in a choked voice to McCarthy, "May God forgive you for that, Senator, for I cannot find it in my heart to do so." McCarthy had tried to pin a Communist connection on one of Welch's aides. Only too accurately, in the personalized style of British reporting, the correspondent of a London newspaper wrote of one session of the hearings, "I watched the great Republic making an ass of itself today."

Eisenhower was sick at heart over the hearings as were many spectators even though, unlike the President, they had not had an Army career. At a news conference, when a correspondent asked him how he would have handled the dispute, Eisenhower almost choked up. He asked to be excused from giving a specific reply. He said he just hoped they would come to an end quickly.

But for all the inherent nonsensicality of the farce on Capitol Hill, one positive value possibly did accrue to the nation from it. An army of TV watchers for the first time saw McCarthy in action, snarling, clawing, flailing about in all directions, interrupting with his nasal "Point of order—point of order, Mr. Chairman," seizing the initiative on every pretext. He was like a trapped bear lunging at his captors. It is difficult to believe that those who had entertained a "favorable opinion" of him before the hearings still retained it when they saw him as he was.

Meanwhile, during the summer, Senator Ralph Flanders of Vermont introduced in the Senate a resolution to censure McCarthy. It read, "Resolved, that the conduct of the senator from Wisconsin, Mr. McCarthy, is unbecoming a member of the United States Senate, is contrary to Senatorial traditions, and tends to bring the Senate into disrepute." It was a courageous action, one of the few during the McCarthy Era, and the general reaction on the Hill that day was summed up by a senator who said, but not for attribution, "Joe'll get Flanders, watch and see."

In December, the Senate voted three-to-one to censure McCarthy.

But by that time, the American voter, indirectly, had delivered the deathblow to McCarthy. In November, the Democrats regained control of the House and Senate in the 1954 elections. Thus, McCarthy lost the chairmanship of the investigative committee, stripping him of his power to act as a one-man Reign of Terror.

Almost immediately, in a curious way, McCarthy seemed to go into a physical decline. The fire went out of him. He looked bloated and shambling. If ever a man nourished himself on headlines and the limelight, in the literal sense, it was Joe McCarthy. When these were denied him he began to starve. He died in 1957.

So, more than four years after the Wheeling speech, the McCarthy Era ended. During that period, Americans in almost every walk of life became suspect on the flimsiest evidence or no evidence at all, government officials, clergymen, schoolteachers, writers, actors, members of the armed forces and certainly anybody who dared criticize McCarthy publicly. It seemed that snooping, spying on one's neighbors through a crack in the curtain, rumormongering, rattling skeletons in the closet—under the guise of hunting Reds—supplanted baseball as the national pastime.

To Eisenhower, these were days of pain and anger. Roy Roberts said that, in a moment of frustration during the McCarthy Era, the President said, "Roy, I wonder if I've made a mistake in being a Republican. Maybe I joined the wrong party." (In asking himself this question, he was not thinking only of McCarthy, of course, but of the other members of his own party who so often failed to support him.) He ignored the criticism, the acid cartoons and scornful denunciations, and held firmly to his conviction that he was following the right course with regard to McCarthy. Eisenhower once said that Lincoln was "more vilified than admired" during his lifetime. He could have said the same of himself in that stormy time.

In retrospect, the America of the McCarthy Era seems to stand in a baleful light, beneath a sheen of paranoia.

"The Cost of One Bomber"

As he labored to advance his legislative program and to remold the Republican Party, Eisenhower at the same time began the search for avenues that conceivably could lead to a thaw in the Cold War.

"The administration about to assume power in Washington will find our foreign relations in stalemate," Hamilton Fish Armstrong, the distinguished editor, wrote in January, 1953. "To break it, they will have to fulfill psychological as well as political requirements both at home and abroad. Our people must be freed...from an oppressive sense of unreality, from the feeling that perhaps their great efforts since the end of the war and the sacrifices of their sons in Korea have not been directed to clear and practicable objectives."[1]

These, the "clear and practicable objectives," were Eisenhower's goals. They had weighed heavily in his thinking when he made up his mind to run for the presidency.

He began the search with certain fixed convictions: One, that Americans could not avoid the heavy responsibility of leadership of the free nations into which they had been thrust; there could be no return to the "good old days" of isolationism. Two, the United States needed allies and should not "go it alone," as some members of the Old Guard advocated. Three, that the Mutual Security Program was not "foreign aid," but an integral part of the security system of the United States itself. Four, that he would be prepared to meet with Joseph Stalin or anybody else at some suitable site if he thought it would do any good and on condition that America's Allies were fully informed of the agenda. He did not say, when a reporter questioned him about this, that he thought little could be done toward reaching even a small *detente* with the Russians so long as Stalin lived, although he probably believed this.

---

1   Armstrong: "Foreign Affairs Quarterly."

On March 5, Stalin died. Did this open the way for a fresh try toward improving relations between the Kremlin and the West? Since the new ruler or rulers were not yet named, Eisenhower could only speculate. But as he turned the matter over in his mind, he came to some conclusions. He said it would be fruitless and stupid to mouth the old indictments of Stalin, valid though they still were, the broken promises, the enslavement of people, the effort to force the Allies out of Berlin, the aggression in Korea. He looked to the future and talked with his aides about specific possibilities.

Out of these ruminations came the famous "Peace Speech." Eisenhower delivered it on April 16, 1953, before the American Society of Newspaper Editors. (He was violently ill with what would later be diagnosed as ileitis when he stepped up to the lectern, sweating, in pain and fearful of fainting.)

He began by citing the meaning of expenditures on armaments. "The cost of one heavy bomber," he said, "is a modern brick school in more than 30 cities. It is two fine, fully equipped hospitals."

Next, he addressed himself directly to the new hierarchy in the Kremlin, saying, "So the new Soviet leadership now has a precious opportunity to awaken, with the rest of the world, to the point of peril reached and to help turn the tide of history."

Then he advanced concrete proposals, an agreement to disarm, international control of atomic energy and universal prohibition of atomic weapons with the establishment of adequate safeguards, a practical system of inspection under the United Nations.

"This government," Eisenhower said, "is ready to ask its people to join with all nations in devoting a substantial percentage of the savings achieved by disarmament to a fund for world aid and reconstruction.

"I know of only one question upon which progress waits. It is this: What is the Soviet Union ready to do?"

The speech rocketed around the world. The State Department took extraordinary measures to give it the widest possible circulation, beaming radio broadcasts to the Iron Curtain countries, showing the President on television, distributing thousands of copies of the text at home and abroad. Churchill gave it high praise and instructed his ambassador in Moscow to personally hand his statement of praise to the Soviet Foreign Minister, V.M. Molotov. Extravagantly enthusiastic editorials appeared in American newspapers, even some publications with strong Democratic leanings. Here was a positive effort to go beyond the established American policy of "containment" of the Communist world, the static holding operation. The basic premises came from Eisenhower's vision and imagination. Richard Rovere, Washington correspondent of the New Yorker Magazine, wrote that the speech "firmly established his leadership and reestablished America's leadership in the world."

Before the year was out, the President was again to command worldwide attention, again seizing the initiative, in the historic "Atoms-for-Peace" speech in the United Nations.

Meanwhile, he directed his efforts toward achieving a truce in Korea. The truce talks had started in 1951 and stalemated during the next two years. Victory had been within sight at that time, Gen. James A. Van Fleet testified before the Senate Armed Services Committee. But in the months that had passed, Eisenhower knew, the Chinese and North Koreans had built defenses-in-depth along the line where the armies stood. As a military man, he could readily estimate the cost in blood and treasure in cracking through these defenses and fighting all the way to the Yalu River, the boundary between Korea and metropolitan China. The alternative would be to agree to the vivisection of Korea, leaving the North in Communist hands—a proposition that fiery old Syngman Rhee said *he* could not and would not accept.

Nevertheless, Eisenhower determined to follow this course.

To hasten the end of the stalemated talks, he took some steps in the war of nerves. He changed the standing orders to the United States Seventh Fleet, patrolling the straits between the Chinese mainland and Formosa where the exiled Chinese Nationalist government had installed itself. The Fleet would still defend them against an attack by the Reds, but the inference of the new order was that the warships would not stand in the way of a Nationalist attack on the mainland. Eisenhower's critics ridiculed this as "unleashing Chiang" and hooted at the possibility of the Nationalist David mounting a serious assault on the Communist Goliath. Evidently, the Chinese Communist command did not find it so ridiculous, however. They moved heavy concentrations of troops into Fukien, a mountainous province directly opposite Formosa.

At the same time, Eisenhower ordered missiles with atomic warheads to Okinawa in the chain of island defenses stretching from Japan through the East China Sea to the Philippines. Again, the inference seemed clear that the President was preparing to take serious action if the truce talks remained mired down.

To make sure that this was understood, John Foster Dulles, the Secretary of State, talked for three days in late May with Jawaharlal Nehru, Prime Minister of India. Dulles told Nehru the United States wanted an acceptable peace in Korea, but he said Eisenhower would not tolerate the stalemate much longer. Most important, he said that if full-scale fighting resumed, it could not be limited, that Manchuria would be bombed. Manchuria, the "privileged sanctuary," as Douglas MacArthur called it, would not remain privileged. It was from this staging area that Chinese hordes entered Korea in the Fall of 1950, almost overnight turning a certain victory into a fighting retreat. The bridges over which they crossed the Yalu could easily have been destroyed and so could the hydroelectric complexes along the river which contributed to the industrial establishment of Red China. Chinese fighter pilots operated from Manchurian bases and troops and supplies massed there without let or hindrance from American planes. It was an Alice-in-Wonderland era of the Korean War, and Dulles told Nehru, it would not recur if Eisenhower felt compelled to fight again. The President and Dulles expected the warning to reach Peking through Nehru, and it probably did.

Whether because of the threat to use atomic weapons, or because Stalin's successors determined to liquidate his costly mistake in embarking on the Korean adventure, the ice seemed to thaw a little as summer came in 1953. In early June, Eisenhower wrote Rhee:

"The enemy has proposed an armistice which involves a clear abandonment of the fruits of aggression. The armistice would leave the Republic of Korea in undisputed possession of substantially the territory which the Republic administered prior to the aggression, indeed this territory will be somewhat enlarged.

"The proposed armistice...assures that thousands of North Korean and Chinese Communist prisoners in our hands...will not be forcibly sent back into Communist areas."

Rhee protested violently. To the end of his days, he pleaded, sometimes almost in tears, for an American green light that would let him "go North," as he always put it. His own forces, given American ammunition and supplies, could do it without American troops, he said. He died in 1965 without the fulfillment of a lifelong dream of a free and unified Korea.

It will long be debated whether the half-a-loaf settlement in Korea, like the Berlin Airlift of 1948, were, in the long run, wise actions. In both instances, they frustrated Stalinist aggression. But all the Airlift accomplished was to prove that a large city could be supplied by air; it did not improve the Allies' position. Similarly, the Korean armistice left South and North in pretty much the positions they had held before the fighting began. The line between them on Parallel 38 had been agreed upon in 1945 purely for administrative purposes in taking the surrender of the Japanese armies in Korea; the Americans had not foreseen that Moscow would create an iron-bound Communist state north of the Parallel. Korea remained half-free, half-Communist after the armistice of 1953.

By that time, nearly 34,000 Americans had died and more than 103,000 had been wounded in the fighting. No one can say how many more would have fallen in an all-out drive to clear Korea of the Chinese. Or whether the Chinese even then would have agreed to an armistice. Or whether the bombing of Manchuria, with or without atomic weapons, would have forced Russia to honor her treaty of mutual assistance with China, thus touching off the Third World War. An American general summed up the feelings of many Americans in and out of government when he said in a speech, "The stakes are too high to indulge in guessing games."

At any rate, the armistice was signed at Panmunjom, July 27, 1953. Acclaim for Eisenhower poured in from around the world and the great majority of Americans approved. It was one of his proudest achievements.

History alone, in the long, unimpassioned view, will judge whether he made the right move on the global chessboard.

In December, he met with Churchill and Joseph Laniel, the Premier of France, at the Bermuda Conference. It was an informal meeting, without agenda. It was notable only because it was Eisenhower's first experience in Summitry as President, and it gave him the opportunity to see the Prime Minister in action. In a letter written the day before Christmas, Eisenhower told a friend, "At times, Winston seemed to be his old and hearty self, full of vim and determination. At others, he seemed almost to wander in his mind. I must confess that occasionally I suspected this latter was almost a deliberately adopted mannerism rather than an involuntary habit. At least it seemed to come over him only when the subject under discussion or the argument presented was distasteful to him."

Churchill, it appears, took a poor view of Dulles and of Eisenhower for permitting himself to be so strongly influenced by the Secretary of State. Lord Moran, the old statesman's physician, has quoted him as saying, "This fellow preaches like a Methodist minister and his bloody text is always the same: That nothing but evil can come out of meeting with Malenkov. Dulles is a terrible handicap."[1]

This judgment, however, must be seen in context. Lord Moran's book makes it abundantly clear that Churchill's mental powers had declined greatly after his second stroke. Moreover, Churchill was desperately anxious to meet personally with Malenkov in the thought that he could quickly come to agreements which would ease world tensions. Dulles never favored such meetings. But Eisenhower's position was more flexible than Churchill seems to have realized: He would not meet with the Russians at the top and merely talk "generalities," but if there was the prospect of agreement on concrete issues, he said he would meet anywhere with anyone.

From Bermuda, Eisenhower flew directly to New York to appear before the United Nations and present an ingenious plan to provide some safeguards against the mushroom-shape clouds of nuclear explosions. This was the famous "Atoms-for-Peace" speech. The President and his assistants had been working out the details for months but the final draft of the speech was not finished even when his plane sighted New York. He instructed his pilot to circle the city until the last page had been typed.

He related the background of his proposal in a personal letter:

"I began to search around for any kind of an idea that could bring the world to look at the atomic problem in a broad and intelligent way and still escape the impasse to action created by Russian intransigence in the matter of mutual or neutral inspection of resources.

"One day, I hit upon the idea of actual physical donations by Russia and the United States with Britain also in the picture…"

Eisenhower credits Adm. Lewis L. Strauss, then chairman of the Atomic Energy Commission, with devising the physical method by which the uranium could be stored, and the proposal to establish an International Atomic Energy Agency.

---

1 Moran: op. cit.

The President was by no means bemused with a quixotic dream of breaking, at one stroke, the impasse with the Russians over control of nuclear weapons, disarmament, an inspection system, etc. He hoped only that it might build, as he said, a "tiny bridge."

On Dec. 8, he brought these thoughts before the General Assembly of the United Nations. He set forth the heart of his proposal in the words:

"…The governments principally involved, to the extent permitted by elementary prudence, to begin now and continue to make joint contributions from their stockpiles of their normal uranium and fissionable materials to an International Atomic Energy Agency. We would expect that such an agency would be set up under the aegis of the United Nations.

"The United States is prepared to undertake these explorations in good faith. Any partner of the United States acting in the same good faith will find the United States a not unreasonable or ungenerous associate.

"The more important responsibility of this Atomic Energy Agency would be to devise methods whereby this fissionable material would be allocated to serve the peaceful pursuits of mankind.

"Of those 'principally involved,' the Soviet Union must of course be one."

Not as a *caveat* to the Russians but to give the world a slight approximation of America's atomic arsenal, Eisenhower said in the speech:

"Today, the United States' stockpile of atomic weapons, which of course increases daily, exceeds by many times the explosive equivalent of all bombs and all shells that came from every plane and every gun in every theater of war in all the years of World War II."

Again, as with the "Peace Speech" of the preceding April, wide applause came from around the world in the form of notes and editorial reaction. For the second time, he had seized the initiative. In effect, he again said, "What is the Soviet Union ready to do?"

At first, it appeared, the Soviet Union was not prepared to do anything. Eisenhower's offer seemed to have taken them by surprise and the Kremlin remained silent about it.

He went ahead, concluding a number of bilateral treaties to provide research reactors to nations around the world.

Eventually, the Russians found that they favored Eisenhower's proposal and went along with it. Eventually, they came into the International Atomic Energy Agency. The "tiny bridge" had been built.

• • •

With his long exposure to foreign affairs before he came to the presidency, Eisenhower, like Franklin D. Roosevelt, could have been his own Secretary of State. But he believed in delegating authority to the men he thought best qualified to administer it. Thus, he delegated wide responsibility to John Foster Dulles, an international lawyer who had hankered since his Princeton undergraduate days to be Secretary of State.

No other Cabinet member stayed closer to the President than Dulles. A day seldom passed when he did not pick up the white telephone, a direct line to the White House, to talk with Eisenhower. He came regularly to the President's office, bringing the draft of a speech (and not necessarily the final draft), a statement of policy or his thoughts on a current problem. When he went overseas, which was very often, he sometimes telephoned Eisenhower to report developments. Or he summarized them in a daily message. This procedure may seem anomalous since, as has been said, Eisenhower wanted to hear solutions, not problems. But his respect and affection for Dulles were so great that, in the Secretary's case, he made exceptions to his own rule. "He always makes me think," Eisenhower said.

Their close partnership gave rise to the assertion that the foreign policy of the United States during Dulles' tenure was his policy, that he formulated ideas and then "sold" them to the President. This may have been true in some instances. Churchill, according to Lord Moran's account, arrived at that conclusion during the Bermuda Conference. The physician quoted Churchill as calling Dulles a "terrible handicap." Eisenhower had the highest respect for Dulles but in the quest for disarmament and peace, the President and Secretary differed on some fundamentals. Nixon, in his statement to the Princeton history project, previously quoted, pointed out some of the differences. He said:

"Dulles was skeptical about Summitry, and Eisenhower was very optimistic about it. Dulles was skeptical also about trade, and Eisenhower thought trade was the answer to everything. When I say 'to everything,' I don't mean to oversimplify. But Eisenhower often used to say—because he had many friends in the business community—he often used to say, 'Well, the more you trade with people the more understanding you're going to have.' And he never could see any harm to be done by trading with even the Iron Curtain countries in the proper circumstances. Dulles on the other hand stood like a rock against any trade unless there were *quid pro quo* concessions."

Nixon said that in 1954, Dulles became deeply frustrated with the British and French, and in this connection first used the often-quoted phrase, "agonizing reappraisal." Nixon told the Princeton interviewers that Dulles requested him to come to his home for a discussion of foreign problems and the former vice president said:

"It was in this period when we were getting very little support from the British and French in our Asian policy, or anything else. I remember going into his library and he said, 'You know, what I am concerned about is that we have done, and are doing, so much for our European allies, and we are getting so little cooperation. I'm convinced that it may be time for an agonizing reappraisal here, and we may have to lay it on the line.' And he even talked in terms of a withdrawal from Europe."

Dulles was a tough, hard-headed lawyer and it was with this approach that he represented his client, the United States of America.

"Foster," the saying went, "has been studying to be Secretary of State since he was 7." It was only a slight exaggeration.

His grandfather, John Watson Foster, a general in the Civil War, had been Secretary of State for Benjamin Harrison. His uncle, Robert Lansing, held the office under Woodrow Wilson.

In 1907, when he was 19, Dulles attended the Hague Convention. Ten years later, during the First World War, Wilson sent him to Central America to devise arrangements for the protection of the Panama Canal. He served as a counsel to the United States delegation at the Versailles Conference.

He graduated at the head of his Princeton class in 1908 and then repeated this feat in the George Washington University School of Law. Dulles also earned a degree in law at the Sorbonne in Paris. When he was 31, he was a full partner in the New York law firm of Sullivan and Cromwell. If Thomas E. Dewey had won the presidency, Dulles would have been his Secretary of State. When Truman was elected in 1948, he named Dulles acting chairman of the American delegation to the United Nations. In 1950, Truman appointed him to the State Department as a consultant.

In short, Dulles came to the office he so greatly desired with almost a lifetime of experience in law and international relations. When he entered it, he luxuriated in it, dedicating himself body and soul to his tasks. He thought nothing of working a 12-hour day or longer and he traveled an average of about 100,000 miles a year. Critics asserted that he "carried the State Department in his hat." But one of Dulles' assistants, Andrew Berding, wrote that it was not unusual for the Secretary to consult with State Department officers from all echelons, high and low. His own knowledge of nations and their problems was encyclopaedic.

When he became Secretary of State he was 64 years old. He was tall, gray-haired, somewhat portly, stoop-shouldered. He often smiled but he was not a humorous man. While reading or listening, he would purse his lips and his mouth puckered and twisted.

He had the Democrats sniping at him before he took office. In the 1952 presidential campaign, Dulles damned the Truman-Acheson policy of "containment" of the Communists as "inadequate and immoral." (The words "moral" and "immoral" often studded his statements on foreign problems.) Next, he got himself into hot water on the question of liberating those European countries that had been enslaved by the Russians after World War II. Eisenhower had spoken of working toward liberation by "peaceful means." Dulles, in a speech on the same subject, omitted the words, "peaceful means." Eisenhower reprimanded him and Dulles thereafter was careful to use the qualifying phrase.

Rather than merely "containing" Communism, Dulles spoke of taking positive action, to *do* something, to "roll back the Iron Curtain." Some of his statements sent cold chills coursing through the chancelleries of Europe.

He missed an opportunity to clarify and perhaps soften such words in an impromptu press conference before Eisenhower's Inauguration. It took place in the Commodore Hotel in New York while Eisenhower was forming his Cabinet.

As men and women emerged from his office, the reporters attempted to buttonhole them to ask what their roles in the new administration might be. Some, like Oveta Culp Hobby and George Humphrey parried the questions, and did so with great charm. Others made a beeline for the elevators. Dulles, however, readily consented to step inside the press room. He seemed eager to talk.

He was asked what he would do about various problems of the Cold War and how his policy would differ from Dean Acheson's. He began contradicting himself and quickly painted himself into some uncomfortable corners. Finally, he ended the conference by saying, somewhat lamely, "Well, I've got a lot of specific thoughts on what we can do but I can't talk about them now."

Dulles held deep religious convictions and one of the main bases of his thinking was that right and justice ultimately must triumph over Godlessness and the forcible imposition of Communist regimes on people. To his critics, this seemed too black-and-white and left little or no room for negotiating agreements. They were soon calling him "inflexible."

He also spoke of "massive retaliation," indicating his belief that if the Communists were convinced that the United States would fight for right and justice, they would be less likely to take further aggressive steps.

In that connection, Dulles stirred up a storm with his statements about what came to be known as "brinkmanship." In an interview with James Shepley of Time and Life Magazines, he was quoted as saying:

"Some say we were brought to the verge of war. Of course we were brought to the verge of war…We've had to look it square in the face—on the question of enlarging the Korean War, on the question of getting into the Indo-China War, on the question of Formosa. We walked to the brink and we looked it in the face. We took strong action. It took a lot more courage for the President than for me. His was the ultimate decision. I did not have to make the decision myself, only to recommend it. The President never flinched for a minute on any of these situations. He came up taut."

Sherman Adams wrote, dryly, that he thought Dulles exaggerated, that in his view, Eisenhower did not come all that close to "the brink" in the three instances cited.

Andrew Berding has written an immensely informative book about foreign policy in which he says Dulles' policy was based, broadly speaking, on six clauses in the Preamble to the Constitution:

"Mr. Dulles extended these ideals into the international sphere. 'To form a more perfect Union' meant to assist in making the United Nations an effective organization for peace. 'Establish justice' meant to promote the sway of international law to bring peace accompanied by justice. 'Insure domestic tranquility' meant to assist other peoples to achieve their just aspirations through peaceful change rather than violence. 'Provide for the common defense' meant to join with other independent nations in a common effort to protect their and our freedoms from any force, particularly international Communism, which sought to destroy them. 'Promote the general welfare' meant to adopt such policies of economic assistance and trade as would stimulate economic development in other nations. 'Secure the Blessings of Liberty' was reflected in all these objectives and also meant to make known to other peoples that the American Revolution was the true revolution for human freedom."[1]

In his Princeton statement, Nixon said Dulles held firmly to four main premises in his dealings with the Communists. They were, Nixon said:

"…in the final analysis that living with the Communists is going to be one of *quid pro quo*, hard bargaining, right down the line.

"Dulles used to say that we must always recognize that we go to conference tables in order to settle differences…they go to conference tables in order to create differences, to increase tensions—always to gain, to win.

"He said, 'We've got to stick and fight and wear them out.' He used to equate it with labor negotiations, where the one who stays awake and keeps at it generally wins…the side with the greatest stamina usually comes out with the best deal.

"Dulles always thought in long-range terms…The Communist thinks in terms of 100 years, and Dulles thought in terms of 100 years."

To further Eisenhower's over-all policy, the framework within which Dulles worked, the Secretary travelled tirelessly. In his six years in office, he logged just under 600,000 miles, flying from capital to capital and conference to conference. The commentator, Murray Kempton, called him "a wandering holy man."

In 1956, Dulles underwent an operation for cancer of the large intestine. He continued to carry on his duties, in spite of sometimes excruciating pain, until illness forced him to resign. When Eisenhower announced this, he had tears in his eyes. Dulles died in May, 1959.

Certainly, Dulles was a controversial figure, a man who stirred strong and utterly contrary feelings about his stewardship as Secretary of State. The opinions of two great statesmen illustrate the point.

---

1 Berding: "Foreign Affairs and You."

Churchill, according to Lord Moran, considered Dulles too rigid with regard to the Russians, and a "terrible handicap" to Eisenhower.

But Chancellor Adenauer, according to C. L. Sulzberger, the distinguished foreign correspondent, saw Dulles as a great man. Writing in The New York Times, Sulzberger said:

"He (Adenauer) makes no effort to conceal his distress with American policy since what he regards as the Augustan Age of John Foster Dulles, his good and equally religious-minded (if Presbyterian, not Catholic) friend.

"Last year, I asked him who and for what reasons he considered the greatest man he had ever met. Without hesitation he arose, not saying a word, and walked over to his desk. He picked up a photograph of Dulles. He handed me the picture, saying, 'There. He thought clearly. He thought ahead with vision of what was coming. And he kept his word. He kept his promises.'"

Eisenhower said of Dulles, "I believe he has filled his office with greater distinction and greater ability than any other man our country has known, a man of tremendous character and courage, intelligence and wisdom."

While campaigning for the Prime Ministership in 1951, Churchill said securing peace was "the last great prize" he sought to win. He did not succeed.

Neither did Eisenhower and Dulles. The Communists brought war to Indo-China and Korea. Their actions in the Formosa Strait and Berlin threatened the peace. They refused Eisenhower's "open skies" proposal as an avenue to disarmament.

Yet it can be said that tensions eased in some degree. Cultural exchanges between the United States and the Soviet Union began in 1955 and continued, varying in numbers with the changes in the temperature of the Cold War. Relations improved with Poland and Yugoslavia. Nixon visited Russia, the first American official of his stature to be seen there in more than a decade. Eisenhower took the bold and imaginative step of inviting Khrushchev to come to the United States in his continuing efforts to build at least a tiny bridge.

Moreover, after the Korean armistice, no Americans died in battle during Eisenhower's tenure. Dulles was instrumental in erecting a set of defensive alliances against the Communists in the Middle East and Southeast Asia. The Suez Crisis of 1956 brought the United States into opposition to Britain, France and Israel but when it was past the Western Alliance held together.

These were notable achievements. History, the long view, will assess John Foster Dulles' role in them.

Crossroads

In 1955, Eisenhower wrote a friend, "No man has ever reached his 70th year in the White House; this may not mean much in itself but... no man has the faintest right to consider acceptance of a nomination unless he honestly believes that his physical and mental reserves will stand the strain of four years of intensive work."

Implicit in this, of course, was the realization that he was nearing 65 and if he attempted to serve out a full second term as President, he would reach his 70th birthday before it ended, a challenge to the historic fact. He appeared to be in perfect health when he wrote the letter. But did it reflect a clairvoyant glimpse of the illness soon to strike him down?

Eisenhower came to dread the thought of slowing down, of failing, through the gradual erosion of mental and physical energies, to fully discharge the duties of the presidency. He wanted to retire anyway and perhaps, as his age advanced, it was right for him to do so. As he neared the crossroads of 1956, Eisenhower could say with Othello, "I do perceive here a divided duty."

The effort began early to wring from him a definite commitment to run for a second term in 1956. One of Eisenhower's first and most powerful supporters, Gen. Lucius Clay, discussed the question with him in 1954. Eisenhower said Clay told him, "I am ready to work for you at any sacrifice to myself because I believe in you. I am not ready to work for anybody else that you can name." It appears to have been a shrewd appeal to Eisenhower's sense of duty. For if Clay and other Republicans of his stature worked only half-heartedly or not at all for another man in 1956 what chance would the party have to elect a President?

As he turned over the pros and cons of the matter, Eisenhower reverted to consideration of his original goals. He had set out to try to advance the outlook for peace in an increasingly dangerous world, to spread the gospel of "dynamic conservatism" and to strengthen and revamp his Party.

Looking back, he found some grounds for satisfaction.

He listed them in another letter which said, "On top of all this, we have made a major tax reduction—the largest single reduction in our history—and if nothing unforeseen occurs, we approach a balanced budget." He took pride in having stabilized the dollar. The cost of living index, he said, varied only one-half to one per cent in his first two years. He called this "possibly the greatest achievement." At the same time, what Eisenhower called "stifling" controls on business had been removed. To further stimulate economic growth he proposed a $101 billion highway building program over a period of 10 years and won Congressional approval for that.

In the sphere of social legislation, he urged Congress to continue a low-cost housing program for another four years and recommended action on slum clearance and broader Social Security coverage. He put through legislation to permit additional immigration in urgent situations.

Eisenhower was highly gratified when the Senate, after years of debate, approved United States participation in the construction of the St. Lawrence Seaway. With Mamie swinging the bottle of champagne, the first atom-powered submarine, Nautilus, slid down the ways. The President announced that the United States would participate in the International Geophysical Year by launching a satellite into outer space.

The Bricker Amendment, designed to limit presidential treaty-making powers, had been defeated after a long and gruelling struggle between the White House and Congressional proponents of the amendment. At the critical point in the fight, Eisenhower sent a strongly worded note to Senator William F. Knowland of California, who had succeeded Taft as Majority Leader. It said, "I am unalterably opposed to the Bricker Amendment…These matters are fundamental…The President must not be deprived of his historic position as the spokesman for the nation in relations with other countries."

He also had to battle Republican conservatives on a quick cut in personal income taxes and the question of extending the excise tax. His principal opponent in these instances was Representative Daniel A. Reed of New York, chairman of the House Ways and Means Committee. Eisenhower used a press conference to make known his views. He disliked the excise tax but he intended to retain it until the way opened for a balanced budget or at least a greatly reduced deficit. The same applied in the question of cutting personal income taxes. He beat Reed on both questions and the cuts in taxes were delayed as he wished.

A business recession had set in but Eisenhower predicted in his 1954 economic message to Congress that it would end soon. By the end of that year, prices on the New York Stock Exchange, which is often a barometer of the economic health of the nation, rose to the highest levels since 1929 and the volume of trading to the highest peak in 21 years. Sherman Adams later wrote, "In fact, 1954 turned out to be the most prosperous year that the United States ever had under a peacetime economy…As one observer said later, in showing that free enterprise could hold its own under pressure with no government intervention other than indirect money control to discourage deflation and inflation, Eisenhower had successfully reversed a 21-year-old trend toward a socialized economy."[1]

But while Eisenhower had a general philosophy about business and the economy he was never doctrinaire in this field. For example he wrote a friend, "Anyone whose business and profits depend upon high protective tariffs is not, by any stretch of the imagination, a rugged individualist."

In contrast with the general prosperity, farm prices and farm income declined. A great hue and cry arose for Eisenhower to dismiss Ezra Taft Benson, Secretary of Agriculture. He refused and was quoted as saying, in a football metaphor, "If I can't stick with Benson, I'll have to find some way of turning in my own suit, or I'll just be known as a damned coward."

In his State of the Union speech of 1953, Eisenhower had touched on the problem of Civil Rights and he pointed to the areas where he said he intended to do something about it. "I propose to use whatever authority exists in the office of the President to end segregation in the District of Columbia, including the federal government, and any segregation in the armed forces," he said.

He put Maxwell Rabb in charge of investigating these sectors and Rabb did a thorough job. Without retracing Rabb's steps through all the labyrinthine structures, an incident that came to light much

---

1 Adams: op. cit.

later is noteworthy. Dr. William Hinton, the first Negro professor at Harvard, stipulated in his will that $75,000 in his estate should be used to establish a Dwight D. Eisenhower Scholarship Fund at Harvard. Eisenhower was not to learn of this until 1962. He wrote:

"Dr. Hinton's will—he died in 1959—provided that this should be done in recognition of steps toward the acceptance of equal opportunities during my administration. When notified by Dr. Nathan M. Pusey, president of Harvard, of the professors sentiments, I told Dr. Pusey that I could not recall having been given a personal distinction that had touched me more deeply."[1]

Moreover, a significant fact was to emerge in a study of the 1956 presidential election. It would show that in 86 urban areas with a high concentration of Negroes, the President increased his share of the votes from 25 per cent to 36 per cent. Southern) Negro precincts which gave Eisenhower 19 per cent of their vote in 1952 would give him 47 per cent in 1956.

On May 17, 1954, the United States Supreme Court ruled unanimously that state-ordered segregation in the schools is unconstitutional and ordered it ended "with all deliberate speed."

Eisenhower foresaw trouble.

In a personal letter, he pointed to "several obvious truths." He said laws are rarely effective unless they represent the will of the majority; Prohibition, he wrote, was an example. He recalled the litigation known as "Plessy vs. Ferguson" in which the Supreme Court in 1896 held that segregation was not unconstitutional. (Plessy, an octoroon, boarded a train in Louisiana and entered a car reserved for white passengers. When he refused to leave, he was jailed. The case eventually reached the Supreme Court which upheld, 7 to 1, the constitutionality of the Louisiana statue under which "separate but equal" facilities were provided by the railroads. One of the Justices' opinion said, "Established usages, customs and traditions, as well as the preservation of public peace and good order must be considered. Gauged by this standard separate public conveyances are not unreasonable nor contrary to the Fourteenth Amendment.") Thus, Eisenhower's letter said, to generations of Southerners, segregation not only was legal but ethical. After 60 years of living with these "established usages, customs and traditions," the Southerner could not be expected to reverse his

---

1   Eisenhower: "Mandate for Change"

beliefs overnight when the Supreme Court of 1954 reversed the ruling of 1896. Eisenhower's letter contained a prophetic note, "When emotions are deeply stirred, logic and reason must operate gradually and with consideration for human feelings or we will have a resultant disaster rather than human advancement."

However, he effectively silenced a diehard who, fulminating against the 1954 Court ruling, said, "There were then (in 1896) wise men on the Court. Now we have politicians."

Eisenhower quietly asked, "Can you name one man on the 1896 Court?"

Relating this incident in a letter, Eisenhower wrote, "He just looked at me in consternation and the subject was dropped."

These were some of the highlights of the domestic scene as the President, looking back in 1955, pondered the question of running for reelection in 1956. The record showed peaks and valleys and Eisenhower was by no means wholly satisfied with it. His feelings about it perhaps are revealed in a letter in which he likens himself to a ship. High winds and waves are battering it, but nonetheless it "manages in spite of frequent tacks and turnings to stay generally along its plotted course and continues to make some, if even slow and painful, headway."

Should he give himself four more years to sail toward his chosen landfalls?

• • •

In his quest for peace, Eisenhower had advanced the plan for an international "atom pool" and it soon became a reality.

Then, in July, 1955, Eisenhower followed this proposal with another and more dramatic offer. He attended a conference in Geneva with Nikolai A. Bulganin, the Soviet Premier, Nikita S. Khrushchev, the new boss of the Communist Party, the British Foreign Secretary, Anthony Eden, and Premier Edgar Faure of France. In the middle of a generalized statement, the President suddenly paused. He turned his head to look directly at Bulganin and Khrushchev and said:

"I should address myself for a moment principally to the delegates from the Soviet Union, because our two great countries admittedly possess new and terrible weapons in quantities which do give rise in other parts of the world, or reciprocally, to the fears, and dangers of surprise attack."

He was speaking from memory, without notes. He continued:

"I propose, therefore, that we take a practical step, that we begin an arrangement very quickly, as between ourselves immediately."

Eisenhower then placed before the Russians the "open skies" plan. It stipulated that the United States and the Soviet Union should furnish each other with complete blueprints of their respective military establishments. Each government would provide facilities for the other to conduct aerial reconnaissance over their respective territories, taking as many photographs as either deemed necessary. Further, "The United States is ready to proceed in the study and testing of a reliable system of inspections and reporting, and when that system is proved, then to reduce armaments with all others to the extent that the system will provide assured results." Eisenhower saw in this project the means of "providing as between ourselves against the possibility of a great surprise attack, thus lessening dangers and relaxing tension."

As before, the Russians were taken aback. They said nothing.

But Edgar Faure said, "I wish the people of the world could have been in this conference room to hear the voice of a man speaking from great military experience. Had this been possible they would believe that something had changed in the world in the handling of this question of disarmament. I am sure that this conference has scored its first victory over skepticism."

The Paris newspaper, Le Monde, never pro-American, said, "Eisenhower, whose personality has long been misunderstood, has emerged as the type of leader humanity needs today."

Prior to this, Eisenhower made a kind of personal appeal to the Russians on the question of unifying Germany. In this instance, he addressed himself to Marshall Georgi Zhukov and said:

"I would particularly like my friend Marshall Zhukov to listen carefully to what I have now to say. I have known him for a long time and he knows that, speaking as soldier to soldier, I have never uttered a single word that I did not believe to be the truth...

"If there is any tendency to delay urgent consideration of the problem of German reunification because of the unhappiness or fear of the united Germany in NATO, then so far as it is possible for the United States to give the assurance of its pledged word, I say here and now: There is no need to fear that situation."

John Hightower, senior diplomatic correspondent of The Associated Press, wrote, "His Open Skies proposal created the most sensational news of the meeting and his private talks with Soviet Defense Minister Zhukov contributed to the impression that he was striving to win the confidence of the Soviet leaders and lay the basis for a Cold War settlement."

But it takes two to make peace and the Communists were not then ready to soften their position nor to halt their global thrusts.

As chief of NATO, Eisenhower had been forced to study the problem of Indo-China where France, for years, had been fighting the Communist-led Viet Minh. The conflict was draining off French strength which was needed in Eisenhower's planning for the defense of Western Europe.

Not long after he came to the White House, the problem of Indo-China had approached the crisis point.

The background of it was this: In the 1860s, using religious persecution of Vietnamese Catholics as a pretext, the French moved to seize by force the Indo-Chinese Peninsula, composed of Viet Nam, Laos and Cambodia. The conquest was completed before the end of the century. As a result of the French intrusion, cleavages soon developed among the Vietnamese, a principal one being between the Buddhists and Catholics, the effect of which has been seen only recently. In 1940, by arrangement with the Vichy government of France, a Japanese army entered Indo-China. Japan occupied the Peninsula until the end of the Pacific War in 1945. Thereafter, as in other parts of Asia, Indo-Chinese nationalists began the drive for independence and an end to the colonial status.

A number of indigenous organizations participated in it, but the Communists, always better organized, took control of the movement. Their leader, Ho Chi Minh, had been working in his country since the early 1920s to prepare for the opportunity that now presented itself. (Under the aegis of France, he had actually been Premier of Indo-China in 1946!) Their military leader was the brilliant tactician, General Vo Nguyen Giap, who directed North Vietnamese operations against American forces. Some of the Viet Minh units had been seasoned in guerrilla operations against the Japanese. The Viet Minh was far more formidable than the French at first realized.

Thus, by the time Eisenhower came to the presidency, about 200,000 French troops and another 200,000 loyal Vietnamese forces had been drawn into the struggle. It had been going on for nearly seven years and little stomach for it remained in metropolitan France.

The President recognized the critical importance of preventing Indo-China from falling into Communist hands. But how to help the French? He made two recommendations to them.

He urged Paris to proclaim to the world that France was not fighting to reimpose colonial rule over Indo-China and to promise the three nations their independence. This the French were unwilling to do until almost the 11th hour of the crisis. Apparently, they feared the effect of such an announcement on the other French colonies, especially Algeria and Tunisia. They gave Eisenhower vague answers on the several occasions when he proposed it.

Second, he worked to internationalize the conflict, to bring in at least token forces from other nations of the Free World, thus making the war in Indo-China part of the worldwide resistance to Communist expansionism. Neither the French nor British responded with any warmth to this suggestion.

And as a military man, Eisenhower was horrified when he learned of the plan to construct a complex of forts at Dien Bien Phu and pen up in them a sizable number of French troops. "You can't do that," he told a French diplomat, "you just can't."

The theory was that the strategically placed complex would force the Viet Minh to emerge from the jungle into the open where French fire-power would decimate them. They did emerge; they were decimated. But slowly they tightened their grip around the fortified area, virtually isolating it from reinforcement and supplies.

Eisenhower considered intervention—but *only* if intervention led to victory. He would not risk the prestige of the United States for anything less. Years later, in another connection, he was to say, "Now I think any time the United States decides to put its hand to anything that is going to be done by force, you've got to go through with it. So when you once appeal to force, a nation such as ours must be successful."

Pessimism increased in France about the possibility of victory. On April 26, the Geneva Conference on Indo-China opened. On May 7, Dien Bien Phu fell. On July 21, the truce was signed. The 1954 Geneva Agreements divided Viet Nam at the 17th Parallel between the Communist North and the non-Communist South.

Eisenhower was not pleased by some features of the Accord but he said in a press conference, "The United States will not use force to disturb the settlement. We also say that any renewal of Communist aggression would be viewed by us as a matter of grave concern."

The Communists did not like the Agreements very much either. One of the first results was the flight of some 850,000 Vietnamese across the Parallel into South Viet Nam. Moreover, during the fighting, the Communists had controlled more of Viet Nam than they now held north of the Parallel. But in all probability, Ho Chi Minh considered the Geneva Agreements only the next-to-last step before the whole of Viet Nam fell into his hands. When the Viet Minh withdrew from the South they left behind in the villages cadres of trained men who set to work clandestinely to convert the politically unsophisticated peasants to Communism. If, as stipulated in the Geneva accord, national elections had been held in 1956, it is wholly probable that Ho Chi Minh would have been elected. However, they were not held.

Eisenhower was determined to keep South Viet Nam free. At about this time, he used his "row of dominoes" analogy to point out that if South Viet Nam fell, the danger of Communist conquest in Laos and Cambodia would increase enormously, and possibly in Thailand and Malaysia.

He took measures to strengthen the new regime in Saigon. He used American naval craft to assist in evacuating about a quarter-million refugees from North Viet Nam. He organized a program of aid for South Viet Nam and ordered that it be implemented directly, rather than through France. When the people overwhelmingly voted to depose the Emperor Bao Dai in 1955 and to establish a Republic under Ngo Dinh Diem, Eisenhower gave Diem all the support he could. He sent American military advisers to train Vietnamese armed forces. In the subsequent Eisenhower years American economic and financial assistance to South Viet Nam increased greatly. But Eisenhower did not commit any American troops. The total of advisers sent to Saigon was less than 1,000.

This program achieved its purposes. Once Diem solved his early political problems, South Viet Nam began to grow stronger. The Vietnamese are intelligent, energetic people. They built a glittering civilization in the past. Left alone, South Viet Nam would have become a showcase for the Free World in the Far East. But it was not to be left alone.

In 1959, a few hundred Communist troops entered South Viet

Nam via the "Ho Chi Minh Trail" from the North. The number increased to about 1,000 in the following year. It was to rise sharply in 1961. But in 1959-60, Diem appeared to be fully in control of the situation. On Oct. 26, 1960, Eisenhower wrote him:

"We have watched the courage and daring with which you and the Vietnamese people attained independence in a situation so perilous that many thought it hopeless. We have admired the rapidity with which chaos yielded to order and progress.

"In five short years since the founding of the Republic, the Vietnamese people have developed their country in almost every sector. I was particularly impressed by one example. I am informed that last year over 1,200,000 Vietnamese children were able to go to elementary school; three times as many as were enrolled five years earlier."

He closed his letter with a pledge—

"Although the main responsibility for guarding that independence will always, as it has in the past, belong to the Vietnamese people and their government, I want to assure you that for so long as our strength can be useful, the United States will continue to assist Viet Nam in the difficult yet hopeful struggle ahead."

Technically, of course, Eisenhower could not guarantee this; he could not commit succeeding administrations to follow his policy. However, on Dec. 14, 1961, Kennedy wrote Diem:

"…we are prepared to help the Republic of Viet Nam to protect its people and to preserve its independence. We shall promptly increase our assistance to your defense effort as well as help relieve the destruction of the floods which you describe. I have already given the orders to get these programs under way."

Nearly four years later, on July 28, 1965, Johnson repeated the earlier statements from Washington. He said:

"…we are in Viet Nam to fulfill one of the most solemn pledges of the American nation. Three Presidents—President Eisenhower, President Kennedy, and your present President—over 11 years, have committed themselves and have promised to help defend this small and valiant nation…We cannot now dishonor our word or abandon our commitment or leave those who believed us and who trusted us to the terror and repression and murder that would follow."

The sound of gunfire in Indo-China had barely given way to uneasy silence before it thundered again in the Far East and reechoed in the White House…Quemoy and Matsu, islands jutting from the sea almost within slingshot range of the Communist mainland.

As the daily plane from Formosa approaches Quemoy, the pilot drops to almost wave-top level in the Straits so that the island's hills screen him from Communist radar on the mainland. Quemoy is mostly rock, naked rock slopes, piles of tawny boulders. Children, long since hardened to shelling from the mainland, play on the boulders and chase each other around the acacia trees. The hills are honeycombed with corridors, gun emplacements, storage rooms, shelters. Usually, some 55,000 Nationalist Chinese troops are massed on Quemoy. From the heights, you can see the streets of Amoy and with binoculars you can read the signs. Quemoy is that close to Communist China. A guard, a tall Manchurian, stands watch on the peak. He gestures toward the mainland. "Some day they will attack," he says. "Let them come. The shrimps will grow fat on their flesh."

On the evening of Sept. 3, 1954, Eisenhower received alarming news about the Offshore Islands. The Communists had been raining shells on Quemoy throughout the day. Throughout the preceding weeks, heavy troop movements into the region directly opposite the islands had been reported. It appeared that the Communists were massing for a major operation. The bombardment could be its prelude.

In a press conference, a correspondent asked Eisenhower "what would happen" if the Communists launched a full-scale invasion of the Offshore Islands and Formosa. He replied, "Any invasion of Formosa would have to run over the Seventh Fleet."

Through the next nine months, the crisis atmosphere continued. It appeared that the Communists, who had often proclaimed their intention to "liberate" Formosa, were now muscling up for the attempt. Eisenhower was prepared to fight if they did.

Formosa has been a controversial subject among Americans and with the Allies of the United States, some of whom recognized Red China, since 1949. In that year, Mao Tse-tung completed the conquest of China. Chiang Kai-shek and some two million anti-Communist Chinese fled to Formosa. Chinese regimes have long considered Formosa an integral part of China, although in the past it was held for long periods by the Dutch, by a rebel leader named Cheng Cheng-kung who used it as a base for fighting the Manchus and by the Japanese. The United States captured it from them in the Pacific War. For both political and military reasons, Truman and Eisenhower kept the Seventh Fleet patrolling the Straits of Formosa to assist in the defense of Formosa.

But Quemoy and Matsu, both about 90 miles west of Formosa, were something else again. If attacked, were they of sufficient value, militarily or politically, to embroil the United States in a war with Red China? Few Americans and virtually none of the Allies of the United States were disposed to fight for some rocky dots in the ocean. What should the President do?

He decided to leave the question unanswered, to keep the Red Chinese guessing. If an attack on the Offshore Islands appeared to be the preliminary to an all-out invasion of Formosa, that would be one thing. But if it were aimed only at the Offshore Islands, that would be another. As a military man, he would make his decision on military grounds.

Meanwhile, he made a dramatic move which he hoped might deter the Chinese Communists. He laid before Congress what became known as the Formosa Resolution, giving him Congressional approval to take whatever military measures he deemed necessary. As Commander-in-Chief of the armed forces, the President already possessed constitutional power to do this. But, remembering the criticism heaped on Harry Truman for not consulting Congress before sending American forces into action in the first days of the Korean War, Eisenhower in effect asked Congress to join him in any action he might be forced to take.

More important, Congressional approval of his request, he said, would clearly demonstrate to the Chinese Reds the "unified and serious intentions" of the United States. His message said:

"In the interest of peace, the United States must remove any doubt regarding our readiness to fight, if necessary, to preserve the vital stake of the Free World in a free Formosa and to engage in whatever operations may be required to carry out that purpose.

"To make this plain requires not only Presidential action but also Congressional action. In a situation such as now confronts us, and under modern conditions of warfare, it would not be prudent to await the emergency before coming to Congress. Then it might be too late. Already the warning signals are flying."

In the Congressional debate that ensued, the President was criticized for not drawing a clear line of defense. Did it embrace Quemoy and Matsu? Or pertain only to Formosa? In effect, his critics asked him to tip his hand to them—and to the Chinese Reds. Among those who supported Eisenhower was Senator George, a Democrat, who said:

"I hope no Democrat will be heard to say that because the President of the United States came to Congress, he is thereby subject to criticism. The President chose a courageous course, a course which would be taken only by a prudent, patient man, who knows the pitfalls along the course and who knows the horrors of war."

Only three senators and three representatives voted against passing the resolution.

In maneuvering for a truce in Korea, Eisenhower had let it be known that he would use atomic weapons unless the Communists agreed to negotiate. When he was asked, in connection with the apparent crisis in the Formosa Strait, whether they would be used, he replied:

"In any combat where these things can be used on strictly military targets and have strictly military purposes I see no reason why they shouldn't be used just exactly as you would use a bullet or anything else. I believe the great question about these things comes when you begin to get into areas where you cannot make sure that you are operating merely against military targets. But with that qualification, I would say, yes, of course they would be used."

Whether the Formosa Resolution plus Eisenhower's clear-cut warning about the use of atomic weapons did in fact deter the Chinese Communists from launching a full-scale attack may never be known. Whatever the reason, the threatened invasion did not materialize.

Eisenhower called this sticky episode "one of the most serious problems of the first 18 months of my administration."

It stands also as another example of his vision and courage. For his hard line, naturally, was unpopular. Fierce criticism arose against the steps he took with respect to Quemoy and Matsu, and the mere mention of using nuclear weapons was, and is, enough to set the world shuddering. Those who did not agree that Formosa was a bastion in the chain of American defenses in the Pacific, those who advocated an accommodation with Red China at any cost, and those who said it would be utter folly to become embroiled in war over two tiny islands—all attacked in full fury, in the United States and in Europe. Eisenhower stood like a rock while the storm beat against him.

It hit Dulles, too. In his Princeton statement, cited earlier, Nixon said:

"But looking at Quemoy and Matsu, there he took on the whole foreign policy Establishment. The State Department was violently against him. I would say that 90 per cent of the career men were cutting his throat day after day. I remember it well, because I agreed with him on the position. I sometimes wonder how he took the heat… The criticism that he received, not only from the undercutting of the people in the State Department, but also the editorials in papers like The New York Times and others, were pretty rough."

Elsewhere in the field of foreign affairs, Eisenhower worked to stimulate foreign trade. He saw Austria and West Germany become sovereign nations again. Solutions were found to the dispute over Trieste, opening the way to Italian participation in the Western Union. His decisions averted a Communist threat in Guatemala.

Yes, he could look back on this part of his record with some satisfaction. But the question remained: Was it sufficient to justify a return to private life? Or should he agree to run again in 1956? Time and again, his thoughts returned to the question.

A glimpse of his state of mind comes from the diary of Lord Moran. The wise and perceptive physician accompanied Churchill to Washington in 1954. After a dinner in the White House on June 25, he related in his diary a conversation with George C. Marshall:

"The President came over and sat down and talked to Marshall about the war. It seemed to be his lot in life to do jobs that he did not care for and he made no secret of the fact that his duties as President came under this heading."[1]

The scene is intriguing. Here is Churchill, failing in health but reluctant to leave office. And in the same room, Eisenhower wrestling with his conscience as to when he can step out of *his*. Of course, like many successful politicians, Churchill had a streak of the actor in his makeup and actors are loath to leave the stage, whereas Eisenhower was no politician and histrionics were totally foreign to his nature.

A little more than a year later, on Sept. 24, 1955, a searing pain in his chest disposed once and for all of the question of running for a second term. Or so he first thought.

---

1 Moran: op. cit.

The Valley of the Shadow

In the dead of night, the sounds in her husband's room wakened Mamie Eisenhower. He seemed restless in bed, fighting the covers. She listened a moment and then crossed the hall and asked him if anything was the matter. He said he felt all right. She returned to her room, but lay awake, listening. She could tell that he had not gone back to sleep. It was after 1:30 a.m. A few moments later, he entered her room and said he had a pain in his chest. He put his hand on the place where he felt the waves of pain.

He swallowed some milk of magnesia and said he was going to try to sleep. Some instinct warned Mamie that he was not, as he thought, merely suffering from indigestion. She telephoned the President's personal physician, Gen. Howard Snyder. She reported the chest pains and described her husband's appearance, flushed and perspiring. "I think you'd better come over," she said.

Snyder at once telephoned for a military car and told the dispatcher the call was urgent. He threw on his clothes over his pajamas and snatched up his medicine bag. In a matter of minutes, he was racing toward 750 Lafayette Street in Denver, the Doud home, where Mamie and the President were visiting her parents.

The President was taking what his aides called a "work-and-play" vacation in Colorado. For four days he had been camping and fishing the trout streams on the western slope of the Rockies with some friends. Up at dawn every day, he had cooked breakfasts himself, sometimes pork sausages or fried mush, sometimes hot cakes and bacon. He had had four glorious days in the open. On Sept. 23, he returned to Lowry Air Force Base, the "summer White House." He appeared to be in top condition, radiating health.

By a strange coincidence, that very day, Sept. 23, Eisenhower dictated a letter to Lyndon Johnson, the Senate Majority Leader, who had been stricken with a heart attack. Johnson was recovering and

Eisenhower expressed his pleasure about this. He wrote, "I most earnestly hope for your sake that you will not let your natural bent for living life to the hilt make you try to do too much too quickly."

The letter was awaiting Eisenhower's signature but he never signed it. A presidential aide, however, sent it to Johnson and when Johnson went to the White House the letter, framed, was placed among his other mementos there.

Eisenhower had eaten a large hamburger and some formidable slices of Bermuda onions at lunch that day. In the afternoon, while playing golf, he felt some distress but attributed it to the raw onions. He went to bed at about 10 o'clock.

When Snyder arrived, he instantly noted the president's color. It was like unbaked biscuit dough. Was he going into shock? By this time, the chest pains had become acute. Snyder administered morphine to stop the pain. The first injection failed to do so and he gave Eisenhower a second one. In a minute or two, the President's eyelids fluttered and he fell asleep. Meanwhile, the physician had checked the President's blood pressure and listened with a stethoscope to his heart beat. He could not yet be certain but he strongly suspected what was happening—a heart attack, coronary thrombosis. He administered drugs to dilate Eisenhower's arteries and to thin his blood.

Snyder did not tell Mamie what he thought a thorough examination would show. He advised her to go back to bed. When she saw her husband in a deep sleep she left the room.

Through the night, the physician sat alone beside Eisenhower's bed, listening and watching. Hours of crisis.

At daylight, an electrocardiogram was taken. It removed any doubt. An artery leading to a front section of the heart wall had been choked off by a blood clot. Deprived of blood, that part of the wall had been "starved," resulting in damage to it.

Snyder now informed Mamie. To the President he said, "We would like to take you to Fitzimmons General Hospital." Rather than taking him downstairs on a stretcher, which would have required tilting it to maneuver around the sharp turns in the staircase, three doctors and Sgt. John. Moaney, his valet, took his weight on their shoulders and assisted him to the street. An automobile waited there. It was a Secret Service car, not an ambulance. At the hospital, he was placed in an oxygen tent. Mamie took a room near his.

The eminent heart specialists, Dr. Paul Dudley White of Boston and Col. Tom Mattingly of the Army Medical Corps, hastened to Denver. Everything that could be done had been done. What might come now lay largely in the hands of fate.

Without knowing Eisenhower's wishes, James G. Hagerty, the press secretary, made a quick and courageous decision when Murray Snyder, his assistant, telephoned the news from Denver. "Play it straight," Hagerty said. "Give it to them absolutely straight." Whereupon, on that Saturday afternoon the nation learned that the President had been felled by a coronary thrombosis. The first announcement called it a "mild" heart attack. Later it was described as "moderate."

When the New York Stock Exchange reopened on Monday, it registered losses estimated at $14 billion, the heaviest in history.

In fact, the question of keeping the nation fully informed about his condition was one of Eisenhower's first thoughts when the effects of the morphine wore off and his mind cleared. "Tell the truth, the whole truth," he said when Hagerty was permitted to see him. "Don't conceal anything."

Thereafter, the doctors issued regular bulletins on his condition. (One, the President thought, was embarrassingly complete; White explained to him that the detail contained in it would hold considerable significance for every doctor.)

There was to be no repetition of the strange situation that had developed after President Wilson was incapacitated by a stroke. For eight weeks then, his wife and his personal physician, Adm. Grayson, ran the country in the sense that they decided which officials could see the stricken President and what matters would be brought to his attention. Mrs. Wilson was quoted as saying, when a group of problem-burdened officials demanded to see the President, "I am not interested in the President of the United States. I am interested in my husband and his health." The business of government, in the full sense of the term, ground to a stop.

This thought, that the business of government must go on, also was uppermost in Eisenhower's mind in the immediate aftermath of his heart attack. Within a week of it, the Cabinet and the National Security Council met. Vice President Nixon presided. Two days later, Eisenhower sent Nixon a note, "I hope you will continue to have meetings of the National Security Council and of the Cabinet over which you will preside in accordance with procedures which you have followed at my request in the past during my absence from Washington."

The constitutional question of Presidential disability did not arise. Eisenhower's recovery proceeded so well that within a short time he was seeing officials and reading reports. He asked Sherman Adams to come to Denver and, on Oct. 1, heard Adams' first report. Thereafter, Adams served as the liaison on matters to be submitted to Eisenhower for decisions.

He began writing long letters to his boyhood friend, Captain Hazlett. They show in detail the questions that most concerned him at this time. They also show that he had not lost his sense of humor.

In one letter, describing the doctors' instruction, he wrote that they told him he must avoid situations which might lead to anger, irritation or frustration. He says he asked them, "Just what do you think the presidency is?"

Again, they advised him against smoking—while smoking themselves. Eisenhower slyly pointed out that he had given up the habit more than six years earlier, and yet he was in a hospital bed while they were up and doing.

He wrote Hazlett that they told him he must eat slowly and that he was finding this admonition hard to obey. "I am always hungry as a bear when I sit down," he said, "and I show it. For 40 years I have been a trial to Mamie. She has done her best but she has made little impression."

Later, he wrote that Dr. White instructed him to lie down for a half hour before lunch "but he does not seem too much concerned whether I actually go to sleep." White prescribed another half-hour rest after lunch but Eisenhower said White did not want him to lie prone then. He could talk or read during the rest period after lunch, provided he avoided controversial subjects.

For exercise after the President left the hospital, White prescribed a short daily swim in a warm pool, a half-hour walk, climbing a staircase of about 20 steps and swinging his golf clubs indoors.

During long conferences, a letter to Hazlett said, Eisenhower was supposed to take 10 minutes out of every hour, leave the room and remain alone "allowing nothing to disturb me."

While he remained in the hospital, he listened to music and to recorded books. His tastes in music ranged from "Claire de Lune" and Beethoven's "Minuet in G" to "Indian Summer" and "Star Dust." He listened to recorded readings of adventure stories, mountain climbing, travel, mysteries and Westerns. His grandson, David, sent him a 25-cent edition of "The McKenzie Raid," a Texas border story.

Nixon visited him two weeks after the attack and later wrote in "Six Crises:"

"President Eisenhower looked startlingly thin and pale, but seemed in good spirits. His mind was agile and he roamed over various subjects including his heart attack and problems of government. I told him he needn't rush to get back to the office, that the team was carrying on his policies without "one iota of jealousy" among us.

A few days after this visit, the President walked a few steps. Then he was taken to the roof of the hospital. There, the photographer snapped a picture of him clad in pajamas of fire-engine red, given him by the newsmen covering the convalescence. The shirt pocket sported five stars and a message, "Much better, thanks."

In another room in the hospital, Mamie began signing her acknowledgments of "get well" messages to her husband. Before she finished, she sent off more than 11,000 replies.

While he rested, steadily progressing, his mind continually turned to political questions, particularly the 1956 presidential election. In one of his first letters to Hazlett, written a month after he entered the hospital, he said he was "vitally concerned" in seeing the Republicans nominate someone who fully subscribed to the Eisenhower program, and moreover, a man who stood a chance of being elected. "This is the tough one," he wrote. At that time, Eisenhower had ruled himself out of the race in 1956. "When I first rallied from my attack on Sept. 24," another letter said, "I recall almost my first conscious thought was, 'Well, at least this settles one problem for me for good and all.'"

A heart attack can be a disaster, psychologically, even after the victim is told he has made a "full recovery." It can bring feelings of failure and even of guilt. There are moments when, inexplicably, he swirls down into the blackest pit of despair. At the most unlikely times, while listening to a symphony or puzzling out a complicated hand of bridge, a sense of dread, waves of reasonless anxiety, may sweep over him. If he thinks about the future, the next birthday or the next Christmas, a question may interpose itself: Will he see these anniversaries?

But opposite to such crumbling introspections, there may come a compulsion to undertake some difficult and demanding task, a challenge which will demonstrate, at least to others, that the cardiac accident has not left him a mental and emotional cripple.

Eisenhower seems to have escaped most of these reactions. If he felt them, his correspondence during that period does not show it. But there was a compulsive note in his eagerness to get back to work, to tackle the full load of the presidency again. Soon after he began receiving visitors, he exhibited signs of impatience if they took much time questioning him about his condition and expressing solicitude; he wanted to get down to business. Dr. White encouraged this. He impressed it on visitors before they saw Eisenhower that cardiac victims do not like to be considered cripples. Moreover, it may have been this rather common compulsion that caused Eisenhower to reverse himself on running again in 1956. Sherman Adams, in "First Hand Report," quoted the President as saying:

"You know, if it hadn't been for that heart attack, I doubt if I would have been a candidate again."

The doctors released Eisenhower from the hospital on Nov. 11, Veterans Day. He spent the weekend at the White House discussing business with Hagerty and Adams. He even went to his office several times on Sunday. On Nov. 14, Mamie's birthday, they drove to the farm in Gettysburg. The first Cabinet meeting was held at Camp David a week later.

He was back in harness and the country breathed more easily again. His life was unchanged except that he was cautioned to avoid fatigue, to keep his weight at 172 pounds rather than the pre-illness 178, and to adhere to a low-fat, low-cholesterol diet, which meant giving up some of the favorite dishes that he cooked himself.

The heart attack was only the first of three potentially fatal illnesses that beset Eisenhower in a period of a little more than two years. On June 9, 1956, an attack of acute ileitis, a disease of the lower intestine, put him in Walter Reed Hospital where surgeons operated to bypass the diseased area. Here, again, the President had the benefit of a quick telephone call from Mamie to Gen. Snyder and a quick diagnosis by the physician, who knew Eisenhower's medical history and suspected he may have had ileitis attacks before. In spite of his heart condition and the condition of his blood, thinned by drugs, he came through the operation without difficulty. As soon as the anaesthetic wore off, he began joking with his nurses and attendants.

On Nov. 26, 1957, he suffered a mild stroke, although the White

House did not use that term to describe the cerebral spasm. For a short time it left him unable to speak or read.

In each instance, the President recovered with remarkable speed. However, each forced him to consider the question: Was he capable of continuing to bear the physical and mental strain of the presidency?

He had little doubt when he returned to Washington after the heart attack. In Denver, in the space of about six weeks, he had discussed problems with 66 officials and other persons. To that degree, he had resumed his duties.

The operation for ileitis came after he had announced his decision to run for a second term. It did not affect that decision; a few days after the operation, he was in a conference with Chancellor Konrad Adenauer of Germany.

After the stroke, he set himself a rigorous test, and then bolstered it with an interesting performance for his own benefit, to determine his fitness to remain in office. This exercise is described in a succeeding chapter.

Through the end of 1955 and the early months of 1956, he continually weighed the pros and cons of seeking a second term. Long letters embodying his thoughts on the question began going to Hazlett again.

The President said he discovered in early November, six weeks after the heart attack, that "a great many people" thought he could and should run again. This astounded him. "I had a letdown feeling that approached a sense of frustration," he said. Continuing, he told Hazlett that if he could have anticipated such sentiment, he would have issued a statement saying he would determine as soon as possible whether his physical condition would permit him to finish out his first term, "but that I would thereafter retire from public life."

His letters reflect less concern about what the crushing burden of the presidency might do to him than what he might do to the office, if without realizing it, he slowed up for lack of physical and mental energy. He recalled that during the Second World War he had put himself in forward positions and flown over battle zones where he could have lost his life. But, he wrote, "great causes, movements and programs not only outlive, but are far more important, than the individuals who may be their respective leaders." He said he had emphasized to many persons that it was of no great importance to him if serving a second term should imperil his life.

On the other hand, he could readily picture himself with failing powers and the dire consequences of this to the United States. He foresaw that loyal subordinates would not be likely to let him know what they could see. He said they would try to make up for his failures and shortcomings and he underscored the word "try."

With cold objectivity, he told Hazlett that he assumed the possibility of another heart attack would be greater "during this year," 1956, than later. He anticipated the "tirades of demagogues and newspaper quarrels" and tried to calculate their effects on his nerves and temper. He indicated that, although he tended to ignore these "venomous" features of an election campaign, he felt that they might enhance the possibility of a second heart attack.

Generally, Eisenhower did ignore personal criticism. Every President, he knew, had been subject to it and he was prone to say that one of his heroes, Lincoln, was "more vilified than admired." But a thread of irritation runs through the letters when his illnesses were used as the basis for attacks. He noted that a man "has taken the trouble" to total up the number of days when the President, allegedly, had been unable to carry out his duties, 143 after the coronary thrombosis and 42 after the ileitis operation, according to this calculation. "Nothing is said about the fact that in Denver, within five days of my initial attack," he had been called upon to make decisions, he wrote, "while in my last operation I had to be functioning again in the space of three days." A critical columnist wrote that ileitis recurs within two years in one out of three cases, whereas the doctors told him it is a "young man's disease" and rarely recurs in a man his age. All this, of course, went into the effort to portray him as a "part-time President." There were suggestions that because of his illnesses he could not be reelected. Grist for partisan political mills. If it was designed to discourage Eisenhower, it backfired. An "I'll-show-'em" note appears in his correspondence.

The letters during this period cite more reasons for running again in 1956 than for moving to the sidelines.

He wrote of his hopes to promote mutual confidence, "and therefore peace," among nations. Similarly, he hoped to convince the American people that they "must avoid extremes" in finding solutions to national problems. "If I could be certain that my efforts would really promote these two things," Eisenhower said, "I shall certainly never have any cause to sympathize with myself—no matter what happens."

These considerations, it appears, lay uppermost in his mind.

Next, he felt a sense of personal responsibility in keeping his Cabinet together and the question of his successor. He wrote, "...I think we have put together in the Executive Branch the ablest group of civilians that has worked in government during the long years I have been around Washington. If I had to quit, no matter who might be elected in my place, there would be a tendency for this band to scatter. After all, two or three of them are even older than I, and most of them have business affairs and interests that attract them to a freer existence than they can lead here."

As to a possible successor, he said he had tried "to acquaint the public with the qualities of a very able group of young men," but none had emerged, he felt. He reproached himself for what he called his "failure."

Apart from these matters, he said (as if Hazlett didn't know!), "I am a competitor, a fighter...reluctant to ever accept defeat."

He found himself awakening early, sometimes at 4:30 or 5 o'clock in the morning. "I think it is fair to say that it is not worry or useless anxiety about the past, *but a desire to attack the future* that gets me into this annoying habit," another letter said. (Italics supplied.) The letter is dated Jan. 23, 1956, about a month before he announced his decision to seek a second term in the White House.

In mid-February, Eisenhower's doctors ran a series of hospital tests on him and having studied the findings, Dr. White said, "Medically, the chances are that the President should be able to carry on an active life satisfactorily for another five to 10 years." The physician added that if Eisenhower ran for a second term he would vote for him.

Meanwhile, although Eisenhower's personal correspondence indicates that he had virtually made up his mind to run, he sought the opinions of members of his family, friends and political associates. The politicians, of course, were unanimous: Run! They told him, knowing his deep concern for peace, that the outlook for it would be enhanced immensely if he remained in the White House. And they said progress had been made toward remolding his party along the lines of his philosophy, as evidenced by the election of 39 new state chairmen since 1952. Family councils were divided. His son, John, and his brother, Milton, (on whose judgment the President frequently leaned) argued against a second term on grounds that it would shorten his life expectancy. Mamie, however, took exactly the opposite view.

She pointed out that for well over a decade he had been in or close to the centers of great power, making or helping to make decisions affecting not only the United States but often the entire world. He had known high drama and great satisfactions. She felt that he might be restless and bored if he retired and that this could be potentially more dangerous than if he continued his work, however heavy.

She may have been thinking about one of his own comments. In a press conference in 1955, Marvin Arrowsmith, a distinguished White House correspondent, had asked him a shrewd question, designed to fathom the President's intentions with respect to running for a second term. Arrowsmith asked him how he now felt about the game of politics. The President replied that he did not like politics when the word was used in the derogatory sense. But he said:

"Mr. Arrowsmith, any man who finds himself in a position of authority where he has a very great influence on the efforts of people to work toward a peaceful world, toward international relationships that will eliminate or minimize the chances of war, all that sort of thing, well, of course it is a fascinating business. It's a kind of thing that would engage the interest—intense interest—of any man alive. It's a wonderful experience."

This was almost the identical thought expressed by Theodore Roosevelt, who gloried in the uses of power more than Eisenhower ever could. Roosevelt had said, "It has been very wearing but I have thoroughly enjoyed it, for it is fine to feel one's hand guiding great machines with at least the purpose, and I hope the effect, of guiding it for the best interests of the nation as a whole."

During the winter months of 1955-56, every gathering in Washington turned into a guessing game about Eisenhower's intentions. Would he run again? The subject dominated all conversations.

The President was playing cat-and-mouse with the correspondents (and obviously enjoying it) when they tried in myriad ways to divine his plans. These evasions were studied closely and interpreted differently. But the majority opinion held that he would not run. On the part of the Democrats no doubt this was wishful thinking. More objective observers arrived at the same conclusion on grounds that his heart wasn't really in his work, that his illnesses had taken more out of him than was generally realized, that he was disillusioned by the lack of support given him by the Republican Old Guard, etc., etc.

However, there seemed little question about the feelings of the average voter. In several cities and small communities, I went from house to house, ringing doorbells, asking questions. The responses were lopsided. The great majority said they hoped he would run and that the possible uncertainties about his health and his ability to complete a second term would not deter them from voting for him. The dissenters in some instances said, "He's such a wonderful man, and I am afraid another four years in that ghastly job would kill him. So I hope he doesn't run."

In his press conference of Feb. 29, while hundreds of reporters sat on the edges of their chairs, unusually still, and poised to begin scribbling like lightning, Eisenhower announced his decision "…my answer will be positive, that is, affirmative."

That night he went on television and radio, talked candidly about the question of his health, explained his decision to run again and described what he hoped to do if reelected.

Some years earlier he wrote in a letter to a friend, "I believe in the jury system and I believe by and large, there is no jury in the world as accurate as the entire American people, even if they make errors occasionally."

He was now preparing to go before that jury again. This time its verdict would be based, not alone on personality and a war hero's glamor, but on his record as President.

He wanted to win an impressive victory, less for reasons of personal satisfaction than for the strong political position it would give him. "Unless I win by a comfortable majority," he wrote Hazlett, "I would not want to be elected at all."

Being limited to two terms by the Constitution, Eisenhower would be a "lame duck" President, Eisenhower's letter continued. As such, he said he might have even less influence in his own party than he had in the first four years. But a massive outpouring of support by the people would demonstrate that he was by no means a "waning star, politically," and he believed, in that case, that the individual Republican officeholder would try to win his goodwill and seek his support in future elections.

He made a second point in this letter, and it is significant in that it foreshadowed a different President from the one Washington had seen so far.

Eisenhower often was accused of being weak-kneed with respect to Congress, of refusing to twist arms and crack the whip to force through desired legislation. In this, he puzzled even some members of his official family when he failed to use the great levers of power at a President's disposal to pressure the men on Capitol Hill. In the letter to Hazlett, Eisenhower said he probably would again need some support for his programs from the Democrats and he wrote "…this strength can be marshaled on both sides of the aisle *only* (his underscoring) if it is generally believed that I am in a position to go to the people over the heads of the Congressmen—and either help them or cause them trouble in their own districts."

Clearly, this was not the Eisenhower of the first term.

By the time he began campaigning in the Fall, the President had been through two serious illnesses. A Massachusetts Congressman had said of George Washington, "Time has made havoc upon his face." Time had left its mark on Eisenhower's. The lines were deeper and it was a thinner face. But his eyes were as searching as ever and when he grinned he seemed little changed.

Nor had the illnesses cut into his energies. Or perhaps he simply drove himself harder as he campaigned. At any rate, on one occasion he returned to Washington at 3 a.m. from a whirl through Oklahoma and was at his desk at 8 o'clock. Two days after his 66th birthday, he delivered speeches in Minneapolis and St. Paul and stood up in his car, waving to the crowds along a 30-mile route that took more than an hour to cover. Then he flew on to Seattle. It was a chilly night and comparatively few enthusiasts lined the route from the airport to the heart of the city. It had been a long, hard day and it might have been expected that he would rest quietly in the car en route. Instead, whenever he spotted a cluster of people waiting to see him, he bobbed up like a jack-in-the-box, arms raised high in the familiar V-sign, and flashing his grin.

After two puzzling incidents, Nixon again was nominated for the vice presidency. First, Eisenhower bewildered him when he told Nixon to "chart your own course" with respect to 1956 and the ensuing four years if the Republicans won the coming election. The President had not meant that he did not want Nixon as his running mate. He thought a major Cabinet office, Secretary of Defense for example, would give Nixon a better showcase in which to display his abilities than would the vice presidency. However, he did not spell out this thought, leaving Nixon in the dark for a time. When Nixon finally said he would prefer to retain the vice presidency, Eisenhower replied that he was "delighted." Then, Harold Stassen, the President's adviser on disarmament, entered the picture. He told Eisenhower that his own polls indicated that Nixon would hurt the ticket and that he intended to launch a movement to advance the candidacy of someone else. Eisenhower, instead of smothering this family squabble at birth, told Stassen, in effect, that he was at liberty to do as he pleased. So, to the Democrats' delight, Stassen started a "dump Nixon" movement. It aborted, of course, and ended in a political farce with Stassen delivering the nominating speech for Nixon at the GOP convention.

The Democrats renominated Adlai Stevenson and named Senator Estes Kefauver of Tennessee for the vice presidency. In a personal letter, Eisenhower said he did not consider this a strong ticket. He wrote that he thought Senators Lyndon B. Johnson or John F. Kennedy would be more formidable. Which indicates that Eisenhower had some political ESP, even though he never fathomed the nuances of politics.

In the opening stages of the campaign, the President ignored the Democrats' attacks on him. But Stevenson stung him when he fired a shot at Milton Eisenhower and he replied to this. Then, Truman described the administration as "this bunch of racketeers in Washington" and Eisenhower began fighting. "This is more than political bunk," he said, "it is willful nonsense. It is wicked nonsense." On Oct. 1, he returned to the attack. "For 20 years," he said in a speech, "the opposition talked about the St. Lawrence Seaway, yet it was repeatedly shelved, bypassed and blocked. This administration acted and got the Seaway going. As a result, two years from now, great ocean ships will dock here in Cleveland." He reminded his audiences that the Department of Health, Education and Welfare came into existence only 81 days after his Inauguration and said more homes had been built "since January, 1953, than in any comparable period in our history."

Characteristically, however, he set boundary lines of propriety in the campaign and refused to cross them for political advantage.

For example, he refused to capitalize on a statement about unemployment attributed to Stevenson. The Democratic candidate was quoted as saying, "All the news is good," in answer to a question about unemployment in Detroit. Hagerty discussed this remark with Adams and then issued a statement excoriating Stevenson for describing jobless workers as "good news" for the opponents of the administration. But when Eisenhower was asked to comment, instead of expressing pious indignation, he defended Stevenson. He said he felt sure Stevenson had been misquoted.

Nor was this the first time he declined a golden opportunity to demean a political opponent. In November, 1953, Brownell broke open a hornet's nest in a Chicago speech about the Harry Dexter White case. He asserted that Truman, although advised by the FBI that White had Communist connections, nonetheless promoted him to a high post in government. Truman hotly denied it. Blasts and counterblasts came from all directions. At Eisenhower's news conference after Brownell's speech, the correspondents put the President on the grill. It was perhaps his roughest session with them, but it was their duty to elicit as much light as possible about the controversy. Out of 32 questions posed that day, 30 concerned the White case. One reporter asked Eisenhower's opinion of Truman's part in it. The President replied, calmly, "I don't believe—put it this way—a man in that position knowingly damaged the United States. I think it would be inconceivable."

Whether the Stevenson and White episodes could be considered legitimate political ammunition depends on the point of view. By Eisenhower's standards, they were not legitimate and he refused to take advantage of them.

The Republican campaign slogan was "peace, prosperity, progress."

Then, toward the end of the campaign, Israel, Britain and France mounted a joint expedition against Egypt after Gamal Abdel Nasser seized the Suez Canal. It posed a grave threat to peace in the world. Eisenhower dropped the campaign and devoted himself full time to the problems of stopping the fighting and searching for a settlement in Egypt.

As for prosperity, the GOP had much to boast about. The Gross National Product soared to $408 billion in the second quarter of 1956, a record. By the end of the year it reached $414 billion. Secretary of Labor James P. Mitchell reported in August that employment also set a record at 66,800,000. The Budget for that fiscal year envisaged a surplus of $400 million.

Some features of what Eisenhower meant by progress were reflected in his special messages to Congress. He asked for an expenditure of $2 billion over a five-year period for public school construction. He announced a billion dollar soil bank plan and asked for legislation to finance a $250 million program for medical research and teaching facilities over a five-year period. He proposed sweeping changes in the immigration laws. In spite of doubters and diehards, he approved a program for increased exchanges of information with the Soviet Union and more reciprocal visits by citizens of the two countries.

In a personal letter, Eisenhower wrote that he felt that the "constructive work" completed in his first term had been overshadowed by the noisy controversies generated by McCarthy, the Bricker Amendment and especially the Dixon-Yates case.

The latter episode gave the Democrats a basis for attacking him as a backer of "give-away" programs. It rose from the 20-year-old struggle between the federal government and the privately owned electric power companies. In 1953, the Tennessee Valley Authority sought funds to build a Steam-generated electric plant at Fulton, Tennessee, because of the growing power needs of Memphis. Eisenhower opposed this and Congress refused to appropriate the money. Then a weird, Rube Goldberg kind of arrangement was devised. The Atomic Energy Commission, largest customer of TVA, would contract with two private utility companies for a certain amount of electricity which the AEC would then relay to TVA for delivery to Memphis. The president of the two companies were named Dixon and Yates. Their two firms, of course, would thus get a slice of the cake. After the contract was signed, it became known that a federal officer who had helped engineer the strange arrangement was an official of the banking firm chosen to finance it. For the Republicans, it was an embarrassing disclosure. However, Memphis rescued the administration in 1955 by announcing it would build its own municipal generating plant.

Eisenhower often said he belonged to neither school, exclusively, in the controversy over public versus private power.

There is much to be said for both sides. When the federal government went into the business of generating tax-free electricity in the 1930s, the privately owned utilities, which pay taxes, found themselves competing at a disadvantage. Why should the taxpayers in the rest of the country subsidize, in effect, the users of electricity in the region served by the Tennessee Valley Authority? Moreover, the utilities assert, they are more efficient and *could*, if untaxed, provide their customers with cheaper electricity than the government does. On the other hand, TVA unquestionably has greatly benefited the region it serves through flood control and development of recreational facilities around the lakes created by the government-built dams. In the 1930s, only about 11 per cent of the farms in the nation were electrified largely because, in a thinly settled region, a private utility would lose money if it strung a power line to perhaps only four or five customers spread over a wide area. The REA co-operatives, financed by the government, solved this problem. The production of aluminum requires a tremendous amount of electricity. Without the great government-built dams, the problem of providing aluminum for the armadas of aircraft needed during the Second World War would have been acute. Other examples could be cited of the advantages of government-generated electricity.

The public versus private power issue is the perfect battleground for the conservative and liberal. Is it "creeping Socialism?" Or is this the object example of government doing for the people what they cannot do, or do so well, for themselves?

In any case, Eisenhower said in his letter that Dixon-Yates and other controversies "have come to mean 'Republicanism' to too many people," and that they obscured what he considered his solid achievements.

He was by no means satisfied with what had been accomplished in his first term and therefore he was anxious to "attack the future" if the "jury" gave him a second mandate.

On the evening of Nov. 6, he heard the verdict. He had carried 41 states with 457 electoral votes and had won a record popular vote. This surpassed the landslide of 1952 when he carried 38 states with 442 electoral votes.

After four years, the people still "liked Ike." Only more so.

Laws and the Man

Over the trans-atlantic telephone, Eisenhower said to Anthony Eden, "I don't give a darn about the election."

The date was Nov. 6, 1956, Election Day. As the President and Prime Minister conferred, millions of voters were registering a preference between Eisenhower and Adlai Stevenson. Eisenhower's thoughts, however, were not on the election. Whatever might happen at home, he was primarily concerned that day with the Middle East and, specifically, with the Suez Canal. From its banks, the shadow of nuclear war rose and spread across the world.

A week earlier, Israeli forces had invaded Egypt and swept to the Canal's edge. There they stopped. Then, following an ultimatum, British troops landed at Port Said and French commandos entered Port Fuad. On Nov. 6, Bulganin issued a series of threats, brandishing Soviet rockets, and expressing "determination to use force to crush the aggressors and to restore peace in the East." He used language seldom found in such exchanges. A letter went to Prime Minister Ben-Gurion accusing Israel of "criminally and irresponsibly playing with the fate of the world." If Bulganin meant what he said, it was a supremely dangerous hour.

Apart from the danger, Eisenhower was heartsick over the events in Egypt. For more than three months, as the crisis developed, he had been arguing against the use of force after Gamal Abdel Nasser seized the Canal. In a radio and television broadcast, he would say, "There can be no peace without law. And there can be no law if we were to invoke one code of international conduct for those who oppose us and another for our friends."

Nor could he, in effect, have simply looked the other way and taken no position at all regarding the aggression against Egypt.

Now he found himself in the painful position of opposing the two oldest allies of the United States. He called the British "my right arm." Further, he knew most of the British leaders personally and considered them his friends. He had worked with some of them during the Second World War. However, he considered that the wrong course had been taken and moral duty compelled him to disavow his friends in this.

He acted as a statesman of high integrity and courage during the Suez crisis. When it had passed he moved quickly to heal the wounds it caused and to search for solutions to the perennial problems that brought it about.

They were deeper than the events that immediately preceded it…

On July 26, Nasser seized the Suez Canal and nationalized the Suez Canal Company. Britain was the largest stockholder in the Company, the head offices of which were in Paris. Both nations reacted vigorously, determined not to let Nasser "get away with it."

In Washington, critics of the administration promptly claimed that Nasser's action came as a result of the United States' "abrupt" withdrawal of an offer of financial assistance in building the giant Aswan Dam on the Nile. Dulles replied that the Egyptians knew, long before they asked for a definite answer, that Congress had taken a position against the loan and that also for other reasons, the answer would be "no." Thus, Dulles said he "suspected" the withdrawal of the offer hid merely provided Nasser with the pretext for an action he had been planning for two years.

Yet, and ironically, Dulles at one time had been courting Nasser. When the Colonel first came to power Dulles seems to have regarded him as pro-Western and an instrument for resisting Soviet efforts to penetrate the Middle East. Egyptian political leaders often said, "Having rid ourselves of one colonizing power we are not so stupid as to fall into the hands of another." Moreover, Nasser seemed primarily concerned with Egypt's domestic problems and indisposed toward foreign adventures. In secret, Dulles established a special desk in the State Department to concentrate on Egyptian problems and to search for avenues to ease the hostility between the Arab nations and Israel. Relations were good between the United States and Nasser.

Then, early in 1955, he opened negotiations for a $27 million consignment of American arms. The State Department stalled. Nasser then turned to the Communists and obtained a much larger consignment from Czechoslovakia. On July 19, the United States withdrew the offer of funds for the Aswan Dam, presumably because the Egyptian economy could not support the heavy burdens Nasser had placed on it.

Dulles' policy of trying to build up the Colonel as a stabilizing factor in the Middle East had backfired.

At any rate, a week later Nasser made his dramatic move. A shudder of dread ran through Western Europe and particularly Britain and France. They felt a garrote around their necks.

It took the form of Middle Eastern oil. In 1955, Western Europe imported 130 million tons of oil, of which 100 million tons came from the Middle East. If Nasser chose to close the Canal and shut down the pipelines bringing oil to the Mediterranean, their industrial establishments would quickly be in desperate straits. Eden estimated that British oil reserves would be exhausted in about six weeks and that smaller European nations had even smaller amounts in reserve.

He immediately ordered the British Chiefs of Staff to work out a contingency plan for military action. The American ambassador to Paris, Douglas Dillon, reported to the President that the French Foreign Minister, Christian Pineau, was comparing Nasser's action with Hitler's seizure of the Rhineland in 1936. Together, the French and British began studying the military factors involved in restoring the status quo ante with respect to the Canal.

But even if Nasser did not close the Canal, and he gave no sign of such intentions, the British and French expressed doubt that the Egyptians would be able to operate it without foreign pilots and technicians.

From the first, Eisenhower considered these fears groundless. It will be recalled that in 1922 he had served in the Panama Canal Zone and had familiarized himself with the operations of that waterway. He knew they were far more complicated than those of the Suez. He had little doubt that the Egyptians could keep it running without interrupting the traffic. Events soon demonstrated that he was right. On Sept. 15, Egyptian pilots brought through a convoy of 13 ships. By the end of the week, 254 ships, without foreign assistance, went through the Canal.

Thus, Eisenhower told Eden, if Nasser abided by the Constantinople Treaty of 1888 which provided for the protection of the "world's biggest public utility," and if the Egyptians demonstrated the ability to keep it running, he could see no moral or legal justification for the use of force now.

He came to believe that Eden and the French were looking beyond the single issue of the Canal to the opportunity to "deflate or remove" Nasser, as he put it in a personal letter, and to restore Western prestige in the Middle East.

In that broader context, Eisenhower saw the main factors.

Hostility between the Arabs and Israel caused a succession of raids and reprisals across the borders, a kind of chain reaction in which civilians on both sides were killed. Ben-Gurion told the Israeli Parliament that "He (Nasser) organized and built up in all the Arab countries special units of murderers who crossed the borders to sow terror among workers in the fields and civilians in their homes...nor did he conceal that his central purpose was to attack Israel at the first suitable opportunity and wipe her off the earth." Of these border tragedies, Eisenhower wrote in "Waging Peace," "Israel often retaliated with what seemed merciless severity."

Nasser envisioned a Pan-Arab Coalition whose twin enemies, he said, were "imperialism" and Israel. Recalling the era of European colonialism in the Middle East was, of course, a powerful bellows for fanning the fires of Arab nationalist emotions. In a speech after seizing the Canal, Nasser said, "Arab nationalism has been set on fire from the Atlantic Ocean to the Persian Gulf. Arab nationalism feels its existence, its structure and strength." The French claimed that Nasser's hand could be seen in the activities of the Algerian nationalists, and the British claimed to see it in Cyprus, one of their principal military bases in the Mediterranean. Anti-Western broadcasts by the "Voice of the Arabs," a powerful radio station in Cairo, brought official protests from the United States, Britain and France. And finally, Nasser's success in obtaining a huge consignment of arms from Czechoslovakia added to the tension building up in the Middle East, especially in Israel.

Another factor was "the Bear," as Western diplomats often call Russia. For centuries, the Russians had been attempting to expand into the Middle East. "The Bear" now saw the opportunity to dip his paw into troubled waters. The Soviets, like Nasser, began denouncing "imperialism" and "colonialism," threatening to meet force with force in Egypt, and in general, attempting the role of friend and champion of the Arabs.

And finally, running through this tangled and increasingly dangerous skein of events, many persons on both sides of the Atlantic thought they saw a parallel in recent history and said the West should draw a lesson from it. In the Era of the Dictators, from Manchuria to Munich, collective action against them might have halted aggression before it finally exploded into World War II. Or so it is often argued. Eden's memoirs reflect almost a preoccupation with the fateful events of those years and the possible parallel in Nasser's case. If Nasser intended to follow a path of aggression, then he must be scotched at once, before he became even more dangerous.

Up to a point, Eisenhower agreed about this. He wrote Hazlett, "I do not quarrel with the idea that there is justification for such fears, but I have insisted long and earnestly that you cannot resort to force in international relationships because of your fear of what might happen in the future."

He rejected the thought of a "preventive war," generally, and certainly in the specific problem now confronting him.

His tactics were to play for time, to apply the brakes against British and French action in Egypt. He sent an envoy, Robert Murphy, to London with instructions merely to "hold the fort." Dulles and the State Department legal expert, Herman Phleger, came later. Weeks of tedious conferences followed in which Dulles used all the lawyer's devices for stalling. Other conferences concerned a proposed Canal Users Club, and technical questions of employing the Club to operate the Canal. Murphy wrote in "Diplomat Among Warriors" about the atmosphere in London:

"I was left in no doubt that the British government believed that Suez was a test which could only be met by the use of force…Pineau did not conceal his contempt for what he called American naivete. He acted as if he had received a blank check from the United States government, but he did not take me into his confidence and I never was privy to French secret plans."

Summer faded into Autumn. The time approached when Eisenhower must begin campaigning, discussing subjects for speeches, itineraries, tactics. But he wrote Hazlett—

"Nasser and the Suez Canal are foremost in my thoughts. Whether we can get a satisfactory solution to this problem and one that tends to restore rather than further to damage the prestige of the Western Powers, particularly of Britain and France, is something not yet resolved."

Whatever the difficulties, the President held firmly to his faith in international adjudication of such disputes. The letter continues:

"In this kind of world we are trying to establish, we frequently find ourselves victims of the tyrannies of the weak. In an effort to promote the rights of all, and observe the equality of sovereignty as between the great and small, we unavoidably give to the little nations opportunities to embarrass us greatly. Yet there can be no doubt that in the long run such faithfulness will produce real rewards."

Negotiations continued in London and the Australian Prime Minister, Robert G. Menzies, went to Cairo for talks with Nasser. Suddenly the news came that Britain and France had ordered the evacuation of their nationals from Egypt, Jordan, Lebanon and Syria. The implications of this move seemed only too clear.

Eisenhower wrote Eden on Sept. 2, "I am afraid, Anthony, that from this point forward, our views on this situation diverge…Even now, military preparations and civilian evacuation exposed to public view seem to be solidifying support for Nasser which has been shaky in many quarters…"

A curtain dropped between the President and the military preparations then taking place. The French had advised him that they had furnished Israel with 12 Mystere fighter aircraft. Then, on the basis of reconnaissance, Eisenhower learned that the number had increased to 60. The volume of radio traffic between Paris and Israel grew much heavier. Dulles was puzzled and unable to interpret the meaning of these moves. Robert Murphy wrote that his wartime colleague, Harold MacMillan, then Chancellor of the Exchequer, kept him informed about Anglo-French plans up to a point—"except French encouragement to Israel. This never was revealed to any American, privately or otherwise."

As for Eden, Eisenhower wrote in a letter to a friend:

"All these thoughts I communicated to Eden time and again. It was undoubtedly because of his knowledge of our bitter opposition to using force in the matter that when he finally decided to undertake the plan, he just went completely silent."

In the evening of Oct. 29, the Israelis struck.

A battalion of paratroopers dropped into the Mitla Mountains, about 30 miles east of Suez. A four-pronged attack by land forces followed. In five days, overrunning fortified positions and slicing through Egyptian infantry along the way, the Israelis gained all their objectives.

Their forces stood on the east bank of the Suez Canal. They captured huge depots of weapons and ammunition and put out of action some 45,000 Egyptian troops. It was a swift and brilliant operation.

On Oct. 30, Britain and France addressed an ultimatum to Israel and Egypt, demanding that both should withdraw their forces to lines 10 miles away from the Canal. Inasmuch as it lies deep inside Egyptian territory, Nasser rejected the ultimatum. Whereupon, Anglo-French forces moved out of Cyprus by air and sea. By Nov. 6, these troops also reached the Canal.

Eisenhower went before the nation on television and radio on the night of Oct. 31. He reviewed the background of the Suez dispute and the military operations then taking place.

"The United States was not consulted in any way about any phase of these actions," he said. "Nor were we informed of them in advance."

The United States would not become involved in the fighting, he said. He pinned his hopes on the United Nations and said, "We went to the United Nations with a request that the forces of Israel return to their own land and that hostilities in that area be brought to a close. This proposal was not adopted—because it was vetoed by Great Britain and France."

The next step would be to bring the problem into the General Assembly, the President continued, where "with no veto operating, the opinion of the world can be brought to bear in our quest for a just end to this tormenting problem." (The General Assembly adopted an American resolution calling for a cease-fire by a vote of 64 to 5.) The President then came to the core of his position and said:

"In all the recent troubles in the Middle East, there have indeed been injustices suffered by all nations involved. But I do not believe that another instrument of injustice—war—is the remedy for these wrongs.

"The peace we seek and need means much more than the mere absence of war. It means the acceptance of law, and the fostering of justice in all the world."

Meanwhile, Bulganin was firing off crudely worded messages to London, Paris and Tel Aviv in which he spoke of "rocket weapons." In other statements, he hinted that Soviet "volunteers" might soon appear in the zone of hostilities in Egypt. He said bluntly that he would use force to "crush the aggressors."

Robert Murphy reported that, on hearing these threats, a highly placed official in the State Department cried out, "We must stop this before we are all burned to a crisp!"

As always in a crisis, Eisenhower remained utterly calm. If, as Sherman Adams later said, this was the President's "worst week" in all the years Adams worked with him, the President did not show it.

To add to his burdens, a group of Republican politicians called on him and told him he might lose the election because, in opposing Israel, he might alienate the many Zionist sympathizers in the United States. Eisenhower conceded that the emotions of these people no doubt were deeply involved but that he believed in their good judgment. In fact, he noted a "courageous" speech by Jacob Javits, a New York Republican, who was campaigning for a Senate seat, defending the administration's position and urging bipartisanship on the question.

Eisenhower also noted, in a personal letter, that he thought Prime Minister Ben-Gurion might feel that, because of the approaching election, Eisenhower would not take a stand against Israel's military operations. He said he instructed the State Department to disregard any political or election considerations in handling the problem. He couched the order in emphatic language.

The Suez Crisis showed Eisenhower's farsightedness and courage. It also revealed his generous nature. He could have let it be known publicly, before the military operations against Egypt began, that the United States government opposed them. In that event, Eden's government might have fallen. Instead, Eisenhower wrote Hazlett that some of his maneuvers "have been handled in secret" and he wrote of his "long, patient and hard work" to dissuade the British and French. "There would have been the greatest political trouble in Britain and probably in France," his letter continued. "*So we just had to let people think that we acted on the spur of the moment and astonished our friends by taking the action we did. Actually, they knew exactly what we'd do.*" (Italics supplied.)

No event in the sphere of foreign affairs brought Eisenhower greater anguish than Suez and, in its aftermath, none gave him greater satisfaction. When it was safely past, he wrote Churchill, "So I hope that this one may be washed off the slate as soon as possible...I shall never be happy until our old-time closeness has been restored."

To that end, he ordered into action a plan to add 200,000 barrels of oil per day to the quota of 300,000 barrels already being sent to

Europe. The Egyptians had blocked the Canal by sinking ships at its mouth when the fighting began. The emergency oil assistance continued until the Canal was reopened. At the same time, Eisenhower began providing financial assistance to Britain to counter a sharp decline in gold and dollar reserves.

Eden resigned and was succeeded by Harold MacMillan with whom Eisenhower had worked in Algiers during the confusing political days after the landings in North Africa. Gradually, the aggravations of what Eisenhower called "a family spat" between the United States and Britain died away.

Long after he left the White House, in reviewing the Suez episode, Eisenhower said he considered the restoration of close relations with Britain, France and Israel one of his biggest successes.

There were important corollaries as well. The course he followed during the crisis strengthened the United Nations and it effectively countered Russian efforts to pose as the champion of the Arabs.

But Eisenhower was not content merely to have stopped the fighting in Egypt and seen the withdrawal of the attacking forces. He began searching for a broad plan to promote peace and stability in the Middle East. Out of these efforts came the "Eisenhower Doctrine."

It was to take the form of bilateral agreements with individual Middle Eastern nations, offering American protection if a government requested it. It was designed principally to block Russian incursions into the Moslem world but, without taking sides, it also applied to Israel. It did not couple the United States with the former colonial powers in the Middle East, France and Britain, nor did it exclude them; it would help preserve Western influence in the Arab world.

The plan encountered some opposition in Congress on the same grounds as had the "Formosa Doctrine," namely, that the President was making Congress equally responsible with him for whatever action the United States might be compelled to take in the Middle East. In the end, however, both houses passed it by large majorities.

The "Eisenhower Doctrine" would soon face its first test. In 1958, the President of Lebanon, Camille Chamoun, sounded out Eisenhower on the response of the United States if he were to call for military assistance against a rebel movement in his country. The rebels, he said, were infiltrating Lebanon from Syria. Before coming to any decision, Eisenhower took steps to bring Chamoun's charges before the United Nations. He called congressional leaders to the White

House to inform them of the situation and to obtain their views. He telephoned Prime Minister MacMillan in London and MacMillan readily concurred. Finally, Eisenhower prepared an announcement of his action to be timed for release when Marines from the Sixth Fleet actually began the landings in Lebanon.

Parenthetically, those of us who rushed to Lebanon found ourselves covering a strange "war." A telephone call to the sandbagged rebel headquarters on the heights above Beirut brought permission to come there. The taxi stopped at a prearranged point and rebel guards escorted correspondents to headquarters. Sporadic fusillades of rifle fire were exchanged, after which the taxi went back down the hill. An effective curfew stopped virtually all movement through the streets of Beirut at night; only Marine vehicles moved unchallenged. The terrace of the palatial St. George Hotel became the press headquarters and at night, between rubbers of bridge, the story was covered from there. The threat, however, was more apparent outside the city. In order to see the border and talk with the United Nations officers on patrol there, I went by automobile to Damascus. Passing through a narrow gulch on the Syrian side, bursts of rifle fire came from both slopes. Fortunately, the rebels' aim was exceedingly poor.

Prior to his decision to send in the Marines, Eisenhower and his aides discussed the possible Soviet reaction. Some were worried. But the President felt that if American action were swift and decisive, Khrushchev would make no move. He was right. Except for the expectable vituperations, the Soviets did not attempt to fish in these troubled waters.

The crisis soon passed. Suez and Lebanon stand as landmarks in Eisenhower's efforts to substitute law for violence in the world.

. . .

Meanwhile, events at home confronted the President with a similar challenge, violence defying law and order.

Newspaper headlines foreshadowed it. The Supreme Court ruling on segregated public schools had said, "…in the field of public education the doctrine of 'separate but equal' has no place. Separate educational facilities are inherently unequal." Early in 1956, the governors of Georgia, Mississippi, South Carolina and Virginia agreed to unite against the ruling. Two months later, 96 Congressmen signed the "Southern Manifesto" pledging themselves to use all lawful means to bring about a reversal of it. While educational authorities in Southern and Border states prepared desegregation formulae, under orders from federal courts, those who held deep convictions about the necessity for segregation prepared to resist, some by violence, some by closing the schools rather than permit Negroes to enter them, some by legal devices.

In Clinton, Tennessee, segregationists bloodied a clergyman's nose when he attempted to escort a group of Negro children into the town's high school. A Negro college student, Autherine Lucy, lay concealed on the floor of a highway patrol car which took her through a mob on the campus of the University of Alabama amid shouts of "Where's the nigger? Lynch her! Kill her!" Variations of these scenes developed in more than one community.

Yet by no means all those who protested were racists, bigots or ignorant "red-necks." Hosts of intelligent, sincere men and women, for reasons that seemed sound and sufficient to them, held that it was wrong to change the pattern of separation of the races in the schools. An anguished era began for them.

Eisenhower understood their feelings as well as any Southerner. His personal letter, quoted earlier, forecast "disaster rather than human advancement" if these deeply rooted feelings were not taken into account, or if attempts were made to go too far too fast. He knew that the millennium in the South would not come over the weekend. He counseled patience and moderation.

He refused to express his opinion of the Supreme Court ruling. "I think it makes no difference whether I endorse it," he said. "What I say is...the Constitution is as the Supreme Court interprets it, and I must do my very best to see that it is carried out in this country." This statement may have led Americans, North and South, to conclude that he opposed the Court's decision or at most was only lukewarm to it. In fact, he simply felt it would be improper for him to take a position, pro or con. His duty was to enforce rulings whether he liked them or not. Moreover, he foresaw that if he stated his view of this Supreme Court ruling, he could scarcely refuse to comment on others. And if he should admit opposition to a Supreme Court ruling, doubts would arise as to whether he would seriously try to enforce it. The law, as he often said, is the only shield against chaos.

After he left the White House he removed any doubt about

his opinion of the Supreme Court ruling. In an interview with The Associated Press in 1963, he said:

"I think there is no question about the legality and propriety of the decision. It was a vote of 9 to 0. The Southerners on the Court participated in that decision. I just say I believe the decision expressed the intentions of our Constitution and therefore is morally and legally correct."

In 1957, he took action in this field. He sent to Congress a Civil Rights bill, and with Brownell, worked hard to get it enacted. Months of debate began as vitiating amendments were introduced to pull its teeth. One applied to cases where the judge might deny a jury trial to a person convicted of contempt in blocking a court order against interference with the right to vote. Senator Lyndon Johnson of Texas said, "The people will never accept a concept that a man can be publicly branded as a criminal without a jury trial." Prominent Negroes urged the President to veto the bill as it stood on grounds that in this instance a half-loaf was *not* better than none. Eisenhower considered it, although he well knew that the Democrats would proclaim that a Republican President had vetoed a Civil Rights bill which they would argue had represented progress. During the debate, Senator Strom Thurmond of South Carolina set a filibustering record. He talked without interruption for 24 hours and 18 minutes before he collapsed. The previous record had been set by Senator Wayne Morse of Oregon, 22 hours and 26 minutes, speaking against the Tidelands Bill. The mysterious processes of the American democracy!

Eventually, it was Lyndon Johnson who effected the compromise. Eisenhower congratulated him.

With that, the first Civil Rights bill in 82 years, since the Reconstruction days, became law. Eisenhower signed it on Sept. 9, 1957. It fell short by far of what he wanted, but he felt that it at least opened the way toward improving the status of Negroes.

Eisenhower said later, "We must counter the notion that the Democrats are for the little people arid that we are for the big corporations and fat cats. This is not so and we should use bills like this (the Civil Rights Act) to stress the opposite."

Even if he had felt a sense of satisfaction, the President was to have no time to savor it. For, during the verbal violence in the Senate, a cruder, more dangerous form was taking shape in the capital of Arkansas, Little Rock.

Little Rock is a pleasant city with a population just under a quarter-million. The people are friendly and courteous. The man in the elevator most likely will say, "G'mawnin'" or "Howdy" to a complete stranger, even one who obviously is a Yankee. The streets in residential districts are quiet, tree-shaded, lined with a high percentage of attractive homes, manicured lawns and flower beds. On one of these stands a handsome school, Central High.

In 1957, the enrollment was near 2,000, all white children. Many of their parents had graduated from Central. The city took great pride in this school. Well over half its graduates went on to college, a high percentage of them on scholarships. The townspeople, whether or not they had attended Central, idolized its athletic teams and followed their fortunes with intense interest. They thought of it as "our school."

On Aug. 30, 1957, Federal District Judge Ronald F. Davies, of Fargo, North Dakota, ordered the Little Rock School Board to proceed with a plan to desegregate Central High which the Board had worked out. Nine Negro children were to be enrolled when the Fall term began, on Sept. 3. Davies had been temporarily assigned to fill a vacancy on the federal bench and the fact that he came from "up North" was to be cited repeatedly as evidence that the federal government was determined to "ram integration down our throats."

Yet, a good deal of integration already had taken place in Little Rock, public transportation, the symphony, the little theater. A not-always-valid generalization holds that resistance to desegregation in a Southern community varies with the ratio of the white and Negro population. In Little Rock in 1957, the population was 75 per cent white. For these and other reasons, the scenes soon to be enacted in front of Central High seemed wildly improbable.

On Labor Day Eve, Governor Orval E. Faubus ordered units of the Arkansas National Guard to take stations around the school. He said he had evidence of "threats of violence" if the Negroes attempted to enter. When they appeared, a crowd of adults and teen-agers confronted them. It was the mixture as before in other Southern communities, some jeers, booing, some curses. The show-offs, adults and youngsters, behaved predictably. The Guardsmen turned back the Negroes and they quietly left the premises.

This appeared to confirm Faubus' assertion about "threats of violence." Mayor Woodrow Mann and the Little Rock police had said they found nothing to substantiate it. True, no violence broke out on that occasion but the elements for it were present, as obvious as a hissing fuse on a stick of dynamite.

Eisenhower had gone to Newport, Rhode Island, to rest and play golf. Faubus wired him there asking for "understanding and cooperation." The President's return message said, "The only assurance I can give you is that the federal Constitution will be upheld by me by every legal means at my command."

A series of legal actions followed. In one of them, Brownell directed federal authorities to petition for an injunction to prevent Faubus and officers of the National Guard from interfering with the desegregation of the high school. Faubus accepted the summons to appear in court on Sept. 20 to explain his reasons for blocking the court's order to enroll the Negro students.

While these procedures ground along, Congressman Brooks Hays, who represented the Arkansas Fifth District, telephoned Sherman Adams and asked whether the President would see Faubus. Hays, a gentle, thoughtful man, was almost universally popular. Adams liked him. In reply to Hays' question, Adams said he felt a meeting could be arranged, provided Faubus showed an intention to comply with the federal court order. Adams correctly guessed the President's reaction. Eisenhower would talk with Faubus and give him the opportunity to explain his problems and his thinking. But the President would not listen to arguments, much less any expression of defiance. So it was agreed that Faubus should come to Newport.

Faubus, through this uneasy period, was anything but a raging, fire-eating table-pounder, mouthing segregationist cliches about race mixin' and the sanctity of Southern womanhood. His manner was low-key. He spoke quietly. Again and again he patiently explained his position vis-a-vis the high school. In press conferences, some Northern reporters went at him like district attorneys cross-examining the defendant in a murder trial. Faubus never lost his temper. He gave soft answers to jagged questions.

His manner, in all probability, would make a favorable impression in Eisenhower since it resembled the President's way, the patient effort to persuade, choking back the hot words that might seem fully justified. However, one remark made it difficult to fathom Faubus' state of mind on the morning he left for Newport. While his party was assembling on the airfield, he took me aside and said, earnestly, "I'm on the ground. I'm in command. They've got to come to me." Then, without amplification of these words, he boarded his plane. Whatever they meant, they hardly sounded conciliatory.

Nonetheless, he impressed Eisenhower as a reasonable man when they met. The President, as might be expected, sought the quiet way out of the impasse. He had no desire to humiliate Faubus nor to leave him without an avenue of retreat. He quietly reminded the governor that in a contest with the federal government, he must surely lose. Then he urged Faubus to reverse the orders to the Guardsmen at the school, to protect the Negro children instead of barring them from its doors. This, he said, would open the way for Brownell to request the judge to dismiss the summons requiring the governor of a sovereign state to appear before him. Eisenhower preferred to see the problem settled locally. Faubus left him with the impression that he was prepared to do this.

When he returned to Little Rock that night, the governor's expression was enigmatic. He hurried into his car without answering any questions.

For nearly a week, nothing changed. The Guardsmen, acting under the same instructions, remained on station outside the school. The Negroes made no further attempts to enroll. Brownell, who had been skeptical from the first about the fruitfulness of the Newport talks, did not request a dismissal of the injunction against Faubus.

On the following Friday, Faubus' attorneys appeared before Judge Davis. The governor remained in his mansion. The lawyers argued that the court had no jurisdiction over the governor of a sovereign state. Then they walked out. Davies ruled that Faubus had "thwarted" the plan to desegregate the high school and issued another injunction which ordered an end to "obstructing or preventing by use of the National Guard or otherwise the attendance of Negro students at Little Rock High School."

Faubus promptly removed the troops. While they were leaving the school grounds, he went on television and said, "As long as this order is in effect, and until its certain reversal on appeal, I will comply...I have instructed my attorneys to exhaust every legal remedy to appeal this order."

The stage was now set for the grim and historic events of Monday, Sept. 23, 1957.

It dawned, a beautiful, warm, blue-and-gold morning. Before 8 o'clock, people began gathering as near the high school as they could come. Police barriers had been placed at the intersections of the streets leading to it. Officers stood behind these, checking through teachers, and others patrolled the area directly in front of the school. Nobody there knew whether the parents of the Negro children would bring the nine students to enroll. Faubus, in his televised statement, had urged them to wait, allowing a "cooling off" period. There had been reports that Negro leaders in Little Rock would comply with his request. Who could say?

In the cool and quiet of the morning, the drifting murmur of voices rose in front of the high school. White students passed through the barriers and then clustered in the windows, watching the scene. There was some horseplay among them. This was fun, more exciting than when the National Guardsmen had been outside. The Negroes might show up now.

A pretty, auburn-haired woman wearing a green jacket leaned on the barrier talking to a policeman. Another held a white portable radio to her ear and said, "I'm getting all the news about what's happening at Central High." She laughed. A gray-haired man replied, "If they're coming, they'll be here soon." It was 8:35.

A moment or two later, a man shouted, "Here come the Niggers." He pointed down one of the streets leading to the school. The people there swung around to look, turning their backs on the high school.

They saw, not the students, but four Negro men, approaching. One carried a news photographer's camera. Another had a press card in his hatband. Some white men surged toward them. The Negroes hesitated a second and then turned to run. The whites caught two of them. They jumped on the back of a tall Negro in a business suit and rode him to the ground, kicking and pummeling. Others smashed the camera and began beating the man who had been carrying it.

If this was a planned maneuver, timed to divert the attention of the crowd away from the school, it succeeded completely.

For at that very moment, a station wagon rolled to a stop near a side door of the school. The Negro students and some Negro adults stepped out. The children were neatly dressed and carrying books. They walked, not hurrying, to a flight of steps. They glanced at the crowd and the police and curiosity showed in their faces, as though they wondered what this was all about. Then they disappeared through the school door, virtually unnoticed because of the scuffling a half-block away.

But not entirely unnoticed. A man roared, "The Niggers are in the school."

The woman in the green jacket cried out, "Did you see them?" She sounded like a mourner keening at a funeral. "Oh, God," she cried, "the Niggers are in our school."

Hysteria spread like lightning. A long block away, where another throng stood near the barriers, a roaring sound rose, pierced with the shrieking of women. At both ends of the street, the crowds pressed forward. A tall man yelled, "Who's going through?" A woman's voice, high-pitched and frantic, answered, "We all are."

With that, a number of men followed by a few women rushed the barriers. Some got through, but none as far as the school. One man reached the lawn across the street and two policemen expertly pulled his coat half way down his arms, pinioning them. They hustled him away. Behind the wood barriers, the police lines swayed back and forth and for a time it appeared they would break. Miraculously, in the close-packed struggle, nobody was killed or seriously injured.

Then, singly and in twos and threes white students began leaving the school. A great shout rose from the crowd, "Good for you, boys… don't stay in school with the Niggers…go back and tell everybody to get out."

Two officers wrestled a boy into a police car and drove away. A man yelled, "That's my kid. Help me get my kid." He sprinted after the car. A girl came out, tears streaming down her face. When some reporters tried to question her, she sobbed, "Leave me alone. Just leave me alone."

Some of the students told stories of wild confusion and disorder in the school, of fights in the hallways and seeing Negroes covered with blood. The details, it turned out, were exaggerated or entirely false.

In the streets, the fighting and yelling went on. And so, at about noon, authorities spirited the Negroes out of the school.

Violence had won the first round over law in Little Rock.

When darkness fell, the city became tense, listening, nerves on edge. Any untoward sound, an automobile backfiring, brought people to the windows. Teen-agers careened through the streets, shouting, "We're going to find us a Nigger." Reports of race rioting were found to be false. Many of the streets in residential areas were dark and silent.

In the Arkansas Gazette building, the lights in every office burned throughout the night. The newspaper had written a glorious page in the history of American journalism, standing against Faubus and the segregationists and pleading for compliance with the orders of the courts. There had been the usual midnight threats against the staff and property of the paper. Its editor, Harry Ashmore, received a telephone call from an officer of the Department of Justice in Washington that night. Ashmore described the situation in Little Rock and said it seemed close to getting completely out of hand.

On the following day, the mayor confirmed this in a telegram to Eisenhower. It said the police could not control the mob, "situation is out of control." Faubus had left the city to attend a conference in Sea Island, Georgia. The lieutenant governor, Nathan Gordon, denied reports that he had alerted the National Guard. "I have to wait for an official request from the city authorities," he said, "and I've had none so far." Instead, the mayor asked Eisenhower to send in federal troops.

The President had issued a proclamation, in effect a cease-and-desist order, on the day of the riots. With the arrival of the mayor's telegram, he determined to take a drastic step.

On two occasions, Eisenhower had prefaced a statement with the words, "I can't imagine any set of circumstances that would" cause him to change his position on something. The first related to his determination not to become a candidate for the presidency. The second came at a press conference during the summer of 1957 when he said he could not conceive a situation in which he would use federal troops to enforce the orders of a court. In both instances, circumstances overruled him.

At noon on Sept. 24, he signed an Executive Order and became the 14th President to use federal troops in a domestic emergency. Just at dusk of that day, Army personnel carriers rumbled through the streets of Little Rock, bringing units of the 101st Airborne Division to the grounds of Central High School.

Except for a few minor incidents in the next few days, this ended the crisis.

Characteristically, Eisenhower immediately began searching for a constructive solution. A week after sending the troops to Little Rock, he met with a committee of governors designated by the Southern Governors Conference to work out a formula for restoring normal conditions in the city. His was simple. He told the governors that if they could persuade Faubus to reverse his position and to assume responsibility for maintaining law and order, the troops would be withdrawn. Owing to Faubus' legal maneuvers, this was not to be effected until May 1958.

Meanwhile, criticism beat down on Eisenhower from all sides. Segregationists called him a "dictator," accused him of having used "storm troopers" in Little Rock, and murmured darkly about the "Second Reconstruction." Partisan critics saw Little Rock as another instance of his "hesitancy" to act, said he was playing golf when he should have been staying close to the emergency, and argued that he could have forestalled the violence if he had acted sooner.

His popularity probably dropped to its lowest point in the aftermath of Little Rock. However, Eisenhower had stood on two principles. He believed local problems should be handled, wherever possible, by local authorities without intervention by the federal government. And he had acted to uphold the sanctity of the law.

There is a parallel in his actions in Suez and Little Rock.

In each case, Eisenhower took steps that were repugnant to him but a matter of duty as he saw it. In each, he had to frustrate persons whose motives he understood, and could sympathize with, but could not condone. And in each, once the crisis had passed, he moved immediately to bind up wounds and find acceptable solutions.

They were painful episodes. They showed a man of vision and principle.

The Bread of Adversity

Between the summer of 1957 and the end of 1958, a succession of alarms and emergencies arose to plague Eisenhower. They came in close order, like storm waves battering a sea wall.

In each, he reacted predictably. He rejected advice prompted by panic and set his face against "crash" programs to meet emergencies. As they arose, he remained calm, in each case awaiting more information before making his decisions. Then, but not before, he acted decisively. He often said, drawing on his experiences in the war, "Planning is essential but plans are useless." And this was his way in the White House when warning lights flashed (the threat to Quemoy and Matsu, for example), to plan in advance of a crisis but to remain flexible until the dimensions of it became clear.

In these 18 months, he passed through a personal ordeal, countered a serious economic recession, and blunted Communist maneuvers in two areas of the world. He saw his party go down to a shattering defeat in the 1958 elections in spite of his efforts to strengthen it. He was forced to deny, again and again, allegations that he had permitted a "missile gap" to develop between the defensive capabilities of the United States and the Soviet Union; for security reasons, he could only couch his denials in generalities. The Democrats' charge that the nation was "leaderless" appeared to take root.

It was a period when the President's fare was the bread of adversity.

During the late summer of 1957, signs of flabbiness began to develop in the economy. It had been booming. Then, inexplicably, the barometer needles quivered and began pointing downward. For the moment, there seemed no cause for alarm.

Next came Little Rock and the dueling with Faubus.

While the President was attempting to deal with this anguished controversy, electrifying news came from Moscow. The Russians announced that they had rocketed a satellite, Sputnik 1, into orbit

560 miles above the earth. The first man-made "moon" began circling the globe on Oct. 4, 1957. It was a brilliant triumph for Soviet science and a psychological victory of stunning proportions. Apprehension, especially in the United States, rose in its wake.

American public opinion often tends to swing in giant arcs from one extreme to the other. During the 1930s, for example, when Hitler seemed unstopable, there were Americans who gloomily concluded that Western statesmen were hopelessly outclassed by him and indeed that the Democracies could not cope with the ruthless efficiency of the Dictatorships. Similarly, with the Russians. After the war, Americans who had served in the Soviet Union brought back countless tales about the ineffable stupidity of the Russians with respect to machines. They invariably ripped out the gears on jeeps, so it was said, and ruined machinery simply by forgetting to lubricate it. They broke their necks in airplanes, having neglected to warm up the motors before takeoff. Countless variations on this theme built up the picture of hilarious inefficiency as against the well-known supremacy of American know-how.

Then came the big swings. Hitler, erstwhile supertactician and Machiavelli, came to be regarded as a ridiculous little paranoiac. And the mechanically inept Russians, with Sputnik I in outer space, suddenly stood 10 feet tall as engineers and scientists.

The reality of Soviet rockets powerful enough to arc across the oceans and deliver nuclear warheads to American cities sent shock waves across the country.

Unquestionably, the administration had been caught completely off guard in having failed to foresee the psychological impact of the Russian success. True, both Washington and Moscow had announced plans earlier to send satellites into outer space as part of the International Geophysical Year, 1957-58. But the Russians had followed through, whereas in Washington a degree of complacency had settled over this sector of the rocket program. Moreover, at first, Sputnik I did not appear to jar the administration. The President did not minimize the Soviet achievement but although he shared the general concern he kept an air of serenity in order to minimize public apprehension. He said his apprehensions had not increased, "not one iota." Keying his attitude to Eisenhower's chord, Sherman Adams spoke of an "outer space basketball game," a remark he later said he regretted.

Nevertheless, public apprehension increased. Why had the United

States been left at the post in the space race? What had happened to American science? What were the military implications of Sputnik I and the 1,100-pound satellite that soon followed it? How did the satellites, looking down at American territory every 95 minutes, affect the nation's defense?

For a time, the general uneasiness presented itself as a fertile field for partisan attacks on Eisenhower. The critics were quick to speak. Some Democrats loudly viewed with alarm and the mythical "missile gap" appeared, a claim that was to survive as an issue in the 1960 presidential campaign. To answer them, it was only necessary to quote the missile expert, Dr. Werner von Braun, who said, "The United States had no ballistic missile program worth mentioning between 1945 and 1951…our present dilemma is not due to the fact that we are not working hard enough now but that we did not work hard enough during the first six to 10 years after the war." In other words, according to von Braun, little had been done during the Truman years, either.

Money and politics also had retarded the space program. In "First Hand Report," Sherman Adams later wrote, "But when Sputnik was launched, the same congressmen who had been cutting funds for scientific research a few years earlier came to the President begging him to make a strong statement that would restore the people's trust and confidence…Congress would not spend money fast enough."

Eisenhower resisted the panicky clamor for huge defense appropriations. He pointed out that spending was no magic wand that would pull increased strength out of a hat. More important, in two speeches he attempted to reassure the nation. Within the bounds of security, he listed some of the main strong points in American defenses. He even considered, but discarded, the thought of disclosing the existence of high-flying reconnaissance planes, the U-2s, one of which was to put him in an exceedingly uncomfortable position a few years later. In summary, he said, "We are well ahead of the Soviets in the nuclear field both in quantity and in quality. We intend to stay ahead."

Whether the speeches achieved their purpose in restoring public confidence was debatable so long as the Soviets held a monopoly in outer space. The most effective way to allay the uneasiness at home, and to reassure the allies of the United States, would be to orbit an American satellite as soon as possible. Eisenhower concentrated on doing this. He called in outstanding scientists and discussed with them the operational and administrative problems relating to that goal. He created a new office, Assistant to the President for Science and Technology. Dr. James R. Killian, president of the Massachusetts Institute of Technology, agreed to fill the position.

Official complacency was gone now. There would still be setbacks, but on Jan. 31, the Army's Explorer I was shot into orbit. It weighed less than 31 pounds and Khrushchev, always quick with his weapons of propaganda, ridiculed it as an "orange," by comparison with the big Russian satellites. But he could not ridicule it out of the skies. In short order, American satellites began pacing the Russians, step for step, in the space race.

Prior to this, the President had planned to deliver a third speech on satellites, rocketry, defense costs and the relations of all this to the federal budget. But this was not to be.

He returned to his office after lunch in the afternoon of Nov. 25 and went to his desk to sign some papers. Suddenly, he felt dizzy. The sensation seemed to pass. He picked up a pen and reached for one of the papers. He found he had difficulty holding it, but worse, when he tried to read the paper, "the words seemed literally to run off the top of the page," as he said. Next, the pen slipped from his fingers. He tried several times to retrieve it but failed. With that, Eisenhower rose to his feet. His head swam and he grasped the back of a chair to keep from falling. He struggled back into the chair and rang for his secretary, Mrs. Ann Whitman, a devoted and highly capable aide. He tried to tell her what had happened. To his consternation, the President heard himself speaking gibberish. The words he spoke were not those he was trying to enunciate. A neurological block had arisen somewhere between his brain and his tongue. It must have been a horrifying experience, but if Eisenhower felt any fright he never admitted it. He simply described the experience as "puzzling" when he came to recount it later. Mrs. Whitman, startled and close to tears, called Gen. Andrew Goodpaster, a top member of the White House staff. They persuaded him to go home.

Eisenhower said later he felt no pain and had no difficulty in walking. He thought he had merely experienced a postluncheon dizzy spell. Still, there was that jarring incoherence, the crossed wires, when he tried to speak—. Without further protest, he went to bed and fell asleep.

Later that afternoon, neurological examination indicated that the President had suffered a vascular "spasm," a mild stroke. Tests later confirmed the diagnosis. It was his third critical illness in three years.

He threw it aside as he had thrown off the first two. In fact, at first he proposed to disregard it entirely.

King Mohammed V of Morocco had arrived in Washington that day. Eisenhower had welcomed him at National Airport and ridden with him to Blair House. A ceremonial dinner in the King's honor was to be held that night. After the doctors left, Eisenhower announced that he would preside as planned at the dinner. Mrs. Eisenhower, John Eisenhower and Gen. Snyder, the White House physician, protested emphatically. Eisenhower said they looked "appalled." He managed to say, "There's nothing the matter with me. I'm perfectly all right." And he insisted on attending the dinner. At which point, it appears, Mamie fired the shot that ended the argument. She said that if he went, she would *not* go. The President capitulated. Masking her feelings, she attended the dinner and none of the guests could have discerned from her expression that her husband had again been stricken with illness. As before, there was a night watch in the President's bedroom, shared this time by his son and Gen. Snyder.

The next day, Eisenhower dressed and shaved himself to prove, at least to himself, that he was "perfectly all right." But he experienced further evidence of impairment of memory for words and in his speech. Instead of becoming frightened, he merely felt frustrated. His famous temper flared, he learned later. He wanted to go to work but agreed to rest a little longer. On the second day after the cerebral spasm, he was permitted to go to his office for routine work, and on the third day, Thanksgiving, he went to church with his wife.

In this illness, he saw a personal problem quite different from the ones presented by his heart attack and the ileitis operation. He had said then that he would not be a "part-time President." Now the thought came to him that, although still alive, he might be rendered incapable of discharging his duties at all. This he would not contemplate. He had written his friend, Capt. Hazlett, when he was weighing the question of a second term after his heart attack, that he was not concerned with what the presidency might do to him. He worried over what he might do to the office and the nation if he "slowed down." But suppose a mere severe spasm left him incapable of expressing, either in speech or writing, his desire to resign?

He determined to forestall that possibility by putting his strength and faculties to a rigorous test. If his judgment told him he had failed to pass it, he would resign forthwith.

The heads of state of the NATO nations were preparing to meet in Paris. Eisenhower advised his family, physicians and associates that he would attend it, as scheduled. Again, they tried to dissuade him but he would not give in. They were unaware that he regarded the conference as a critical test for himself. He knew the sessions would be demanding, physically and mentally. He felt they would give him the information about his condition that he needed to form his decision. In December, leaving a pall of misgivings behind him, he flew to Paris.

He attended all the plenary sessions, and not merely as a passive figurehead. He made his contributions to the discussions. More than that, he met privately with MacMillan, Adenauer and the Premiers of France and Italy, Gaillaut and Zoli. As he anticipated, the conference was fatiguing but he went through it without feeling overtaxed. This all but settled the question of whether he should resign or finish out his term.

Without telling his staff, Eisenhower then undertook one further step, an unrehearsed little speech.

He drove from Paris to Marly, the Supreme Headquarters of NATO, on a sunny afternoon. He entered the office he had occupied nearly six years earlier and chatted briefly with the officers, some of whom had been on his staff. Then he walked outside to the head of the broad flight of steps leading into the building. A sizable crowd had assembled there, men and women in uniform, others in civilian dress, children. A microphone had been set up. The President stepped up to it. He could see the expressions of surprise and even dismay on the faces of his Washington aides. He began speaking, expressing his thoughts about the meaning of NATO, the importance of the duties the officers were discharging, and his sense of personal involvement with the organization. A touch of nostalgia warmed the statement. But the important part of it, for him, was that not once did he stumble or pause, groping for the word he wanted. The little talk went off so smoothly and so fast, in fact, that I had difficulty getting it all in the notebook. I was amazed when I learned later that Eisenhower had spoken extemporaneously.

Now he was over the hurdle, finally and completely.

Nonetheless, he was 67 years old. And this was the Nuclear

Age when life-and-death decisions might have to be taken within a matter of minutes. His iron constitution had carried him through three serious illnesses but he concluded that the question of presidential disability could no longer be left to chance. The nation's safety might depend on a plan for the quick transfer of power if he should be incapacitated.

On March 3, 1958, James Hagerty announced that the President had worked out an arrangement in which, should another emergency arise, Nixon would take over the duties of the presidency. Eisenhower had discussed the plan with the attorney general and Hagerty said its terms "are consistent with its (the Constitution's) present provisions and implement its clear intent." In essence, the arrangement contained three stipulations. The President—"if possible"—would notify Nixon of his inability and Nixon would serve as acting President until the inability ended. But if the President became incapable of speaking or writing, then Nixon alone would assume the responsibility of whether, and when, to take over. Eisenhower wrote him that he "hoped" Nixon would consult with medical authorities and members of the Cabinet and White House staff but he emphasized that the decision would be Nixon's. Finally, Eisenhower said he himself would decide when he could return to his duties.

The arrangement was unique in the history of the presidency. It bespoke Eisenhower's rugged integrity and his confidence in Nixon. Other Presidents had been partially or completely disabled in office for varying periods of time but none had taken a step of this magnitude.

Little Rock, Sputnik and the mild stroke were sudden and explosive emergencies for Eisenhower. While he was busy coping with these, a less dramatic but equally disturbing development arose before him. A full-blown business recession appeared to be glowering on the horizon.

Through the summer of 1957, the economy had been setting records. It hit 10-year peaks in total production and foreign investment. The Gross National Product (the total value of all goods and services produced) stood at an all-time high of $445 billion. Then, toward the end of the year, the trend rapidly reversed itself. During the first six months of 1958, unemployment reached a figure of nearly six million.

Analysts later attributed the sharp dip to a combination of technical factors, the size of productive capacity and inventories, a decline in investment spending, etc...But an imponderable—loss of confidence in Eisenhower—also may have contributed to the downturn. His efforts to reassure the nation after Sputnik I, and before the United States put its first satellite in orbit, seemed less than successful. People were uneasy on that score. The Democrats had been hammering on the theme the nation was "leaderless." This, of course, was partisan politics. But then came the astonishing sequence of events with respect to the Federal Budget for the fiscal year, 1957-58, projected at $73.8 billion.

In order to discourage Congress from authorizing even more spending, George Humphrey, Secretary of the Treasury, prepared a letter to the President which would be made public. It contained a passage that seemed to suggest that Humphrey considered the figure of $73.8 billion too high. The letter commended all those who had worked on the Budget for their "painstaking and conscientious" efforts to cut out the fat. However, it said, "But it is not enough. The over-all net results are not sufficient. Only the most drastic action will suffice." That certainly sounded like an invitation to Congress to get out the axes and begin whacking away at the President's Budget. The letter was discussed in a Cabinet meeting. Some of those present objected to it, but Eisenhower himself did not. He had great admiration for Humphrey, who was persuasive and strong-minded. So the letter went out. And then, at a press conference, Humphrey added an off-the-cuff remark that rocked the reporters back on their heels. He said, "If we don't (reduce expenditures) over a long period of time, I will predict that you will have a depression that will curl your hair."

Confidence is like a thin film of oil lubricating the huge American economy. When it evaporates, as it did in the 1930s, the engines are in trouble. Humphrey's qualifying phrase, "over a long period of time," put his statement in a less frightening light. But what was largely remembered was the warning about "a depression that will curl your hair."

In the hullabaloo that arose, Eisenhower stood by Humphrey. Regarding the letter, the President said, "I not only went over every word of it, I edited it, and it expresses my convictions very thoroughly." And, he added, if Congress could find parts of the Budget that could be cut, it was Congress' duty to do so.

Confusion compounded. Eisenhower had pledged economy in government during the 1952 campaign. Now it appeared that his own

Treasury Secretary was criticizing the administration, suggesting the Budget was too fat, and uttering the dire word, "depression." And the President was publicly agreeing with him.

Congress whacked away gladly. Deep cuts were made in the Budget and some were restored. More important, the President had stumbled into a major political (and perhaps, economic) blunder. For a time, he seemed the epitome of uncertainty.

But he soon appeared in a different light.

As the recession deepened later in the year, cries for federal "crash" programs to ameliorate it came from both sides of the aisle in Congress and from powerful labor union leaders. They were accompanied by calls for an immediate reduction in taxes.

Eisenhower turned a deaf ear to these urgings. He abhorred the thought of creating "huge federal bureaucracies of the PWA and WPA type." These make-work programs of the 1930s, he knew, had produced only temporary relief in the Great Depression. (In the summer of 1937, after the beginnings of recovery, the whole economy went into a decline again. Roosevelt's Secretary of the Treasury, Henry Morgenthau Jr., told him, "We are headed right into another depression. The question is, Mr. President: What are we going to do about it?")

Confronted with the same question, Eisenhower held firmly to his natural stance as a middle-of-the-roader, opposing extremes. When Congress passed a bill authorizing $168 million for rivers, harbors and flood control, he vetoed it. He also vetoed legislation to freeze farm prices. The off-year elections were approaching and these measures would have been politically popular. But Eisenhower called the rivers-and-harbors bill "stupid" and considered the farm bill harmful to the interest of the country as a whole.

One of the myths that grew up about Eisenhower pictured him as a man who held few convictions of his own, a President who merely acted according to the majority opinion of his Cabinet and advisers.

But two instances at this time deny the legend. The Senate Republican policy committee voted 17 to 14 to request him to sign the farm bill. When he let it be known that he would veto it, five of the senators called on him to try to argue him out of doing so. He refused. Similarly, on reducing taxes, he disagreed with economic advisers whose judgment and expertise he valued greatly. He insisted that the economy would soon begin to recover, said he would await more information from all sectors, and then, balancing all the pros and cons of cutting taxes, he would make his decision. If the recession was like an economic Battle of the Bulge, he would not be stampeded into charging off in all directions on the basis of reports from the first few hours of fighting.

He did take some positive steps. He submitted to Congress a program to extend the period of federal-state unemployment insurance from 26 to 39 weeks. Moves were made to stimulate construction and housing starts. He proposed a $2 billion measure to modernize post office buildings and equipment, plus spending for other projects he believed would create useful jobs, especially in the cities hit hardest by unemployment. It was a moderate program. The Republican Minority Leader, Senator William F. Knowland of California, strongly supported it. And the Democratic Congressional leaders, Lyndon Johnson and Sam Rayburn, disappointed the advocates of pump priming in their party by generally going along with the President.

In about six months, the economic trend began to reverse itself. By autumn of 1958, the Gross National Product returned almost to the level it had reached when the recession started. The stock market, which had dipped, rose to new highs. At the end of 1958, unemployment dropped from 6,000,000 to 3,800,000. The President, of course, could not be given all the credit for the upturn. Built-in stabilizers in the economy played their designated roles. Nonetheless, while sticking firmly to the middle of the road, he saw the sharpest business decline since World War II checked and a vigorous recovery begin.

Meanwhile, Communist moves in the Middle East and Far East again threatened the peace. Eisenhower acted promptly to put out the fires—with the use, if necessary, of small atomic bombs.

In July, he rushed 15,000 Marines to Lebanon when President Camille Chamoun appealed to him for assistance. Nasser and the Communists cried "imperialism" but made no counter moves. (In fact, a highly placed Egyptian told me in Cairo that Eisenhower's action in Lebanon put Khrushchev almost in a state of jitters and that he strongly counseled Nasser against taking any step that might aggravate the danger of war.) In response, Eisenhower said he would withdraw the Marines if a legitimate Lebanese government requested it, or if machinery could be set up to meet any future threats to peace in the Middle East.

In August, the President addressed the United Nations General

Assembly, presenting a six-point program to stabilize the region, plus a plan for international economic development there. The United Nations adopted a resolution largely conforming to the program. On Oct. 26, order having been restored in Lebanon, Eisenhower withdrew the Marines.

Coincidentally, and possibly timed to meet with the flareup in the Middle East, the Chinese Communists suddenly posed a new threat to Quemoy and Matsu, the Nationalist-held offshore islands. On Aug. 22, shore batteries hit them with more than 20,000 shells. A buildup of Communist ground forces and fighter aircraft had previously been spotted in the mainland provinces opposite the islands.

With one exception, it looked like 1955 all over again. The exception was that, during the three years, Chiang Kai-shek had built up the garrisons on Quemoy and Matsu until, it was estimated, about a third of the Nationalist ground forces were stationed there. Eisenhower considered the buildup ill-advised. He thought the islands should be garrisoned only to the extent of being strong outposts for the defense of Formosa. Now, if the Communists overran them, the Nationalist forces would be greatly reduced and the threat to the main bastion greatly increased.

In the succeeding days, the heavy shelling began to interfere with shipments of supplies to Quemoy and Matsu. If the interdiction continued, the garrisons could be starved out.

Eisenhower ordered ships of the United States Seventh Fleet to escort Nationalist supply convoys, but to remain just outside the three-mile limit. At the same time, he added aircraft carriers and destroyers to the Fleet. He publicly announced these moves so that the news of them would reach Peking.

What he did not disclose was the fact that if the Communist threat increased to a point where it imperilled Formosa itself, he would use small atomic bombs on mainland airfields. Then, depending on developments, he might go further, hitting military targets deeper inside Red China. Eisenhower foresaw that there would be a worldwide wave of revulsion to unleashing the terrible weapons, even though of small yield and against strictly military targets. At the same time, he considered the balancing effect of such drastic action, demonstrating to friend and enemy alike his determination to defend Formosa. Fortunately, he never had to make that decision.

The supply problem eased. The Reds' next move was to announce that they would suspend the bombardment if American warships stopped escorting Nationalist convoys. A cease-fire began. Public opinion in the United States had been divided about the wisdom of Eisenhower's actions in this ticklish situation and there was almost universal opposition to them in Europe. It was said that Chiang Kai-shek was trying to involve the United States in a war with Red China in order to fulfill the perennial cry, "Back to the mainland." But when the guns fell silent, Eisenhower stood vindicated and his prestige rose sharply. Then came a bizarre development—the Communists announced that they would bombard the islands only on odd-numbered days. As the poet said, "For ways that are dark and tricks that are vain, the heathen Chinee is peculiar." In this case, the dark ways probably were designed to save face after Eisenhower showed his firmness of purpose.

The President then set about to persuade Chiang to reduce the number of troops on Quemoy and Matsu. He sent Dulles to Formosa to emphasize the necessity of renouncing the use of force as a means of returning Chiang to the mainland. Chiang, of course, could not agree to this, but he did agree in principle to reduce the islands' garrisons.

With that, Chou En-lai, Premier of Communist China, announced that talks would be resumed in Warsaw between his ambassador to Poland and the American ambassador, Jacob D. Beam. They were fruitless but at least they indicated that for the moment another crisis involving the United States in the Straits of Formosa had passed.

For Eisenhower, the year ended on two unhappy notes, Sherman Adams and the November elections.

During the summer, it came to light that Adams had accepted some gifts, including a vicuna coat, from a Boston industrialist, Bernard Goldfine. Adams made no attempt to deny this, nor that Goldfine had paid some hotel bills for him in Boston. But he said he and Goldfine had been friends for many years, and that he had often given presents to Goldfine. Adams said he had made some written and telephoned inquiries to government agencies at Goldfine's request. But he strongly denied that he ever attempted to obtain favors for the manufacturer or to intercede on Goldfine's behalf. He summed up his position later with the statement, "If I had those decisions before me now, I believe I would have acted more prudently."

The situation seemed all too redolent of what the Republicans had called the "Truman administration scandals" when Eisenhower first campaigned for the presidency. At that time, GOP politicians expressed pious dismay over gifts to White House Democrats. And when the storm broke over the "Nixon Fund" during the campaign, Eisenhower said it must be shown that Nixon was "clean as a hound's tooth" if he were to remain on the ticket. Now it was the Democrats' turn.

Moreover, as White House chief of staff, Adams had made enemies. They came at him now.

Eisenhower attempted to defend Adams. He said in a press conference statement, "I personally like Governor Adams. I admire his abilities, I respect him because of his personal and official integrity. I need him…"

This failed to silence the clamor for Adams' head within the GOP itself. He was advised that he had become a political liability, that some important contributors to the party's campaign chest might be less than generous with their checkbooks if he remained in office. Whether Adams' troubles affected the elections in Maine would be hard to say, but they badly jolted the Republicans. They were held in September when the uproar was at its height. When the ballots were counted, the Democrats had elected a governor, Edward S. Muskie, a congressman, and won a number of state offices. Adams now concluded that he should resign in the interests of the President and the party.

Adams said Eisenhower did not ask him to leave office. He made the decision himself and stepped out on Sept. 22. He declined an invitation to a square dance given in his honor by the President before he left office.

Traditionally Maine was a harbinger of the national elections. Sensing the trend, Eisenhower campaigned hard in an effort to reverse it. At first he keyed his speeches to mild dissertations on his moderate philosophies of government. But toward the end of the campaign, he started to go after the Democrats in earnest, attacking the "dominant wing" of that party as "radicals and spendthrifts."

His efforts went to no avail. The Democrats elected 13 senators, bringing their total to 62. They rolled up a net gain of 47 congressmen for a total of 282. They increased the number of Democratic governors by five.

Was this a repudiation of the Eisenhower administration? The President said he did not see it that way. He said it was a victory for "the spenders" and vowed to fight that philosophy with all his strength in his remaining two years in the White House.

Surprises were in store for his friends and foes alike.

Commander-in-Chief

In 1959, a cartoon in the Akron, Ohio, Beacon-Journal pictured Eisenhower astride a donkey, the Democratic-controlled 86th Congress, holding a big stick, the veto, and grinning while the donkey drinks from a trough captioned "Moderation." Nothing could have illustrated more accurately the change in tactics that he adopted during the last two years or so of his second administration. If he had seemed diffident and vacillating in his dealings with Congress before, he gripped the levers of executive power with a firm hand now. He came to resemble one of his heroes, Abraham Lincoln, who had occasion to growl toward Capitol Hill, "I will show them at the other end of the Avenue whether I am President or not."

It was not only that Eisenhower used the veto more often, or brandished the threat of it, to kill unwanted legislation. He seemed to abandon the civics textbook concept that what Congress did was its own business, not his. He began his own form of lobbying. By notes and telephone calls to the Hill he expressed his appreciation for votes or other actions supporting him. Also, he began writing letters to influential men and women in all parts of the country, semipersonal letters explaining his views and actions on current issues.

The list of these correspondents eventually grew to 500, and since it is highly flattering to receive a communication from the President of the United States about his problems, Eisenhower could be certain that the recipients would pass along his thoughts to a host of other persons. A man would be less than human if he did not have his secretary make dozens of copies and send them out with a covering note which probably began, "Dear Joe: I am enclosing a copy of a letter I have just received from President Eisenhower that I'm sure will interest you..." The President estimated that in one such chain reaction he reached more than 20,000 people.

He adopted two other techniques to enlist public support for legislation he wanted. He went on television and radio to set forth the type of labor-reform bill he considered desirable, and in the process to point out what he said were the shortcomings of a labor bill sponsored by the Democrats.

He also took steps to present his points of view more directly to the Washington newspapermen. Up to that point, the majority of them probably would have characterized his attitude toward them as courteous, willing enough to answer questions in press conferences, but otherwise standoffish. Unlike some of his predecessors he did not play poker with reporters nor address them by a first name or nickname. During the war in Europe he had become friendly with a few correspondents, but the circumstances were different then: censorship protected him and a correspondent who broke the rules could be disaccredited and sent out of the theater. In the presidency, Eisenhower seems to have started at least with a somewhat jaundiced view of newspapermen. Perhaps some of them deserved it. At any rate, on Dec. 24, 1953, Eisenhower wrote Hazlett that the Bermuda Conference proved to be "…a good example of how useless it is to tell the full truth to the press—at least when the representatives of that Estate want to believe otherwise." However, in his new approach, Eisenhower began organizing dinners at the White House for small groups of Washington correspondents. The first took place July 20, 1959. About a dozen writers where invited. They were escorted first to the Oval Room upstairs for cocktails. Dinner followed. Then the President led the way to the library and the discussion of current questions went on for about two hours. The entire evening lasted some four hours. During the entire time, questions were asked and Eisenhower answered them. He ranged over the full spectrum of foreign and domestic problems. The correspondents took no notes but when the evening ended, they gathered in a nearby hotel to reconstruct together, from memory, what the President said. They were free to publish what he told them without naming him as the source. Two days later, at a regular press conference, he was asked if he had been the source of the stories that appeared after the dinner. He acknowledged that he had been, said he considered the meeting a useful one, and added that he planned to have other such gatherings. Which he did.

Neither the televised "fireside chat" nor the off-the-record dinner for newspaper correspondents was a wholly new gambit. But they were rather new for Eisenhower.

This was a more aggressive President, taking a course different from the Eisenhower who had said, during the filibuster against the Civil Rights Bill, "I do not normally comment on the procedures of either the Senate or the House because it is their business and it is not for me to interfere or to say how they will do things."

Now he was, in effect, throwing down the gauntlet. In 1959 he said, "There are a number of things I have recommended to Congress, and when my intuition tells me they are right, I'm going to use every single influence I can from the Executive Department to get Congress to see the light. If that's lobbying, I'm guilty."

What he called "responsibility in fiscal affairs" had been, from the outset, one of his objectives. The Democratic landslide in the 1958 elections troubled him particularly because in his view it marked a victory for "the spender" and he determined to use every weapon at his disposal to thwart them. On the day after the elections, discussing balanced budgets and what he considered excessive government spending, he said, "I promise this—for the next two years, the Lord sparing me, I am going to fight this thing as hard as I know how. And if we don't, I just say that, well, in the long run, every kind of person that has got the brains to see what is happening to this country with our loose handling of our fiscal affairs has got to fight it."

And so he twice vetoed an omnibus housing bill, signing the legislation only after Congress reduced the original figure by $375 million. He also vetoed bills providing for changes in controls on prices and production of wheat and tobacco, airport construction, and financing for cooperatives in the Rural Electrical Administration. The first of his 147 vetoes to be overridden was on a water projects bill which he considered "pork barrel."

In four of his eight years in office, Eisenhower produced balanced budgets. But due mainly to the recession of the previous year, he also had the biggest peacetime deficit in history, $12,540,000,000 in fiscal 1959. Then, as the economy bounced back, and as he went on killing spending legislation right and left, the trend reversed and he claimed a surplus of a billion dollars in fiscal 1960.

Defense spending, however important, was by no means sacrosanct to Eisenhower. It presented the greatest problem in his ceaseless efforts to achieve balanced budgets. He knew he was well qualified to make judgments in this field and he expressed his concern about the potential dangers of overspending for defense in a personal letter. He wrote:

"Some day there is going to be a man sitting in my present chair who has not been raised in the military services and who will have little understanding of where slashes can be made with little or no damage. If that should happen while we still have the state of tension that now exists in the world, I shudder to think what could happen to this country."

An object example of his efforts to affect pending legislation by going directly to the people came in his television speech on the kind of labor-reform bill he wanted. A Senate Investigating Committee headed by Senator John McClellan of Arkansas, and with a young chief counsel named Robert F. Kennedy, had uncovered an amazing story of racketeering and corruption in some labor unions. Eisenhower considered inadequate a reform bill introduced by Senate Democrats. In conferences with legislative leaders he warned them that he would not accept legislation which failed to correct the abuses disclosed in the McClellan Committee hearings. They replied that such a bill would be hard to pass. He thereupon scheduled the television appearance. After describing the kind of law he wanted, Eisenhower said:

"Now let us examine what Congress has done so far this year. Has its action measured up to the minimum requirements I have outlined to protect the American people? I regret to say that the answer, as yet, is No."

The upshot of the speech, plus his threat of another veto, produced a bipartisan-sponsored bill bearing the names of Representative Philip M. Landrum, a Georgia Democrat, and Representative Robert P. Griffin, Republican of Michigan. The Landrum-Griffin Labor-Management Reporting and Disclosure Act was the first major labor legislation since 1947. Griffin said, "Eisenhower's wonderful support was the thing that made the difference in obtaining fair and constructive reform legislation."

After he left the White House, Eisenhower declined to agree that he changed greatly during his second term. "I just worked in a different way," he said. But in Washington he looked like a very different man and it became a commonplace to say, "Ike has discovered how to rule and not just reign."

His "team," of course, had changed. George Humphrey and Herbert Brownell resigned in 1957. Sherman Adams left in 1958.

In April, 1959, John Foster Dulles resigned, felled by the illness that took his life a month later.

In Congress, Representative Charles A. Halleck of Indiana supplanted Representative Joseph W. Martin Jr. of Massachusetts as GOP Minority Leader. Energetic, tough and shrewd, Halleck was credited with "knowing the deck," as the Washington phrase goes, meaning that he knew the particular interests and motivations of a wide circle of congressmen. He gave Eisenhower invaluable assistance in revitalizing the GOP and in forming coalitions with conservative Democrats to pass legislation. When Knowland resigned to run for governor of California in 1958, Senator Everett McKinley Dirksen of Illinois replaced him. A strong-minded man, Knowland had had his differences with Eisenhower, especially in foreign policy, but they nevertheless had worked well together. Eisenhower called him "an effective party leader in the Senate."

Dulles' death was a great personal loss to Eisenhower. A strong bond had grown between them. Nothing so draws men together as a shared experience, especially one of danger or adversity, and as Dulles wasted away with cancer, Eisenhower, sitting beside his friend in the hospital, remembered that the first sign of it had appeared in 1956 when they were passing through the anxious days of Suez together. The President visited him frequently in the hospital until May 24, 1959, when Dulles died in his sleep.

The era of presidential travels, of private talks with many heads of state, of efforts to establish contacts with the Russians was about to begin.

Not long after the death of Dulles, Eisenhower moved into the field of foreign affairs. He never conceded, after he left the White House, that Dulles' policies in the Cold War were too "rigid" nor that the lines he followed were different. Perhaps not. But Dulles formed alliances and remained skeptical of Summit meetings whereas Eisenhower, searching for means to break the East-West stalemate, began exploring avenues of personal contacts with the Communists to see where they might lead.

Thus, in the summer of 1959, Richard M. Nixon went to Moscow to open the American Exhibition there. Earlier in the year, Anastas I. Mikoyan, deputy premier of the Soviet Union, had visited Washington. Nixon sat next to him at a small private dinner. Their conversation was a prelude to the vice president's dramatic "kitchen debate" with Khrushchev a few months later. It covered the whole range of Soviet-American hostility, the arid deserts and forbidding mountains of policy standing between the two governments. Much of it concerned Berlin. Khrushchev had announced his intention to conclude a separate peace treaty with East Germany on May 27 which, he argued, would abrogate the Western Allies' right to remain in Berlin. Once again it appeared that they might have to send armed convoys to shoot their way into the city. Nixon emphasized to Mikoyan that Eisenhower would not back away from that threat. (In West Berlin they were saying, "Nervous? Our nerves have callouses on them.") Nixon handled himself well. His conversation with Mikoyan suggested the possible usefulness in further informal talks between American and Soviet officials at all levels. The opening of the American Exhibition, with Nixon attending, could be used as a test. It would give him an opportunity to fathom Khrushchev's thinking and to gather information without being in a position to make any commitments. Nixon consulted Dulles in the hospital when the idea was under discussion. Dulles not only approved, he strongly urged a go-ahead. Nixon was the most important American official to set foot in Moscow in 12 years.

The unusual "debate" with Khrushchev began in the model kitchen installed in the American Exhibition but it continued wherever they met. It turned into a rough-and-tumble as the vice president and the Soviet Premier argued about the captive nations and the relative merits of Communist and Democratic systems. In the kitchen, and recorded on television, Nixon broke in on Khrushchev and said, "The way you are dominating this conversation..." And then he proceeded to dominate it himself. Later he delivered a statement over the radio in Moscow in which he said one of Eisenhower's overriding objectives was to improve the outlook for peace and that the question of melting some of the ice in the Cold War was "up to Khrushchev."

Nixon then went on to Poland to be greeted by tremendous crowds, showered with flowers, and everywhere given expressions of friendliness. His journey was an unqualified success, not on a government-to-government basis, but as a reflection of the desire of the people for a changed climate in the world.

Government—and People...

How to hurdle governments and reach the people directly not only in Communist countries but in the unaligned nations? How to correct misconceptions and counter propaganda by contacts with the man on the street and the farm? Eisenhower had been working on a plan for a large-scale exchange of students with the Russians, as many as 10,000. He had advanced an imaginative proposal, a People-to-People program to bring together Americans in all walks of life with their counterparts in other countries.

A highly constructive and successful development came of this. Eisenhower interested a Washington physician, Dr. William B. Walsh, in the People-to-People program and Walsh came up with a brilliant idea: Why not bring a Navy hospital ship out of mothballs, refit her and sail her into regions where millions of persons badly needed medical attention? In February, 1959, the President gave Walsh the green light. Walsh got his ship (after a terrific struggle with Washington bureaucracy), persuaded specialists, nurses and technicians to interrupt their work at home, and sailed away to islands and poverty-ridden communities where few of the residents had ever seen a doctor before. What could be more person-to-person than the act of an American surgeon removing a six and one-half pound parotid tumor from an Indonesian woman? Or an American woman pediatrician fighting to save a child's life in a remote region of Viet Nam infested with Viet Cong guerrillas? No strings were attached, no quid pro quo, as is often the case when Washington extends aid to another government. Each of the multitudes who came aboard the ship, renamed HOPE, received a simple message printed in his own language. It said the ship was not a government project, that all the cost of supplies, equipment and operation came out of gifts from American individuals, corporations, labor unions. The last sentence said, "The American people wish you well." The ship brought a shining image of America to thousands and thousands of people in Asia, Africa and Latin America and Walsh has presented evidence to show that her missions even converted persons who considered themselves Communists.

The effects of all such actions, Nixon's visit, cultural exchanges, Person-to-Person, of course cannot be measured. In the majority of the nations of the world, the average man or woman does not make official policy, nor can he affect the making of it very much. However, Eisenhower was looking ahead to the day when younger men would replace the hard-bitten old revolutionaries in the upper echelons of the Communist regimes. If he could reach younger people, cause them at least to wonder about the daily blasts of anti-American propaganda, perhaps the future might hold a brighter hope. (The point is probably even more cogent today in the case of Red China.) At any rate, what he initiated represented efforts to try something new, to start even a small forward movement toward a better prospect for peace. They showed a man of vision and enterprise.

Next he made a move that would be described as the "boldest gesture" in more than a year. Word reached the President, through a newspaper report, of a Khrushchev hint that he would like to visit the United States and thought Eisenhower should follow with a visit to the Soviet Union. The report intrigued Eisenhower. Was it possible, barely possible at all, that he could sit down alone with the Soviet Premier and convince him that it would be advantageous to all the major powers to relax the tensions? Eisenhower immediately discussed the question with Christian A. Herter, successor to Dulles, and decided to issue the invitation. The gears seem to have slipped somewhere in the liaison between the White House and the State Department concerning the terms of Khrushchev's visit, a fact which greatly irritated the President. In effect, he chewed out the officials involved. But then, as he often did, he shouldered the blame for the slipup himself. "After a bit of cool reflection," he said, "I realized that the cause of the difficulty lay more in my own failure to make myself unmistakably clear than in the failure of others to understand me."

On Aug. 5, at a press conference, he announced that Khrushchev would come to the United States in mid-September. He anticipated that there would be adverse reaction to this as well as to his own projected trip to Russia. But he said, "Any President who refused flatly to use…the last atom of his energy in the quest for peace…ought to be condemned by the American people."

The New York Times applauded. On Oct. 16, the newspaper said, "Mr. Eisenhower's surprise announcement two weeks ago that he had invited Premier Khrushchev to the United States and that he would visit Russia this Fall is by far the boldest gesture in American diplomacy since the landing of the Marines in Lebanon a year ago. That this was his own decision can scarcely be disputed."

Eisenhower's announcement stirred degrees of anxiety and even dismay in Bonn and Paris. Was the President about to negotiate a settlement on Berlin and other East-West frictions on his own, without consulting Adenauer and DeGaulle? Partly to erase any such misconceptions, and partly to renew his wartime acquaintanceship with DeGaulle, who had returned to power in 1958, Eisenhower mapped a trip to West Germany, England and France in advance of Khrushchev's arrival in the United States.

Unforgettable scenes formed around the President everywhere. Those who had followed him were accustomed to seeing huge throngs turn out in American cities to see him, but they were amazed by the size of the crowds in Bonn, London and Paris. In each capital, his car passed between solid walls of people lining the streets, shouting, cheering, waving banners and homemade signs..."We like Ike and Konnie" (Adenauer) in West Germany..."Welcome back, Ike" in London..."Vive le President" in Paris. As they always do, correspondents tried to estimate the numbers lining the route Eisenhower's car followed from the airport to the center of Bonn. Hundreds of thousands, obviously, they told each other. One suggested the figure might be as high as a half million. A gifted lady columnist, always less than enthusiastic about Eisenhower, snapped, acidly, "Make it a million, boys. That's the way history is written."

These were the people Eisenhower's forces had bombed and blasted and overrun 14 years before. Now he came on a mission of good will. The spirit shone in his face and the Germans responded to it with Teutonic lustiness.

Since the distance from London Airport to Grosvenor Square is much greater than the route the President covered in Bonn, there probably *were* a million Londoners cheering him when he entered the city. Wartime associations, memories of his magnificent Guildhall Speech, plain curiosity, all no doubt motivated them. But I witnessed a little tableau that is worth recounting in this connection. Eisenhower joined MacMillan at the Prime Minister's country residence, Chequers. Once he was inside the house, I went looking for a sandwich and found a milk bar in a small village nearby. A woman there put down her tea cup and said to the little boy with her, "Now, Charles, you must always remember that you saw the President of the United States today, in this very street, and a great man he is, too."

"Is he greater than Mr. Churchill, Mummy?"

"Well, no, of course not. Nobody is as great as Mr. Churchill. But Mr. Eisenhower is a very great man."

From England he went to Paris. The magic spell of personality seemed not to affect the residents of an outlying district of Paris. Only clusters of people watched Eisenhower and DeGaulle ride past. The

President later learned that DeGaulle twice ordered the chauffeur to stop and let down the convertible top on the car so the people could see them. The driver ignored the orders until the car had gone several miles further. Then he stopped and the top came back. They had passed through a predominantly Communist district.

Then, suddenly, the streets were jammed to the point of endangering glass store fronts and the gendarmes, arms locked, swayed back and forth under the pressure of the thousands behind them. The French love of drama and spectacle brought even greater numbers to L'Etoile when Eisenhower and DeGaulle marched to the foot of the Tomb of the Unknown Soldier. They stood, erect and soldierly, in the traditional moment of silence during the ceremony and complete silence fell over the throngs choking the noble avenues that converged on the Arc de Triomphe. When the plangent notes of a bugle sounded, salvos of cheers, "Vive Ike," "Vive le President," thundered across the great plaza. The newspaper, LeMonde, concluded its report of Eisenhower's Paris tour with the words, "You like this great and simple man."

A great and simple man…a President whose expression reflected honesty, straightforwardness and as always a fundamental humility. And so the journey was a personal triumph for Eisenhower. The implications, however, went beyond that. For by 1959, American policy had come to be regarded by many Europeans as haughty, sterile, unimaginative, unlikely to produce any solutions to the world's problems. As a British newspaper editor phrased it to me, "We feel tied to the American chariot and unable to touch the reins." But now the President was listening and talking to MacMillan, Adenauer and DeGaulle. He had made a significant gesture in his agreement to exchange visits with Khrushchev. And the millions who saw Eisenhower in the three capitals recognized that here was no imperious and inflexible man, presiding over Pax Americana.

The lady columnist, without intending it, had been right. History was being written on this journey.

In mid-September, Khrushchev arrived in Washington. Eisenhower met him at Andrews Air Base. The President was carefully correct. His normally warm expression lay hidden behind a mask of impassivity. He read a brief prepared statement of welcome, utterly astringent in tone. In reply, Khrushchev used the occasion to remind Americans of another Soviet step in space, guiding a rocket around the dark side of the moon. But he also spoke of peace and said it would be "sheer madness" to permit disagreement between "neighbors" to lead to war. So far so good for peaceful coexistence.

His visit was mapped in two sections, first a cross-country tour that would take him to California and back, followed by a stay at Camp David and informal conversations with the President. (Eisenhower would have liked his itinerary to include a visit to the Belle Springs Creamery in Abilene where the Soviet Premier would have been told that Eisenhower, as a young man, had worked an 84-hour week.)

Khrushchev was an original. He was tough, blunt-spoken, witty, sharp as a piece of broken glass. His highly skilled interpreter, Oleg Troyanovsky, probably filtered out many of the vulgarisms in Khrushchev's remarks but a startling number nevertheless survived. One of his favorite terms was the Russian equivalent for Shakespeare's "whoreson," which was rendered into English as "ruffians" or "riffraff." A reference to the ruthless suppression of the Hungarian uprising invariably brought a scowl and the statement from Khrushchev, "That question is a stinking dead rat that sticks in the throats of some people." He was a consummate actor who appeared to fly into a rage at a dinner in Los Angeles, accusing the mayor, Norris Poulson, of discourtesy and threatening to break off his tour then and there. But on a seeming impulse in a steel mill in Pittsburgh, Khrushchev suddenly unstrapped his wrist watch and gave it, with a warm hug, to a puddler. He found the crowds of Americans who turned out to see him not unfriendly but largely curious. He was all smiles on such occasions, beaming with a kind of porcine charm.

The tour finished, he joined Eisenhower at Camp David. An agenda for their conversations had been prepared by their respective staffs but they largely ignored it. Of several objectives, the President planned to emphasize one: That Khrushchev had the opportunity to go down in history as a great statesman if he would make some positive moves to relax East-West tensions. In light of Khrushchev's subsequent actions, it seems doubtful that Eisenhower's urgings made much of an impression on him.

At any rate, a Soviet Premier had visited the United States and the President would soon make a reciprocal visit to Russia. These steps, in themselves, suggested the possibility of improving the climate in the world. The optimism of the day was reflected in the term, "The Spirit of Camp David." Eisenhower never used this expression himself for, in fact, little was accomplished at Camp David. Khrushchev did abandon his deadline for attempting to change the status of Berlin and forcing the Western Allies out of the city. And the way opened for a conference preparatory to a Summit meeting with Khrushchev in 1960. Further, when he returned to Moscow, Khrushchev publicly described Eisenhower as a man sincerely working for peace.

But Khrushchev was a political chameleon. He would soon be raging at Eisenhower and calling him "my fishy friend."

For the moment, however, the toothy grin remained on Khrushchev's face. Probably as a result, Eisenhower's prestige rose to the skies in public opinion polls. One showed that 62 per cent of the persons questioned in the autumn of 1959 approved of his actions in domestic and foreign affairs. Had he been running for reelection, such ratings would have produced an even greater landslide than those of 1952 and 1956.

Eisenhower's next move demonstrated the extent of his popularity around the world. Having taken the bit in his teeth as a roving diplomat, he embarked in December on a tour of 11 countries, Italy, Turkey, Pakistan, Afghanistan, India, Iran, Greece, Tunisia, France, Spain and Morocco. He travelled 22,000 miles in 19 days, which was rather striking testimony to his physical condition. In each country, roaring, flower-throwing multitudes massed around him. Those in India, he said, exceeded even the giant victory celebrations that burst around him after the Second World War. At one point, entering New Delhi, the throngs stalled his car completely for nearly a half hour while the Prime Minister himself, Jawaharlal Nehru, attempted with a stick to force his way through. The arrival of police reserves finally opened a lane. In lesser degrees, the same demonstrations rose around the President wherever he went.

As might have been expected, Eisenhower minimized his own part in these great outpourings of cordiality. At a press conference after he returned to Washington, a correspondent said the acclaim had probably been greater for him than any man in history and asked his explanation of the phenomenon. Eisenhower said he believed the millions had come out, not because of him, but out of a desire to express their feelings of friendship for the United States. "I believe it is just that simple," he said. "Certainly, so many young people never heard of an old soldier of World War II…they didn't come out for any personal thing, particularly."

Then why, since the Indians and Pakistanis presumably felt equally friendly toward the Soviet Union, had Khrushchev and Bulganin received only a lukewarm reception when they visited those countries?

When the trip ended, Marvin Arrowsmith wrote an open letter to Mamie—

"Dear Mrs. Eisenhower:

"You were somewhat worried three weeks ago about your husband taking on the arduous tour from which he returned last night. You'll recall he told us about the concern of his family on Dec. 2, the day before he left.

"The President also said, however, that he felt a compulsion to make the trip—that he simply had to do what he could in behalf of world peace.

"Now that he is safely back with his family for Christmas, perhaps you would like to know how well he seemed to stand up during the gruelling three-continent journey that sometimes had us reporters almost on the ropes. In short, his performance from a physical standpoint amazed us. At 69 years of age, he wore us younger fellows to a frazzle.

"We're sure of course that he is tired. But on the second to last day of the tour he came down the ramp from his jet airliner at Madrid with the bounce of a man just home from a month at the beach.

"As he has in every other nation on arrival, he was on his feet for miles—waving, bowing, smiling everlastingly to the huge crowds which jammed the roadside.

"His berth aboard the jet must have looked mighty good. We heard that he grinned and said to an aide:

"'Wake me up when I awaken.'"

In February, 1960, the President was on the move again, this time to Latin America. He stopped first in Puerto Rico and then went to Brazil, Argentina, Chile and Uruguay. On the whole, as in his other travels, he was warmly received. Here and there he heard shouts of "Yankee imperialism" from students but by contrast construction workers in Brasilia, the new capital of Brazil, greeted him like a hero. He returned to Washington after two weeks satisfied that he had made a contribution toward strengthening the ties between the United States and the South American nations.

Taken together, the two journeys gave Eisenhower every reason to hope that before the end of his term, now in its last year, he could also contribute to insuring peace in the world. The problem was to open more lines of communication with the Communists. He had made a start with Khrushchev and he hoped to make further progress at the Summit Conference to be held in Paris in May.

All these hopes were to be extinguished in the crash of an airplane near a city named Sverdlovsk.

• • •

Toward sunrise on the morning of May 1, 1960, a black airplane with a huge wingspan taxied down the runway of an air base in Adana, Turkey. The wings were so wide that they had to be supported by removable wheels which dropped away when the aircraft became airborne. This was a U-2 and she was starting on another mission of espionage over the Soviet Union.

The pilot, Francis Gary Powers, of Pound, Virginia, had logged more than 500 hours in U-2s. His present mission was to carry him from Peshawar, Pakistan, across nearly 3,000 miles of Russian territory to the terminus of the flight in Norway. As usual, he would fly at an altitude well above 60,000 feet which, heretofore, had been beyond the range of Soviet fighters or antiaircraft artillery. A specific task was to determine whether the Russians were building their first Intercontinental Ballistics Missile base and, if so, to photograph it.

The U-2s had been making such flights for nearly four years. The Russians knew about them and Washington was aware that they knew. Why, then, had Khrushchev remained silent? Why had he not fired off salvos of protests, indignantly proclaiming to the world that American planes were violating Soviet air space and, moreover, doing so for purposes of spying? The reason probably was that to make this announcement the Soviets would have had to admit that they were powerless to reach and destroy the U-2s in flight. Time and again, Russian fighter pilots rose toward a U-2 only to feel the controls become mushy in the rarefied atmosphere and then feel their planes falling away. Evidently, Khrushchev preferred to endure the overflights rather than concede that he could not keep them out of Russian skies. Improved detection systems and the advancing science of rocketry extricated him from the predicament on May 1.

Russian radar probably locked on Powers the instant he crossed the border, and began tracking his flight. Over the city of Sverdlovsk, at an altitude of 68,000 feet, something hit the U-2. At his subsequent trial, Powers said he felt rather than heard an explosion and saw "an orange flash or an orange-colored light behind me."

The word reached Eisenhower later in the day that an American "reconnaissance" plane flying out of Turkey was overdue and probably lost. The President suspected that what had long worried him had now happened—a U-2 was down inside the Soviet Union. He prepared to face the storm that would soon be raging around his head. He had authorized the construction of the U-2s and their flights over Russia.

It may be that there are states, such as Monaco or Liechtenstein, that do not engage in espionage, but most nations do, in one form or another. Eisenhower had offered the Russians his "open skies" plan in 1955. Not long after they rejected it, he started his own, using the U-2s. The planes brought back tons of information from Russia. Sometimes, it was reported, so many thousands of feet of undeveloped film piled up in the Central Intelligence Agency that the flights were suspended until the photographs could be processed. The cameras that took them were spectacularly efficient. During the excitement over the Powers case, the administration released a picture of an automobile parking lot in California, taken from an altitude of more than 13 miles. The details were so sharp and clear that the white stripes marking the parking stalls were easily visible. Eisenhower never made, nor felt impelled to make, any apologies for the aerial espionage over Russia. Dealing with a closed society, he felt justified in using any means necessary to prevent a repetition of Pearl Harbor, Russian-style.

What came next rattled the windows in chancelleries around the world. The President assumed personal responsibility for Powers' flight.

In the early sequence of events, the administration issued a "cover" story—a prepared lie—about the missing U-2. It said the plane was known to be missing and added that the pilot reported difficulty with his oxygen equipment in flight. Then, the story said, "It is entirely possible that having a failure in the oxygen equipment could result in the pilot losing consciousness, the plane continued on automatic pilot for a considerable distance and accidentally violated Soviet air space."

Plausible enough but for an ace stuck in Khrushchev's sleeve. A day or two later, he played it. He announced that Powers was alive, a captive and talking. Photographs showed the debris of the U-2 and the array of articles in Powers' equipment, the camera, the destructor unit, bank notes of different national currencies, a pistol equipped with a silencer.

Now, manifestly, the "cover story" would not mislead a child.

Eisenhower's instinct from the first was to say, in effect, "Yes, it was an espionage mission. Spying is a dirty but necessary business in this world and the Soviets are among the greatest practitioners of it." He proposed to take the responsibility himself. Conflicting advice came from all sides. Manifestly, Washington could not maintain a stony silence in the customary manner of a government when one of its spies had been caught. The evidence was too conclusive. It was suggested that a subordinate be made the scapegoat. Eisenhower rejected this out of hand. Finally, he determined to bring the whole matter into the open. Under Herter's signature, a statement (the fourth since Powers was downed) was issued. The key sentence said, "In accordance with the National Security Act of 1947, the President has put into effect since the beginning of his administration directives to gather by every possible means the information required to protect the United States and the Free World against surprise attack…"

This was unprecedented. But it was completely consonant with Eisenhower's character. As a soldier he had always been prepared to assume responsibility for a setback. Now, again, he stepped into the open.

Meanwhile, he went ahead with intention to attend a Summit in Paris, scheduled to open in less than a week, where he would confront Khrushchev across the conference table. On arrival, he learned that Khrushchev would demand a personal apology from him, punishment of those involved in the U-2 flights, etc. This, the President said, was out of the question. The possibility of any tangible results accruing from the meeting, if it ever existed, now seemed wholly foreclosed.

The four heads of state met in the Elysée Palace. It had been agreed beforehand that Eisenhower would speak first. But DeGaulle, presiding, had barely finished his statement opening the meeting when Khrushchev demanded the floor. DeGaulle glanced at Eisenhower and the President nodded, indicating he had no objection. Khrushchev then wheeled out all his histrionic artillery, pouring a barrage of invective on Eisenhower. He said the President had ordered the acts of espionage, which was true, had refused to condemn them, also true, and had said they would be continued, which was not true. This American policy, Khrushchev continued, "dooms the Summit

Conference to complete failure in advance." He suggested, with his eye on the approaching presidential elections in November, that Eisenhower's successor might be more favorable to "peaceful coexistence" and that therefore the Summit should be postponed until the new President took office. Then he shot the final barb: Eisenhower could no longer be greeted by the Russian people with "the proper cordiality" and so his visit should be postponed, too.

Through it all, the President kept his temper. While the Soviet Premier was fulminating, Eisenhower penciled notes on the statement he prepared to make. His voice was calm when he began speaking. He disavowed any aggressive intent on the U-2 flights and corrected Khrushchev on one point, that they would be continued. (Obviously, if the Soviets now possessed rockets capable of reaching a U-2, there would be little point in sending them over Russian territory.) The President said he had ordered the flights to be stopped.

DeGaulle and MacMillan advanced arguments for going ahead with the Summit but Khrushchev and his aides walked out. The French President called another meeting. Khrushchev said he would attend only if its purpose was to cover his demands for an apology and assurances from Eisenhower.

On the following day, with no signs of another meeting, Eisenhower scheduled a helicopter flight to Chartres to see the famous stained glass windows in its cathedral. Bad weather canceled the trip. He spent a large part of the afternoon in Notre Dame examining its treasures.

So the Summit aborted.

Khrushchev's reasons for coming to Paris at all may remain forever a mystery. He may have concluded that he could wring no concessions from the Allies on Berlin or in the area of disarmament. He may also have decided not to run the risk of seeing the President acclaimed in Moscow as he had been in so many other capitals. What the Soviet leader did achieve was to extract the maximum propaganda value from the sad event by using an international forum to tell Eisenhower he would not be welcome in Moscow.

He then further insulted the President, and issued a thinly veiled threat at a gigantic press conference attended by some 2,000 correspondents in the Palais de Chaillot. He was asked why he had not discussed the U-2 flights with Eisenhower at Camp David. Khrushchev replied that the thought had crossed his mind, since "the atmosphere was so convivial." But he said he concluded that "there was something about this fishy friend of mine and I didn't broach the subject." Then came the implied threat. Recalling his boyhood, Khrushchev said, "Whenever we caught a cat in the pigeon loft, we took it by the tail and banged its head against the wall, and that was the only way it could be taught some sense."

Gone now were Eisenhower's hopes of achieving at least a modicum of understanding with the Soviet leader. Perhaps a foundation for them never really existed. Or perhaps Khrushchev's apparent change of heart came from a power struggle in the murky depths of the Kremlin that forced him to return to the hard line.

But the President's prestige seemed undiminished by the events in Paris. On the way home, he stopped in Lisbon and the familiar scene of applauding crowds greeted him. When he landed in Washington, several thousand people cheered him at the airport and many more lined the streets on the way to the White House. His car passed beneath an arch bearing the words, "Thank you, Mr. President." His effort to reach the Russians had failed but people were grateful for his having made it.

In that very hour, as he rode down Pennsylvania Avenue in Washington an explosion that would involve him was building to a climax on the other side of the world.

Hundreds of thousands of Japanese were snake dancing and screeching in the streets of Tokyo, demonstrating against the renewal of the Security Treaty between Japan and the United States. Communist influence tinctured the rioting but the frenzied hordes were by no means all Communists. Nor were they anti-American. They were anti-Treaty.

The roots of their opposition to it were deep and strong. When the Pacific War ended the overwhelming majority of Japanese said to each other, "Never again." They had suffered terribly and the horrors of Hiroshima and Nagasaki had burned indelibly into Japanese memory. Article 9 of the postwar Constitution reflected these feelings. It bound Japan to "forever renounce war as a sovereign right of a nation." It further stipulated that "land, sea and air forces or other war potential, will never be maintained."

The United States then undertook the defense of Japan. A treaty was signed in 1952.

As the Cold War developed, and especially when the United

States used Japan as its main base in fighting the Korean War, Japanese of all walks of life became deeply concerned. The majority, probably an overwhelming majority, feared that Japan would become involved in the East-West struggle. They passionately desired to remain clear, totally neutral. Many opposed the organization of "Self Defense Forces," small land, sea and air units, contending that this brought Japan even closer to the United States. They even opposed providing the police with proper equipment, remembering the 1930s when Japan was a Fascist state with a ruling clique supported by the armed forces, a dreaded secret police and the conventional police.

Eisenhower had accepted invitations to visit Japan, the Philippines and Formosa. He had planned to fly to the Far East from Russia, arriving in Tokyo June 19. When Khrushchev withdrew the invitation for him to come to Russia, the President simply prepared to fly to the Orient from the United States.

Meanwhile, the Security Treaty came up in the Diet (Japan's Parliament) for revision and renewal. Socialists, Communists and other political opponents of Prime Minister Nobosuke Kishi set out to block the ratification. The Communists particularly blazoned the U-2 incident as evidence of the dangers of American policy. Khrushchev had warned the governments of countries where U-2s had been stationed that Soviet missiles were "zeroed in" on these air bases—and Japan, due to the presence of U-2s on its soil, was among these. The Leftists cried havoc. No doubt their arguments echoed in many an uneasy Japanese heart.

As for Eisenhower's impending visit, Kishi's opponents asserted that its underlying purpose was to ensure the renewal of the Security Treaty.

Riotous scenes developed in the Diet. The debates continued for more than 100 days. Then, while members of the Opposition were absent from the Diet, Kishi rammed through the ratification.

With that, gigantic demonstrations began. Miraculously, only one person, a university coed, was killed. An organization of university students, the Zengakuren, which could rightly claim to speak for hundreds of thousands of students, and Sohyo, the biggest labor group, spearheaded the demonstrations. However, thousands of Japanese who were not affiliated with either group also participated. They simply were passionate neutralists, as they often took pains to explain to Americans who stood watching the snake dancing.

Kishi took his bold step on May 19 and the new Treaty would become effective a month later, June 19, the date of Eisenhower's arrival.

As the days passed, violence increased in Tokyo. The police were ill-equipped to control the mobs, lacking riot weapons and restrained from using the strong-arm tactics of the prewar police.

However, on June 9, Kishi went on nationwide television and said the government could guarantee the safety of Eisenhower when he came to Tokyo. Events swiftly overtook this assurance.

On the following day, Hagerty and Thomas Stevens, another White House aide, came in to map the arrangements for the President's visit. At Haneda Airport, a huge mob immediately surged around their car, rocking it and beating it with sticks. The demonstrators made no effort to physically injure Hagerty and Stevens. On the contrary, Hagerty reported, one man who jostled a Secret Service agent bowed low in apology—and then went on banging the hood of the car with a stick. When it became apparent that the police could not open a way for the car to move, a helicopter extricated Hagerty and Stevens and took them to the United States Embassy in Tokyo.

This scene, the demonstrators warned, was only a small sample of what they would organize when Eisenhower's plane landed at Haneda.

Ironically, it appears that Eisenhower did not want to undertake the Far Eastern trip, not because of Hagerty's experience, but simply because he was tired of traveling. Someone present at the Cabinet meeting of June 9 and attempting to keep fragmentary notes of the proceedings, scribbled these words of the President. "don't want any part of this trip...don't want to go...duty for America...will mean good will for America..."

Nevertheless, he left for the Far East on June 12. He made a brief stop in Alaska and then flew on to the Philippines. In Manila, at least one million persons thronged into the streets in another great demonstration of affection. Manila held a special meaning for the President. A quarter of a century earlier, Lt. Col. Eisenhower had been stationed here.

The unhurried past, like a dislocated frame of motion picture film, now merged with the burdened present. Eisenhower was reviewing a military parade in Luneta Park in Manila when the news came from Tokyo. The Japanese government announced that it would ask him to postpone his visit.

The Communists could proclaim this as another humiliation of

Eisenhower and a heavy blow to the prestige of the United States. At first blush, it appeared so.

But this ignores the texture of public opinion in Japan at the time. When the excitement died away and a thoughtful Japanese would try, with great difficulty to explain his feelings, this line of reasoning (or visceral foreboding) emerged: The Treaty, a military pact, tied Japan more closely to the United States, therefore it heightened the possibility of involving Japan in another war. This was not anti-American, it was simply the desire to remain clear of involvements. Better to leave Japan totally undefended, without one man under arms, than to be atomized. Yes, your friend would concede, this was perhaps an ostrich-head-in-the-sand position. Perhaps it was unrealistic. But perhaps, too, Japan could make her own accommodations with Communist China and Russia while remaining friendly with the United States.

One such conversation seemed especially significant. It took place during a long afternoon in an inn in Kyoto with two members of Zengakuren. Both were law students at the University of Kyoto. Both had participated in the demonstrations. Both said they were Marxists.

They said Red China and Russia were "peace loving" nations whereas the "ruling clique" in the United States was bent on aggression. Therefore, Japan's best interests lay with the two Communist countries. Manifestly, these interests could not be served so long as military ties bound Japan to the United States. They followed the standard Communist line, often blinking the facts, often performing incredible contortions of reasoning to support their conclusions. It was old stuff, banal and boring, except in one surprising respect, Eisenhower.

"Your President," one of the students said, "is a good and sincere man. He does not want war, it is the American militarists who try to push him. The Japanese people like Mr. Eisenhower. We hope he will come to Japan now. We demonstrated against the Treaty, not Mr. Eisenhower."

Even here among the Japanese Marxists, it seemed, if these two could be considered typical, the tendency to "like Ike" remained unshaken.

And so it was at home. Political critics might gloat in private over the "humiliations" of Paris and Tokyo and mourn in public over the damage to American prestige in the world. But the President's popularity remained unmarred. The phenomenon, elusive, hidden in the mysteries of personality, had often been noted during his seven and one-half years in the White House. When something went wrong, a Little Rock or a decline in farm income, public censure tended to center on a Cabinet officer or a department of government, not on Eisenhower. Criticism of the administration seldom translated itself into criticism of the President. "He was badly advised," people would say. Or, "Ike's trying to do his best, it's the politicians who mess things up."

Through thick and thin, Eisenhower retained the affection of the overwhelming majority of Americans. They responded to the shining qualities of his spirit.

• • •

Eisenhower now began the last six months of his tenure in office. They were not to be quiet reaches of the sea before he came into harbor.

On New Year's Day of 1959, a bearded Cuban giant approached the outskirts of Havana. His name was Fidel Castro and he was by no means unknown in the United States. For some six years, he had been working and fighting to unseat the dictator, Fulgencio Batista. Now he had succeeded and for a short time it appeared that the unhappy history of Cuba had taken a new turn. Who was Fidel Castro? What did he stand for? Conflicting reports about him reached Eisenhower. On the one hand, he had promised free elections, social reforms, an end to corruption in Cuba. On the other, he was said to have Communist support and Nixon, who had a long talk with him, said in a report that Castro either was naive about Communism or "under Communist discipline."

In short order, Castro began to emerge in his true colors. He announced that the Communist Party in Cuba, previously held underground, would now be permitted to operate legally. Mass executions of his opponents began. He betrayed his promise to hold free elections, announcing they would be postponed for two years. The CIA reported the probability that Communists would participate in Castro's government. When he learned of this, Eisenhower said he was "provoked" that the estimate had not been given to him earlier. The rest is history, tragic history.

The President immediately began studying possible areas of counteraction. He concluded that his first step should be in the field of personal diplomacy. This inspired his tour of South America in the early months of 1960, one purpose of which was to organize collective opposition to Castro in the Latin American republics, He learned something of economic and social conditions there and that Castro had captured the imagination of those Latin Americans who desired reforms. The President saw one placard which read, "We like Ike. We like Fidel, too." Soon after, steps were taken to formulate a plan to assist the Latin American governments to raise living standards and bring about social reforms with American financial assistance. This culminated in the signing of the Act of Bogota in the autumn of 1960. In "Waging Peace," Eisenhower wrote of this plan:

"'Nonintervention' had given way to a new idea—the idea that *all* American nations had an interest in ending feudalism, the vast hereditary gulf between rich and poor, the system that assured to a handful of families opulence without labor and condemned millions to near starvation without opportunity."

He also studied proposals aimed at bringing Castro's downfall through economic sanctions. He first radically reduced the quota of Cuban sugar purchased by the United States and then cut off the sugar imports entirely.

By secret Executive Order he authorized the arming and training of Cuban refugees, guerrilla forces for possible counterrevolution in Cuba. The plan never crystallized to that point, in part because no Cuban political leader emerged with whom the administration could deal. And after he left office, Eisenhower emphasized that no specific strategic or tactical plan for military operations in Cuba were formulated during his administration.

Only a few months in office now remained to Eisenhower. The problem of what, specifically, should be done about Castro was to be left to his successor.

When he returned to private life, he frequently was asked to comment on the fiasco in the Bay of Pigs. He consistently refused to criticize or "second guess." But in one conversation, he said:

"I don't know whether I would have ever agreed to the Bay of Pigs operation. I know that when the plan was set up the details were finally approved by the military authorities, and I have the greatest respect for their strategic concepts and their common sense. Now the plan was changed somewhat at the very last minute.

"The only thing I would say is this: If I had gone into any movement like that, I would have made sure it was a success. I think any time the United States decides to put its hand to anything that is going to be done by force, you've got to go through…When you appeal to force, a nation such as ours must be successful."

In September, while Eisenhower was watching the campaign duel between Richard Nixon and John F. Kennedy, an unprecedented number of heads of state prepared to attend the sessions of the United Nations General Assembly. MacMillan, Khrushchev, Nehru, Nasser, Sukarno of Indonesia, Diefenbaker of Canada, Tito of Yugoslavia, Janos Kadar of Hungary, Prince Norodom Sihanouk of Cambodia, Nkrumah of Ghana and Castro, along with the heads of newly independent African states, announced their intentions to come to New York.

As a result of the disturbances in the Congo, the United Nations had come under severe attack from the Russians. They had attempted to capitalize on the trouble there and had been unceremoniously booted out. Troops under the aegis of the United Nations came into the country to provide assistance in restoring law and order. The United States, rapidly mobilizing fleets of planes, provided the bulk of the logistical support in the inception.

Eisenhower foresaw that Khrushchev would use the Assembly forum to attack the United Nations and the Secretary General, Dag Hammarskjold. So the President determined to address the General Assembly on the opening day of the sessions. In his speech, he strongly defended Hammarskjold and offered a five-point program of assistance to the emerging African nations, under the United Nations.

As expected, Khrushchev followed with one of his bulldozer speeches, attacking Hammarskjold. He said the actions of the Secretary General in the Congo were "shameful," and by inference called him a "stooge" of "colonialists." He pulled out all the stops, volleying and thundering.

The delegates of the newer Asian and African nations could not fail to mark the contrast between Khrushchev's approach and Eisenhower. If the Soviet leader intended to impress them, he failed utterly. In talking with correspondents, they expressed astonishment and dismay. MacMillan evidently found the same reaction. "A feeling is growing that Khrushchev has badly overplayed his hand," he told the President.

Weird, if not inspirationally memorable, scenes took place in the Assembly…Khrushchev banging his shoe on the desk in an afternoon of uproar...Castro, bearded and wearing jungle fatigues, losing his audience (except for the Communist bloc) during a speech that lasted more than four hours...Sukarno, a pouter-pigeon little figure, grandly handing pages of his speech, as he finished reading them, to a bemedaled aide standing behind him...The Assembly President, Frederick H. Boland of Ireland, banging his gavel so hard that it broke and then abruptly recessing the session "in view of what has happened here this afternoon"...Khrushchev interrupting MacMillan and the Prime Minister, first pausing to hear a translation of the insults, urbanely proceeding with his speech...

A nation's prestige in the world cannot be measured with total accuracy. But if the United States suffered setbacks in 1960 from the events in Paris and Tokyo, Khrushchev and the Communists engineered their own loss of prestige when the new and/or uncommitted nations saw the saloon-brawling tactics of the Soviet leader and his minions.

Eisenhower seized the opportunity in this United Nations session to talk privately with a number of chiefs of state, especially those he had not met before, Tito and Nasser, Norodom Sihanouk and Nkrumah, Prime Minister B. P. Koirala of Nepal and Sylvanus Olympio of Togo. His purpose was two-fold, to hear in detail about their problems and to explain the objectives of American foreign policy. In such a setting, informal, man-to-man, the President could be very persuasive.

On Oct. 14, Eisenhower celebrated his 70th birthday, the only man to ever reach that age while presiding in the White House.

More important to him, however, time was running out in the election campaign and it appeared that the Democratic candidate, Senator John Fitzgerald Kennedy of Massachusetts, was leading Nixon. The President's role in the electioneering had been fixed in conferences with Nixon and the GOP captains soon after Nixon's nomination. In the early stages of the campaign Eisenhower would appear before nonpartisan audiences and in the closing weeks he would deliver some major political speeches.

Eisenhower was prepared to do everything in his power to help Nixon win, not only because he wanted a Republican in the White House, but because he considered Nixon well qualified to be there.

By the nature of presidency, no man can be wholly qualified for the office. It is a matter of degree; some men are better equipped than others. The expression, "on-the-job-training," is pointedly applicable to a new President.

However, Eisenhower had sought to prepare Nixon for the office by assigning him to a wide spectrum of tasks, at home and abroad, with which the President must deal. As early as 1957, Eisenhower wrote the vice president a memorandum outlining the work he wanted him to undertake in such areas as mutual assistance, technical and direct aid, trade policy, monetary matters and defense. Later, he made Nixon chairman of a Cabinet committee to watch price stability and the nation's economic growth. The vice president also presided over the Government Contracts Committee, an office that exposed him to the problems of racial and religious discrimination in business firms with government contracts. In the steel strike during the summer of 1959, the President assigned Nixon to work with Secretary of Labor Mitchell in bringing together the parties in the dispute. Some of these meetings took place in Nixon's Washington home. Eisenhower sent Nixon on liaison missions to Congress. In internal matters, such as the events that eventually led to the resignation of Sherman Adams, Eisenhower frequently asked Nixon's advice. Nixon sat directly opposite the President in meetings of the Cabinet and the National Security Council, where, of course, he heard discussions of and participated in, the whole, brain-numbing range of governmental business.

Nixon made his biggest splashes, however, outside the United States. The "kitchen debate" with Khrushchev sent his political stock rocketing. So did the wild demonstrations in Latin America which appeared to endanger the lives of his wife and himself. Eisenhower sent him on long travels through Asia and Africa. Nixon went to London while the memories of Suez still rankled with some Englishmen. Randolph Churchill, Winston Churchill's son, wrote of his activities there, "Good for Nixon! He had to do well and he did brilliantly." Evidently, however, the vice president did not win over all English hearts. Earl Mazo, his biographer, recalled that a Lord Winster wrote a letter to the Baltimore Sun saying, "By and large he did a solid good job…(but) he is not what we would call our cup of tea."

These varied undertakings, plus Nixon's wide acquaintance with Republican officers at all levels, made his nomination in 1960 a foregone conclusion.

The decision to engage in televised debates with Kennedy came soon after the nomination. Eisenhower did not approve, but he did not propose to manage Nixon's campaign. And so thousands of Americans laid eyes for the first time on Kennedy. They saw a slim, good looking, but forceful young man, quick with the riposte, surefooted in his positions. The general consensus was that Kennedy "won" the first debate. Nixon made better showings in the next two, but who made the best impression was a matter of opinion. (After the election, in his father's home in Hyannis Port, Kennedy told a group of reporters he was sure he could not have won, but for the debates.)

Eisenhower entered the lists in late September. In October, he increased the pace. He began drawing heavily on his physical reserves. He returned to Washington after one speech to find that his blood pressure had gone up. By that time, he was replying directly to Kennedy's principal contentions—that the nation was "standing still," that it had lost prestige in the world, and that Eisenhower had permitted a "missile gap" to put the United States behind Russia in armaments. (This alleged "missile gap" disappeared mysteriously some six months after Kennedy took office.) Eisenhower hit back by citing the specifics of the nation's economic growth and social progress during his administrations. Militarily, he said, the United States had become the most powerful nation on earth. He called the prestige issue "an exercise in calculated confusion."

Whether Eisenhower could have tipped the balance in Nixon's favor if he had entered the campaign earlier and made more speeches will long be debated. In fact, he said, he came into the fray when Nixon asked him to do so, and made more speeches than originally had been planned. A number of Republican candidates rode into office on Eisenhower's coattails in 1952, but they failed in subsequent elections to wrap the mantle of his popularity around their shoulders. Nor, in all probability, could Eisenhower have done it for Nixon. It had been tried before in a different setting. At a gigantic press conference in Chicago in 1956, with searchlights playing and cameras grinding, Harry Truman threw his arm around Averell Harriman and enthusiastically endorsed him for the Democratic presidential nomination. And the convention then nominated Adlai Stevenson.

At any rate, through the long night of Nov. 8, 1960, and the next day's interminable morning, it became apparent that Nixon had lost the election. Kennedy won by the narrowest margin in 72 years, 113,000 votes. As the political slide rules showed, a change of about 12,000 votes in five states would have elected Nixon.

To Eisenhower, the election result came as one of the most grievous disappointments of his eight years in office. He believed in his programs and took pride in the achievements of his administration. Now, he feared, "the spenders" would have their hands in the cash box again. He said he felt as though he had been "hit in the solar plexus with a baseball bat."

However, he lost no time probing his bruises. There was urgent work to be done, the first item of which was to arrange for the orderly transition of power. He had set the wheels in motion for this during the summer.

Not long afterward, he held his first meeting with Kennedy. The President-elect drove to the White House alone, without any jubilant advisers, and this impressed Eisenhower favorably. They talked about the balance-of-payments problem, North Vietnamese depredations into Laos, Berlin, and Castro, with whose government Eisenhower would soon break relations.

On the evening of Jan. 17, Eisenhower addressed the nation for the last time as President. His statement contained a warning:

"The conjunction of an immense military establishment and a large arms industry is new in the American experience. The total influence—economic, political, even spiritual—is felt in every city, every state house, every office of the federal government. We recognize the imperative need for this development. Yet we must not fail to comprehend its grave implications. Our toil, resources and livelihood are all involved; so is the very structure of our society.

"In the councils of government we must guard against the acquisition of unwarranted influence, whether sought or unsought, by the military-industrial complex. The potential for the disastrous rise of misplaced power exists and will persist.

"We must never let the weight of this combination endanger our liberties or democratic processes…"

Here was a man who knew both sides of the coin, the soldier's and the President's.

He held his final briefing session with Kennedy two days later. They had come to like each other. A little banter, a little laughter, passed between them as Eisenhower again went over the pending business awaiting the new President. Yet the solemnity of the moment weighed heavily on both men, one about to depart the room where he had given so much of himself, the other about to shoulder the awesome burdens of office.

From having wished to retire at the end of his first term, Eisenhower had come to see the presidency as "a fascinating business." As the day approached when he would leave the White House, he appeared to feel a twinge of regret. Pointing to the reviewing stands erected along the route of the Inaugural parade, Eisenhower said, "I feel like the fellow in jail who is watching his scaffold being built."

His last press conference, No. 193, was more nostalgic than newsworthy on the part of both the President and the correspondents. He said he had always enjoyed the conferences, that on the whole he felt the reporters had done a good job of reporting to the nation about his administrations, and that he had come to regard some as good friends. No, he said, the "penetrating questions" (some of which might better be described as "needling") had not annoyed him. When he turned to leave the stage, they gave him a standing ovation. At the door, he paused and looked back into the room. He was blushing.

On Inauguration Day, only moments after the end of the eternally impressive ceremony, Eisenhower and his wife slipped quietly through the crowd in front of the Capitol to a waiting automobile. Before nightfall they were driving toward the farmhouse on the outskirts of Gettysburg and a family reunion.

Dwight D. Eisenhower was a private citizen after nearly a half century in the service of his country and the world.

Fulfillment

In retirement, Eisenhower settled gratefully into the house on a gentle knoll, surrounded by ancient oaks, white pines, flowers bright as paint, more or less in the center of his farmland. In a sense, the wheel turned full circle when he came to spend his last years in the Pennsylvania Dutch country. For the Reverend Jacob Eisenhower had moved west from this region in the Spring of 1878. His grandson, Capt. Dwight Eisenhower, had returned to it in 1918 as an instructor at nearby Camp Colt. The camp had vanished long since, but Eisenhower never forgot the countryside, rolling hills and handsome farms, the changing moods of sunshine and lowering clouds, the site of Lincoln's Gettysburg Address, which he regularly visited. For years, in Army barracks, hotels, apartments and then in official residences, he had pictured his own home on the farm. At last the day came. A new life (but not the leisurely life he anticipated) opened before him in the house on the knoll. These were to be the golden years.

He had passed his 70th birthday when he left Washington but his ruddy cheeks and quick, firm step belied his age. The electric blue eyes, so expressive that they usually signaled his mood before he spoke, were as bright as ever. He settled down, secure in a sense of accomplishment, and prepared to reconcile his private and public life in the days ahead.

Eisenhower for years had been an early riser. On the farm, he fell into the habit of taking a walk before breakfast, often breasting a boisterous northwest wind. He walked from the house to the front gate and back. On the macadamed driveway, he strolled through an allee of trees, 50 white pines, (his favorite tree), each the gift of a state Republican Party. At the gate, he could picture the bivouacs of a gray-uniformed host, the Army of Northern Virginia, just before the glory and tragedy of Cemetery Hill. The troops must have encamped on the north section of what became Eisenhower's property. A marker close to his fence says that Gen. LaFayette MacLaw's Division arrived here shortly after dark on July 1, 1863. A step or two away, another marker indicates the site of Gen. James Longstreet's headquarters. To Eisenhower, long since a student of the battle, his own acres were hallowed ground.

Turning back toward the house, he looked across a shallow valley and in the distance he could see the Blue Ridge Mountains, shouldering through the Western sky. He passed, on his left, the barn, farm buildings and the pens for his Black Angus, and on his right, the flat stretch where a helicopter could land when he called for one. A powerful searchlight, set beneath the ridgepole of the barn and visible for 15 miles, guided in the helicopter pilots and smaller lights on the ground showed them the flarepath. Eisenhower could be in Washington in a matter of minutes when, as often happened, John F. Kennedy and Lyndon Johnson requested him to come to the White House.

A few steps more and he reached his front door. The round trip to the gate had covered exactly one mile.

At that early hour, when the sky is nacreous, the larger section of his house, painted white, gleams like fresh snow in the morning sunlight. Adjoining it is a smaller section with walls of dun-colored native stone. A little white structure nearby looks for all the world like a one-room country schoolhouse and it may have been so in another era. Now it has two rooms and serves as a guest house. A screened porch, trimmed with wrought iron like the balconies in New Orleans, faces east from the main dwelling. It overlooks boxwood and flower beds, Eisenhower's putting green and the "tea house," where he could preside over a barbecue.

When they settled on the farm, Mrs. Eisenhower made the selection and care of the flowers her special preserve. She planted daffodils, lilies, crocus, narcissus, gardenia, geraniums, tulips, pink and purple lilacs, a species of rose named for the former Chancellor of Germany, Konrad Adenauer, and columbine, the official flower of her native Colorado. Eisenhower named one of his presidential airplanes The Columbine. A metal plaque standing in a flower bed beside the porch speaks of flowers—

"The kiss of the sun for pardon,
"The song of the birds for mirth.
"One is nearer God's heart in a garden
"Than anywhere else on Earth."

The farm became the focal point of Eisenhower's new life. He busied himself with crops and cattle, reading, playing bridge, holding political meetings and, best of all, entertaining his friends. (Richard Nixon has observed, "Eisenhower is not a man who gets close to people easily, despite his outward affability. Eisenhower is a very reserved man and very cautious in the extension of his personal friendship...when he makes friends he keeps them for a long time.") Now he had the leisure to enjoy his friends.

He soon acquired a second center of activity, a two-story building on the University of Gettysburg campus which became his office. Under federal law, the government provides a former President and five-star general with funds for an office and staff. When the university building became available, it was leased for Eisenhower. Considering the work he had mapped out for himself, he badly needed it.

A room facing Carlisle Street in Gettysburg became his private office. A circle of five stars was engraved on the glass door. He placed a small bronze figure of Lincoln, half-reclining on a bench, just outside the door. Eisenhower expressed his feelings about busts in a letter to a friend, written in 1957. He said, "Statues and busts of Lincoln were not made until after he died, if for no other reason than while he was alive he was more vilified than admired. While here and there I have seen busts of other Presidents...there is no single one of them that has ever provided me with any feeling of satisfaction, much less inspiration. All of which convinces me that I have sworn off sitting for sculptors for ever and ever. Amen!"

The great majority of the hundreds of awards, medals, jewels, ceremonial swords and other mementos of his glittering career went to the Eisenhower Library in Abilene but he kept some in the Gettysburg office. The facsimile of a newspaper hangs on one wall, announcing in skyscraper type the fall of Cherbourg, the first major city in Europe to be taken after the breakout in Normandy.

The nucleus of Eisenhower's staff had been with him in the White House, his aide, Brig. Gen. (Ret.) Robert L. Schulz, his personal secretary, Lillian Brown, and Dr. Kevin McCann and William Ewald who, along with his son, John, assisted him in the research of his books.

He would be at his desk by about 8 o'clock in the morning. He spent the first half-hour or so reading newspapers. A typewritten card, just as in the White House, listed his appointments in and out of the office for the day. Secretaries duplicated them in an appointments book. They ushered in the first caller at about 8:30.

The lists of visitors, over the years, reflects the range of Eisenhower's interests in retirement—national and foreign affairs, politics, religion, economics, military affairs, business. The books record visits from Dean Rusk, Arthur Goldberg, Cabot Lodge, Senators Barry Goldwater and Thruston Morton, Nixon, Hagerty, Ray Bliss, the Republican national chairman, Adm. Arthur W. Radford and Gen. James Doolittle, Lewis L. Strauss, former chairman of the Atomic Energy Commission, Amory Houghton, former ambassador to France, William Paley, communications executive, Roy Wilkins, executive secretary of the National Association for the Advancement of Colored People, Gen. Francis W. deGuingand, a British wartime associate, and many others. An entry for May 18, 1962, said, crisply, "George Romney here. No publicity."

He reserved his afternoons for writing, letters, a speech, an article or work on his books. A machine to record telegrams had been installed in another office and whenever Eisenhower made a speech or wrote for publication, the recorder would begin spinning off messages by the hundreds. A tremendous response came from his moving memorial to Winston Churchill at Churchill's funeral. Some days earlier, the British Broadcasting Company had telephoned Eisenhower to tell him that Churchill's last illness was irreversible, and asked Eisenhower if he would prepare a memorial statement. Eisenhower consented but then he puzzled for several days over what he should write. Millions of words had been written about the old statesman, reviewing his life and probing deeply, or trying to, into every facet of his character. What more could Eisenhower say? Finally, a thought came to him: He had enjoyed a unique relationship, sometimes stormy, always stimulating, with Churchill during the war and while each was chief of state. He began scribbling on a pad of yellow, legal-size paper, "The Churchill I Knew." When he had finished, he showed it to his wife. "It's wonderful, Ike," she said. "Now don't go changing it." The reason for her admonition was that Eisenhower is a fastidious, often nit-picking, rewriter. When he returned from London, he found a mound of letters and telegrams. People wrote that they wept when they heard him delivering the tribute to Churchill and one expressed, in simple American, the thought that threaded through many others: "You did us proud at Churchill's funeral."

From time to time, Eisenhower contributed to national magazines and one article is notable for what it reveals of himself. The topic was "Leadership." He listed five qualities for a leader, "selfless dedication, fortitude, humility, attention to homework, the power of persuasion." No doubt he attempted to conduct himself in conformity with this formula. But leaders more often have exhibited ambition and ruthlessness, not selflessness and humility. He wrote an article about D-Day for a Paris magazine, about faith for a religious publication, a number of statements about politics.

His mail averaged more than 150 letters a day long after he left the White House. Those that pricked his interest received answers, often at length. A schoolteacher in Georgia wrote Eisenhower that his pupils frequently posed questions about national and international problems which he found difficult in answering. He listed a number. Eisenhower dictated a reply that ran to four and one-half typewritten pages. He also initiated a wide correspondence. He would write friends, enclosing a newspaper report or editorial on a current topic and say, "I would appreciate having your thoughts on this."

Meanwhile, he worked steadily on the record of his two administrations. In four years he completed "Mandate for Change" and "Waging Peace." To organize the enormous mass of pertinent material, he first wrote a list of major and secondary subjects to be covered, hundreds of topic headings. That done, he would begin to dictate, "off the top of his head," as an assistant put it. Then a staff of researchers attacked the mountain of documents written at the time of these events. John and Dr. Milton Eisenhower assisted in this. His memory remained so clear, however, that the researchers found few errors of detail. When his secretaries delivered the typescript of his dictation, Eisenhower went to work to revise and rewrite. This was a long and painful process. He might be careless about the spoken word but he took infinite care with his writings, changing words, recasting passages, arguing with his staff about the use of "whom" or "who." When he came to narrate his role in the Second World War and his years in the presidency, he willingly stretched himself on the writer's torture rack, trying to be crystal clear.

The books about the White House years were thorough and detailed, admirable records of his two terms. Historians reviewed them favorably. However, they revealed little of the chief actor in these great events, Dwight D. Eisenhower. Historians and students found few clues to Eisenhower's character and personality in them. He seldom permitted his feelings to color the passages about even the most trying events. He wrote that he was "provoked" on one occasion and that a contretemps impelled him to "lecture" his staff on another. Yet each was a serious development that would seem to have warranted stronger words. Sherman Adams reported that Eisenhower, out of frustration with the Republican Old Guard, toyed with the thought of trying to organize a third political party, but if so, Eisenhower did not choose to describe his frustrations. Of all the fumbling and crossed wires in the Administration's statements in the U-2 case, Eisenhower wrote mildly, "The big error we made, of course, was in the issuance of a premature and erroneous cover story. Allowing myself to be persuaded on this score is my principal personal regret…" When Taft lost his temper and pounded the table over the proposed budget in 1953, Eisenhower's version of the incident leaves no doubt that it thoroughly angered him. But his book merely said Cabinet small talk gave "me time to cool off." The dismay that he felt as the Suez expedition approached its climax, feelings vividly set forth in personal letters, does not appear in his memoirs. Harsh events are related without rancor.

In part, the explanation lies in a statement he made during one of his earliest press conferences when he said he would not "deal in personalities." To have revealed his feelings about the wounding events of the White House years, the moments of disappointment or anger, would have meant naming names and reopening old quarrels. This was foreign to his nature. He simply buried them. Nixon said in his Princeton statement, "Eisenhower, we have to realize, is not the simple, direct type that people think. He is a man who is very complex in his thinking and in his handling of people." The two books tend to support this assessment, not so much in what Eisenhower wrote as what he left unsaid. "The four most miserable years of my life," said John Quincy Adams, "were my four years in the presidency." And even the strong-willed Andrew Jackson said, "I can with truth say that mine is a situation of dignified slavery." No doubt there were times when Eisenhower would have subscribed fully to these sentiments but they are not related in his books.

The early years of retirement were not, as he had expected, quiet and leisurely. Nixon's defeat in 1960 left Eisenhower the most prominent member of his party. Politicians, especially as the presidential year of 1964 approached, beat a path to his door. Loyalty to the GOP and his sense of duty impelled him to yield to the many demands for speeches and statements on current questions. Washington correspondents frequently sought him out for interviews.

Both John F. Kennedy and Lyndon Johnson called him to the White House for consultation or telephoned him, especially during the Cuban missile crisis and later about the war in Viet Nam.

On the 20th anniversary of D-Day, Eisenhower returned to the Normandy beaches and narrated the course of the battles in a television program for the Columbia Broadcasting System. Whenever he traveled, his secretaries telephoned ahead to his former associates and friends, inviting them to lunch or dinner. When the company assembled, no time was spent, usually, in reminiscing. Eisenhower wanted to discuss questions of the day. Once, a number of his former White House associates gathered at the farm. Suddenly, as in a Cabinet meeting, Eisenhower was going around the table asking each of them, "What are your thoughts on this?"

Delegations from all parts of the world came to Gettysburg to see him. In the space of a little more than a month, he received a group of Irish schoolteachers, some professors of political science from West Germany, a troupe of Korean entertainers and the representatives of a Japanese Little League baseball team.

He often accepted invitations to speak to groups of students, even junior high school pupils. He enjoyed this. He never "talked down" to them. Years before, while Eisenhower was chief of NATO, he said he liked to have young people come there to question him about the organization and he wrote in a letter, "Sometimes I get quite weary of talking to the old, the fearful, the cautious. I like to meet young people with their fresh outlook." Another letter said, "I do not despair of the younger generation because I believe the younger generation has more sense than ours so far has displayed."

He also enjoyed showing visitors around the sites of the principal actions in the Battle of Gettysburg and the spot where Lincoln delivered the Gettysburg Address. Eisenhower thought that Lincoln's eloquence that day probably shortened the Civil War.

So the days passed, days of fulfillment and peace, a happy blend of family life, work and doing the things he liked.

They were not all sunny, however. Eisenhower was attending a United Nations luncheon on the terrible afternoon of Nov. 22, 1963, when an assassin's bullet ended the life of John Fitzgerald Kennedy. Eisenhower immediately canceled all appointments and flew to Washington. He stood for long moments beside the coffin in the East Room of the White House. An expression of shock and infinite sadness dimmed his eyes.

Then, Lyndon B. Johnson, sworn in only hours earlier, called him into conference.

At Johnson's request, he undertook to set forth some thoughts and observations that he felt might be helpful to the new President. For more than two hours, Eisenhower scribbled away, writing on long sheets of yellow paper, after which he dictated a statement from these notes. Johnson, the master politician, found them useful.

He later disclosed that "some of the things I said to the joint session of Congress" were suggested by Eisenhower.

In the small sitting room adjacent to his office, Johnson kept a photograph of Eisenhower, along with those of Johnson's father, Sam Rayburn and John F. Kennedy. Another memento, a framed letter from Eisenhower, stood near them. This is the unsigned letter Eisenhower wrote Johnson on the day Eisenhower had his heart attack.

"I like him," Johnson said. And referring to his years as Senate Majority Leader, in opposition to Eisenhower, he said, "He was a wonderful man to work under."

The events preceding the nomination of Barry Goldwater for President in 1964 brought Eisenhower some unpleasant moments. At the same time, he dismayed many of his admirers by not openly opposing Goldwater's candidacy.

In the early maneuverings, Eisenhower took the position that the interests of the GOP would best be served if a number of prominent Republicans contested for the nomination. As for himself, he said he had no favorites and would endorse nobody. Apart from that, he said privately that he did not believe his endorsement would carry any great weight.

On Sept. 29, 1963, The New York Herald Tribune published a statement written by Eisenhower in which he said, "I keep hearing and reading that I am 'anti-Goldwater.' This is simply not true. At this point, I am neither against nor specifically for any one candidate…" He then proceeded to name some 10 men whom he believed would make acceptable candidates.

About two months before the convention in San Francisco,

Eisenhower wrote another statement for The Herald-Tribune which was regarded as a statement of principles to which the nominee should subscribe. He referred to previous GOP platforms and wrote, "These platforms represented the responsible, forward-looking Republicanism I tried to espouse as President." He then itemized, at length, actions taken in the field of social legislation during his two administrations. It was an impressive record, especially to those who cherished the fiction that Eisenhower and his party generally opposed such legislation. Further, Eisenhower reminded his readers that during his eight years in office, "the nation made more progress in civil rights than in the preceding 80...through passage of the Civil Rights Acts of 1957 and 1960, the first such acts passed since Reconstruction." Finally, in reviewing the record on foreign affairs, Eisenhower said there was no room for "impulsiveness."

Perhaps the use of this word, more than anything else in the statement, seemed to strike directly at Goldwater. True or not, he had continually been charged with being "impulsive" in speeches on foreign and military affairs. He was regarded as opposed to the type of social legislation that Eisenhower stressed. Critics pictured him as a Neanderthal reactionary and a dangerous jingoist.

Naturally, therefore, Eisenhower's statement was widely interpreted as his way of saying to his party, "Don't nominate Goldwater." In the tidal wave of newspaper editorials that followed, the majority came to this conclusion.

The Rochester, New York, Democrat & Chronicle said, "By defining what the Republican Party stands for...he pretty well disqualifies front-running Senator Barry Goldwater." The Portland Oregonian said, "Former President Eisenhower's refusal to name his favorite candidate...does not obscure the evidence that Goldwater is not his favorite candidate." The Des Moines, Iowa, Register said, "The statement has been interpreted as reflecting an anti-Goldwater attitude on the part of Eisenhower. We think that interpretation is correct." The New York Times said, "The statement of principles drawn up by Former President Eisenhower as a guide to the selection of a Republican presidential nominee is plainly designed to throw the influence of the party's most distinguished leader against Senator Barry Goldwater and the backward-looking philosophy he espouses."

When he read these and many other editorials keyed to the same chord, Eisenhower was stunned. He telephoned a number of his newspaper friends and said, "I just don't see how anybody could read that into what I wrote."

Similarly, he was irritated by the speculative interpretations placed on a conference he had with William Warren Scranton, the personable young governor of Pennsylvania. It took place just before Scranton left to attend a Governor's Conference in Cleveland. Soon after Scranton won the governorship of his state, his name went on the list of potential candidates for the GOP nomination. He said he would not seek it and would only respond to a genuine draft. Eisenhower, in their meeting, urged him to take a less rigid position, so that, as the phrase went, there would be "a Convention and not just a Coronation" in San Francisco. Eisenhower consistently argued that public discussion of differences in views between candidates would be healthy for the party. Hence, the conference with Scranton.

No endorsement was asked and Eisenhower gave none. What exactly passed between him and Scranton remains foggy, but Scranton said he came away "with the distinct impression that he would support me." A crisp communique from either Scranton's headquarters or Gettysburg would have clarified the question, but none was issued. Thus, within hours after their meeting, newspapers and the airwaves were filled with reports that it signaled Eisenhower's intention to back Scranton for the nomination. When he reached Cleveland, the governor said he found a message asking him to telephone Eisenhower in Gettysburg. He did so. The governor said Eisenhower expressed astonishment over the wide speculation and said to him, "I don't want to be part of a 'stop anybody' cabal, and I don't think you should be." Scranton had been prepared to announce his candidacy that same day on a television program, but after his conversation with Eisenhower, he said, he had no choice but to be inimitably vague. Confusion reigned supreme at the conference.

Nevertheless, Scranton made a brave 11th hour attempt to win enough delegate support to give Goldwater a fight at the convention. It was an exercise in futility. The ultraconservatives who locked up the nomination for Goldwater had started organizing in late 1961. By the time of the convention, they were in a position to dictate the choice of their candidate and their kind of platform.

Both episodes, the second statement to The Herald-Tribune, and the conversation with Scranton on the eve of the Governor's Conference, reflected Eisenhower's innocence of the vagaries and totems of politics. With his towering prestige, anything he said or did during the preconvention months was closely scrutinized for a possible meaning with respect to any potential candidate. He could not seem to realize this.

He went to San Francisco and appeared in the role of a commentator, discussing the convention proceedings on television. He held a press conference which, as always, he enjoyed. After Goldwater's nomination, Eisenhower made a speech which delighted those unusually turbulent galleries.

The result of the election came as no surprise to him. He did not consider the Republican ticket a strong one and he sensed that the emotional aftershock of the tragedy in Dallas would swing a great many votes to the Democrats.

After the debacle at the polls, Eisenhower busied himself with the effort to strengthen his party. He delivered speeches and conferred regularly with Republican leaders. Although he was suffering from an attack of arthritis, he attended an event honoring the memory of Herbert Hoover at Hoover's birthplace, West Branch, Iowa. On a blistering day in the summer of 1965, Eisenhower erected tents on his farm, moved in equipment to air-condition them, and assembled 400 Republicans for lunch and a political conference.

In June of that year, accompanied by his wife, he attended the 50th reunion of his class at West Point. It was a happy occasion for him. In the afternoon, Eisenhower and Omar Bradley sat behind home plate during the baseball game between Army and Navy. The Cadets obliged him by winning it, 7 to 2. When the day ended, he said, "The whole thing has been an inspiration, seeing all of my old pals. Of course, we're all getting older. But we come here to renew our faith in America."

Not long after these events, he went to Washington to lecture and answer questions at the National War College. Here he was in his element. He went on answering questions until an aide, becoming increasingly nervous as the time passed, reminded him of his afternoon appointments in Gettysburg. When the session ended, an officer said to Eisenhower, "This has been a memorable occasion." The General smiled and replied, "It is for me, too. Ten years ago today, I had my heart attack."

At the time, he appeared to be in excellent health. He came to his 75th birthday on Oct. 14. The publication of his second book about the presidency, "Waging Peace," had been timed to coincide with his birthday and his publishers organized a heavy schedule of appearances for him in connection with the book. He went through the day like a man of 40, holding press conferences, presiding at a luncheon, appearing on television. A woman timidly asked if he would autograph a copy of the book. Eisenhower replied, "Why, certainly, Ma'am, I'm always flattered when somebody asks me for an autograph." His mood was relaxed, contemplative, sometimes playful. In a press conference, a reporter referred to him as a "statesman." Eisenhower's forehead crinkled. Then he grinned broadly and said, "Actually, what most people in the Congress cynically say is that a statesman is nothing but a defeated politician, and—"

The reporter interrupted, "But you were never defeated."

"Well, then," Eisenhower said, "I'm probably not a statesman."

From New York, he scurried back to Phoenixville, Pennsylvania, to spend the rest of the day with his grandchildren. In Gettysburg, meanwhile, so many telegrams were pouring in that the machine in his office ran far behind. Every hour, a messenger came to the door, bringing another stack. Before the day ended, more than 10,000 birthday telegrams and letters piled up on the desks, testimonials to the extent of the affection that followed him into retirement.

He had the time of his life on his birthday, unaware that he stood on the threshold of another critical hour.

In November, Eisenhower and Mamie went to Georgia as usual and settled into "Mamie's Cottage" on the grounds of the Augusta National Golf Club. A stabbing pain in his chest awakened him in the early morning hours of Nov. 9. For several weeks he lay in an oxygen tent in a nearby hospital. More messages came "We are praying for your recovery."

His stout heart rallied again. By Christmas he was back on the farm, opening presents with his grandchildren.

Throughout his last years, Eisenhower's interest in national and international developments never flagged. He sought to make his nation aware of its moral responsibility and strength. He commented on everything from miniskirts to Supreme Court rulings. He backed President Johnson's Vietnam policy, going further in suggesting that Congress consider declaring war. He reminisced about the past and on June 16, 1967, brought out his fourth book, relaxed, autobiographical vignettes, entitled, "At Ease: Stories I Tell to Friends."

Politically he could no longer remain neutral. He implied, but never said, that his silence concerning Republican choices in 1964 may have been a mistake. It would not happen again. In 1968, despite illness and flagging strength, he lent his popularity to Richard Nixon's bid for the Presidency. Abed in Walter Reed Hospital, recovering from two more heart attacks, Eisenhower called a news conference on July 18 and announced his choice. He was breaking his silence, he said, because "the issues are so great." The effect was immediate. In a few days public opinion polls showed a rise in Nixon's popularity.

Nor did Eisenhower stop there. He shocked his doctors with his insistence that he address the Republican convention from his hospital room over closed circuit television. The speech was short, but it was vintage Eisenhower, stressing the simple American virtues, the common sense solutions.

The next day he suffered another heart attack. But as always his remarkable constitution and resiliency amazed doctors. He told a friend he wanted to go on living "as long as I can be useful to somebody." By October he was able to go to the third floor window of Walter Reed's Presidential Suite to salute the military band playing birthday greetings to him from the yard below. He was 78.

Still adversity and age pursued him. He encountered an intestinal obstruction and doctors operated, much against their will, on Feb. 23, 1969. He stood the 2 hour and 20 minute operation well but came down with pneumonia afterwards. Antibiotics fought off the infection but the combined assault left him weak. His heart, scarred by seven attacks, could not sustain him. Doctors noted in mid-March that he had suffered serious congestive heart failure. His wife almost constantly at his side, he endured bad days and good. Then, at 12:25 p.m., March 28, the Kansas farmboy who rose to be General of the Army and President of the United States, died quietly after what his doctors called "a long and heroic struggle." Twenty-one minutes later the last hospital bulletin spread through the world leaving grief and shock in its wake.

Said old friend, consultant and former President Lyndon Johnson:

"His death leaves an empty place in my heart as it will in the hearts of men and women everywhere. America will be a lonely land without him, but America will always be a better nation—stronger, safer, more conscious of its heritage, more certain of its destiny—because Ike was with us when America needed him."

Leaders of more than 50 nations including the Soviet Union flew to Washington to pay homage. Among them were France's President Charles de Gaulle, Germany's Kurt Kiesinger. The mourning period, planned by Eisenhower in 1966, was short, but filled with military and religious meaning.

There were the simple services at Washington National Cathedral, the slow-time march to the Capitol, the artillery caisson bearing the $80 soldier's steel coffin, the riderless horse, the boots reversed in the stirrups, the strains of "Hail to the Chief" and "Ruffles and Flourishes," the 21-gun salute, all sounding for him for the last time. And finally the 40-hour train trip home to Abilene and burial in an Army uniform and Eisenhower jacket beneath the chapel of the Eisenhower Center.

And a nation sorrowfully savored his last words: "I've always loved my wife. I've always loved my children. I've always loved my grandchildren. I've always loved my country."

Ike's Enduring Legacy

For two decades, from 1941 through 1960, Dwight D. Eisenhower presided over a succession of powerful offices. Yet, until he consented to run for the presidency in 1952, he did not seek, much less fight for, any of them. This is the phenomenal aspect of his story, that a man so selfless rose so high. Captains and kings have seldom been selfless. More often, history shows them driven by the familiar human motivations, megalomania, the desire for power or wealth, some compelling personal ambition. By contrast, Eisenhower was perhaps overly modest and his ambitions were primarily impersonal, to promote the best interests of his country and to contribute to maintaining peace in the world.

He was highly skilled, to be sure, as a soldier and he possessed a rare gift for organizing and directing great politico-military structures. Without these talents, he would not have reached the apex in the Army or become Supreme Commander. On the other hand, in the rarefied upper atmosphere of the Military, ability and devotion to duty do not automatically guarantee recognition and rapid promotion to high command. Nor do they in any large public or private organization. In a sense, Eisenhower was thrust into the high offices he occupied. Thus his career developed outside the norm, that pattern of success in which an intensely ambitious man, single-minded and unswerving, drives for his goal and finally attains it. The chart of Winston Churchill's course through public life, for example, follows that pattern. As a young man, Churchill fixed his eyes on the Prime Ministership, and thereafter, through more than 40 years, through his political "wilderness" and years of unpopularity, the office remained his polar star. At 65, he attained it. Eisenhower's personal ambitions, however, were sharply limited. It will be recalled that before the Second World War he merely hoped for a Colonel's eagles before he retired. He called himself "small fry" in the Army, even when it began expanding. When he received his first star, Brig. Gen. Eisenhower thought he might, with luck, be given command of an armored division. When the hour came for naming an American Commander in Britain, he did not attempt to maneuver himself into that position; he recommended a colleague for it. Instead, George C. Marshall, the Chief of Staff, named him. Next, he knowingly risked this first great career opportunity, as Robert Murphy pointed out, when he approved the unpopular "Darlan Deal" in North Africa. Eisenhower concluded that it was the best thing to do from a political and military point of view, and if his own career were to suffer as a result, so be it. He was as surprised as anyone else when Roosevelt and Churchill agreed to appoint him Supreme Commander for the invasion of France instead of Marshall. (Marshall, a great-souled man, generously sent Eisenhower the President's handwritten announcement of the appointment for his mementos of the war.) The next high office, Chief of the North Atlantic Treaty Organization, also came out of the blue; President Truman advised Eisenhower that the Western governments had turned to him, unanimously, and he asked Eisenhower to undertake the heavy assignment. Eisenhower did so, although he would have preferred to remain president of Columbia University. These were the main stepping-stones to the presidency and Eisenhower sought none of them.

As for the highest office, Eisenhower's personal letters to friends clearly show that he did not want it. The evidence in them is more weighty than in his public statements, for an ambitious man may take one position publicly and quite a different one privately. He wrote at one stage, "Once this war is won, I hope never again to hear the word 'politics.'" And somewhat later, he wrote a friend, "I occupy the enviable position of a man who wants nothing." These statements, along with others in his private correspondence, express the essence of Eisenhower's desire to leave public life. He then put it as forcefully as he could in the famous reply to Leonard V. Finder, the New Hampshire publisher, which was published. This, he assumed, settled the question and would remove the pressure. And he wrote his friend, Capt. Hazlett, that he was now "experiencing a great sense of relief."

This was in 1948. By 1951, his position was changing. A number of friends and men whose judgment he respected, notably Cabot Lodge and Roy Roberts, argued that it was his duty to run for the presidency. They touched the sensitive nerve in his makeup, his strong sense of duty. Eisenhower was an internationalist; if Taft were elected, they said, he might lead the nation back to the isolationism of the 1920s. (Indeed, not many years later, Taft did advocate that the United States "go it alone.") On the other hand, if a Democrat won the presidency, the "spenders" would have the mandate to continue spending. Ergo, it was Eisenhower's duty to make himself available. Excerpts from his personal letters reflect Eisenhower's instinctive response to the word, "…this principle is that every citizen is required to do his *duty* for his country, whatever it may be"…"the necessity for earnest obligation to *duty*." The word appears again and again in his letters.

His concept of duty was not the only factor but it was a compelling one in his decision to run for a second term. Before his heart attack in the autumn of 1955, Eisenhower had thought of resigning. His illness, he wrote a friend, seemed at first to have taken the decision out of his hands. The potential consequences to himself of undertaking a second term were secondary in his thinking; uppermost was the well-being of the nation if a semi-invalid sat in the White House. The blocked artery in his chest and the damaged heart wall at last had closed the book on his public life. This, he said, was his first thought when he regained consciousness. But his constitution was sturdier than he realized and as strength and energy returned second thoughts intruded. In four more years as President, he might achieve or at least bring within reach the goals he had set for himself. Therefore, it was his duty to run for office a second time.

Eisenhower goes into history as one of the most popular of Presidents, in whom Americans recognized an earnest, kindly, sincere man of unquestionable integrity. As a politician, he was almost unique in that he was wholly without the "jugular instinct," the urge to destroy an enemy; he was more prone to turn the other cheek. Even after he left the White House and came to write his story of the presidential years, he made no attempt to settle old scores. He also was one of the most selfless Presidents, less concerned for his popularity and the expedient actions that might enhance it than what he considered the well-being of the United States and her Allies. His actions in Korea, Lebanon, the Suez Canal crisis and the Formosa Straits contributed to maintaining peace. His efforts to reach understandings with the Russians, the proposal for an international pool of fissionable material, the "open skies plan," the invitation to Khrushchev to visit the United States, demonstrated his vision and courage and enhanced the prestige of his country. In the fields of civil rights, budgetary responsibility, the assurance of prosperity, and in other domestic spheres, his achievements were notable. He was right to send U-2 reconnaissance aircraft over the Soviet Union but wrong to suppress his instincts and permit the prepared falsehood to stand until the Russians punctured it. There are those who will not forgive him for not publicly denouncing Joseph R. McCarthy, those who ridicule him on grounds that an inept politician is an ineffective President, those who scorned his whole concept of the presidency vis-a-vis Congress, and those who were disappointed when he refrained from taking a clear-cut position in the choice of the Republican nominee for President in 1964. Apart from these concrete issues, the pluses and minuses, there is an intangible to consider: When Eisenhower came to office, bitterness and rancor divided the nation; when he left, an era of good feeling had replaced the sense of divisiveness. The credits far outweighed the debits in his presidency and if he could (and would) have run for a third term there can be little doubt that he would have been swept into office on the crest of another landslide.

In his "Oxford History of the American People," Samuel Eliot Morison described Eisenhower's presidency as "memorable," although he qualified this judgment. Other historians have been more critical.

The problem confronting historians, especially in evaluating contemporary Presidents, is that the record seldom is complete down to the last fact and last shred of information. More importantly, other factors, atmosphere, unrecorded counsels and arguments, a President's health, elements that may have influenced a particular decision, are difficult to discover and to weigh.

Arthur Schlesinger Jr. illustrated the problem in an anecdote about John F. Kennedy, who was an earnest and careful student of history. Schlesinger related that Kennedy, while President, was asked to participate in a poll of historians evaluating the Presidents, "great," "average" or "failure." The ballot came to Kennedy and he began to fill it out. But then he stopped. Schlesinger wrote that Kennedy said, "How in hell can you tell? Only the President himself can know what his real pressures and real alternatives are. If you don't know that, how can you judge performance?" Schlesinger wrote, "Some of his greatest predecessors, he would sometimes say, were given credit for doings things when they could do nothing else."[1]

---

1 Schlesinger: "1000 Days."

Eisenhower inscribed his own gauge of greatness. It embraced, he said, the qualities of vision, integrity, courage, understanding and the ability to communicate. If he was least successful in the last of these, he demonstrated the others again and again in full measure.

As an American and as a President, he marked an illustrious place for himself in the history of the decades of danger and a swiftly changing world.

The "Great Deception"

The story of the elaborate and intricate arrangements by which the safety of President-elect Dwight D. Eisenhower was guarded for six days while he flew to Korea and toured the battlefields.

By Don Whitehead
Associated Press Staff Writer

WITH EISENHOWER IN KOREA, Dec. 5.—It was 5:30 a.m. (E.S.T.) on Saturday, Nov. 29, when two men stepped quickly through the doorway of the residence at 60 Morningside Drive in New York City into the cold, starlit night.

Their overcoat collars were turned up as though against the chill. They strode swiftly to the limousine that had pulled up at the curb a few feet from the doorway, ducked into the car, and it drove away. The street was bare and silent once again.

One of the men was United States Secret Service Agent Edward Green and the other was President-elect Eisenhower. This was the beginning of the Eisenhower mission to Korea, where he hoped—as millions of Americans did—that a way could be found to bring an honorable end to the bloody fighting which in two and a half years had claimed 126,000 American dead, wounded and missing.

As the Eisenhower car drove toward Mitchel Field, the Air Force base on Long Island, other automobiles in other parts of the city moved in a precision pattern, also converging on Mitchel Field. There two big Air Force Constellations waited in the darkness.

A few minutes before Eisenhower had left his Morningside Heights residence, Defense Secretary-designate Charles E. Wilson had strolled out of the Waldorf Hotel and entered a cab. He told the driver to drop him off at the southeast corner of 58th St. and Fifth Ave.

Wilson Waited for Car on Fifth Ave. Corner

This gray-haired, distinguished industrialist—president of the General Motors Corp—stepped from the designated spot, paid the driver, and then stood on the street corner for a moment.

The sounds of the city were muted at this hour. A few cruising cabs drove by and a few pedestrians walked quickly in the cold streets. A car drew up beside Mr. Wilson, the door opened, and he stepped inside. It drove off into the pattern that was forming.

From half a dozen different points, six reporters and photographers quietly left their lodgings and converged on Pennsylvania Station, which sounds like an improbable place for secrecy in movements.

But the six were lost among the other early travelers waiting for their trains, lounging in doorways and trying to kill time.

A black limousine drove down the ramp to the unloading platform and the six news men strolled one by one to the car driven by Secret Service Agent Ed Sweeney. The group was joined by Eisenhower's press secretary, James Hagerty.

Mr. Sweeney moved out quickly toward the East River, across the big Triborough Bridge over the East River and out on Long Island to a back road paralleling Mitchel Field. The car stopped at a gate, a light was flashed, and someone said the magic words, "Secret Service," to a major who then identified the occupants by name.

The gate opened and we followed a car that swung suddenly into the gate to guide us. Then the big Constellation loomed ahead. We stepped out into the sharp, chill wind.

2 Constellations Waited at Mitchel Field

"I'm sorry we don't have coffee," an Air Force general said, "but security cuts down the number of people we can use at this hour."

There were two Constellations, one for Gen. Eisenhower and his party of seven. They included Gen. Eisenhower's old friend, Gen. Omar N. Bradley, chairman of the Joint Chiefs of Staff, who had flown up from Washington; Maj. Gen. Wilton B. Persons (retired), his close friend and White House assistant-to-be; Herbert Brownell, of New York, who will be the Attorney General in the Republican administration; Mr. Wilson; James Rowley, Secret Service agent in charge of the White House detail, and Lt. John Davies, who was to act as Gen. Eisenhower's secretary.

The second plane carried the newspaper men; Col. Paul T. Carroll, of Woonsocket, R.I., temporarily assigned to the party; Mr. Hagerty, and Secret Service Agent Richard Flohr.

In addition, both planes carried double crews of twenty-two men. This was a total of thirty-nine on board the ships.

The Eisenhower plane took off at 5:55 a.m., just as the blackness was turning gray. The second plane followed ten minutes later. At 2:25 p.m. and 2,641 miles later the planes set down at Travis Field near San Francisco to refuel. An hour later they were off for the long overseas flight to Hickam Field, Hawaii.

No one left the planes at Travis. The ships paused just long enough to take on the fuel and then they roared westward again.

It was just after midnight when the lights of Honolulu showed on the horizon, sparkling in the dark sea like jewels reflecting the brightness of the round moon. The planes swept out of the darkness onto the Hickam Field runway and taxied to a secluded part of the field. Again no one left the planes as crews swarmed into the wings to fill the tanks. Minutes later we were air-borne again.

Midway Island Was Next Stop

Midway Island was next—1,320 miles and 4 hours 50 minutes later. Gulls, terns and those ridiculous members of the albatross family known as gooney birds, wheeled overhead or gathered in conclaves near the apron of the field.

The gooney birds—some with wingspreads up to nine feet—appeared to be putting on a show just for the amusement of the General and his party. They waddled toward each other, touched bills, bowed, curtsied, and then danced about in solemn and absurd tribal rites.

Our ships were traveling under false identifications and numbers, but there was tight security across the whole Pacific from San Francisco to Korea to guard against any leak that Gen. Eisenhower was en route.

It was Sunday, Nov. 30, when we left Midway on the longest oversea hop of the trip—the 2.695 miles to Iwo Jima. But a few minutes after leaving the island it was Monday. Our ships had crossed the International Dateline.

Our press plane was less than halfway to Iwo Jima when the No. 1 engine began losing power. Maj. Thomas E. Dye, of Somerset, Ky., was forced to feather the prop and we flew with only three engines. A fuel pump had gone bad.

Maj. Dye headed for Wake Island for emergency repairs and radioed his decision to the Eisenhower plane. "Message received" was the only reply, a curt reminder that security even prohibited any talking back and forth between the planes. But we learned later that Gen. Eisenhower and his group were concerned over our safety until they learned we had limped into Wake Island safely.

It seemed to us the whole population of Wake had turned out to see our plane land and we wondered if the news of Gen. Eisenhower's trip hadn't already swept around the world.

Newsmen Allowed Off Plane at Wake

But Richard Fisher, United States Commissioner on the island and Pan American Airways base manager, came aboard and assured us that the island had been "secured" and communications were being watched so that inter-island traffic would reveal nothing unusual.

With this assurance, the Secret Service and security guard permitted us to leave the plane for the first time since we had left New York.

Three hours later the faulty fuel injector had been repaired and we were roaring off Wake toward Iwo Jima.

The Eisenhower ship landed on Iwo Jima at 3:30 p.m. and we landed five hours later.

One of Gen. Eisenhower's first acts on Iwo Jima was to visit the Marine memorial on Mt. Suribachi—that knob of a hill where a gallant little band of warriors in February, 1945, raised the American flag in defiance of the Japanese making a fanatical defense of this island.

There the General stood looking out across the black beaches where 21,000 men were killed or wounded in trying to storm the stronghold. And he was told the story of Iwo Jima by Col. W.W. Buchanan, of Athens, Ga., who was the assistant operations officer for the 4th Marine Division, and by M/Sgt. Robert T. Fox, of Honolulu and Long Beach, Calif., who had been with the 2d Battalion of the 24th Marine Regiment on the assault.

The General turned in early—before 8 p.m.—to get a good night's rest. He hadn't been off his ship until Iwo, and most of this time he had spent in getting briefings from Gen. Bradley and reports from the Korean warzone.

Captain Got General on Phone by Mistake

The General had just gone to bed when Capt. Wayne Melvin, of Los Angeles, rang his telephone—thinking it was the number for the base commander.

Telling the story later, Capt. Melvin said:

"I rang No. 10 and after a while somebody answered and I asked if Maj. Weldon was there.

"This guy said, no, Weldon wasn't there and I asked if he knew where I could reach Weldon.

"He said: 'No, I'm just a visitor here.' And then I knew I was talking to Eisenhower."

The island had begun to buzz with excitement the day before when planes began landing and depositing V.I.P.s, a staff car and six brand-new refrigerators for the officers' quarters.

Second Lt. Eugene G. Hobbie, of Red Level, Ala., said he figured it had to be Gen. Eisenhower who was coming to Iwo.

"When they brought those refrigerators in from Japan and then a staff car," he said, "I couldn't see them doing it for anybody but Eisenhower. So I went around making bets with the guys on who was coming in.

"Most of them figured it was a command staff meeting and I got $60 bet that it would be Ike."

Then another plane came in to Iwo carrying security police, special cooks and waiters and service personnel to handle the influx of visitors.

These men had received only an hour's notice to pack and get ready to move to an unknown destination.

Second Lt. William H. Thompson, of Chicago, said he was told to get ready for an emergency assignment. He was the food supply officer at the Air Force base at Tachikawa, Japan.

"I said I had a day off coming to me and I wasn't supposed to work that day," Lt. Thompson said with a grin. "The man said, 'that's just too bad, because you are leaving in an hour.'"

Party Was Billeted Near Invasion Beach

The Eisenhower party was billeted in spanking clean Quonset huts just a few yards from the beach where the Americans stormed Iwo Jima in one of the bloodiest battles of World War II. Sentries patrolled the huts throughout the night and Secret Service agents kept watch with them.

A young officer said to me:

"They told us to give you everything you wanted—and if you asked for the battleship Missouri, then I was to call for the island commander and he would see what he could do about that."

The first time reporters saw Gen. Eisenhower on the trip was at breakfast next day, Dec. 2. He came into the officers' mess about 7:30

a.m. looking rested and in top condition. He grinned and waved to those in the room.

"By golly," he said, "I got into bed at 7 o'clock last night and I woke up at 4 o'clock this morning and had a devil of a time going back to sleep."

After breakfast, the General agreed to go back up Suribachi so that cameramen could get the picture they had missed the day before. He rode in a Chevrolet sedan to the foot of the Suribachi and then climbed out to transfer to a jeep for the steep climb up a dusty trail cut out of the side of the hill.

Mr. Wilson asked the driver why the change was being made from the sedan to the jeep.

"That hill's too steep for the Chevrolet to make it," the driver said.

"Are you sure?" Mr. Wilson asked.

"I'm damned sure. Sir," the youth replied.

Later, the driver was told he had been talking to the next Secretary of Defense and the man whose company makes Chevrolets.

"Oh, lordy," he exclaimed. "I put my foot in my mouth, didn't I?"

He was assured he had—both feet.

No Welcoming Committee On Hand at Seoul Field

Gen. Eisenhower's plane took off at 2 p.m. from Iwo for the 1,700-mile flight to Seoul. The overnight stop at Iwo had been planned so that he would arrive in Korea after nightfall.

It was 7:57 p.m. Korea time (5:57 a.m. Tuesday in New York City) when the General's plane touched down on the icy runway near Seoul. It had spanned the 10,836 miles between New York and Korea in 47 hours 15 minutes' flying time. The temperature was 10 degrees above zero.

Armed guards and secret service agents waited on the field—but there was no welcoming committee. Gen Mark Clark, Supreme Allied Commander in the Far East, had remained at the United States 8th Army headquarters in Seoul with Gen. James Van Fleet, 8th Army commander. The only newspaper men present were those in the Eisenhower party. Their plane had landed twenty minutes ahead of the General's.

Gen. Eisenhower stepped from his plane wearing civilian clothes and only a medium-weight brown camel's hair overcoat to shield him from Korea's wintery winds, the coldest of the season.

The General quickly climbed into a waiting sedan with Gen. Bradley and Mr. Wilson. Two Secret Service agents—Messrs. Rowley and Flohr—were in the front seat. Then the heavily guarded caravan moved quickly across a land of frozen rice paddies into the war-battered city of Seoul.

Only President Syngman Rhee of the Republic of Korea had any notice of the general's arrival. But there was plenty of evidence that President-elect was expected. Banners and arches across the streets carried messages of welcome—and appeal.

They said "Welcome President-elect Eisenhower." Others read: "Drive Away the Chinese Reds"—"Strengthen R.O.K Forces"—"We oppose Withdrawal of United Nation Forces."

At 8th Army headquarters, Gen. Eisenhower was warmly welcomed by Gens. Clark and Can Fleet—and the first thing he asked for was hot chocolate. He retired shortly after dinner.

Eisenhower Briefed By Clark and Van Fleet

The general was up early on Dec. 3 and spent the morning being briefed on the Korean situation by Gens. Clark and Van Fleet and others.

Gen Clark later told this reporter: "We gave him the whole story including the problems that lie ahead for us." He didn't say what the problems were.

After lunch, Gen. Eisenhower was flown in the L-19 "puddle-jumper" plane to an airfield where he visited a fighter interceptor squadron and the 67th Tactical Reconnaissance Wing headquarters.

This time he wore regular Army issue winter clothing—with no insignia. The winter clothing had been issued to the general and those in his party during the morning. He was accompanied by the entire group which had traveled with him from New York—and by his son, Maj. John Eisenhower, who is stationed in Korea as assistant operations officer for the 3rd Infantry Division.

Maj. Eisenhower had flown from the front early in the morning to see his father and to stay with him during his Korean visit. It was the first time he had seen his father since July.

Outside the squadron headquarters, Gen. Eisenhower stopped to shake hands with Capt. Herbert Weber, of Brattleboro, Vt., a jet pilot just back from a mission along the Yalu River.

"Did you get any MiGs?" Gen. Eisenhower asked.

"We saw some." Capt. Weber said, "but we didn't get into any fights."

On the apron of the field, Gen. Eisenhower stopped to chat for a moment with Lt. Ira M. Porter, of Fort Worth, Tex., a twenty-three-year-old jet pilot with two MiGs to his credit—and a Silver Star for heroism in action.

A few minutes later, he was flying from the airfield toward the 1st Marine Division headquarters on the fighting front while F-86 Sabre jets swept the skies on the lookout for any enemy planes trying a sneak attack from the north.

Frozen Land Below Showed Battle Scars

The frozen land below—white with ice and snow—showed the scars of old battles.

The little planes carrying the Eisenhower party set down on an airstrip six miles from the actual battle line. But in this area a sniper had shot a Marine two nights before.

The Marine band—waiting in 8-above-zero weather—played "Ruffles and Flourishes" for the President-elect. Just as the echoes faded into the bleak hills there was the sound of sharp explosions.

"What are they dropping in here?" Gen. Eisenhower snapped.

The officers nearby laughed and explained that a pilot had just fired four rockets into enemy positions—the sound carrying for miles in the sharp, cold mountain air.

Gen. Eisenhower was given a secret briefing of the situation along the Marines' front. And then when he was ready to visit another unit his son couldn't be found. He had wandered away for a moment.

When he returned, Gen. Van Fleet said: "You're the general's aide. That's your job. Stick with him." But the rebuke was given with a smile.

In mid-afternoon the general arrived at 1st Corps headquarters where units of fighting men from fifteen nations stood stiffly at attention in the bitter cold. Gen. Eisenhower had changed his G.I. hat for an overseas cap. He "trooped the line" and then stood on a platform at the edge of the airstrip while the troops marched in review with a color guard carrying the American and United Nations flag.

The Australians came first—tall men with wide-brimmed hats—and then the British, Belgians, Canadians, Colombians and Ethiopians. There were Frenchmen, Greeks, Koreans and Dutchmen, New Zealanders, Filipinos, Thailanders and Turks and finally units of the United States Army and Marines.

Flew Back to Seoul For Talk With Rhee

Loud speakers had been set up with a microphone on the stand—and every one expected the General to make a talk to the troops who symbolized the effort of the free world to resist aggression. But Gen. Eisenhower remained silent.

From the reviewing stand, he went to corps headquarters, where he received another briefing on the battle situation in this zone of the front. Then he flew back to Seoul for an hour-long talk with President Rhee, who came to 8th Army headquarters.

One source said Mr. Rhee had proposed a seven-point program calling, in part, for a few and unified Korea; strengthening of the R.O.K. forces and U.N. aid for reconstruction of Korea.

But there was no report that the General had made any promises on what he might so—although he has advocated building up the military strength of South Korea in order to lift some or all of the burden of fighting from American troops in Korea.

Gen. Eisenhower's second day in Korea—Thursday, Dec. 4—was a whirlwind visit of United Nations combat units in the snow-covered valleys near the front.

I asked soldier after soldier how he felt about the President-elect's visit—and there was not one who did not say he was glad the general had made the trip and that he hopes Gen. Eisenhower would find a way to end the war.

Sgt. Joseph Kililea, of County Roscommon, Ireland—in the British Commonwealth Division—put it this way: "If anybody can end it, Gen. Eisenhower can. He's the man to do it, sir."

Lt. John Condit, of Baltimore, said: "The boys all hope Ike can do something. But they aren't expecting miracles."

Corp. Paul Morrissey, of Trenton, N.J., said: "We feel at least he might come up with something to end this thing."

And so it went—a feeling that somewhere, somehow the general would find a way out for them in this stalemated war.

Gen. Eisenhower traveled from unit to unit by plane—an L-19—hopping over the frozen mountains from valley to valley sometimes in sight of the front, where Air Force and Navy planes were hitting the enemy positions with napalm and bombs.

During the day, the general visited the Commonwealth Division, the R.O.K. 1st Division, a surgical hospital, a R.O.K. cavalry unit, and the United States 2d and 3d Divisions. After more than thirty-four hours, only a few of the front-line troops knew he was in Korea.

At the 3d Division command post, Gen. Eisenhower ate lunch with members of the 15th Regiment—the battalion which he commanded only twelve years ago as a lieutenant colonel. The soldiers didn't know they were to lunch with Gen. Eisenhower until they saw him climb from a jeep.

While Gen. Clark, Gen. Van Fleet and the other generals and V.I.P.s went into a mess tent for lunch, Gen. Eisenhower sat on a pine box in the near-zero weather to eat and chat with Sgt. Jack R. Hutcherson, of Frankford, Mo., Corp. James A. Murry, of Muskogee, Okla., and Pfc. Casper Skudlarck, of Avon. Minn.

The social atmosphere was a bit strained as newspaper men and photographers crowded around them to watch every bite and to picture every move. The general—again wearing no insignia—cleaned his tray of pork chops, mashed potatoes, gravy, sauerkraut, peas and apple pie.

Watched R.O.K. Unit Practice Hill Assault

Later, he watched a R.O.K. unit assault a hill in realistic training maneuvers. Mr. Wilson, Gen. Bradley, Gen. Clark, Gen. Van Fleet, Mr. Brownell and President Rhee were among the spectators.

When it was over, Mr. Rhee presented Gen. Eisenhower with a big silk Republic of Korea flag and the general said: "I assure you, Mr. President, that it will hang in a suitable place where people will see it and not forget it."

Mr. Rhee and the South Korean generals have made it clear to

Gen. Eisenhower during his visit that they favor his plan to build up the strength of the South Korean Army.

Gen. Eisenhower returned to 8th Army headquarters in the mid-afternoon and one of his visitors was Maj. Gen. William Chase, who heads the United States military mission in Formosa. This conference was a hint that Gen. Eisenhower also was getting a fill-in in Chiang Kai-shek's Nationalist Chinese Army and its capabilities.

The general's third day in Korea was reserved for a news conference and further talks with Gen. Chase and other military men. He refused to talk politics and concentrated on the problem of peace.

DON WHITEHEAD became one of the best-known war correspondents in World War II, making so many landing with troops that he was called "Beachhead Don." In 1951 he was awarded a Pulitzer Prize and a Sigma Delta chi Distinguished Service Award for his coverage of the Korean War. In 1952, Whitehead became part of the AP team of special correspondents assigned to outstanding news stories. He was the author of "The FBI Story," which became a film in 1959. Whitehead died in 1981.

Selected References

Adams, Sherman—*First Hand Report*, Harper, 1961.
Armstrong, Hamilton Fish—*The World Is Round*, Foreign Affairs Quarterly, January, 1953.
Aron, Raymond—*An Explanation of De Gaulle*, Harper, 1966.
Bell, Jack—The *Splendid Misery*, Doubleday, 1960.
Bennet, G. Vernon—*Grant to Eisenhower*, Comet, 1956.
Berding, Andrew—*Foreign Affairs and You*, Doubleday, 1962.
Bradley, General Omar N.—*A Soldier's Story*, Henry Holt.
Brown, John Mason—*Through These Men*, Harper, 1953.
Bryant, Arthur—*Turn of the Tide, Triumph in the West*, Doubleday, 1959.
Butcher, Harry—*My Three Years With Eisenhower*, Simon & Schuster, 1946.
Carell, Paul—*Invasion—They're Coming*, Dutton, 1963.
Childs, Marquis—*Eisenhower, Captive Hero*, Harcourt Brace, 1958.
Churchill, Winston—*World War II*, Houghton Mifflin.
Ciano, Count Galeazzo—*The Ciano Diaries*, Garden City, 1946.
Clubb, O. Edmund—*20th Century China*, Columbia University Press, 1956.
Columbia Broadcasting System—*D-Day, 20 Years After*, 1964.
Corwin and Koenig—*The Presidency Today*, New York University Press, 1956.
Davis, Elmer—*But We Were Born Free*, Bobbs Merrill, 1953.
Davis, Kenneth—*Soldier of Democracy*, Doubleday, 1945.
Davies, John Paton—*Foreign and Other Affairs*, W. W. Norton, 1964.
Dayan, Major-General Moshe—*Diary of the Sinai Campaign*, Harper, 1966.
Department of State—*Berlin-1961*.
Department of State—*United States Relations With China*, 1944-49.
De Toledano, Ralph—*Nixon*, Henry Holt, 1956.

Duff Cooper, Alfred—*Old Men Forget*, Dutton, 1954.
Eden, Anthony—*The Reckoning*, Houghton Mifflin
Eisenhower, Dwight D.—*Crusade in Europe, Mandate for Change, Waging Peace*, Doubleday.
Gellhorn, Walter—*American Rights*, MacMillan, 1960.
Goebbels, Josef—*Diaries*, Doubleday, 1948.
Grew, Joseph—*Ten Years in Japan*, Simon & Schuster, 1944.
Gunther, John—*Eisenhower: Man and Symbol*. Harper.
Hand, Learned—*The Spirit of Liberty*, Alfred A. Knopf, 1960.
Hughes, Emmet—*The Ordeal of Power*, Atheneum, 1963.
Hyman, Sidney—*The American President*, Harper, 1954.
Jameson, Henry—*Heroes by the Dozen*, Shadinger-Wilson, 1961.
Liddell Hart, Captain B.H.—*The German Generals Talk*, William Morrow 1948.
Liu, F. F.—*A Military History of Modern China*, Princeton University Press, 1948.
Mazo, Earl—*Richard Nixon*, Harper, 1959.
McCann, Kevin—*Man From Abilene*, Doubleday, 1952.
McGill, Ralph—*The South and the Southerner*. Little Brown, 1959.
Moley, Raymond—*After Seven Years*, Harper, 1939.
Moran, Lord Charles—*Churchill*, Houghton Mifflin, 1966.
Morgenstern, George—*Pearl Harbor*, Devin Adair, 1947.
Mosley, Leonard—*Hirohito*, Prentice Hall, 1966.
Murphy, Robert—*Diplomat Among Warriors*, Doubleday, 1964.
Nixon, Richard M.—*Six Crises*, Doubleday, 1962.
Office of the Chief of Military History—*German Army Records*.
Pogue, Forrest C.—*George C. Marshall*, Viking, 1966.
Potter, Charles—*Days of Shame*, Coward McCann, 1965.
Rommel, Field Marshal Erwin—*The Rommel Papers*, Harcourt Brace, 1953.
Rovere, Richard—*Senator Joe McCarthy*, Harcourt Brace, 1959.
Schoenbrun, David—*Three Lives of Charles DeGaulle*, Atheneum, 1966.
Sherwood, Robert—*The Roosevelt and Hopkins Papers*, Harper.
Smith, Merriman—*The President Is Many Men*, Harper, 1948.
Snell, John L.—*The Meaning of Yalta*, Louisiana State University Press, 1956.
Snyder, Louis L.—*Documents of German History*, Rutgers University Press, 1958.

United States Army—*Command Decisions*, Harcourt Brace, 1965.

Warburg, James P.—*The United States and the Postwar World*, Atheneum, 1966.

Wechsler, James—*The Age of Suspicion*, Random House, 1953.

White, William—*Citadel: The United States Senate*, Harper, 1956.

Whitney, *Courtney*—*MacArthur: Rendezvous With Destiny*, Alfred A. Knopf, 1965.

Workman, William D. Jr.—*The Case For the South*, Devin Adair, 1960.

Acknowledgments

The Associated Press would like to thank Valerie Komor, Val Nicholas, Sara Nordgren, Francesca Pitaro and Retired Col. Jack Jacobs for their contributions to this project.

RELMAN MORIN was a two-time Pulitzer Prize-winning Special Correspondent of The Associated Press. He began his career at the AP in 1934 and served in Los Angeles, New York, DC, London, Algiers, Tokyo, Cairo, New Delhi, Italy and Korea until retiring in 1972. He authored several books including "Assassination: The Death of President John F. Kennedy" and "The Associated Press Story of Election 1968." Mr. Morin died in 1973.

ALSO AVAILABLE FROM AP BOOKS

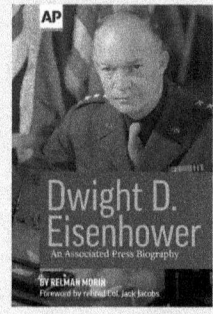

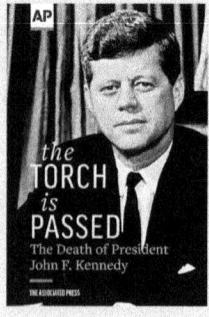

ap.org/books

www.ingramcontent.com/pod-product-compliance
Lightning Source LLC
Chambersburg PA
CBHW071647090426
42738CB00009B/1442